SOCIOLOGY IN THE WORLD TODAY

SOCIOLOGY IN THE WORLD TODAY

Edited by
JOHN W. KINCH
San Francisco State College

ADDISON-WESLEY PUBLISHING COMPANY
Reading, Massachusetts
Menlo Park, California · London · Don Mills, Ontario

This book is in the
ADDISON-WESLEY SERIES IN SOCIOLOGY

 Printed in the United States of America. Published simultaneously in Canada. Library of Congress Catalog Card No. 71-136124

To Sally Jo,
Linda Kay,
and Cathy

PREFACE

Sociology in the World Today has been compiled with one idea in mind: to bring the perspective of sociology into the world of the student. Designed for the introductory course in sociology, it draws on material almost exclusively from nonprofessional popular sources. The criteria for selection were these: (1) Each article must have appeared in a popular source with wide distribution (usually a national magazine). (2) It must be of high literary quality and sociologically sound. (3) It must be relevant and interesting to the student using it as a text.

Several considerations went into the decision to use this type of article. First, the conventional practice of relying heavily on professional journals for articles has not always proved satisfactory. After all, these are written by sociologists for the consumption of other sociologists, not college freshmen. It is no insult to the student to suggest that he would find these articles, with their technical jargon and often poor literary quality, both difficult and boring.

The second motivation was to find articles that would be useful in describing sociological concepts in such a way that the student would be able to see their usefullness in his everyday life. This required articles that were on topics that were relevant to the lives of the students and written in a style that would enable him to see where *he* fits in the complex scheme of society.

A third concern was with providing the student with some guidances in dealing with the world in which he will live the rest of his life. Hopefully, many students will be motivated by this book to take more courses in sociology, but realistically we know that most of them will not find it possible to take more courses. With a single course in sociology, the best service that can be done for the student is to provide him with a few useful concepts and tools for understanding the world about him. But we try to go one step further. The student will not have his textbooks, the library, or an instructor to carry with him throughout life. But he will have access to the popular magazines that are introduced here. If, after taking this course, he is better equipped to read and derive more value from these materials and if, from this book, he is introduced to sources that he will continue to use in his everyday life, then the course and the book have been a success.

In the process of meaningfully responding to the various readings in this book the student should be developing one of the most essential skills needed to cope with the world today—the ability to critically analyze ideas and opinions and to form accurate judgments. Within the readings presented in this book the student will be confronted with contrasting ideologies, competing views, and opinionated materials. It is expected that the student will read the articles carefully, looking for the biases of the authors, their motives and aims. The authors are frequently trying to persuade the reader of their particular points of view. It is up to the student to appraise the material, critically evaluate it, and determine its validity. We encourage open discussion of the articles in the classroom as a valuable aid in developing the student's ability to make critical judgments.

In the introductory notes to most of the sections you will find questions about the selections that follow. This is done as a guide in directing the student to certain dimensions of the articles that the editor feels are important. They will make him aware of the purpose for which the article was selected and help him in making critical analyses of the material. Each section is followed by a more structured set of questions or issues for consideration. These should prove valuable for both individual review and group discussions.

It is my hope that this book will help the student to better understand himself and the society in which he lives. If it is a first course in his college career, I hope it will instill in him the idea that college can be an exciting adventure, but most importantly, that education can be a stimulating lifetime experience that need never end.

San Francisco, California J. W. K.
November 1970

CONTENTS

Introduction 1

1 A Case for Sociology
Robert K. Merton, *The New York Times Magazine*, 1961 7

2 The New Sociology
Time Magazine Staff, *Time*, 1970 12

PART ONE / SOCIAL ORGANIZATION 17

Unit A Interpersonal Relationships 23

3 Growl to Me Softly and I'll Understand
William Hedgepeth, *Look*, 1970 24

4 The Fund of Sociability
Robert S. Weiss, *Trans-Action*, 1969 29

Unit B Social Norms and Roles 39

5 A Rose for Emily
Justin Kaplan, *Harper's Magazine*, 1969 40

6 Role Playing: A Judge is a Cop, A Cop a Judge
Richard Hammer, *The New York Times Magazine*, 1969 45

7 Psychology Constructs the Female
Naomi Weisstein, 1968 53

Unit C Institutions 57

FAMILY

8 The Swing to Small Families
Mary Seton, *Parents' Magazine*, 1967 59

EDUCATION

9 The Schools vs. Education
John Goodlad, *Saturday Review*, 1969 65

POLITICAL

10 Turning off "The People"
Andrew N. Greeley, *The New Republic*, 1970 73

RELIGION

11 The New American Jesuits
John L'Heureux, *The Atlantic Monthly*, 1969 78

COMMUNICATION

12 The American Media Baronies
The Editors of *The Atlantic Monthly*, 1969 89

Unit D Social Group 97

13 The Split-Level American Family
Urie Bronfenbrenner, *Saturday Review*, 1967 98

14 Reading an Organization Chart for Fun and Survival
Donald Winks, *Harper's Magazine*, 1967 105

Unit E Culture 112

15 The Culture of Poverty
Oscar Lewis, *Scientific American*, 1966 113

16 Renaissance and Repression: The Oklahoma Cherokee, *Trans-action*, 1969
Albert L. Wahrhaftig and Robert K. Thomas, *Trans-action*, 1969 123

Unit F Collective Behavior 133

17 Profile of Disorder: Newark 1967
National Advisory Commission on Civil Disorder, *The Kerner Report*, 1968 134

PART TWO / SOCIAL DIFFERENTIATION 147

Unit G Social Class: The Rich and the Poor 151

18 Even the Saints Cry
Oscar Lewis, *Trans-Action,* 1966 152

19 The Upper Crust: Review of *The Right People*
Paul D. Zimmerman, *Newsweek,* 1968 162

20 The Forgotten American
Peter Schrag, *Harper's Magazine,* 1969 164

Unit H Race: Black and White 171

21 The White Race and Its Heroes
Eldridge Cleaver, *Soul on Ice,* 1968 175

22 The Unknown Price of Success
Jack Olsen, *The Black Athlete, A Shameful Story,* 1968 184

Unit I Residence: The City and the Country 192

23 We Won't End the Urban Crisis Until We End Majority Rule
Herbert J. Gans, *The New York Times Magazine,* 1969 193

24 Is Main Street Still There?
Peter Schrag, *Saturday Review,* 1970 205

Unit J Sex and Age: Man and Woman, Young and Old 216

25 The Curse
Margot Hentoff, *The New York Review of Books,* 1969 217

26 Who Cares for the Aged
Robert Burger, *Saturday Review,* 1969 221

27 In Praise of Young Revolutionaries
John D. Rockefeller III, *Saturday Review,* 1968 229

Unit K Deviance: The Good and The Bad 235

28 Deviance and Deviates
Howard S. Becker, *The Nation,* 1965 236

29 The Condemnation and Persecution of Hippies
Michael E. Brown, *Trans-action,* 1969 245

30 The Respectable Criminal
Donald Cressy, *Trans-action,* 1965 257

31 Pot: A Rational Approach
Joel Fort, *Playboy,* 1969 265

Epilogue: Social Change 274

32 Tobacco's Double Revolution
Dwayne E. Walls, *The Nation,* 1970 276

33 The Coming of the Humanoids
Neil P. Hurley, *Commonweal,* 1969 281

34 The American Academy 1970
Judson Jerome, *Change,* 1969 287

INTRODUCTION

A new type of student has emerged on our college campuses over the past several years. He talks about wanting his college experience to be "relevant." He wants to see the connection between what he learns in college and what he experiences in the world in which he lives. Wherever he goes he looks for explanations of the preplexing world with its wars and riots, problems and promises. It is little wonder that sociology becomes a more popular course each year. It sounds as if it is relevant; it looks as if it has something to offer. The purpose of this book is to introduce sociology to the student in such a way as to demonstrate both its relevance to his world and the ways in which it can help him in his search for understanding in that world.

What is sociology? Perhaps the most frequent definition used is that it is simply the *science of society*, with society referring to a group of people who share a common interdependent life through interaction and interrelationships. We might say that sociology is a particular (scientific) means of making discoveries and explanations regarding *human social behavior*. To clearly understand what sociology is, however, we must see it in three different dimensions. *First*, we must have some general idea of the subject matter that sociologists are concerned with. *Second*, the student must be aware of the methods prescribed for the study of the subject matter. The *third* dimension to sociology, which is sometimes overlooked in introducing the subject to students, is the conceptual frame of reference for the analysis of human social behavior which the sociologist brings to his subject matter.

Man is a social being who has developed extremely complex schemes for relating to his fellow men. Thus within the subject matter of sociology we find everything from dating practices, which involve the way two people relate to each other, to industrial practices, which may involve hundreds of thousands of persons. No textbook or book of readings tries to cover the entire subject matter of sociology.

The objectives of sociology are to discover and explain the nature of human social behavior. To obtain this objective the sociologist applies the rules of science. This method restricts the sociologist to those data that are revealed through observation or experience—i.e., empirical data. Discovering what is and what is not is by no means an easy task; to insist that it be done with precison and accuracy makes the job even more difficult.

But the sociologist is charged with more than just discovering what *is*, for he must go further and try to explain *why*. He must develop propositions that attempt to account for human social behavior and test these propositions so that we can be confident they will hold up in the future. For example, consider the findings of a study reported in one of the articles in this book.* In this study it was discovered that children from lower-class homes showed a considerable variation in intellectual achievement: some did well in school, some did poorly. Since this finding came from a carefully conceived and executed research project, we can be reasonably certain that it is accurate. How do we account for this difference? What "causes" some children to do well while others fail? The investigators looked at several factors—the varying per-pupil expenditures of the schools, the size of the child's class, etc.—but none seemed too important. The one factor that seemed to make a difference was the pattern of characteristics of the other children in the same school: "If the lower-class child had schoolmates who came from advantaged homes, he did reasonably well; but if all the other children also came from deprived backgrounds, he did poorly."

Thus we have begun to *explain* the findings by further observations and discovery of the fact that peer relationships (associating with advantaged children) is a factor in determining intellectual achievement. The student should see this as a step in the development of a theoretical idea. More investigation is always needed and the ideas must be elaborated on, but our tentative answer to the question of how children achieve has been derived from empirical observations.

Science is sometimes described as the *interplay of ideas and observations*. Our example demonstrates this interplay. The sociologists had some ideas as to what caused differences in intellectual achievement; they thus looked at the types of schools the children came from, the size of their classes, etc. Although they had to reject some ideas, they found others to be consistent with their observations. Their discoveries will now lead to new ideas (did peer relationships affect psychological development as well as intellectual achievement?), which immediately suggest new observations. The observations in turn inspire new ideas, and so the process goes. It is this interplay of ideas and observations which makes up the foundation of any science.

In the study of sociology we accumulate generalizations about human social behavior. We recognize that our observations are always limited and open to question, but such is the nature of science. The ultimate goal

---

*Example from James Coleman's study, reported in Urie Bronfenbrenner's article on the family, p. 98.

of sociology is to build up sets of verified generalizations which present the discoveries and explanations that have been made about human social behavior in such a way that they increase our understanding of the topic.

There is one more important aspect of the method of sociology that is central to our understanding of it. This is the conceptual frame of reference—a set of tools that provides the framework within which the explanation is to be given. Every science has a set of such concepts. Whereas physicists talk about mass and force, the sociologist is likely to use concepts such as social class, social role, and institutions. These concepts are not unique to the discipline, but their particular connotations and the combination of concepts used in the discipline define its limits. Although some of its concepts change as sociology grows, many remain constant and become the focus of the discipline. Thus we might say that sociology explains human social behavior in terms of such concepts as interaction, groups, norms, social structure, social differentiation, and so on.

The central concepts of sociology are the basis for the organization of this book: if you look at the headings you get a picture of the ideas or concepts that the sociologist uses in explaining human social behavior. Note that the book is divided into two parts—social organization and social differentiation. In the first part we deal with those concepts that have to do with the organization of relationships between persons. Starting with simple interaction between two persons, we move to groups and their structure as seen in roles and norms. We then consider the more stable dimensions of human social life, which we call institutions, and those persistent patterns of behavior known to sociologists as culture. The section ends with a brief discussion of collective behavior, or behavior that is not organized through the conventional means of roles and norms but is still very social in nature.

The second part of the book deals with social differentiation. Here the sociologist tries to explain behavior not so much in terms of the organization of its parts, but rather in terms of the differentiations that members of society make in classifying other members and their corresponding rights and obligations. We find people divided by social class, race, age, sex, residence, and conformity.

The final section of the book deals specifically with social change. Note that, for the most part, the terms used by the sociologist to refer to his concepts are familiar. But the sociologist gives them special meanings, which are important for the student to learn. In the case of social change the sociologist refers particularly to changes in the social organization of society. It is particularly interesting to observe how changes in one realm of the social organization affect or instigate changes in other realms.

(Changes in the economy, for example, affect the functioning of the family.)

To each area that the sociologist studies he brings his own frame of reference, that is, his set of concepts. It is along these lines that we can differentiate between the various social sciences. Anthropology, political science, economics, history, and sociology all apply scientific methods to the study of human social behavior; they differ in the frame of reference that they use in their analyses.

In its 100 to 150 years of existence, sociology has undergone a number of changes. We shall not in this volume try to trace all of its origins and influences. Man has found the application of the methods of science useful in understanding human social behavior; thus sociology has persisted. Although there is wide agreement as to the important concepts and the general framework of sociology broadly defined, beyond that point we find areas of increasing disagreement. There are those who insist on an extremely rigid scientific model closely paralleling that of the physical sciences, emphasizing mathematically precise measuring instruments and clearly validated evidence. At the other extreme there are those who feel that sociology can be practiced as an art; the sociologist must experience his subject matter and find intuitive answers. Most sociologists fall somewhere in between; they respect rigorous scientific methodology, but realize that some deviation from the model of the physical science is needed to tap the fruitful sources of sociological data. The article by the widely respected sociologist Robert K. Merton answers those who suggest that perhaps sociologists have nothing constructive to offer to the understanding of human social behavior. This type of criticism is not at all unfamiliar to the socioligist.

There is another source of controversy which comes to the forefront every few decades and seems particularly relevant today—the question of the sociologist as an activist. Traditionally, the notion has been perpetuated that science—thus sociology—must be value-free. As scientists we are exclusively interested in knowing the truth; the determination of what is right or wrong is left to others. It was long felt that the sociologist should present his findings and let others do with them as they wished, but times have changed. Sociologists, like the students referred to in the first paragraph of this chapter, are beginning to feel that they want to become involved in the world. Many now feel that it is their obligation, because of their special expertise, to play a significant role in encouraging social change. In the article from *Time* we read a report on this new sociologist.

1 / THE CASE FOR SOCIOLOGY

Robert K. Merton

Once again the season of the anti-sociologists is upon us. The academic year has ended and professors are ready to turn from talking to writing. A self-selected few will dust off and publish yet again the litany that fiercely imprecates sociology and all its works. This year, the avowed conservative professor of political science, Russell Kirk, got in first. His version will serve to exhibit the curious admixture of illogic and sentiment that makes up the creed and canons of anti-sociology.

Some sociologists find these assaults tiresome. To me, they have the peculiar charm of testifying to the need for the very kind of sociological inquiry they caricature. For each jaded version reads as though it were written by a sociologist-*manqué*. Each purports to describe the behavior of sociologists, to explain that behavior and, even more ambitiously, to describe and explain the responses to it.

With practiced ease, for example, Mr. Kirk reviews the work of thousands of social scientists and promulgates the first canon that "the representative" specimen is an "empiricist of the positivist variety; emotionally, he is often a secular evangelist." Had Mr. Kirk allowed himself to profit from the introductory course in sociology he so deplores, he might have learned of the danger of creating out of his private impressions a stereotype of the aims and behavior of large numbers of people, all the while pretending to have caught hold of the representative reality. But amateur sociologizing has no place for disciplined inquiry. Rather, it assumes that statements become authoritative simply by being put into the black and white magic of print.

The second canon declares the absurdity and impiety of statistics dealing with the behavior of men in society. For nothing significant about man's behavior can be counted. If it could be counted, it would be immoral to do so. Everyone knows that no good can come of it.

To support this canon, Mr. Kirk cites Carlyle, who knew little about the primitive statistical methods of his own day and nothing, obviously, about the mathematical bases of modern statistics. As further proof, he quotes the attack by the sociologist Pitirim A. Sorokin on "quantophrenia"

---

or an uncritical devotion to faulty statistics. Unlike myself, Mr. Kirk has not had the benefit of having been Professor Sorokin's student, and so does not know, apparently, that Sorokin used vast arrays of social statistics in every one of his major works and, in "Social and Cultural Dynamics," states that "quantitative judgments . . . in verbal form" are inevitable in any substantial work of history.

No doubt it is more inviting to assume statistics of human behavior. The amateur sociologist will explain, for example, why it is that we have such high rates of mental illness in what Mr. Kirk feels free to describe as our age of "twentieth-century social disintegration." But while the amateur sociologist explains *why* this is so, the disciplined sociologist proceeds first to find out whether it really *is* so. Only through painstaking analysis of the statistics of mental illness—as in the work of Herbert Goldhamer and Andrew Marshall—do we find that we had best postpone our ready-to-hand explanations, if only because it now seems probable that the rate of confinement for mental illness is no higher today than it was during the past century.

Turning up like death and taxes, the third canon of the anit-sociologists declares the sociologists to be both perpetrators and victims of jargon. Here, the anti-sociologist knows himself to be on altogether safe ground, for just about everyone can be counted on to be "against jargon" in the same penetrating sense that President Coolidge's minister declared himself against sin.

Perhaps it is time to distinguish between jargon and that essential of all disciplined thought, technical language. Technical language is a more precise and condensed form of thought and communication than colloquial language. It is designed to fix definite meanings to which each word has ideally only one denotation and is deliberately deprived of connotations. Jargon, in contrast, is a muddled and wordy imitation in technical language.

The mere unfamiliarity or unesthetic quality of language is no criterion. Jargon and technical language sound alike to someone untrained in the discipline where the language is employed.

All this is only prologue to the pair of canons central to the anti-sociologists' creed. Briefly put, these hold, first, that sociological truths cannot be discovered, for there are no detectable uniformities in human behavior, since man is incorrigibly unpredictable. And second, that sociologists constitute a danger to society, for they provide the knowledge through which men can be molded to fit a new and obnoxious social order. I need not burlesque the logic of the anti-sociologists, for they have preceded me here. I need only review it.

It would seem clear that, if there are no discoverable uniformities about man in society, there can be no sociological knowledge employed to regiment him. Should anti-sociologists admit that there are such uniformities, they can scarcely argue that these uniformities can be discovered by the defective sociology of today, with its inapplicable statistics, its tattered jargon, and its total misunderstanding of human nature.

Forced to acknowledge that there are discoverable uniformities in social life and that modern sociology, for all its limitations, discovers some of them, would they then propose to exercise this knowledge for fear that it might be used to violate civilized values? On this last line of retreat, the anti-sociologists would join forces with the anti-intellectuals and totalitarian regimenters of thought they ostensibly combat. They would declare themselves guardians of us all, alone able to distinguish dangerous from undangerous knowledge.

The remaining canons of the anti-sociologists are transparently trivial. Criticism among sociologists, for example, is described by the anti-sociologists in the militant metaphors of "warring camps" and "internecine warfare." Perhaps they should pause before advocating monolithic agreement on intellectual issues. It would be a curious reading of the history of thought to suggest that the absence of disagreement testifies to a developing discipline.

As for the anti-sociologists' canon that gives them alone access to the recorded wisdom of the past—from Plato to Montesquieu and Burke—this need only be stated to refute itself.

Since the anti-sociologists impose their grotesque versions of the methods of sociological inquiry upon a public too busy to look for themselves, a few words should be said about those methods. Social scientists believe it no longer sufficient to describe the behavior, attitudes, values and social relations obtaining in a complex society simply on the basis of a large but scattered array of documents, both public and private, and on educated guesses about what people are thinking and feeling. Studies of the historical past, of course, have no alternative. But in the study of present-day societies, these procedures are giving way to systematic, though far from perfected, methods.

One such method is the "sample survey," which sounds out the practices and attitudes of a group selected as representative of the larger population from which they are drawn. This type of survey is now part of the intellectual landscape. However, the "opinion polls" in the popular press do not begin to reproduce the analytical uses to which such surveys are put by academic sociologists.

Furthermore, it is with this instrument as with the rest: the most devastating criticisms of its misuse have come, not from the anti-sociologists who know about it only through casual inspection, but from the professional sociologists who are prepared to study their sometimes disappointing experience with it. For they, at least the best of them, know that, whatever the worth of one or another tool of inquiry, it is the questions put into the inquiry that determine the significance of the results. If the questions are trivial, then the answers will be trivial.

For sociology as for most other scientific disciplines, the electronic computer has emerged as a new resource. Contrary to the imagery of the anti-sociologists, this machine is not the universal mind of our day. It must be told what to do. But, as with most technical creations, the computer has a capacity for deflecting men from the pursuit of purposes that genuinely matter. It tempts its tenders to cast all manner of raw data into its maw and wait for the thoroughly digested product that will itself be senseless if the thought of its managers is without sense. The potential victims, by their professional training, are best qualified to recognize and to counter this danger.

With or without the computer, today's sociology makes no attempt to substitute science for ethics and esthetics or to displace humanism with scientism. Every responsible sociologist, and there are not a few, knows that his knowledge is no substitute for artistic thought.

The thinking humanist, for his part, recognizes that the social scientist who knows his business seeks only to provide an understanding of certain, not all, aspects of the behavior of men and the organization of human society. The intellectual gulf between humanist and social scientist has begun to be bridged. The late Gilbert Murray, critic and classical scholar, said that sociology is "destined to bear abundant and ever-increasing fruit." The political journalist Richard Rovere, has observed that "those of us who have been educated in the twentieth century habitually think in sociological terms, whether or not we have had any training in sociology."

After all this, it is only natural to ask: what is going on in sociology and what does it all amount to? It would be foolish to answer this question by staking out the boundaries of sociology, as though it were a piece of real estate. That is not the character of intellectual property. But we can, in this short space, at least hint at the answer.

In the large, sociology is engaged in finding out how man's behavior and fate are affected, if not minutely governed, by his place within particular kinds, and changing kinds, of social structure and of culture. This means that sociology moves across a wide, varied and, to the layman, often bewildering range of topics and problems.

In doing so, one of its principal functions is to subject popular beliefs about man and his works to responsible investigation. As I have implied, the sociologist asks about many of these beliefs, "Is it really so?" The popular assumption, for example, that the rate of social mobility in America has recently declined has been put in question by systematically assembled data.

The alleged breakdown of the American family, with obsequies read regularly over the remains by those who should know better, has been found to be specious; thorough analyses of data on divorce and death find American marriages remaining intact more often now than they once did. Or, to tackle one last widespread assumption, people who reject orthodox religious beliefs are not more apt to engage in crime than people who hold fast to such beliefs.

Some of the findings of sociology take a considerable time to enter the public domain. For more than a generation, sociologists have found that complex organizations of widely different kinds—economic, political, military, educational—exhibit the same tendencies. These tendencies make for the "bureaucratic man," who is shaped by organizationally induced pressures to conform to the rules even when this means that conformity gets in the way of doing the job effectively. How far this is inevitable remains to be seen, and inquiries are now under way to find out how these tendencies can be counteracted.

Basic to sociology is the premise that, in the course of social interaction, men create new conditions that were not part of their intent. Short-run rationality often produces long-run irrationality. Public health measures may go awry; financial incentives may lead to a decline rather than an increase in production; intensified punishment may aggravate rather than curb crime. Growing recognition of this has become one of the sources of an enlarged use of sociological research in such fields as medicine and public health, social work, law, education, the ministry, architecture and city planning, business, organized labor and agriculture.

Yet it must be added, that sociologists, perhaps better than the anti-sociologists, know they are just beginning to acquire the knowledge needed to cope with the many social ills man has the inveterate capacity to contract.

We sociologists need to be saved from the anti-sociologists only in respect to the exaggerated claims they make for our prowess and accomplishments. It is they, not we, who say that "sociology is a power in the land." It is they, not we, who make the absurd claim that sociology has the power and the intent to turn men into robots and to construct a new social order. The men and women at work in sociological inquiry have more modest and less sadistic hopes. Like their colleagues in other scholarly and scientific disciplines, they recognize that this "very new science of an ancient subject" has still a long way to go. And undisturbed by the cannonades of the anti-sociologists, they are methodically proceeding on their way.

2 / THE NEW SOCIOLOGY

Time Magazine Staff

The public image of the sociologist—if there is a public image—is that of a fusty pedant who writes books that nobody understands. He is esoteric, obfuscatory, exclusive and elusive. The stereotype is not too far from reality. There are such men, and they preside jealously over an academic fiefdom whose efforts to be recognized as a science are barely a century old.

But the image is no longer adequate. Sociology is changing, perhaps more rapidly than any other discipline. The field is generating a highly visible, adventurous and activist new type of scholar who respects no scientific boundaries, least of all his own, and who rejects the traditionalist's antiseptic analyses of how society works in favor of passionate prescriptions for its betterment.

PREMEDITATED EFFORT

No one more vividly personifies the new practitioner than Irving Louis Horowitz, 40, a shaggy, disarmingly unprofessorial professor who lectures without a tie, lambastes most of his colleagues, and delivers endless *sotto voce* manifestos. "I'm making a conscious, premeditated effort to radicalize sociology," says Horowitz. In pursuit of this goal, he passed up more lucrative offers last summer to accept the chairmanship of the sociology department of the Livingston campus of New Jersey's Rutgers University.

The youngest of Rutgers' four colleges, Livingston is itself a living experiment in the new sociology. Housed since last fall in what was once a U.S. Army barracks at deactivated Camp Kilmer (named for the arboreal poet), it attracts the young from the very constituency that Horowitz has staked out as his own: "The poor and the blacks, society's deviants of all kinds." More than half of Livingston's 750 students are black or Puerto Rican, and nearly all of them are poor. Horowitz can rap with them—and they with him. As one of his Negro students said recently: 'Irv is the blackest of any white man around here."

In company with most of the new sociologists, Horowitz is bent on redefining the traditionally accepted symptoms of social deviance: divorce, homosexuality, crime and revolution. In a white-dominated society, for that matter, a man can be labeled deviant just because he is black. "But how do we know what is and is not deviant?" asked Horowitz. "When 41 per cent of all marriages end in divorce, for example, must we still regard divorce as a social problem?" Instead of asking the question, "What went wrong with the marriage?" he suggests, the sociologist should ask: "What's wrong with the institution?"

NOT STASIS BUT CHANGE

This approach owes much to the late C. Wright Mills, the contentious Columbia University sociologist who died at 46 in 1962. Mills hurled his books like Molotov cocktails at the sociological myths of the time: that order prevailed, that the national institutions evolved by civilized societies remain forever faithful to their designers. An impetuous and often outrageous writer, Mills dismissed the classic image of American democracy as a "fairy tale."

Horowitz has become executor of Mills' literary estate and the most fervent advocate of Mills' central thesis: that human society is characterized not by stasis but by radical change. Born and raised in Harlem, the son of an illiterate immigrant Russian-Jewish locksmith, Horowitz rubbed elbows with his constituency before he recognized it. In sociological field trips to South America, where social fissures are far more visible than in the U.S., he developed the humanist approach that places responsibility to mankind before the obligations of science. He helped found and still edits *Trans-action*, an excellent magazine and one so remote in spirit from the old sociology that only 10 per cent of its 70,000 circulation goes to social scientists.

THE WORLD AS LABORATORY

One trouble with the traditional discipline was that it was—and in many respects still is—a private club with rigid rules. These have been summarized by Bennett M. Berger, a sociologist at the University of California at Davis. As he sees it, the traditionalists demand "ethical detachment as the appropriate posture of the sociologist toward his work, the selection of research problems not primarily for their importance but for their scientific manageability, and the maintenance of a strict separation between the sociologist's responsibilities as a scientist and his moral and political responsibilities as a citizen."

Horowitz and the new sociologists, in contrast, regard the world as their laboratory, not the laboratory as their world. They show little respect for either the old rules or the interdisciplinary fences that once divided the life sciences. By their definition, a sociologist is anyone who studies man. When Psychologist Hans Toch of the State University of New York at Albany wanted to study prisons as breeding places for violence, he recruited as his research assistants six inmates of California's San Quentin prison with a total of 83 years behind bars. To these investigators, other convicts opened up with a candor that the old methods could never have prompted. In New York City, Richard A. Cloward of Columbia University's School of Social Work has been dramatically successful in organizing one of the most unorganizable of all social subcultures, the welfare recipients.

Another of the new activists, David Gottlieb of Michigan State, played an influential role in the formation of the Job Corps. When, earlier this month, the National Commission on the Causes and Prevention of Violence proposed an annual report on the social state of the nation, the commission was only endorsing a suggestion that has been repeatedly urged by such men as Horowitz and Herbert J. Gans, professor of sociology and planning at M.I.T., who was also one of the first to blow the whistle on the bulldozing school of urban redevelopment. In Boston, Gans has played a sociological role by calling attention to the demolition of old but otherwise structurally sound tenements by landlords who no longer found them profitable. Gans' critique spread to other cities and helped rescue from condemnation many a building whose destruction might have served everyone's purpose but the tenants'.

The new men are less concerned with what is right in the world than with what is wrong. Since they are not afraid to be wrong themselves, they have naturally attracted criticism. "What we've really learned," Horowitz told *Time*'s Steve Englund, "is that the doctors are as sick as the society." With considerable validity, the traditionalists have faulted the innovating physicians for romanticism and for shoddiness of method—for the ease with which they advance outrageous and sometimes unsupportable hypotheses. Princeton University's Marion J. Levy, Jr. typically accuses Horowitz of "making a virtue of thinking with his heart, not with his head." Of his own approach, Levy says: "I do not regard myself as being concerned with helping my fellow man."

Partly as a result of Horowitz and his colleagues, who are indeed concerned with helping their fellow men, many colleges and universities are enjoying a boom in sociology. Enrollment of sociology students at Princeton is up 200 percent (to 1,500 students) in four years. At San Jose State College, it has risen 350 percent in three years. What is sociology's new appeal?

In an age of mass democracy and vast, impersonal institutions, it promises the individual a way to regain self-determination. "History," says University of Michigan's Anatol Rapoport, "is determined by forces over which man has no control, so long as he is unaware of those forces. When he becomes aware of them, he can determine his future history. This is also similar to the Freudian view: man is a slave to his compulsions when their roots are repressed; exposing the roots makes man free."

Whether the new approach will make man free any more than Freudian analysis did remains to be seen. In the meantime, it is certainly and excitingly freeing sociology.

AIM OF THE BOOK

Now that you know something of what sociology is all about, it seems worth while to take some space to explain the format of the remainder of this book. The first aim is to communicate with you, the student. Within the profession of sociology the conventional means of communication is through the use of professional journals. All disciplines have their journals (sociology has more than 15) in which scholars publish the results of their studies or argue the merits of their latest ideas. Although these are common sources of material for books of readings, we have chosen not to include them. Since they are designed and used as vehicles by which sociologists communicate with each other, they tend to use technical language and are frequently difficult for the beginning student.

For this reason, all of the articles we have chosen were written for popular consumption. Most of the articles included appeared in national magazines which you could pick up at a newsstand. They were chosen because of their good literary style and their sound sociological presentation of interesting and stimulating subjects. Because we were concerned with presenting material with which the student could identify and in which he could see reflected his own experiences, most of the articles deal with American Society. Sociology, of course, is concerned with developing generalizations that have universal application, but for a beginning it is best to stay with the familiar. Because we live in a rapidly changing world, it should not be surprising that many of the articles deal with social change of one type or another.

However, we are concerned with more than simply presenting you with good reading material. Some articles were chosen because it was felt they were written in such a way as to be relevant to the student's interests and concerns—enough a part of his everyday life that he could relate to the material and begin to understand how sociological concepts can be used in the discovery and explanation of that particular aspect of social life. That is, to help the student apply the *sociological perspective*. Others were chosen because they provided good examples of scientific research. And some were chosen because we felt that they did a particularly good job in communicating important sociological propositions.

The value in a book such as this is determined to a great extent by what the student puts into it. It is designed to allow you, the student, to fill in the gaps and sift through the ideas and opinions to determine their relevance. To get the most out of the articles, it is a good idea to consider each of the following questions while studying the article: What are the author's intentions? Is he presenting fact or opinion? What is ideology and what is evidence? How does the material fit in with the topic being covered in the section? At the end of each section ask yourself: What have I learned about the concept under consideration by my reading of the material presented?

PART ONE
SOCIAL ORGANIZATION

When people act in relation to each other their actions are called *social.* In this section we shall make an effort to explain ways in which this behavior can be meaningfully understood. First, consider the concept of *social organization.* This term suggests that social interaction is not random, but rather patterned or organized. As people relate to one another over periods of time they begin to develop organized ways of responding and corresponding expectations for the responses of others. It is thus apparent that we are born into a complex, organized society in which most of the patterns of expected behavior have already been established for us. The customs of our society, its language, and its habits are all part of its social organization. Therefore, when the sociologist attempts to understand human social behavior, he soon realizes that one of his first tasks is to understand the underlying organization that determines the expectations that members of society have for themselves and others.

Human social organizations vary tremendously. Some are short-lived and flexible, as in the case of two persons who meet for the first time, exchange ideas, and depart. Other organizations are formal and last over generations with little change, as in the case of institutions like the church. When faced with the variety and complexity of human social organizations the sociologist finds it useful to introduce several important concepts.

Of crucial importance to the understanding of social organizations is the concept of *social norms—the rules or standards for behavior which are shared by the members of the group or the society.* These are the ways in which the person is *expected* to behave as a member of society. They range from simple etiquette to complex laws. Since not all persons behave exactly as they are expected to, society develops what are called *sanctions,* or responses to deviant behavior which tend to force the deviant back toward conformity. Sanctions, too, vary considerably—a frown directed at the person who eats with the wrong utensil and the imprisonment of a criminal who commits a serious crime are both examples of sanctions.

Sociologists have noted that deviation from the norms of society is frequently not an individualistic act, but often performed by groups of individuals who form an organization. Thus when the gang member steals from the corner store he may be violating the norms of the larger society, but he is living up to the expectations of his group.

These norms emerge out of the necessity for cooperation that arises in order for the group or society to function. The emergence must be seen as a long evolutionary process through which the expectations or norms are passed on from generation to generation—the process known as *socialization.* The young child is socialized as a part of his growing up, i.e., he is taught what will be expected of him as an adult member of society. However, this is not the only type of socialization; whenever a person joins a new group he must become socialized to its norms.

In dealing with the broad concept of norms, we shall find it useful to introduce additional concepts to handle its complexities. Those norms that refer to expectations for individuals because of their characteristics or the positions they hold in the group or society are called *roles.* For example, when he speaks of the role of the woman in American society, the sociologist is referring to those sets of expectations that society sets for individuals who have this characteristic. In our society we learn to expect that women will be allowed to enter a room before a man, dress in a particular way, have certain responsibilities for the care of children, and so on. These role expectations take many forms. Sometimes they are *rights* and *privileges,* while at other times they are *duties* and *obligations.*

Of course, society does not always agree on what the role-norms should be, which can lead to confusion and frustration for the persons involved. Take, for example, a foreman in a large factory. One segment of society, his fellow workers, may expect him to be a friend and make the work easy for them, while another, the management, may expect him to work the men hard to increase productivity. The foreman is caught in between and may well be sanctioned by one segment or the other for not conforming to their norms.

Institutions are the complex sets of norms and roles which are oriented around the basic needs of society. The family as a social institution provides an excellent illustration. In order for a society to survive there must be some mechanism for procreation; thus in every society we find something resembling the family. Those norms, roles, and values which are oriented around the maintenance of the family and the fulfillment of its functions make up the institution of the family.

Institutions are characteristically stable and persist over long periods of time. An arrangement whereby a man and woman enter into a legal contract of marriage, raise their own offspring, and live in an exclusive household is not the only way a society can reproduce itself, yet this practice has endured for many generations in our society and we have come to place great value on its continuance. This does not mean that institutions do not change, but rather that they are likely to become so ingrained in society that when change comes it is slow and frequently painful to those committed to the institution's values.

Sociologists do not always agree on just how many *basic* institutions ought to be considered, but most agree that familial, political, educational, economic, and religious institutions exist in all societies. Lately, some sociologists have suggested that there are other needs which emerge in a complex society such as ours that are just as basic to the survival of society as those listed. For example, mass communication, recreation, transportation, and science might all be considered social institutions in our society. Think of the complex set of norms and roles that are oriented around mass communication—the newspaper reporter, editor, publisher and newsboy, the TV correspondent, the movie maker, the actor, and the sportscaster all conform to certain norms in fulfilling their function in the process of communicating to the public.

A *social group* is usually defined by the sociologist as any number of persons who interact over a period of time. The interaction that makes up the group activity is patterned by the norms and roles that are brought to the group by its members or that emerge as time passes. The group as a social organization can be seen as a set of relationships among members, with the relationships defined in terms of the expectations the members have for each other. Take the example of a family as a group: the very labels that we give to the various position imply relationships—father, mother, husband, wife, son. To refer to a person as a father implies that he is part of a relationship with at least one other person—a son or daughter. If we were to study one particular family we would find that the father would have certain norms that governed his behavior because the family was part of American society (he would be expected to take the financial responsibility for his children), and other norms that applied because he was a member of that *particular* family (he might be expected to spend an hour with his children each evening after dinner, not because society demands this of him but because he has always done it and his family has come to expect this of him).

The concept of *culture* is widely used in the social sciences. It can be thought of as the total of the ways of behaving, feeling, and thinking which are *learned* by man as a member of society. Social norms are at the very core of culture; they define for the members of society what is considered the proper way of life. However, culture is the more encompassing term. If we were to combine in our analysis all social institutions, organizations, groups, norms, and roles of the society in order to determine styles of life, we would be studying culture. The same idea can be useful in considering a segment of the larger society as a sub-culture. Thus, in studying the culture of poverty the concern is with how being poor in an affluent society affects one's way of life. What are the norms that govern the behavior, thoughts, and feelings of a low-income person in regard to his family, his job, his religion, his relationships with peers, etc.? How does his way of life differ from that of middle-class or rich persons?

The study of *collective behavior* in some ways deal with the other side of the coin. Under this heading falls discussion of those forms of behavior that have social origins but do not fit the organized patterns of norms and institutions. When people are together in a tenuous setting and they do not have norms or roles to guide their behavior, they may become highly suggestible and act according to aroused impulses. Crowds, riots, and mobs demonstrate this type of behavior. Although the concepts of roles and norms are of little help in the analysis of collective behavior, the behavior is social in the sense that it constitutes reactions of man to others in a social setting. In the social organization we assumed man to respond rationally, whereas in the crowd we find him reacting more on an emotional level.

UNIT A INTERPERSONAL RELATIONSHIPS

The relationship between two persons lies at the very foundation of human social behavior. Communication is essential to the establishment and maintenance of such relationships, and communication in a complex society relies heavily on language. It is understandable, then, that language should play an important part in much sociological analysis.

In this section we start with the basics of the relationships between persons. Hedgepeth, a writer for *Look* magazine, suggests that we need a new language in order to find meaningful communication in our rapidly changing world. Weiss, a sociologist, is concerned with more fundamental questions regarding the importance of relationships with others to the individual's well being. Both writers feel that the changes taking place in our society add to the urgency of their appeals. Is it possible to relate the two articles in a meaningful way? Take Hedgepeth's notions about the difficulty of communication and ask yourself how they would affect the categories of relationships that Weiss lists. Now you can easily see that if Weiss is right in his assumption that the loss of relationships can be traumatic, then effective language, the vehicle for human relationships, is of central importance.

There is another important lesson in comparing the two articles. Note the difference in approach between the first article, written by an excellent writer, and the second, written by a competent sociologist. The first is a clear expression of opinion in which the author, using the best creative writing techniques, attempts to sell you on his ideas. In the second the sociologist is much more cautious. He tells you what ideas he started with, what evidence he gathered, and how he was forced to revise his ideas and come up with new ones to explain his findings. Both men are attempting to communicate their ideas; both are worth listening to. It remains for the reader to sort out biases and prejudices and determine what he has learned about human social behavior.

3 / GROWL TO ME SOFTLY AND I'LL UNDERSTAND

William Hedgepeth

Bands of light beam from the rear—flare, pale, flutter: blue, green, yellow, red; now it's red. Janis is red, writhing, wrenching words right out her pores. "Puh . . . Puhleeazzze . . ." up straight from her toes, shot through cosmos, amplified 2,000 watts. Stompstompstompstomp. Oh, Momma! Janis Joplin! Room booms: thousands out there, in the dark, feel the vibes. Supercharged. Slow glow grows in eyes: Does she *mean* it? Does she *mean* it? "WAH!" Mike jammed to her teeth, kicking, stomping, keeping time. Crouch down, up slow, louder now—tell us, tell us—"Awww wah hoo heee." Cymbals: crash, crash. Drum thump. Silent. Now it's over. Stunned hush. Did she mean it? Did she? Wah? Yes! Yes! The hall explodes. Message gotten. Yes! Yes! And then—*wham*—out of the grayish-hazy auditorium air rolls a long, blurry clap-whistle-roar like a rattling of the world's largest sheet of tin. Janis drops the mike, shoulders suddenly limp, bleats a teeny "thankya" and turns away from the crowd to grope for a paper cup (Dixie Cup) of Southern Comfort sitting on the organ. Then back to the mike.

No pukey, careful-metered lines sung here. And who here can possibly disentangle more than a few bare words out of that jammed-together thunderation of wailed syllables? ("AhheeeWOGPleaghuhh woo," she

---

From *Look*, Jan. 13, 1970. Reprinted by permission of the editors of *Look* magazine.

erupts again.) Not me, anyway. But everybody gets the point. The point is how she feels, and they are eager to pick it up, share it, feel it with her. They are primed for this kind of thing. People don't speak this way to them anywhere alse—even at home. No one lays it on the line; no one translates deep-felt feelings into language and says it like they sense it.

Probably because most often they can't. And because they can't say it, they can't imagine it being said. And because of that, if, somehow, they were able to, the chances are they wouldn't—at least not right off. So, as it turns out, there's a whole vast range not only of emotions but of newly grasped sensations that seems doomed to lie locked up, unwordable, in our heads. Our language, in its present shape, just can't handle it; and people —particularly young people—are slowly becoming aware of this flaw in their tongue.

They're becoming aware that—as a vehicle for conveying new sensibilities, perceptions of consciousness and the huge input of new ideas and information—straight English is inadequate. And because, at present, it's untrained to operate in this dimension, people are feeling around elsewhere for ways to express the new reality in words (or in wails, grunts, growls, shrieks or sounds no one's yet labeled). In parts of California, for example, young people are evolving a speech form some call "Sunbear." "It's based on how things sound and feel. It's street talk, family talk," says a turned-on girl in Palo Alto. "But our parents would never understand a word we're saying. Like, when we start rapping, we stop all the usual connections between thoughts."

"LAAww, ahh wahh..." (and louder) "OOOHHHh hooowooo Unngggghh" (like a stomp in the chest). Janis is looking out into the rotating multicolored spots and undulating against them and against the sexual pulse-bump-mega-beat of the band. She humps and bumps, howling, and, for a moment, becomes an upright elastic gyration in the stuttering quick-flicker of the strobes. "Uhh uhhhh huh, awoooooo"—low, and with much anguish. Some near the front nod in sympathy. She is speaking now to them beyond words. Ahhhh.

Words develop from a mental tagging of experience. Today, though, the sudden gush of new sorts of experiences—in both inner and outer space—has not only outpaced the development of our language but also shown up the limitations of its structure. It's not that conventional language has become inadequate for communicating fresh concepts merely because of a lack of new words; it's because of the whole way of thinking that it forces us into.

Psychologists say all higher levels of thinking depend on language. But at the same time, the structure of whatever language we use affects the way we see the world—influences, in fact, our attitudes and thought processes themselves. The difficulty today is that our brains have out-evolved our tongue. Every major language, says Dr. Mario Pei, started as a rough-hewn tool "fit only for material communication, and then proceeded to polish and refine itself to the point of becoming a vehicle for abstract, cultural thought."

Obviously, our language has done well in keeping its technological terminology polished up. But just where we need it most today, it lets us down. It's clear that there are important new realms of the mind, of interpersonal involvements and levels of perception that defy its ability to convey or communicate—or even to conceive. The whole business nowadays of people talking about ineffable vibrations they receive from this or that suggests the existence of dimensions of reality beyond the outer limits of our language's vocal range. Our language, after all, is a thought trap: when certain sorts of notions don't fit into its framework they remain unrecognized. It's a monstrous handicap. We are so crippled we haven't even the words to think about all those thoughts that might-have-been.

Then, too, there are concepts expressible in other tongues that simply don't translate into ours—except, perhaps, as vague approximations. The Hopi Indians, for example, can put forth ideas and feelings we can't even think about. The Hopi have a whole conception of time and space that's so far removed from *our* frame of reference it seems the work of Martians. What this means, in other words, is that there are other ways of regarding reality. "A change in language," wrote Benjamin Whorf, "can transform our appreciation of the Cosmos."

But today, our awareness of the Cosmos, our exploratory experiences (whether psychedelic or otherwise) into human consciousness, the whole content of our collective minds, in fact, have grown beyond the present capability of *any* conventional language to express. At the same time, the growing global nature of the human community is about to place enormous demands upon our capacity for interpersonal communication. "Our new environment compels commitment and participation. We have become irrevocably involved with, and responsible for, each other," says McLuhan. Our future, then, requires more than everyone becoming merely multilingual. What we need is a new basis for communication—a new language and, along with it, a newly understood function for language itself.

As it stands, we are harnessed to a tongue that's actually doing bad things to us. Much of our tradition-bound speech is structured in a way that creates a polarity between us and everyone (and everything) else. Our language forces us to conceive so much of life as an endless, goal-focused struggle, a war. And success, in even the most mild endeavors, is depicted in outright battlefield terminology: We grapple with, strive, clash, cross swords, lock horns, tussle, contend, engage, fight for or take the offensive to achieve (with flying colors) a triumph, victory, conquest, a win, a mastery, a put-down, a killing, etc. Roget's Thesaurus devotes 28 lines to "Peace" and 162 lines to "Warfare." Thus, at a time when we need to be dismantling barriers to human unity, we continue to generate tension as we talk—and our talk, in turn, influences our behavior. We tend, too, in this way, to use language not as a means of touching souls with others but as a defense, a barrier, with words deployed as little bricks to wall us in and hold other people off. Language tries to deal with reality by manipulating symbols of reality. It hinges on the mind's ability to link sounds with meanings and thereby transfer those meanings. Until we all become telepathic, we can't hope to grasp more than a hazy fraction of what's in another head; but meanwhile, we have to clear our existing channels of communication of all the subterfuge and conflict-laden verbosity that stand between us and what we could be.

Among young people, at least, a real frustration factor enters in here. For too long now, abstract feelings have largely been left in nonlinguistic limbo while our language has developed itself among more "practical" lines. To make things worse, so much irrational emotional baggage has been heaped on so many words that our ability to voice a gut-felt notion is stifled—unless we fall back on euphemisms that remove us even further from reality. If words are sounds that symbolize meanings, it's obviously the meanings not the sounds that are the things we try to get across. OK? Then why do you persist in the idea that "intercourse" or "lovemaking" is acceptable while – – – – is an unprintable moral affront? It's a perfect example of thinking backward, reacting to the symbol rather than the subject—a response so senseless that no one even knows why he does it. Somewhere along the line, things just got so turned around that now people are scared of their own words. We make ourselves feel guilty about our speech and sull up like treed possums when "unmoral" words are uttered—or perhaps it's just those word-sounds that touch a nerve or feeling or say a thing directly.

So, while the framework of our language hamstrings the brain's ability to think, we cramp our speech even further, just out of sheer perverseness. As a result, we go about transmitting at almost inaudibly low intensities with equipment that's inadequate to begin with.

If there is transfer of meaning, there is language. But this transfer doesn't have to be in sequential order nor in sentences nor even in words. Numbers or tones or computer beeps will do it. There are some American Indian tongues in which the verb can include the subject, object and all modifiers so that the entire sentence is a single word. The key element in this is a community of understanding, a willingness to comprehend each other's feelings, a group-consciousness—a quality of "us-ness." And it is precisely this aspect of speech—already a feature with many young people—that can spread worldwide.

Present national languages are a product of fragmentation. Today, though, due to global electronic communication, growing literacy, population density and travel, the drift is toward putting things back together. We're moving toward a world culture and ultimately universal consciousness. Eventually, an international language will supersede national languages—but hopefully sooner, for the lethal potential of this planet is already too great to tolerate continued mass misunderstanding, concealment of feelings and anything less than undistorted universal rapport.

Whatever it may be, our new language must serve this new function: as a common ground for interpersonal honesty; and, by way of that honesty, a greater breadth of nonverbal understanding—i.e., "us-ness." New language, too, can mean a new freedom of thought. We will, at last, use words at peak capacity, and without guile, to make clear who we are and how we feel, to feel our own words and to level with each other by committing ourselves to what we say.

On a personal level, there'll be no need to cling to formal grammar to convey meaning. Speech doesn't have to be linear; it can come out as a compressed overlay of facts and sensations and moods and ideas and images. Words can serve as signals, and others will understand. The way a man feels can be unashamedly expressed in sheer sound, such as a low, glottal hum, like the purring of a cat, to indicate contentment. People need only enough openness about themselves not to feel silly about an honest sound. If it says it, say it. Feelings have meaning. Sounds have meaning. Open language can be a joy—a language we can grow with, growl with. Words can cramp your style.

Janis glares out across the darkened auditorium with a pained grimace and an "Ohhh ahh hoo hiweee" that tears at the very root of the heart. She leans back now and moos some sorrowful something into the mike—low, now high, shrill, other worldly, like a haunt, a siren, wraith, denizen of the darks, dawn goddess, knobby nymph, mooncalf, Ophelia: "UUnnh hoo youpleuzz Yeahhh." Lord, she can't live through this—being eaten inside out with pain. Run to her. Clasp her shoulders, cradle her tortured head. "PUHleazzee. . . ." (Crowd: yeh, yeh, do it, do it.) "Yawhoo oo. . . ." Up now, quick, before she dies, seize her. Cool her. Blow in her face. Marry her. Kiss her cheeks. Ply her limp lips with Southern Comfort. Anything, anything. Oh God . . . Janis, Janis, you've not said a word but I understand. We're in love. We don't need words, just meanings, just sounds of feeling, noises that say things. Oh, roar, hiss, bleat, bark, purr to me, snarl sweetly to me. Ahhhh . . . snaarrrll . . . ahhhhh, yes, I know, I know. . . .

4 / THE FUND OF SOCIABILITY

Robert S. Weiss

Why do people require relationships with one another? What needs are being expressed? We recognize constantly, sometimes with surprise, how important relationships are to us. Newly divorced individuals are distressed by loneliness, even as they congratulate themselves on having ended a conflict-laden marriage. Individuals who work alone, such as writers, complain of isolation, even as they prize their autonomy. Travelers on shipboard, separated from their network of friends, may find themselves greeting with enthusiasm an acquaintance from their home town who, in other circumstances, they might have barely acknowledged. In all these ways social needs express themselves. What can be their nature?

In trying to find answers to this question, people have generally taken two lines of argument. One, associated with some schools of sociology, has been to assert that relationships which are close, so close they may be called primary, provide the individual with his understandings of reality, his moral values, his goals, even his sense of self. Relationships are important because through them the society organizes the individual's thinking and acting. Essentially, the society teaches its members what they want.

The second view, associated more with psychology than with sociology, has been that people have a number of needs or requirements which only relationships can satisfy, and that without appropriate relationships the individual will suffer. These needs are intrinsic to the individual, and are not formed by the society in which he lives. They may include needs for recognition, for affection, for power, for prestige, for belonging, and many more.

How can we move from these fairly general theoretical positions to a testable formulation of why people require relationships? Perhaps the simplest hypothesis we can phrase, one which would seem to be an implication of the first view but not of the second, is that of the "fund of sociability." According to this idea individuals require a certain amount

---

of interaction with others, which they may find in various ways. They may with equal satisfaction have a few intense relationships or have a large number of relationships of lesser intensity. They would experience stress only if the total amount of relating to others was too little or too great.

The "fund of sociability" idea seemed to us to be a useful starting point in our effort to learn more regarding the assumptions, content, and functions of social ties. The research strategy that seemed to us a promising way to test this hypothesis was to seek out a group of individuals, all of whom had lost an important relationship but who also had the opportunity for unlimited sociability. It might then be seen whether increased sociability in some way compensated for the loss of the relationship.

For about a year, a colleague and I attended meetings of the Boston chapter of Parents Without Partners, a national organization of people who have children but who are living alone because of separation, divorce, or the death of their spouse. By listening to discussions of their past and current problems, and also from interviews with a good many members and former members, we hoped to be able to specify the nature of the losses sustained by these men and women with the end of their marriages, and the way in which membership in Parents Without Partners was useful to them.

We found that most members had joined simply because they were lonely, although there may well have been other reasons, including concern for their children or the desire to help others. The loneliness resulted directly from the absence of the marital relationship, rather than from such secondary factors as change in social role.

According to the "fund of sociability" hypothesis, we should expect to find members reporting that they had been lonely and restless after the dissolution of the marriage, but that interaction with others in Parents Without Partners had made up some part of that loss. We found, however, that although Parents Without Partners offered its members help with a host of difficulties, the sociability of belonging did not particularly diminish the sense of loneliness. Dating helped a good deal, but friendship did not. Although many members, particularly among the women, specifically mentioned friendship as the main contribution they received from Parents Without Partners, and these friendships sometimes became very close and very important to the participants, they did not compensate for the loss of the marriage. Friends and activities (discussion groups were perhaps the best) made the loneliness easier to manage, but they did not end it or even appreciably diminish it. One woman said, "Sometimes I have the girls over, and we talk about how hard it is. Misery loves company, you know."

SIMPLE SOCIABILITY NOT SATISFACTORY

Clearly the social needs satisfied in marriage, and, apparently, in dating, were not satisfied by simple sociability, no matter how much of it there was. But this raised the question of whether friendship was simply inadequate to supply the kind of interaction required, or whether friendship supplied something quite different, something that might not be found in marriage.

It seemed to us that friendship did offer something distinct from what marriage provides. But how to test this? We needed to find people who were married, but without friends. If friendships met social needs distinct from those met by marriage, then people without friends should be in distress, even though married. However, if friendship provided only a kind of time-filling sociability, then married people without friends should get along almost as well as married people with friends.

We began with a pilot study of six couples who had moved to the Boston suburbs from at least two states away. Our respondents were all middle-class and they had moved to Boston because of the husband's job.

Soon after the move, all but two of the wives were seriously unhappy; they were feeling a sense of social isolation similar in intensity (albeit shorter in duration) to the sense of emotional isolation that seemed to follow the dissolution of a marriage in others. The problem appeared to be that the housebound wife had no one with whom she could share the concerns of her daily life. Husbands could not really discuss with interest the dilemmas of child care nor the burdens of housework, and though they sometimes tried, they simply could not function properly as a friend. They might even compound the difficulty by saying they couldn't understand what was happening to their wives, and sometimes be downright unsympathetic because of what they felt were their own more serious problems of proving themselves on the new job. They were not troubled by the lack of people with whom they could share common interests, because at work they found men to talk to about the things that concerned them; the job, politics, sports, the local driving patterns, and the like. Two of the men with whom we worked listed for us the people they talked with during the day, and the number was impressive.

Meanwhile, the newcomer wives were likely to become painfully bored. In the absence of anyone with whom they could share their interests, they found housework and child care increasingly unrewarding. One wife who had been socially active and had considered herself reasonably happy in her former home began to drink heavily. Another wanted her husband to give up the promotion that had brought him to the Boston area, and to return to her parents' home town.

Of the two wives who did not seem to suffer from newcomer blues, the first was a woman who had no children and who immediately solved the problem of social isolation by going to work. The other was married to a man who in a previous move had bought a house in an old and settled neighborhood where friendships were well-established. To escape social isolation, she began taking night-school classes, and as her husband said when he talked with us, he hardly saw her except when they passed each other in the driveway. This time the husband moved into a new development where other homes were also owned by newcomers to the region, and spent his first weekend making friends with the new neighbors.

It now appeared clear to us that just as friendships do not provide the functions ordinarily provided by marriage, neither does marriage provide the functions ordinarily provided by friendship. Our current work on the nature of marriage suggests that marriages may vary in this, but nevertheless we believe that even in the most companionate of marriages, some important interests will not be shared within the marriage, and for women in the social group of the newcomer sample and even to a greater degree among poorer women the conerns of managing a family are not shared with the husband.

At this point, the hypothesis of a "fund of sociability" could be confidently rejected. It was clear that there were different kinds of relationships, providing different functions. The question then arose, how many relationships seemed to be necessary, and what functions did they seem to provide?

On the basis of further work with Parents Without Partners, we have been led to develop a theory that might be characterized as "the functional specificity of relationships." We believe that individuals have needs which can only be met within relationships, that relationships tend to become relatively specialized in the needs for which they provide, and as a result individuals require a number of different relationship for well-being.

Although there are many variations in the way people organize their lives, one can in general say that relations with kin seem to be reliable as sources of help, but not as sources of companionship; friends offer companionship, but not intimacy; and marriage or a near-marital relationship offers intimacy, but rarely friendship. We are not sure why this specialization develops. Undoubtedly, much has to do with underlying cultural definitions of the relationship. If wholehearted commitment between friends is difficult—and this seems the case in adult American life—then it will be possible for friends to share interests, but extremely difficult for them to develop the level of trust which would permit emotional intimacy.

The marriage relationship may be an exception to the generalization that relationships are specialized in function. In marriage each spouse provides for the other a degree of emotional integration, and also provides collaboration in managing the mechanics of life. But even here there may be conflicts between the way of relating to one another that is associated with the one function, and that associated with the other. In terms of the collaborative relationship, for example, it may be reasonable for a wife to criticize her husband's capacity to earn, but since she is also a source of emotional integration, her criticism can be devastating.

The specialization of relationship is probably always incomplete. Undoubtedly every friendship involves some emotional exchange and has the potential for more. Yet going beyond the understood assumptions of the relationship can endanger it. When it happens, for example, that one partner in a friendship seeks to move the relationship to one in which there is an assumption of the unbounded trust, the more usual assumptions of the friendship may be temporarily flooded out. The consequence is likely to be uneasiness when the friends later find it necessary to return to the old basis. Generally there is so much resistance to changes of definition of a relationship that if a person loses the relationship that provided a particular function—as through the death of a spouse—he will be able only temporarily to alter his remaining relationships to fill the gap. Among members of Parents Without Partners, for example, we found a good deal of bitterness that stemmed from the failure of their friends to respond to their new relational needs.

FIVE CATEGORIES OF RELATIONSHIPS

On the basis of our material we believe we can identify five categories of relational functions, each for the most part provided by a different relationship. All these functions seem to us to be necessary for well-being.

1. *Intimacy*, for want of a better term, is used to characterize the provision of an effective emotional integration in which individuals can express their feelings freely and without self-consciousness. It seems to us that this function of relationships prevents the individual from experiencing the sense of emotional isolation that is expressed in the term "loneliness." For a relationship to provide intimacy, there must be trust, effective understanding, and ready access. Marriage provides such a relationship and so, often, does dating, at least for a time. Occasionally a woman may establish a relationship of this kind with a close friend, her mother, or a sister. And under some circumstances a man may establish a relationship of this sort with a friend.

It may be noted, parenthetically, that the relationship between sexual involvement and emotional intimacy, when the individuals concerned are potentially appropriate sexual partners, is quite complex and may well vary by social group and by circumstance. Certainly sex and intimacy are not necessarily associated. Still, rather fragmentary evidence suggests that in the groups we have worked with, individuals who are potentially appropriate partners may find it difficult to maintain a non-sexual emotionally intimate relationship. Where individuals are not appropriate sexual partners there is no apparent difficulty in maintaining such a relationship.

2. *Social integration* is provided by relationships in which participants share concerns, either because of similar situations ("we are in the same boat") or because they are striving for similar objectives (as in relationships among colleagues). Such relationships allow a good deal of sharing of experience, information, and ideas. They provide the basis for exchange of favors, and sometimes for more substantial help (though not for help continued over time). Among women this function is usually provided by friendships; among men, by relations with colleagues, as well as by friendships. The absence of this relationship may be experienced as a sense of social isolation and will, we suspect, be accompanied by feelings of boredom.

3. *Opportunity for nurturant behavior* is provided by relationships in which the adult takes responsibility for the well-being of a child. Our impression, based on experience with Parents Without Partners, is that men seem able to act as foster fathers to children not their own, but that it is much more difficult for women to act as foster mothers. The conditions for the expression of nurturance—and the nature of nurturance—may be different in men and women. We suspect that absence of this function may be signaled by a sense that one's life is unfulfilled, meaningless, and empty of purpose.

4. *Reassurance of worth* is provided by relationships that attest to an individual's competence in some role. Colleague relationships, and the social support and mutual respect they imply, can do this for some men, particularly those whose work is difficult or highly valued. Successful family life may function in this way for other men, competence or worth here depending not on particular skills, but on the ability to support and defend a family. Women who work may also find their employment a source of reassurance of worth. Women who do not work must look to relationships with husbands, children, and acquaintances for recognition of their competence in making and managing a home. The loss of any system from which recognition of work, value, or competence may be gained will, we believe, result in decreased self-esteem.

5. *Assistance* through the provision of services or the making available of resources, although a primary theme in kin relationships, may be provided by a number of other relationships as well, including friendships and relationships with neighbors. However it seems to be only among close kin that one may expect assistance that is not limited in time and extent. It is the importance of this function for the poor that leads to the development of relational patterns in which kin ties are of primary importance. We suspect that the absence of any relationship providing the assurance of assistance if needed would be reflected in a sense of anxiety and vulnerability.

In addition, there seems to be a sixth function which can be provided by relationships that some people find important. This function might be characterized as *guidance*, and may be provided by mental-health professionals such as social workers or psychiatrists, or by ministers and priests, among others.

Undoubtedly there are individual differences in capacity to withstand the absence of one or another of the functions without giving way to restlessness and to the development of such symptoms as loneliness and boredom. On the basis of accounts of individuals who have successfully weathered long periods of isolation, one might suspect that individuals who have more rigid character structures might be better able to forego the absence of some relational functions. One device that seems to have helped these men and women was to establish a detailed daily routine from which they did not deviate.

It is difficult at this point to say that any one of the relational functions is more important than another. The absence of intimacy can clearly be disorganizing for many individuals, and for most it would be accompanied by painful loneliness, but we are not able at this time to say that it is a more serious deficit than the absence of opportunity for nurturance. I have known childless couples to be as downcast by difficulties in adopting a baby as a lonely person might be by difficulties in finding love. It seems as though the absence of any relational function will create some form of dissatisfaction, accompanied by restlessness and occasional spells of acute distress.

This theory, like any theory of human nature, has implications for the way in which we might deal with individuals in difficult situations. We might consider two possible areas of application of these ideas: to the problem of relational loss, and to the problem of aging.

There are many forms of relational loss. There is the loss of friends that comes with moving from one area to another, the loss of colleagues that accompanies retirement, the loss of newly adult children from home, the loss of a spouse through death or divorce. Each of these losses would seem to have two aspects: first, the trauma that accompanies the damage to the individual's life organization; and, second, the deficit in the individual's life that is a result of the continuing absence of the functions once provided by the now-lost relationship. When individuals move from one area to another, the trauma aspect may be nothing more than sadness at leaving old friends and old associations, and not especially serious. The primary problem of relocation is that of deficit in the wife's relationships, the absence of new friends in the new situation. In conjugal bereavement, the loss by death of a spouse, the pain of loss is ordinarily very great and, for a good while, the trauma of the loss will be the primary source of distress. Yet even when this has been resolved, the life of the widow or widower is apt to continue to be unsatisfactory because of problems of relational deficit. It can be helpful to a widow or widower to recognize these two consequences of loss and to acknowledge that loneliness may be an unavoidable response to an unsatisfying situation rather than an inability to resolve the disruption of loss. Being able to identify what is wrong makes it easier to find remedies.

To turn to aging, the theory alerts us to the disturbances of social relationships that come with time. These include departure of children, retirement, possibly the loss of spouse, and, as a result of all the preceding, painful and sometimes bewildering reorientation of central life concerns.

When their children leave, the older couple may find a freedom they have not known for decades, but they also lose their opportunity for nurturance. They may continue to help their now-grown children, and they may be able periodically to indulge their grandchildren, but they probably will never again have the sense of being essential to someone else, which is at least one of the functions small children seem to provide for their parents.

RETIREMENT REMOVES IMPORTANT BASIS FOR SELF-ESTEEM

Retirement varies in its implication, but for many men, as Eugene A. Friedmann and Robert J. Havighurst have shown, it removes from their lives an important basis for self-esteem. The parallel, for a woman, would be the loss of a home to keep up. This too can occur in time, but usually at a considerably later point in a woman's life than retirement occurs in a man's. It must be said, though, that the loss of children from the home may constitute a partial retirement for women.

With bereavement, the aged person may have no access to intimacy, and despite remaining relationships with grown children, other relatives, and friends, may begin to experience chronic loneliness. The absence of an intimate tie, we suspect, makes it difficult for an individual to maintain an even emotional balance. Since his emotional responses are not communicated and responded to, they go unchecked, uncorrected by another's perceptions. The result may be distortions either in the direction of pathological distrust or in the direction of depression which are difficult to interrupt.

The aged will lose friends through death, including old friends with whom so much is shared that the relationships are irreplaceable. But they also may give up friends because the interests and concerns that were central to the frienship no longer have meaning for them. Losing her husband may change a woman's life so much that she may no longer have anything in common with her married friends. Retirement may make irrelevant a man's relationships with former colleagues. And at the same time these bases for former friendships are lost, the afflictions of age—sickness, limited income, dependence—may produce new central life concerns which can be shared by few others. The aged who become seriously ill, or crippled, or have a chronic condition that requires frequent medical care, cannot share with anyone their feelings about these physical problems, even though they may well find them the central concerns of their lives. Small wonder, then, if an aged person who is ill seeks out a doctor just to talk about his condition, even at the risk of being thought a hypochondriac.

The aged, therefore, are vulnerable to relational losses that bring in their wake feelings of loneliness, boredom, and worthlessness, and a sense that they are no longer of critical importance to anyone else. These feelings, taken together, have sometimes been characterized as a psychological syndrome that accompanies age. A simpler explanation is that these feelings are normal reactions to relational deficits, reactions that would be found in any group similarly afflicted.

This appraisal suggests that the social and emotional distresses that accompany age can be remedied, but only by relationships that supply the required functions. It gives us a guide to the sort of relationships that may help and the sort that probably will not. For the retired, activities that clearly benefit others, or display competence in an important or valued way, may substitute for employment; but a make-work task, a hobby, or just keeping busy will not.

The appraisal also suggests that relational losses can be repaired. Should loss take place, and this is almost inevitable with age, then the view taken here suggests that it would be better to advise such people that they attempt to establish new relationships that will provide the same functions, rather than "gracefully" accept constriction.

But this recommendation could be made universally. Beyond a certain point we cannot limit our relations with others without incurring serious loss. Just as it is bad advice to tell a widow to live for the children, or to tell someone who is aged to accept the inevitable losses, it is bad advice to tell a young person to forego intimacy for a time while he concentrates on his studies.

UNIT A / ISSUES FOR CONSIDERATION

1. How does the framework of our current language inhibit social relationships?
2. List several forms of "relational loss" and describe their consequences for the individual experiencing the loss.
3. How would Hedgepeth's notions about the difficulty of communication affect the five categories of relational functions discussed by Weiss?

UNIT B
SOCIAL NORMS AND ROLES

The key to understanding the perspective of the sociologist may lie in an understanding of the concept of *norms*. Most of sociology is based in one fashion or another on the assumption that man acts according to his perception of what is expected of him in social settings. These standards for behavior are what we call norms—the social rules that tell the individual how he is supposed to behave in a given situation.

There are a great variety of norms. What is important to remember is that they are the *expectations* that society, or the group, has for the way the individual should act. When these norms pertain to the individual because of a particular position he holds in the group or society, we refer to them as *role-norms* or simply *roles*. You already know something about the role of the sociologist. Elsewhere in the book we will learn about role-norms for such varied positions as priests, athletes, white collar criminals, and many more.

Since most selections in this book deal with norms in one way or another, we have chosen for this section articles that are of direct relevance to the topic. The review by Kaplan of the 12th edition of *Emily Post's Etiquette* is a specific attempt to deal with norms in American Society. Although most persons do not learn what is expected of them by reading books on etiquette, the very existence of such a book reveals an effort by at least one element of society to impose its standards on others. Most efforts, however, are more subtle, as is clear from Naomi Weisstein's article on women. Note how this psychologist, after considering psychology's understanding of the role of the woman in American Society, ends by explaining woman's behavior not in psychological terms, but in terms of society's expectations of women.

Sometimes the most dramatic way to become aware of role-norms is to be required to step out of your role and play that of another. Hammer's article describes judges playing the role of prisoners and vice versa. The experiment demonstrates the complexities of a single role. For the prisoner, there are expectations for how he should behave held not only by fellow prisoners, but also by the judge who sent him to prison, the guard who keeps him there, and all others whom he confronts. Could one of the problems for the prisoner be a conflict in role-expectations?

When an individual or group does not conform to the expectations of society, there is usually some device to get him or it back into line. The sociologist refers to these devices as *sanctions* and the process as *social control.* When the individual violates the more serious or valued norms of society he is likely to be sanctioned by imprisonment or even death. The valued norms are called *mores*; those less serious, such as rules of etiquette, are referred to as *folkways.* In the latter case the sanction may take the form of a frown.

5 / A ROSE FOR EMILY

Justin Kaplan

Emily Post, *Etiquette: In Society, In Business, In Politics, and At Home.* A replica of the 1922 edition. Funk & Wagnalls, $10.

Elizabeth L. Post, *Emily Post's Etiquette,* Twelfth revised edition. Funk & Wagnalls, $6.95.

Visiting this country in 1831, Mrs. Frances Trollope (the novelist's mother) observed that a typical American theater audience was like noth-

---

ing she had known at home. "The noises were perpetual, and of the most unpleasant kind," she wrote. "Men came into the lower tier of boxes without their coats." "The spitting was incessant." "The mixed smell of onions and whiskey" made her regret she was not back in her room working on other notes for *The Domestic Manners of the Americans.* Her book caused considerable anguish on this side of the Atlantic, and along with other accounts of our domestic manners, such as Dickens' *Martin Chuzzlewit,* it helped stir up, in loyal and corrective response, a home-grown literature of etiquette and improvement books big enough to deserve its own excellent history (Arthur M. Schlesinger's *Learning How to Behave,* published in 1947). Even so, that literature was possibly bigger than it was availing. Ninety years after Mrs. Trollope's book Emily Post still had to remind her readers (all of whom, by the ingenious conventions of her book, aspired to belong to or at least imitate "best society") that in the theater it is "very inconsiderate to giggle and talk" and to drag your coat "across the heads of those sitting in front of you." She also reminded her readers that by the strict code which governs behavior in opera boxes as well as drawing rooms, a gentleman removes his rubbers before entering.

Mrs. Post's *Etiquette: In Society, In Business, In Politics, and At Home,* published in 1922 in a modest edition of 5,000 copies, went on, of course, to a position of commanding authority in its field. Now, 47 years, about a million copies, and 99 printings later, we have a "replica" of the first *Etiquette* and also a new twelfth edition, revised by Elizabeth L. Post, who is married to Emily Post's grandson and divides her time between Westchester and Martha's Vineyard. By these two editions, social history and social utility are being served simultaneously and with varying degrees of success.

Emily Post, as she herself recognized when she wrote her book, was something of an anachronism, the product of a family, background, and bank account which, it seemed, had been put on earth in order to turn little girls into *grandes dames.* Born in Baltimore in 1873, a spectacularly popular debutante in 1892, married to a society banker in New York, she turned to writing partly to support herself and her two sons when her marriage broke up. Young and handsome, already the author of a couple of novels, she was one of the literary ladies (along with Willa Cather and Dorothy Canfield) who celebrated Mark Twain's seventieth birthday at a stagy formal banquet at Delmonico's in 1905. Seventeen years later, when she wrote her etiquette book, the word "party" (according to a newspaper column of 1922 discussing F. Scott Fitzgerald's *The Beautiful and Damned*) had "come to mean a gathering of persons who have a 'good time' only when highly stimulated by strong waters." Reacting against hip-flask America, Mrs. Post was determined to protect and perpetuate the decorums of her own upbringing: she believed in *jeunesse dorée* but not in flaming youth. Still, as a writer of considerable skill and alertness, she saw the need to make some concessions to the fantasies of her potential readers and to the realities of their relation to "best society." Writing out of nostalgia for the past and distress with the present, from the vantage point of Tuxedo Park, New York, and with an Annie Oakley eye for dead center, she devised a remarkably effective strategy.

She dangled before the reader a definition of "best society" which was fearfully exclusive but still seemed to have room for almost everyone. Moving up with Mrs. Post must have had the same paradoxic double appeal as the original Loop the Loop at Coney Island which was supposed to be both desperately dangerous and perfectly safe. "Best Society is not a fellowship of the wealthy," she wrote, "nor does it seek to exclude those who are not of exalted birth: but it *is* an association of gentle-folk, of which good form in speech, charm of manner, knowledge of the social amenities, and instinctive consideration for the feelings of others, are the credentials by which society the world over recognizes its chosen members."

Further on in *Etiquette* it turns out that more than a little cash is necessary, too—one cannot entertain at all adequately, we are told, with fewer than three in help. And even when she is at her most philosophic, Mrs. Post's metaphors show she has not lost sight of what makes it all go. "Life . . . is a bank in which you deposit certain funds of character, intellect, and heart. . . . And the bank honors your deposit, and no more. . . . You can draw out nothing but what you have put in." Still, even the humble reader who, not having much of a bank account anywhere, had to consult the public library's copy of *Etiquette* in order to find out whether to tip his soup toward or away from himself, would have been caught in Mrs. Post's net.

By page four he is thrown into heady confrontations with the President and Mrs. Harding and with King George V, and soon he is with Mrs. Post all the way in shunning such undesirables among her cast of actors as the Richan Vulgars, Mr. Parvenu, Mr. and Mrs. Gotta Crust, and "that odious Hector Newman." The reader has also learned to share Mrs. Post's scorn for the parvenu vices of bad form in speech ("Pardon *me*!"), tactlessness ("Twenty years ago you were the prettiest woman in town"), ostentation ("Nothing is more vulgar than a display of 'ice' on a man's shirt front, or on his fingers"), and abasement ("It was so good of you to come to my horrid little shanty").

The reader has been co-opted, as in other absorbing works of the imagination—he has been bribed into assent by the promise or illusion of probationary membership. With Mrs. Post by his side, he becomes Everyman going on a journey upward toward the wealth and dazzle of Mr.

Robert ("Bobo") Gilding and his wife, the former Lucy Wellborn, who live at Golden Hall. "The house is a palace," says Mrs. Post, bringing Everyman to the purlieus of the Celestial City, "the grounds are a park."

Mrs. Post hints strongly that *Etiquette* is also a sort of *roman à clef* "To you my friends," she says in her dedication, "whose identity in these pages is veiled in fictional disguise." If we had been in the swim we should have been able to identify "Bobo" and his Lucy (who "smokes like a furnace and is miserable unless she can play bridge for high stakes"), Mr. and Mrs. John Kindhart, the Toploftys, the Worldlys, the Oldnames, and a stand of New York blades—Frederick Bachelor, John Hunter Titherington Smith (whose name is too long for his visiting card), and the elegant Clubwin Doe—who dine out at the Toit d'Or and the Fitz-Cherry. In the world these vivid figures inhabit there is a great deal of room for detail and punctilio (usefully organized for reference) but very little room, it seems, for "intellect" or even for "character" and "heart." In the "well-appointed" country house, for example, a man and wife are invited to share a guest room only "if the hostess is sure beyond a doubt that they occupy similar quarters when at home." Each guest room must have a palm-leaf fan and a flyswatter, which, by association, brings us to Professor Bugge, the one apparent intellectual we meet among Mrs. Post's characters. The one "artist" we meet in best society also has a derisive name—Frederick Dauber. Mrs. Post's years as a toiler in literary upper bohemia may have left her with grudges to settle.

She is at her brilliant best in scenes of broad social comedy in which she gives her characters their head. One of these scenes, an evening at the Newlyweds ("How a dinner can be bungled") has the overtones of a Witches' Sabbath. The Gildings, Mrs. Toplofty, the Kindharts, Mr. Clubwin Doe, and some others enter Mr. and Mrs. Newlywed's smoke-filled drawing room. "Everyone begins to cough and blink. They are very polite, but the smoke, growing each moment denser, is not to be overlooked. Mrs. Toplofty takes matters into her own hands and makes Mr. Doe and your husband carry the logs, smoke and all, and throw them into the yard." "Dinner's all ready," the cook shrieks from the dining room, and the guests file in. They begin with an oyster course, which is all right, but they balk at the next hurdle, a "greasy-looking brown" soup served at room temperature. The meal moves on from disaster to disaster. What passes for conversation is punctuated by clash and rattle—as the waitress (named Delia, apparently because she has a habit of dealing plates around the table, Mrs. Post says, "like a pack of cards") clears, stacks, drops, and spills. By the end of the evening Mrs. Newlywed, who had innocently overextended herself as hostess, knows what she is in for. Her nobby guests, "without malice, but in truth and frankness" (say Mrs. Post, forgetting about "heart" among other things), are going to tell everyone, "Whatever you do, don't dine with the Newlyweds unless you eat your dinner before you go, and wear black glasses so no sight can offend you."

Most of the old characters, along with their Margaret Dumont antics, have been retired over the years and are missing from Elizabeth Post's twelfth revised edition of *Etiquette*. True, some names are still here—Mr. Stocksan Bonds, Mrs. Rich, Mr. and Mrs. Brightmeadow, Miss Jenkins (who "writes as Grace Gotham"), and Mr. Alan K. Greatlake, seen in the act of ordering a chair and a rose quilt from a store in Evanston. Now, instead of New York, with its glittering opera house and the Fitz-Cherry, these people appear to inhabit a generalized place called "Homeville." The geographical center of the book has moved westward, its standards have moved downward from "best society" toward a sort of large, house-broken community, and, in general, the successive revisions that have taken place since 1922 reflect a process of leveling, denaturing, and deformalizing that has taken place in the country. High social goals are no longer so forbidding—but they no longer are so alluring, either.

The concept of the book, too, has shifted over the years from a guide to forms and etiquette to a general encyclopedia of modern living which now gives practical and for the most part sensible advice on how to conduct yourself at a radio or television interview ("You are really a guest in the home of the listener or viewer") and an audience with the Pope, how to run a bar mitzvah, how to terminate a telephone conversation ("My bath is running over") and a cocktail party ("Remove the liquor and close the bar"), how to shield your beach picnic from gusts of sand, how to "make contact" and how to behave on a first date, how to announce a legal change of name ("Mr. and Mrs. John Original-Name Announce that by Permission of the Court They and Their Children Have Taken the Family Name of Miller"), and even what to do before starting on a car trip ("Your fuel, oil, brakes, and automatic transmission fluid should be checked").

"Although we have many fine American authors," the book concedes, readers are cautiously urged to turn to Rebecca West and Winston Churchill for instructive "sources of pure English." The function of books, aside from this, is still mainly that of conversational pump primers or mild sedatives in guest rooms and trains. Our one intellectual, Professor Bugge, is still with us in 1969 and is handled more gingerly than ever at dinner parties: "Professor Bugge might bore *you* to tears, but Mrs. Entomid would probably adore him."

It would be unfair to expect either Emily or Elizabeth Post to say other than, "An unmarried girl should not go alone on overnight trips with any young man, even with her fiancée." But when the current Mrs.

Post tells you that "screaming is not only ear-splitting but is also extremely bad form," that you should avoid critical discussions of religion or politics, and that you must "never write a letter to *anyone* that would embarrass you were you to see it in a newspaper over your signature"—then you know that things haven't changed all that much in Emily Post's world in nearly fifty years. Despite the striving for comprehensiveness and realism in this new edition, my impression is that nowhere in 721 pages is the word "sex" used except in such phrases as "the opposite sex." This fits in with another impression, which is that the new *Etiquette*, for all its strenuous updating, still has some of the ostrich, or at least backward-looking, qualities of the old one. Under twelve layers of writing and revision there is still Emily Post's Troy, a rather crusty place.

6 / ROLE PLAYING: A JUDGE IS A COP, A COP IS A JUDGE

Richard Hammer

Annapolis, Md.

For nine days this summer, the grassy, groomed and venerable campus of St. John's College in Annapolis was the scene of a remarkable confrontation. The college kids and their professors were off on vacation, and the "great books"—the core of the St. John's curriculum—had been laid on the shelf. In place of the faculty and students were 21 convicts from three state prisons and about 100 lawyers and judges, prosecutors, policemen, prison officials and state legislators and some "interested citizens." Before the nine days ended, the participants had been enlightened and, in some cases, emotionally scarred by their experiment, a "Workshop in Crime and Correction."

This was anything but a gathering of dreamers and bleeding hearts concerned over the failures of the prison system. Those failures, of course, are beyond argument. The "correctional institutions," as they call themselves these days, neither correct nor rehabilitate; more than half, some say more than 70 per cent, of those released from the nation's prisons end up behind bars again, and what they usually learn behind those bars is how to make better "hits," how to be better burglars or bank robbers the next time they walk free. The non-prisoners at the workshop were not ignorant of these facts, but they lacked an appreciation of the personal and emotional realities behind the statistics. That appreciation was provided in psychodramas, seminars, all-night bull sessions and in hours spent as "inmates" themselves in three Maryland prisons.

The workshop had the best "establishment" credentials: It was financed with $67,000 from the Social and Rehabilitation Service of the Department of Health, Education and Welfare and was sponsored jointly by the Maryland Governor's Commission on Law Enforcement and the Administration of Justice and the National College of State Trial Judges, which claims the membership of more than 4,000 jurists in all 50 states.

Directing the conference were the Berkeley Associates, a consulting organization formed by three Californians whose experience in the prison system has left them disillusioned. They are: Dr. David Fogel of the University of California at Berkeley, a heavy-set, bearded, emotional sociologist who worked seven years in the Marin County jail system; Dr. Richard Korn, a U. of C. criminologist who resigned after three years as a psychologist at a New Jersey prison farm "when I found one night that I could lock up my assistant, a prisoner, in his cell and walk away without feeling anything," and Douglas Rigg, a public defender in Berkeley, a former associate warden at San Quentin who once resigned as the warden of a Minnesota state prison after his reform efforts led to charges that he was "coddling convicts."

Given the workshop's credentials the conference organizers found it easy enough to round up participants among the professionals. Finding the right convicts, however, was another matter. Berkeley Associates did not want a group hand-picked by prison administrators, but a representative sampling of both men and offenses. Above all, they sought the right to select the 21 convict participants themselves. Ultimately, they settled for a compromise: Prison officials chose a group of more than 100 inmates from which Berkeley Associates picked the 21 they wanted.

The convicts came from three institutions in Jessups, Md.—the Maryland House of Correction, a medium-security prison with a reputation as little more than a warehouse for men convicted of anything from nonsupport to murder and rape; the Maryland Correctional Camp Center, a minimum-security institution where some inmates are on a work-release program, and the Patuxent Institution, a maximum-security prison for "defective delinquents," all of them serving indeterminate sentences.

Some of the 21 men chosen for the workshop were serving terms as short as two years, others had been sentenced to "life plus"; some had been behind bars for only a year, others for 20 years or more. Their crimes ranged from possession of narcotics to burglary to rape and murder. One participant was even an alumnus of death row; his sentence had been commuted to life shortly before his date in the gas chamber.

As a group, the participants were not entirely representative of Maryland's 6,000 convicts. They were articulate and intelligent, with considerable insight into themselves and others. Most of them seemed to retain some hope for a future life beyond the walls. As the workshop progressed, however, it became evident that most of the participants from the outside world looked upon the *con*-sultants (as they called themselves) not as a select group but as a random sampling of the prison population. The effect of their words and actions during the conference was thus generalized—and magnified.

A typical day began at 8 A.M. as the convicts, dressed in casual sports clothes, arrived at St. John's by bus. More than one prisoner was amused at the thought of breakfasting with the judge who had sentenced him—a judge dressed in Bermuda shorts and a flowered shirt.

The business session usually opened with a speaker after breakfast, then a psychodrama, a brief play in which the magistrates and the miscreants were the cast, sometimes playing their real-life roles and sometimes trading roles. The scene was always one having to do with the judicial process: a disciplinary hearing for a policeman accused of having used abusive language; a grand jury session; a parole hearing; the arrival in prison of a new con. Fogel or Korn set the scene and the actors improvised as the plot developed. Members of the audience were allowed to interrupt if they thought the portrayals lacked realism.

Later in the day, the workshop broke up into seven groups for discussion and more psychodrama. After the prisoners had returned to their cells for the evening, the "outside" participants heard another speaker, then attended informal bull sessions that typically lasted until 4 or 5 A.M.

In the first days of the workshop, there was a tentative feeling, a sparring for openings, an evident wariness. The cops sat in a back row, isolated; the judges sat together; the cons sat in a group. A psychodrama about a policeman's being reprimanded for the use of a racial epithet produced only yawns and bored rustling.

What broke the conference open was a psychodrama on prison life. Fogel set the stage: The action was to be the arrival in prison of a new con, a first offender sentenced to four years for assault. To play the new con Fogel selected a young, blond correctional officer who looked indeed as though he could be in that position. The inmates who processed him into the prison were played by real cons. The only other roles in the play were two prison officials, a guard and a counselor, played by men whose real-life roles these were.

The drama began as "Scag," a black inmate who supposedly worked as a runner in the prison storeroom, led the new con, "Frank," from the storeroom, where he'd been issued prison clothes and other gear, to the tier where he would be locked into a cell.

Scag: You know anybody here, anybody can help you?
Frank (shaking his head): No, I don't know anybody.
Scag: Not nobody at all?
Frank: Nobody. I don't think I belong here.
Scag (laughs): That's what everybody says. You know, you gonna need some protection.
Frank: Protection? From what?
Scag: Man, you is gonna be approached.
Frank: What for?
Scag: Man, I ain't got to tell you.
Frank: Well, I don't want any part of it.
Scag: You ain't got no choice.
Frank: If they come to me, I'll fight.
Scag (laughs): You can't fight three-four men at a time.
Frank: What can I do?
Scag: Man, you can avoid it.
Frank: How?
Scag: You can pick somebody to protect you. . . . You got any money?
Frank: No. But I've got a ring and a watch.

Reaching the tier that contains Frank's cell, Scag holds a mumbled conference with Slim, a black inmate assigned as a runner in the tier.

Scag: We got a new chicken here.
Slim: Yeah, what we gonna do with him?
Scag: I'll tell you. I'm gonna play his friend. You make him think he's got to turn to me to protect him from you.
Slim: Yeah, that's right, I'll scare him right to you and we'll split what he's got. Only don't do like you did the last time and hit me when you're protecting him.
Scag: Don't worry, we'll play this cool.

As Scag leaves, Slim explains prison life to Frank, telling him that he can order once a week from the commissary and that he must come out of his cell immediately when the bell rings for a meal or an exercise period in the yard or he will be locked in again. Slim offers to give Frank a pack of cigarettes in exchange for two packs after Frank has received his order from the commissary. Then a bell rings and Slim patrols the tier, chanting, "Yard time. Yard time."

The scene shifts to the crowded prison yard, and when Frank appears there are whistles. "Say, man," says one con, "that's a real sweetie." Another yells: "Hey, baby, I think you need a protector." The action then moves back to the cell tier.

Slim: Where you been?
Frank: In the yard.
Slim: How come you didn't tell me you was going?
Frank: I did.
Slim: Man, I says you didn't! You callin' me a liar?
Frank: No. I thought. . . .
Slim: Man, you want to go someplace, you tell me. Whenever you go someplace, you don't go without you let me know, dig?
Frank: Why are you jumping all over me?
Slim: Man, you is askin' for it. I gonna come in that cell with you and lock the door you don't watch out.

Scag suddenly appears, telling Slim to leave the new inmate alone. After Slim wanders off, Scag offers to take Frank into the yard during the next exercise period and walk around with him, explaining: "That'll let everybody know I'm protecting you." He says it will cost a carton of cigarettes a week. Frank says he will think about it and stays in his cell during the next few exercise periods. A few days later, against Slim's urgent advice, he insists upon seeing an officer.

Frank: It seems there are all these guys who want to be my buddies. They want to protect me. But they want cigarettes and they seem to want my watch and ring and shoes, too. And they seem to be able to do anything they want and nobody stops them.
Guard: When did all this start? When did they approach you?
Frank: As soon as I got in here.
Guard: Can you identify them?
Frank: I'm afraid. I don't want it to get back to them.
Guard: Well, anytime you want to tell me anything, you just ask. I'll come. You just ask. We'll protect you.
Frank: I'm scared to tell.

The realization that the guards cannot effectively protect him sends Frank back to Scag. At the next yard call, they go out together and Scag introduces Frank to other cons, among whom blacks outnumber whites by more than two to one.

Fogel interrupted the action to ask several of the convicts what they were feeling as Frank was being introduced. Among the answers were these:

"I'm feeling that colored guys have all the goodies. I feel like they must feel out in the streets. I'm a minority in here, and I'd like a crack at that goody."

"I don't care what Scag or the rest of the black guys do as long as they don't touch my man."

"I've got a feeling of fear. I know what happens to young cons like him; it happened to me."

"He's a white boy, and I don't care what happens to him."

The action resumes in the office of a counselor with whom Frank has requested an interview.

Frank: I've had some weird things happen since I came in here. There's a lot of homosexuals running around loose and they all seem to be looking at me.

Counselor: Well, what would you like us to do?

Frank: I don't know. I think I'm more afraid of the inmates here than I am of the institution itself, and I thought it would be the other way.

Counselor: What do they want?

Frank: Everything I've got. My watch, my ring, my shoes, all my personal possessions. Can I send them home?

Counselor: Yes. If you give them to me I can have them sent home for you.

Frank: They want my tail, too.

Counselor: I'm afraid I can't send that home. You want to tell me who these guys are who are doing these things to you?

Frank: If I tell you, what will happen to me?

Counselor: We'll try to protect you.

Frank: How?

Counselor (*burst out*): I'll adopt you! . . . Seriously, the only assurance I can give you is close supervision.

The psychodrama ended there, amid shouts and cries from the convicts in the audience. "Man, you can't give him no protection. He'll have boiling coffee thrown at him even if you lock him up in solitary," said one. "He ain't got no assurance. You think his only salvation is in protection and custody, but that won't work. Somebody'd get to him."

"Maybe you'd put him in B-3, where they keep all the sissies," said another con, "and then he'd be branded one, and he'd be branded a rat, too, and that wouldn't be no protection."

"There's a million ways to get to him," a third convict warned. "We'd be in contact with him and that would be that." Another added:

"Nothing anybody can do will make any difference because it's a jungle we live in. The only ones who can do anything for him or against him are the other inmates."

One of the prison administrators asked the actor who had played Slim, "Would you protect him for a guaranteed parole?"

Slim stared at him. "For a guaranteed parole? Man, I guess so."

Another con leaped up: "And who would protect Slim? Then who would protect the next guy and the next? You gonna let us all out on parole to protect this one guy?"

As more members of the workshop joined the discussion on prison life and its purposes, one inmate rose and asked: "What's rehabilitation? I've never seen it. We come in laborers and go out laborers. All we learn in here is how to make [license] tags, and there ain't no place outside where you can make tags. We're the same guy when we go out, and that's where it's at, baby."

The psychodrama had shaken the workshop. For many in the audience—judges, policemen, lawyers and even some prison officials—it was the first good look at what goes on behind the walls and at criminals as real people. Save for the criminal himself, almost everyone's contact with the problems of crime, correction and justice is severely limited. The average citizen's only glimpse of crime occurs when he is a victim, and even then the contact is usually just the discovery that something is missing from his home or car; the policeman's contact with the criminal begins with the arrest, often a dangerous and charged confrontation, and ends at the station house or in the court-room; the judge and attorneys see the criminal only when his behavior is circumscribed, when he is wearing a face that is often not his real one; prison officials see him only as a number, and parole officers only when he has finished his term and is again free.

The emotions released by the psychodrama were heightened the next day when the conference adjourned behind prison walls. A third of the delegates went to each of the three prisons, where most of them were led on tours by the inmate conferees, unhampered by guards and officials. And at each of the prisons, three or four of the outside workshop members, including a couple of judges, were processed as though they were new inmates. The convicts and guards who processed them were—officially, at least—unaware that they were not real prisoners, though it was evident that word had leaked out.

While the rest of the outside visitors entered the prisons through the main gates, the men chosen to be pretend-convicts were handcuffed and shackled together, put on prison vans and driven into the processing areas. There they were checked in, stripped and made to sit naked on wooden benches while being interviewed. Then they were forced to undergo a flashlight examination under the arms, between the legs, in all the hairy parts of the body—"we're looking for crabs, narcotics, you know, things like that," said the inmate-clerk conducting the examination at one of the prisons. The new "convicts" were showered, given prison clothes, mugged, fingerprinted and asked other detailed questions about their lives. Then they were led to cells and locked in.

When the doors closed, one "convict," an elderly white-haired state representative, sank onto his cot, put his elbows on his knees and buried his head in his hands. "I can't tell you what this did to me spiritually," he said later. "I knew that anytime I wanted to get out, all I had to do was yell and they would come and let me loose. What if I had known that I couldn't get out, that I was to be locked in there for years?"

A judge who had sentenced scores of men to the prison through which he was processed suddenly pretended to be a mute. Later, he was to say that he had enjoyed the experience, but those who saw him doubted it. He was certain, he said, that he had been spotted, "and I didn't know whether I was going to get a knife or just be pointed out to everyone else." Within a couple of hours, he asked to be released from his cell.

When another judge left his cell for lunch, a knife was planted in it by one of the few guards who was in on the pretense. The judge was pulled out of the lunch line and thrown into solitary confinement in the "hole" next to a black convict who was lying on his cell floor, his legs in the air, screaming, "White mother-f----s, white mother-f----s . . ." (The judge later said he had not heard a word.)

After a half hour in the hole, the judge was brought before a five-man disciplinary board, none of whose members knew that this was all a pretense. The judge was dressed in prison slacks and shirt, white socks without shoes; his hair was tousled, his face distraught.

The board chairman asked, "Do you know why you're here?"

"They told me you found a knife in my cell."

"That's right. Can you tell us how it got there?"

"No. I can't think how."

"Did you bring it in with you?"

"No. Somebody must have put it there."

"When did you get here?"

"This morning."

"Do you know anybody in here?"

"No."

"Does anybody in here have anything against you?"

"No."

"Then why would somebody have planted a knife in your cell?"

The judge, knowing that he was innocent, was sentenced to 30 days in the hole.

7 / PSYCHOLOGY CONSTRUCTS THE FEMALE

Naomi Weisstein

It is an implicit assumption that the area of psychology which concerns itself with personality has the onerous but necessary task of describing the limits of human possibility. Thus when we are about to consider the liberation of women, we naturally look to psychology to tell us what "true" liberation would mean: what would give women the freedom to fulfill their own intrinsic natures.

Views from men of high prestige in psychology, such as Harvard's Erik Erikson, reflect a fairly general consensus: liberation for women will consist first in their attractiveness, so that second, they may obtain the kinds of homes, and the kinds of men, which will allow joyful altruism and nurturance.

The central argument of my article, however, is this: psychology has nothing to say about what women are really like, what they need and what they want, essentially, because psychology does not know. I want to stress that this failure is not limited to women; rather, the kind of psychology which has addressed itself to how people act and who they are has failed to understand, in the first place, why people act the way they do, and certainly failed to understand what might make them act differently.

The kind of psychology which has addressed itself to these questions is in large part clinical psychology and psychiatry, which in America means endless commentary and refinement of Freudian theory. Here, the causes of failure are obvious and appalling: Freudians and neo-Freudians, and clinicians and psychiatrists in general, have simply refused to look at the evidence against their theory and their practice, and have used as evidence for their theory and their practice stuff so flimsy and transparently biased as to have absolutely no standing as empirical evidence. But even psychology which conforms to rigorous methodology has gone about looking at people in such a way as to have limited usefulness. This is

---

Paper delivered at the Meetings of the American Studies Association, University of California, Davis, Calif., October 1968. Printed by permission of author. A revised edition of this paper appeared in *Psychology Today* in October 1969.

because it has been a central assumption for most psychologists of human personality that human behavior rests primarily on an individual and inner dynamic, perhaps fixed in infancy, perhaps fixed by genetalia, perhaps simply arranged in a rather immovable cognitive network. But this assumption is rapidly losing ground as personality psychologists fail again and again to get consistency in the assumed personalities of their subjects and as the evidence collects that what a person does and who he believes himself to be, will in general be a function of what people around him expect him to be, and what the overall situation in which he is acting implies that he is. Compared to the influence of the social context within which a person lives, his or her history and "traits", as well as biological makeup may simply be random variations, "noise" superimposed on the true signal which can predict behavior. To summarize: the first reason for psychology's failure to understand what people are and how they act, is that clinicians and psychiatrists, who are generally the theoreticians on these matters, have essentially made up myths without any evidence to support these myths; the second reason for psychology's failure is that personality theory has looked for inner traits when it should have been looking at social context.

Two theories of the nature of women, which come not from psychiatric and clinical tradition, but from biology, can be disposed of now with little difficulty. The first argument notices social interaction in primate groups, and observes that females are submissive and passive. Putting aside for a moment the serious problem of experimenter bias (for instance, Harlow of the University of Wisconsin, after observing differences between male and female rhesus monkeys, quotes Lawrence Sterne to the effect that women are silly and trivial, and concludes that "men and women have differed in the past and they will differ in the future"), the problem with the argument from primate groups is that the crucial experiment has not been performed. The crucial experiment would manipulate or change the social organization of these groups, and watch the subsequent behavior. Until then, we must conclude that, since primates are at present too stupid to change their social conditions by themselves, the "innateness" and fixedness of their behavior is simply not known. As applied to humans, the argument becomes patently irrelevant, since the most salient feature of human social organization is its variety; and there are a number of cultures where there is at least a rough equality between men and women. Thus, primate arguments tell us very little.

The second theory of sex differences argues that since females and males differ in their sex hormones, and sex hormones enter the brain, there must be innate differences in "nature." But the only thing this argument tells us is that there are differences in physiological state. The problem is whether these differences are at all relevant to behavior.

In brief, the uselessness of present psychology with regard to women, is simply a special case of the general conclusion: one must understand social expectations about women if one is going to characterize the behavior of women.

How are women characterized in our culture, and in psychology? They are inconsistent, emotionally unstable, lacking in a strong conscience or superego, weaker, "nurturant" rather than productive, "intuitive" rather than intelligent, and, if they are at all "normal," suited to the home and the family. In short, the list adds up to a typical minority group stereotype of inferiority: if they know their place, which is in the home, they are really quite lovable, happy, childlike, loving creatures. In a review of the intellectual differences between little boys and little girls, Eleanor Maccoby has shown that there are no intellectual differences until about high school, or, if there are, girls are slightly ahead of boys. At high school, girls begin to do worse on a few intellectual tasks, such as arithmetic reasoning, and beyond high school, the achievement of women now measured in terms of productivity and accomplishment drops off even more rapidly. There are a number of other, non-intellectual tests which show sex differences; I choose the intellectual differences since it is seen clearly that women start becoming inferior. It is no use to talk about women being different but equal; all of the tests I can think of have a "good" outcome and a "bad" outcome. Women usually end up at the "bad" outcome. In light of social expectations about women, what is surprising is not that women end up where society expects they will; what is surprising is that little girls don't get the message that they are supposed to be stupid until high school; and what is even more remarkable is that some women resist this message even after high school, college, and graduate school.

My article began with remarks on the task of discovering the limits of human potential. Until psychologists realize that it is they who are limiting discovery of human potential, by their refusal to accept evidence, if they are clinical psychologists, or, if they are rigorous, by their assumption that people move in a context-free ether, with only their innate dispositions and their individual traits determining what they will do, then psychology will have nothing of substance to offer in this task. I don't know what immutable differences exist between men and women apart from differences in their genitals; perhaps there are some other unchangeable differences; probably there are a number of irrelevant differences. But it is clear that until social expectation for men and women are equal, until we provide equal respect for both men and women, our answers to this question will simply reflect our prejudices.

UNIT B / ISSUES FOR CONSIDERATION

1. What sanctions are placed on a woman in our society who insists on becoming a business executive?
2. List some of the norms of etiquette that your family accepts and describe what methods of social control are used to encourage members to conform to these folkways.
3. What are some of the norms of prison life that the judges learned through their role-playing in the experiment Hammer describes?
4. Does the review of the successive editions of Emily Post's *Etiquette* reflect changes in American society? If so, what are the limitations of this type of analysis?
5. To what degree and in what direction do you think the role of the American woman will change in the next ten years?

UNIT C
INSTITUTIONS

Perhaps no other aspect of sociology better reflects the changing nature of the world today than does the study of *social institutions*. Institutions incorporate those systems of social relationships that embody the ultimate values of men and are characterized by formality and continuity. Usually seen in terms of the functions they perform, institutions were described earlier as those persistent norms and roles that are oriented around the fulfillment of the basic needs of society. Thus, assuming that the bearing and rearing of children are societal needs, we would say that those lasting norms, roles, and values that develop around the fulfillment of those needs make up the institution we call the family. The norms governing dating, marriage, and sex, the roles of father, mother, and child, and the values placed on the maintenance of the marriage relationship are all part of the familial institution in America.

The educational system continues the socialization of the child by transmitting the expectations of society and certain parts of its cultural heritage. The economic system provides food, clothing, and shelter. The political institution fulfills the protective need by enforcing laws, rules, and standards. The religious institution establishes systems of morals and ethics and attitudes toward the supernatural. In addition to these more universal institutions of the family, education, economics, religion, and government, one might find institutional aspects of recreation, mass communication, transportation, health, and many other components of our complex society.

The articles in this section emphasize three points about social institutions: their complexity, their interrelationships, and their reaction to the changing world.

In the first article in this section we find a discussion of some reactions to changes in the American family. A large family has long been held in high regard in our country; thus it is not without some pain that this value is replaced with one that honors the small family. In some respects the author is providing her readers with a justification for their small families—telling them that it is all right not to have as many children as their parents did. The perceptive student will detect the norms, roles, and values reflected in the descriptions of these families. As you read this material, ask yourself if it would be justified to generalize the author's observations to apply to all American families, or if it is wiser to conclude that she is talking mostly about upper middle-class families?

The article on education demonstrates clearly how an institution, once it becomes formal and rigid, may not adapt well to changes in the rest of society. The school was set up in American society to educate the young, but schooling is not educating. Goodland, a professional educator, applies sociological principles to his vast experience in schools and suggests the need for some radical changes in our school system. Can you detect the principles of education that the author would subscribe to?

Hammer presented a view of one small aspect of the political institution in American society in an earlier article on the prison system. Quite a different dimension of this institution is evident in Greeley's article on the white ethnics. Effecting changes in the American political system is a complex matter. Can you see how the structure of the political institution (e.g. democratic elections) affects the strategy that must be used in bringing about change?

Change is also central to an analysis of the religious institution in modern society. Perhaps no other institution has been questioned more. Does the church fulfill any meaningful function in modern American society? There are some who would be quick to answer no, and indeed, there is a clear indication that adherence to any religious body is on the decline in American society. But there are others who say that we need as never before guidelines for moral and ethical conduct, and that the church can provide them if it can free itself from the rigid shackles of tradition, ritual, and exclusiveness that have made it stagnate. L'Heureux's article on "The New American Jesuits" offers a firsthand look at some of the problems of change in a large, long established religious organization. The modern members of this Roman Catholic order, recognizing the disjunction between its old established regulations and the religious needs of modern society, wonder if change can be accomplished before the order is destroyed by obsolescence.

Not all institutions are discussed in the articles in this section. We have dealt primarily with those institutions that sociologists usually consider to be universal. When a society becomes as complex and differentiated as modern American society has become, other institutions emerge. Take, for example, the complex system that has developed around the need for communication in our heterogeneous society. While at one time the beating of a drum might have been enough to call persons together to hear the latest news, our large society now has hundreds of thousands of persons working full time to gather, analyze, and distribute the news. The editors of *The Atlantic Monthly* describe some problems this institution faces in American society today.

As you read through this section, keep in mind the functions of these institutions, the structural forms they take, and the relationships that exist between them. How does the relationship between social institutions affect their response to change?

FAMILY

8 / THE SWING TO SMALL FAMILIES

Mary Seton

Last year our national birth rate dropped to 18.5 per thousand of the population—virtually the same figure as the all-time low during the depression years. In spite of this, our national population is increasing significantly—alarmingly, many experts feel—due to the great numbers of young men and women born during the baby boom of the post-war years who are just now getting to the marrying age.

Although population experts are still cautious about calling the downturn in the birth rate a trend, it does look as if there is a definite

From *Parents' Magazine,* October 1967. Reprinted by permission of the publisher.

swing to small families among young couples today. An extensive survey of urban and suburban families, conducted by a Midwestern university, showed that most young couples think of a happy life as something they can best achieve around the nucleus of a small family.

Of course, there is no magic ingredient for happiness. We have all known small families who were unhappy and large ones who seemed to live in a state of permanent good humor. But I think no one would deny that most couples with two or three children have more time, energy, and money to do the things they want to for themselves and their children than those with four or five youngsters.

I think of my good friends, Steve and Joy Harrison and their two sons, aged eight and ten. The Harrisons, parents and children both, have a wonderful quality of vitality and enthusiasm. They expect a lot out of life and they get a lot out of it. They don't have a great deal of money but they do the things that some people think you need a lot of money for.

The Harrisons live on the outskirts of a small town—a long way from the big city where I first met them and where Steve still works. It's quite a train ride for him to and from work, but living where they do Steve can afford to have a big house with land around it, trees to climb, a brook running through the property which he dammed up to make a swimming hole, and all the other country things city-bred Steve and Joy wished they had had when they were kids.

Sometimes when parents strive to give their children the particular pleasures they feel they missed out on as children, it works out ironically, being mainly a rejection of their own experiences, rather than a creative search for a satisfying style of life. But the Harrisons haven't turned their backs on the riches of the city. They're enjoying the best of both worlds.

"I've got a good job with a big insurance company," says Steve. "It's never going to make me wealthy, but it enables me to live the way I want to live. Some men get great personal rewards out of the work they do. My job isn't like that, but it does allow me the kind of home life I want, and that's the most important thing to me. I guess you'd call me a family man. I've got a wife who understands me and two wonderful boys, and though costs are high, I figure I'll be able to see to it that the boys get a good education, and the chance to fit themselves for the kind of lives they want."

Right now, Steve spends lots of time with his children, swimming and sailing (his special hobby) in the summer, skiing, and skating in the winter, not because he feels this is what a good father should do but because this is how he likes to live.

The Harrisons have a houseful of books and records, and the boys are good and enthusiastic students. This fall they both joined a Saturday morning nature and science program run by a nearby museum where they've been having a fine time helping to take care of some of the animals—raccoons, deer, foxes—which are native to their area, and where they are helping a naturalist on the staff of the museum run a research project. As for Joy, their mother, she has no intention of letting rustic life turn her into a know-nothing or a household drudge. She rides into the city with Steve a couple of times a week (the children get to the city frequently, too) to visit a museum or art gallery, see a show, or just stroll on the city streets, sometimes to special parts of town, where the foreign food markets are, or to a manufacturing center.

Once I remarked to her on how much more "up" on events in the city she was than I who live right in town. She laughed and said she could understand that. "Before I moved to the country," she said, "I didn't do half the things I do now. I guess I figured they'd always be there and so would I, so I let most things slide. Now that I live so far away, I don't want to miss out on anything special so I keep up with what's going on. I know I've been to more good concerts in the last year than I used to get to when I lived here."

Joy told me that a couple of years ago when Teddy, her younger son, started school she got quite upset and depressed for a while, not knowing what to do with herself all day, feeling as if there wasn't much point to her life and that somewhere she'd missed the boat. She thought of having another baby—though she and Steve didn't specially want another child, and had settled way back on having two.

"I talked it over with Steve," Joy said, "and he wasn't dead set against having another child if I really wanted one, but knowing me he thought that I was considering it more out of fear of an empty future than anything else. I think he was right. At any rate he persuaded me to pick up some of the things I used to like to do. I've always been good at languages, so I started studying Italian again. I read a lot in it now. We subscribe to a couple of Italian magazines and I enjoy them a great deal. Not only for the fun of reading another language but because it's fascinating to compare their interests and points of view with our own. I'm also the family expert when it comes to interpreting those lines in Italian movies which don't seem to get written on the bottom of the screen. You know there will be what sounds like a two paragraph speech, and then only the words, 'I have to leave. My wife is waiting for me,' or something like that, will appear."

Joy has it in the back of her head that she might teach some day, depending on how she feels and what kind of preparation she would need. She certainly would make a good Italian teacher—her knowledge of the language, her interest in it, and her warm and relaxed appreciation of children, her own and others, make her well-suited to the job. In the meantime, she's living now—as is her husband—the way she wants to, and both of them are giving their children as good a life as they can.

Another family I know, my neighbors, Herb and Lillian Powell, are very different from the Harrisons, save for the quality one recognizes in them of having chosen a satisfying style for themselves and their children. Lillian, herself the oldest of five children, has told me about her childhood, so different from the life her two children know.

"I liked being the oldest, feeling important and being the one my mother could trust. If we kids went somewhere on our own I always got to hold the money, and that sort of thing. But lots of the time I felt sorry for myself and put upon, having so much responsibility. I have to admit that I don't remember feeling sorry for my mother then, but now when I look back on those years, I do. It seems she always had a baby underfoot, with diapers to change and bottles to warm up. My mother loved to sculpt and paint but she had so little time for it. I don't mean she had a bad life. I just know it's not what I want for myself."

As soon as the Powells' two children, Janie and Joe, were both in school, Lillian went to work part time for a friend of hers who runs a small travel agency. Now a few years later, Lillian has her own clients and is quite happy and successful doing a job she enjoys, which has, as she puts it, "terrific advantages for the whole family. I get discounts traveling and the kids have been to places I never even heard of when I was a child.

"Though I work away from home three afternoons a week (I have a mother's helper for those times), I'm sure the children aren't suffering a bit from my absence. At their age they like to go places with their friends after school, anyway."

Lillian knows, as do all sensible mothers, whether they work at jobs out of the house or not, that being a good mother doesn't mean hovering over one's children or always being home. It means treating them with love and sensitivity, which includes letting them do more and more things on their own as they grow older.

My own observation of the Powell youngsters reveals that they feel anything but neglected. For example, recently I was involved in an instance which showed Janie's self-confidence and the good feeling both children have about their family life. A few weeks ago my husband was out of town on business and Janie invited my son and me to dinner which she was going to prepare, she told me proudly, all by herself. I knew that twelve-year-old Janie often made dinner for the family, not because her mother expected her to, but because she loved to cook. And we were to be her first guests. The dinner really was fine, especially the dessert which Janie specializes in. Even her nine-year-old brother, who generally looks with great suspicion at new foods, was so pleased that she had made his favorite dish for a main course that he boldly took a good-sized helping of a stewed tomato dish he had never seen the like of before.

What the Powell children have in common with the Harrison youngsters is a feeling of camaraderie which reflects, I think, the generally good-humored and optimistic outlook of their parents. It would be too much to claim that this good spirit prevails in these families because they have only two children. Obviously, the important thing is that these are parents who have chosen the way they want to live. They feel relatively in command of their lives, and not like victims of chance and circumstance. It is significant, however, that so many young couples today do actively choose and work for a kind of life they have a vision about, and that this vision so often includes planning for no more than two or three children.

Obviously, the conditions of modern life, first among them the high cost of living—of food, rent, camps for the children, education, and particularly college—make having a large family a luxury few of us can afford and still manage to live well. But it isn't only the cost of bringing up a family, or the crowded conditions of our increasingly citified lives, which are the arguments most young couples consider when they decide how many children to have.

It's also likely that it isn't the world population explosion which causes couples to refrain from having large families. However admirable it would be to act in one's personal life directly in response to a threat to the community at large, the fact that this planet, including our own portion of it, may be unlivably overcrowded a generation or two from now isn't what makes most of us decide for or against having another child now.

We should, indeed, take the population explosion right here in our own country seriously. However, it's more likely that the swing toward smaller families mainly reflects an unspoken belief most of us have about the meaning of life. A belief that its moral purpose is to live responsibly—and joyfully.

Partly because of the great medical and industrial advances which have been made in the last generation, and which we take for granted now, confidently anticipating even greater benefits, most of us have been relieved of the fear of disease, of disability, of poverty in our old age. We look forward to a secure future with more and more time to spend as we please. And so our attentions have been freed to focus on ourselves, in our search for that responsible and joyful life style.

A decade or so ago, many young couples, the women particularly, seeking this kind of personal fulfillment, quite definitely planned to have large families. Wanting to be good mothers and responsible citizens, as young women do now, they saw both these conditions satisfied at once by having many children. To be the mother of a big family seemed to prove a woman's femininity and showed her trust in herself and society. Now it seems that women no longer feel it necessary to demonstrate their motherliness by numbers, as it were. Motherliness we now recognize is not proven by the quantity of one's children, but by the quality of their lives.

Moreover, many women have found that their gift of motherliness and their sense of responsibility can be satisfyingly and less selfishly engaged by helping others outside of their families, not just their own children. I know many young mothers who give some time and plenty of thought and energy to volunteer community projects. A friend of mine started with limited aims, to help the foreign speaking children in her neighborhood grade school learn to read and write English. After three months, she became so interested in the work that she enrolled in a summer course for teaching beginning English to foreigners. She now spends several hours tutoring youngsters, and she knows she is accomplishing something worthwhile. Another woman I know who has a degree in fine arts started a supplementary art course for fourth graders in a school in a poor neighborhood. The hour she spent became so popular that she was asked to take on further grades and to accept a salary for her work.

However mothers spend their days—whether most of their time is taken up in raising their families and running their households, or whether they work, part or full time—young mothers today feel close to their children in a fond and easy way, not with self-conscious togetherness but with an unpressured and humorous appreciation of their children as dear and distinct beings.

So many of the young couples whom I have seen—fathers and mothers both—are succeeding at giving their children the best of themselves, as well as the things that money can buy. And in this time and place, a great many parents believe that the way they can give the best, and be the best, is to aim for quality over quantity in family life.

EDUCATION

9 / THE SCHOOLS VS. EDUCATION

John Goodlad

The years from 1957 to 1967 constituted the Education Decade for the United States. It began with Sputnik and the charge to education to win the cold war; it ended with a hot war and the growing realization that education is a long-term answer to mankind's problems and must not be confused with short-term social engineering. The danger now is that we are becoming disillusioned with education, without realizing that we are only beginning to try it.

During the Education Decade, the school years were extended upward and downward, the school curriculum was revised from top to bottom, the Elementary and Secondary Education Act of 1965 brought the federal government into education as never before, the schools became both a focal point for social protest and a vehicle for social reform, and schooling joined politics and world affairs as leading topics of social discourse. "Innovation" and "revolution" were used interchangeably in discussing the changes taking place in the schools.

But the education scene today remains confusing. Put on one pair of glasses and the schools appear to be moving posthaste toward becoming centers of intense, exciting learning, marked by concern for the individual. Put on another, and they appear to be mired in tradition, insensitive to pressing social problems, and inadequate to the demands of learning.

Where are the schools today? How widespread have been the changes during the decade since Sputnik? What kind of changes are needed in the 1970s, and what lies ahead for the balance of the century?

While conducting studies of new approaches to school curricula during the early 1960s, I visited many schools and classrooms. Although the Education Decade was well underway, the reforms it espoused were not conspicuously present. Was the sample of schools visited inadequate, or were proposed changes losing their momentum before reaching their target? Several colleagues joined me in an effort to probe more deeply as we visited some 260 kindergarten through third-grade classrooms in 100 schools clustered in or around the major cities of thirteen states.

If the most frequently discussed and recommended educational practices of the Education Decade were already implemented, what would constitute a checklist of expectations? The following would seem reasonable. First, teaching would be characterized by efforts to determine where the student is at the *outset* of instruction, to diagnose his attainments and problems, and to base subsequent instruction on the results of this diagnosis. Second, learning would be directed toward "learning how to learn," toward self-sustaining inquiry rather than the memorization and regurgitation of facts. Third, this inquiry would carry the student out of confining classrooms and into direct observation of physical and human phenomena. Fourth, classrooms would be characterized by a wide variety of learning materials—records, tapes, models, programed materials, film strips, pamphlets, and television—and would not be dominated by textbooks. Fifth, attention to and concern for the individual and individual differences would show through clearly in assignments, class discussions, use of materials, grouping practices, and evaluation. Sixth, teachers would understand and use such learning principles as reinforcement, motivation, and transfer of training. Seventh, visitors would see vigorous, often heated, small and large group discussions, with the teacher in the background rather than the forefront. Eighth, one would find rather flexible school environments—marked by little attention to grade levels—and extensive use of team-teaching activities involving groups of teachers, older pupils, parents, and other persons in the teaching-learning process. And, certainly, it would be reasonable to expect to find innovative ways of dealing with special educational problems such as those presented by environmentally handicapped children.

Although these expectations seemed reasonable at the outset of our visits to schools, they did not constitute an accurate description of what we found. We were unable to discern much attention to pupil needs, attainments, or problems as a basis for beginning instruction, nor widespread provision for individual opportunities to learn. Most classes were taught as a group, covering essentially the same ground for all students at approximately the same rate of speed. Teaching was predominantly telling and questioning by the teacher, with children responding one by one or occasionally in chorus. In all of this, the textbook was the most highly visible instrument of learning and teaching. If records, tapes, films, film strips, supplementary materials, and other aids to learning were in the schools we visited, we rarely saw them. When small groups of students worked together, the activities engaged in by each group member were similar, and bore the mark of the teacher's assignment and expectations. Rarely did we find small groups intensely in pursuit of knowledge; rarely did we find individual pupils at work in self-sustaining inquiry. Popular innovations of the decade—non-grading, team teaching, "discovery" learning, and programed instruction—were talked about by teachers and principals alike but were rarely in evidence.

On a more general and impressionistic level, teachers and students did not appear to be intensely involved in their work. Only occasionally did we encounter a classroom aura of excitement, anticipation, and spontaneity; when we did, it was almost invariably a kindergarten class. This is not to say that classroom inhabitants were uninvolved but rather to suggest that it may be erroneous to assume that teaching and learning in the schools, more than other human enterprises, are characterized by excitement and enthusiasm. On the positive side, however, the teachers we observed were warm and supportive, and not sadistic as some polemicists have pictured them to be.

From the data, we were unable to differentiate practices in schools enrolling a high proportion of disadvantaged or minority group children from practices in other schools. Our descriptions of classrooms enrolling predominantly Mexican-American children, for example, were not distinguishable from our descriptions in general. Nor were there marked differences in our respective descriptions of classrooms in the inner city, on the fringe of the urban environment, and in suburbia.

It is dangerous to generalize about something as large, complex, and presumably diverse as schooling in the United States, or even about the first four years of it. As far as our sample of schools is concerned, however, we are forced to conclude that much of the so-called educational reform movement has been blunted on the classroom door.

Yet, the responsibility for this situation does not rest entirely with school-teachers and principals. The elementary schools were anything but the "palaces" of an affluent society. In fact, they looked more like the artifacts of a society that did not really care about its schools, a society that expressed its disregard by creating schools less suited to human habitation than its prisons. These artifacts reflect the strange notion that learning proceeds best in groups of thirty, that teachers are not to converse with each other, that learning should be conducted under rather uncomfortable circumstances, and that schools proceed best with their tasks when there is little or no traffic with the outside world.

We had hoped to conduct sustained interviews with the teachers we observed, but there were rarely quiet, attractive places to confer. We held our interviews on the run or, more favorably, when we were able to have breakfast or dinner together. These teachers wanted to talk about education: what "good" things we had observed elsewhere; what we thought about current innovations; whether we had any suggestions for improving the teaching we had just observed; and on and on. Interestingly, those with whom we talked had a rather favorable image of what they were doing in the classroom; they thought they were individualizing instruction, teaching inductively, and encouraging self-propelled learning. Neither principals nor teachers were able to articulate clearly just what they thought to be most important for their schools to accomplish. And neither group was very clear on changes that should be effected in the near future.

Both our observations alone and those with teachers lead to several disquieting conclusions. Public schooling probably is the only large-scale enterprise in this country that does not provide for systematic updating of the skills and abilities of its employees and for payment of the costs involved. Teachers are on their own as far as their in-service education is concerned, in an environment designed for "telling" others, yet one that is grossly ill-suited to intellectual pursuits with peers. Teachers, we presume, can readily cast aside their old, inappropriate ways and acquire markedly different ones through some process of osmosis.

Sixteen or more years of schooling should educate teachers and others for self-renewal—and this frequently is the case. But general failure to do so for large numbers of people constitutes the greatest failure of our educational system. In the colleges as well as in the lower schools, the processes and fruits of human experience are so cut up in the curriculum and so obfuscated by detail that cohesiveness, relationships, and relevance are obscured.

Another aspect of our educational malaise is that an enormous amount of energy goes into merely maintaining the system. Studies have shown that administrators favor teachers who maintain orderly classrooms, keep accurate records, and maintain stable relations with parents and the community. Other studies reveal that middle managers in the educational system, such as principals and supervisors, tend to be recruited from among teachers who demonstrate these orderly qualities. Because they are rewarded for maintaining the system, administrators are not likely either to challenge it or to reward subordinates who do.

Just as teachers and principals appear to be uncertain as to what their schools are for, the communities they serve provide no clear sense of direction or guidelines. There is evidence to suggest that parents are somewhat more favorably disposed toward educational change than are teachers or school administrators, but legions of educators who push at the forefront of innovative practice stand ready to show their community-inflicted scars. Many parents are more interested in changes in the abstract or for someone else than in changes involving their own children. Social change is a formidable enterprise under the best of circumstances; schooling too often presents only the worst of circumstances, with resistance being built into both the setting and the internal structure.

It should come as no surprise, then, that comprehensive experiments in schooling are the rarest of all educational phenomena. Small wonder that teachers practice so little individualizing instruction, inductive teaching, non-grading, team teaching, or other recently recommended practices. They have not seen them. If teachers are to change, they must see models of what they are to change to; they must practice under guidance the new behaviors called for in the exemplary models. If teachers are to change, the occupation itself must have built into it the necessary provisions for self-renewal. The creation of these conditions is an important agenda item for the decade ahead.

Seers of bygone decades occasionally asked whether our schools had outlived their usefulness—and we laughed. The question is no longer funny. The schools are conspicuously ill-suited to the needs of at least 30 per cent of their present clientele: the large numbers of children from minority groups who live in harsh environments; the tens of thousands who suffer from crippling mental, physical, and emotional handicaps; and a few whose rare gifts separate them sharply from their peers. But the lack of "fit" between school and client extends into other realms until one is forced to ask whether our educational system serves even 50 per cent of its clientele in reasonably satisfying ways. Learning disabilities evidenced in the primary grades often go undiagnosed, persisting throughout life and seriously limiting human relations participation. Talents in music, art, and creative writing lie largely outside the school's scope and are usually brought to fruition in the home where parents can afford to, or not at all where parents cannot. The human models in these fields, so necessary to refinement of childhood talent, are inaccessible to the school because of teacher certification restrictions or sheer failure to recognize their powerful role in educating the young.

It is also questionable whether those students who appear to be adjusting well are acquiring desirable traits and repressing undesirable ones. Success in school seems to assure further success in school; good grades predict good grades. But academic success neither assures nor predicts good work habits, good citizenship, happiness, compassion, or other human virtues. The incidences of dropouts, non-promotion, alienation, and minimal learning reinforce our apprehension that schools have become or are fast becoming obsolete. They appear to have been designed for a different culture, a different conception of learning and teaching, and a different clientele.

The task of rehabilitating the schools, then, is indeed formidable. We dare not ask whether we *should* rehabilitate our schools, although this is a good question. Impotent and irrelevant though much schooling may be, the schools are at present the only educational institution deliberately created and maintained for inculcating something of man's heritage, for developing the basic tools of literacy, and for instilling some powers of rational thought and criticism. Although our civilization abounds in educational institutions and media, from scuba-diving school to television, none is centrally committed to this basic, cultural role. By seeking to rehabilitate the *educational* role of the school, rather than its various ancillary functions (baby-sitting, social stratification, economic investment, etc.), perhaps we will keep the meaning of education before us, experiment with improved means, and ultimately transfer the process to new and better institutions should the schools fail us and we them.

A brief analysis of television serves both to illustrate what I mean by rehabilitating the *educational* role of the school and to project us into the varied possibilities of an electronic educational future. Some of us still remember those wonderful evenings of intellectual discourse with friends, before that glass-faced monster took over. At first, exposure to the glass face meant only a few hours' diversion each week, watching the favorite programs we had only heard before. But now there are "hot" and "cool" stimuli, Marshall McLuhan's non-linear communication, and a television generation. From birth to high school graduation, today's young man or woman spends an average of 15,000 hours before television sets and just over 12,000 hours (1,000 hours each year) in school. I do not believe that these hours of schooling provide anything like an antidote for the formidable array of violence, cruelty, dishonesty, prejudice, and inhumanity to man provided by newspapers, magazines, movies, and television.

Our schools have not adopted television; nor has television adopted the schools. An occasional educational television program becomes a "tack-on" to the curriculum. During the Education Decade, a national network occasionally found it mildly profitable to feature a "special" on the schools. Meanwhile, however, television has gone about its business and the schools have gone about theirs. Television has not yet taken on the essentially educational function of humanizing the content of experience for teaching and learning. It seeks only to entertain, to hold the viewer. But neither have the schools been markedly successful in producing an intensely human environment in which children are caught up in man's adventure, whether in the arts, politics, the sea, or outer space.

Herein lies our dilemma. On one hand, a powerful medium has caught the attention—indeed, the very lives—of our children. But it lacks significant substance to nurture a civilization and appears to care not, despite its protestations, whether it uplifts or debases. On the other hand, the only institution charged specifically with the performance of educational functions fails to grip a significant portion of its clientele. Unfulfilled educational promise lies between.

In schools run by humans, we have not succeeded in developing intensely humanistic learning environments—not in process, not in content, and not in perspective. The schools do not, in general, foster man's most creative traits, nor grapple with his great ideas, nor relate these ideas and talents to the contemporary environment where man's dramas are continuously re-enacted. The schools are bogged down with routine, trivialities, and the lesser literacies. In the rat race to cover what is in the textbook, schooling has lost sight of education as an end in itself and has become instrumental to the next textbook, the next grade, higher education, and the Gross National Product. And now—at a critical time in the history of schools, education, and man—an electronic teacher of great power, the computer, comes into this human-based environment. The instructional era now on the horizon is one of man-machine interaction. Will the computer dehumanize learning and teaching even more? The choice is ours.

On an experimental basis, computers are demonstrating their usefulness in teaching spelling, mathematics, reading, and a host of cognitive skills. Tapes, video-screens, records, and other devices are combined with computer memory to produce a unique instructional system of sight, sound, and touch. Current writings on computer-aided instruction present a picture of instructional efficiency and the freeing of human teachers to do those truly *human* educational things. But what are these things? And have teachers been prepared to engage in them?

Already it is clear that computers, unlike television, are more efficient by far than humans in performing routine instructional tasks and in assuring error-free performance on the part of learners in those basic skills to which teachers devote so much time. It is clear, then, that computers have a viable, albeit threatening, role in the schools. The critical problem is how computers and people are to live together productively in the school environment. If educators continue to confuse instruction in the basic skills with education, then teachers will merely monitor the computer and, in time, become its servant. Under such circumstances, in due time, there would be no need for schools as other than custodial agencies, since computer terminals might more readily and profitably be placed in homes. State and local budgets, together with some transportation problems, would be substantially relieved.

A happier alternative, however, is that there will be a separation of those instructional tasks most appropriate for electronic teachers from those educational activities most appropriate for human teachers. Efficiently taught in the basic tools of their culture, young people would have much more time than is now the case to pursue education as a way of life. With the processes of providing these tools freed from the restraints of the human time and energy for teaching them, they would become readily accessible to all. But this alternative, too, destroys or drastically changes the school as we have known it.

The tireless computer is fully capable of working twenty-four hours a day every day. It can recall the same material and teach the same lesson over and over, and it can provide subject matters singly or in various combinations and sequences. No need, then, to confine teaching to the hours between 9 in the morning and 3 in the afternoon; nor to delay certain subjects until high school or college; nor to complete sixteen units of work in four years. Suddenly, we come to realize that schools as we know them are largely the product of limitations and conventions in the use of human energy. Introduce a new source of instructional energy and learning is unshackled.

But still to be accounted for in schooling are "those educational activities most appropriate for *human* teachers." Their human character demands libraries, seminar rooms, museums, studios, art galleries, courts of law, government offices, airports, housing developments, fields, ponds, counseling centers, hospitals, quiet study corners, work experiences, visits with exemplary models of accomplishment, and on and on. Take the educational environment beyond school and classroom and learning can be humanized.

With fundamental learning effectively taken care of, perhaps we can then correct our myopic perspective that equates education with schooling, and go beyond the utilitarian boundaries we have set for both ideas. We can then tend to the urgent need to value education for its own sake, to grapple with education's first question: What kinds of human beings do we seek? But even before looking toward where we want to be, perhaps we should ask fundamental questions about where we are. To what extent is each individual being provided with opportunities to develop his unique potentialities? To what extent is each individual developing a deep sense of personal worth—the kind of selfhood that is prerequisite to self-transcendence? To what extent are our young people coming into critical possession of their culture? And to what extent are our people developing a mankind identity—an identity that transcends all men in all times and in all places?

POLITICAL

10 / TURNING OFF "THE PEOPLE"

Andrew N. Greeley

It doesn't take those patriotic parades of "hard hats" to demonstrate that there is immense dissatisfaction in the country with "radical protest." And it is not new. One study of the 1968 election showed that only about a tenth of the population supported the Chicago demonstrators, despite the rather favorable presentation the protests got in the mass media. Only about a quarter of those identified as "doves" on Vietnam disapproved of the behavior of the Chicago police. About three-quarters of the general population approved of the Chicago conspiracy trial. Similarly, the outrage in academia not withstanding, it appears that more than half of the American people blame the Kent State killings on the students themselves!

However virtuous the present radical movement may be, it has turned off somewhere between 60 and 90 per cent of the American people. To put the matter bluntly, one could make a persuasive case that a large segment of the organized peace movement has been self-defeating—if its goal is to make converts. William Kuntsler, David Dellinger, Abbie Hoffman, Daniel Berrigan, Dr. Spock and Noam Chomsky may be folk heroes among intellectual elites and a substantial number of the young; they are *not* folk heroes among the white ethnics or, one suspects, among a substantial majority of the country. If white ethnic groups (not all of them "blue collar" by any means) are told in effect that to support peace he must support the Black Panthers, women's liberation, drugs, free love, Dr. Spock, long hair, and picketing clergymen, he may find it very difficult to put himself on the antiwar side.

From *The New Republic,* June 27, 1970. Reprinted by permission of The New

We may dismiss the white ethnics' loyalty to the country as quaint and old fashioned, as super-patriotism, but that does not make it any less powerful. Most of these people are the children or grandchildren of peasant immigrants who had behind them centuries of landlessness and oppression in Europe. Through hard work (as they see it) they have obtained land, home, financial stability of a sort, and personal freedom. From their point of view, a nation which makes possible both financial security and personal freedom for so many of its citizens *deserves* vigorous defense. To those who point out that we still have our poor and oppressed, the white ethnics respond that they, too, were once poor and oppressed but managed to struggle their way up the economic and social ladder.

The white ethnic, then, simply cannot understand why the children of the well-to-do are so eager to "knock" American society. Hasn't that society permitted them a "college education"? Granting that there are social wrongs, even granting that the war might be a mistake, the white ethnic is appalled at the hatred for the United States that he observes (on the television screen) among young radicals and some of their faculty patrons. Burning the American flag or waving the Vietcong flag may be an exciting or an exhilarating experience for the son of a well-to-do family, but it's an astonishing and disgusting spectacle to a white ethnic. I don't know the exact cost to the peace movement of burning the American flag or waving the Vietcong flag, but my impression is that these incidents have been of extraordinary symbolic importance.

Anti-Communism is now unfashionable among the American intellectual elite (which is not to say that it might not become fashionable again at some later date). The revisionist historians now would persuade us that the cold war was mostly of American doing. Others who are not willing to go quite that far, point out the disunity in the international Communist movement and observe that given the schism between China and Russia (and the many lesser schisms all about the Communist world) it is no longer meaningful to speak of an "international Communist conspiracy." These arguments are far too subtle to gain much credence among the white ethnics. In their perspective, it was the international Communist conspiracy that blighted the bright hopes of peace after the Second World War, which dragged us into the Korean "police action," and which is responsible for the present conflict in Vietnam. The white ethnics read the newspapers and know about Hungary, the Berlin Wall, and Czechoslovakia, and wonder how anyone can doubt the Communist menace. They are also painfully aware that many of their old homelands are under Communist control and will be until the "captive nations" are "free." It comes as a surprise to many liberal intellectuals to be told that Poles, Lithuanians, Czechs, Slovaks, Hungarians, Estonians, Latvians, and Ukranians accept the Moscow-controlled regimes in these countries about as cheerfully as American Jews would accept Nasser's armies of occupation in Tel Aviv.

Such an attitude may be unrealistic, unappreciative of the complexities of international diplomacy or of the economic progress made in some of the "Iron Curtain" countries in the last quarter-century; it is nevertheless an extremely important reality for American ethnics. For many of them, the same people who "betrayed" the Captive Nations are now advocating "surrender" in Vietnam.

The Establishment, too, is seen quite differently by the white ethnics and student radicals or their faculty supporters. From the perspective of the Polish TV watcher on Milwaukee Avenue on the northwest side of Chicago, the long-haired militants are every bit as much part of the Establishment as are the presidents of corporations, Wall Street investment bankers, and other Anglo-Saxon and Jewish members of the power elite. In their frame of reference, Richard Nixon to some extent, and Spiro Agnew, to a very considerable extent, are *anti*-Establishment figures, and someone like David Dellinger with his Yale degree is an Establishment personage. They see the protesters and the militants as sons and daughters of the well-to-do, who have attended elite colleges and are supported financially by their parents through all their radical activity. A Harvard graduate is, after all, a Harvard graduate whether in a picket line or in a board room of a large corporation. The peace movement is seen as an Establishment movement, working against the values, the stability, and the patriotism of the American masses—which masses, incidentally, are seen as footing the bill for Establishment games and amusements.

American ethnics are deeply troubled at what they consider to be the "changing of the rules," a phrase I have heard over and over again. *They* had to work to achieve the social position they presently occupy, but other groups in American society are demanding these positions as a matter of right. *Their* children had to pass entrance exams to get into college; other men's children (they think) do not. *Their* fathers had to work long hours to support their families; other men's fathers seemingly did not. *They* fought bravely to defend America in World War II and in the Korean War, and now it is being alleged that those who fight and die in wars are immoral or foolish. *They* lived according to the American ethic of sobriety and respectability, and now they see on TV the spectacle of the drug smoking hippie at a rock festival. In other words, the white ethnic feels that he is being told that the rules no longer apply, that others are to achieve what he has achieved (frequently, it seems to him, with his picking up the tab) by doing exactly the opposite of what the rules prescribed.

There is obviously something incomplete, perhaps something paranoiac, about this "change of rules" analysis. But Mr. Agnew's success is the mark of the plausibility it enjoys. He who wishes to make converts to the cause of peace among those who think the rules are changing has his work cut out for him.

I must confess that I have rather little confidence that such persuasion is going to occur. The intellectual and moral strains among the liberal elite groups run directly counter to strains in the white ethnics and other members of middle America. Not to put too fine an edge on the matter, the liberal elites are strongly tempted to view white ethnics with profound contempt. The elites are far better educated, far more articulate, far better informed, far more sophisticated and, in their heart of hearts, convinced that they are far superior morally. The white ethnic might not himself be a "pig," but he probably has brothers or cousins or uncles who are "pigs," and one simply does not try to make converts among pigs.

If one were trying to convert substantial segments of the white ethnic population to the cause of peace, it would not be hard to outline some components of the strategy:

Peace must be separated from the peace movement, particularly from its radical fringes. Militant protests, demonstrations and marches are what peace does not need. One is appalled at the risk of self-defeat involved in the closing down of school before the next election. My own hunch is that white ethnics will not be at all offended by youthful political activity, but they will be offended by the "changing of the rule" implied in a shutdown of schools to permit campaigning. After all, no one shuts down their factories or their offices so *they* can campaign. Demonstrations, protests and violence during the last two weeks of the campaign (and given the nature of American extremists at present, such actions are almost inevitable) will make matters worse. My own fear would be that a Children's Crusade during the last two weeks of October would virtually guarantee one of the biggest right-wing majorities in Congress since the 1920s.

Appeals for peace should be rooted in American patriotism rather than in "hate America" rhetoric. Unquestionably, there is a chauvinistic, if not imperialist, strain in our tradition, but there is also an altruistic one. It should, I think, be emphasized that we have honored—always in theory and frequently in practice—the principle of self-determination for small countries. It could also be emphasized that America's claim to be a first-rate power could scarcely be an issue in Vietnam, and that indeed the measure of greatness in the contemporary world is that a nation is able to permit other nations to make their own decisions. As a matter of fact, it might be argued that only a very strong and powerful nation can afford to get out of a war without winning complete victory. Even in the War of 1812, America settled for something less than complete victory, rather than needlessly prolong a foolish conflict. In the Mexican-American War we did not choose to conquer all of Mexico, though we could have done so.

In the Spanish-American War, while we had mixed feelings about Cuba and the Philippines, we were willing to permit them, more or less, to go their own way. Emphasis, then, on the altruistic strain in the American tradition should be more helpful in winning converts among the white ethnics than emphasis on Professor Chomsky's assertion that we are the most imperialistic country that ever existed, an assertion which has historical problems of its own.

It also seems to me that a point can be made that the United States is under no obligation, indeed ought not to try, to defend another country that is not capable of or interested in providing for its own defense, a notion which I gather is currently called the Nixon Doctrine, though 25 years ago it was called the Truman Doctrine. It could thus be argued that the mistake was not so much trying to resist Communism in Vietnam, as trying to do it by ourselves, the South Vietnamese being either unwilling or unable to do so. It might be asserted that it is their war and not our war, and that it was a mistake on our part ever to take it over and make it our war. One could at least say that if the South Vietnamese government is not able to fend for itself now, it never will be.

It might also be asserted that at least some objectives in Vietnam were achieved; India, Thailand, and especially Indonesia are now much more secure from Communist takeover than they were in the early 1960s. There is little doubt that this claim would be true about Indonesia, perhaps somewhat more doubtful about Thailand. But at least some kind of case could be made for the position.

The important point about this last argument is that it is counterproductive to describe the war as a complete waste. Too many white ethnics (and others, too, for that matter) have lost relatives in the war to be able to accept the notion that it was a total loss. On a more subtle level, I think one could reasonably argue that many lessons have been learned by the United States which will not be soon forgotten (though, heaven knows, a lot of people said after Korea that we would never get involved in a land war in Asia, much less a guerilla war), but I do not think these subtle arguments will be very effective with white ethnics. Thus, one is forced to take the stand that perhaps some good things were accomplished.

All of these approaches may seem weak, if not dishonest. I would reply that weak they may be, but reality is too complex, too ambiguous, and too uncertain for any definitive judgment to be made today about all the functions and dysfunctions of Vietnam. Dysfunctions aplenty there were, but it will take the historians of the future to perceive them clearly. It is surely true that the enthusiasts of the peace movement at the present time, and even many of us who are not part of the formal peace movement, see the war as a clearcut disaster from every possible viewpoint, with few, if any, mitigating qualities. And yet, if that be the case, it is one of the few major events in human history which is not shrouded in mitigating ambiguity and complexity. My only suggestion is that if one wishes to engage in any dialogue with the white ethnics, one must be prepared not to dismiss them as blind or immoral because they do not see the issues quite as clearly as we do, but rather to try to sympathetically understand the complexities and ambiguities as *they* see them.

I rather doubt that this will take place, if only because I am not persuaded that the elite groups in American society have the humility or the patience or even the personal security necessary to try to establish, or perhaps reestablish, dialogue with the rest of the nation. There seems to be some extremely important payoff in being alienated from the larger society, indeed, even in suspecting the "fascist mass" is out to get you. One cannot escape the impression that some commentators are eagerly awaiting an "era of repression" so that they can experience the same kind of "subpoena envy" they experienced in the McCarthy era. Why intellectual elites take secret pleasure in the fantasy of Slavic stormtroopers pounding on their doors is an important subject, but beyond the subject of this article.

RELIGION

11 / THE NEW AMERICAN JESUITS

John L'Heureux

"Absolute obedience" was the command on which Ignatius Loyola founded the Society of Jesus more than four centuries ago. Today the word "obedience" is rarely uttered when young Jesuits get together. Their ranks include protest marchers, draft-card burners,

bishop-baiters, and jailbirds. The community of 8,000 American Jesuits is caught in profound internal ferment, as one of them here explains.

"What we've really been saying is that we're fighting over the last deck chair on the *Titanic.*"

The Jesuit who spoke was summarizing the first day of discussions about the situation of the Society of Jesus—the Jesuits—within the larger context of the American Church. Ten Jesuits, all of them around thirty and all of them friends, came together during the Easter holidays to talk about the future of their religious order, and—more important to them—what their future within that order might be. An extraordinary aspect of the meeting was that religious superiors who had been neither consulted nor informed nonetheless sent their blessings on the project and asked to be informed on opinions and decisions. More extraordinary still was that this meeting was convened at a time when vast overhauling of the structures of religious life was under way and when the occasions for expressing dissident opinion were practically unlimited. These young Jesuits were not concerned, however, about the opinions or plans of superiors or about expressing grievances. They were pursuing something far more essential to their lives: a way of living out their religious commitment which would assure some kind of effectiveness in their work, affectivity in their social life, and some sense of corporate unity more meaningful than merely the wearing of similar clothes and the sharing of a common house.

"All the Jesuits coming along have decided to do their own thing," one remarked. "They've even been encouraged to do their own thing. And that's fine. But if you're going to do *just* your own thing, be a spiritual loner, then you might as well do it outside the Jesuits. What we've got to discover is in what way we are a special group, what our corporate identity is. Because the Society of Jesus is going to be what we make it. We are the Jesuits just as surely as we are the Church."

What the Jesuits are is a phenomenon far more difficult to describe than what they do. Primarily they are educators. The largest order in the Church, the Jesuits today number more than 34,000 men, almost two thirds of whom are involved somehow in education, whether in teaching or administration or as students in Jesuit schools. Of the 8,000 Jesuits in the United States some 2,400 are studying for the priesthood and another 700 are vowed Brothers who live the religious life of the Jesuits but who will not be ordained priests. These 8,000 men run twenty-eight colleges and universities, from the vast sprawling complexes of Fordham and Georgetown and the University of San Francisco to the relatively small and specialized Wheeling and Holy Cross. They also run fifty-four high schools, which enroll 38,000 students. Though surveys show that only 42 per cent of American Jesuits are involved in teaching, these figures are misleading, since another 20 to 25 per cent are preparing for teaching careers, and most of the men on mission duty also are involved in education.

Jesuits engage, of course, in numerous other occupations; in limited numbers they are retreat masters and army chaplains and editors of religious publications; in even smaller numbers they are employed as lawyers, psychiatrists, labor arbitrators. But their principal work traditionally has been and today remains education. And this is perhaps the single most debated point in the Jesuit program of renewal: whether they own their schools or whether the schools, limiting mobility, imposing huge financial and manpower obligations, have come to own the Jesuits.

The Easter meeting at which the ten young Jesuits discussed their own and their order's future was one of the more hopeful, positive signs of the dramatic changes occurring in the Jesuits today. For well over five years the Jesuit order has been under heavy and unrelenting attack from outside and from within. It is the men on the inside who have brought about the most impressive changes. Protest marchers, draft-card burners, professional rebels were at first rebuked by their superiors and some, like Daniel Berrigan, exiled by them. But time passed. Massive and highly publicized defections from the priesthood which once embarrassed Jesuit officials now merely dismay them. What remains utterly baffling is the new spirit of indifference. The new American Jesuit acts in consultation with his conscience and his friends; how his superior will react is not a matter of importance to him. This because, so he feels, authority has ceased to be a problem: by its years of righteous inconsideration for the individual it has phased itself out. Today the word "obedience" is rarely mentioned when Jesuits get together.

Yet it was upon the concept of absolute obedience that Ignatius Loyola in 1540 founded his Society of Jesus. The religious order he established was at once an amalgam of what he found effective in traditional religious orders and what he intuited would succeed for his times: a highly centralized monarchical government controlling widely dispersed and highly mobile apostolates. In such an organization, unquestioning obedience was essential, and it is not by accident that he chose the traditional monastic representation of that virtue as "blind" and compounded the image in his Constitutions: "Each one should convince himself that they who live under obedience must allow themselves to be carried and ruled by God's Providence through their superiors as though they were a dead body which allows itself to be carried in any direction and to be treated in any manner whatsoever." Ignatius had been a soldier before his conversion, and when he founded his religious order, he elevated and spiritualized military obedience; it remained total and unquestioning; only the motive for obeying was changed. It was his genius to make such absolute obedience a liberating rather than a constrictive force.

From the beginning Ignatius placed heavy emphasis on teaching and on missionary work. Though not founded as a direct response to the Reformation, the Society of Jesus won its greatest fame in combating the sweepingly successful Protestantism in France, Central Europe, and the Low Countries. And at the Council of Trent, Rome's belated response to Luther's success, it was again the members of the Society of Jesus who as *periti* prepared the speeches and framed the documents which made Church reform possible for the first time in centuries.

By 1650 there were on the Continent at least five hundred colleges run by Jesuits. This is the great baroque period when Jesuit drama, ballet, art, and music flourished. It is also the period when the accusations of "Jesuit pride" began, the political machinations of court favorites that would finally lead to the suppression of the Jesuit order.

The third century of Jesuit existence saw expansion of institutions and membership, but little of the brilliance or sanctity which characterized Ignatius' early Society. Not surprisingly after 1750, the Jesuits who had so fiercely battled heresies and the men who made them now found themselves battling for their own existence. But their schools and their pulpits were too great a threat to the absolutist monarchs of France and Spain and the Two Sicilies; cooperating for the first time in a common effort, they brought such pressure to bear on Pope Clement XIV that in 1773 he suppressed the Society of Jesus for unspecified reasons which were "suggested to Us by the principles of prudence and which We retain concealed in Our breast."

Restored in 1814 the Society of Jesus was at once the same and immensely different. Constitutions, ascetic ideals, and educational policies remained as they had been. But the spirit was gone. The effort to regain what was irrevocably lost led Jesuit superiors, and principally the Superior General Roothaan, to a blindly conservative dedication to rules and procedures; emphasis was on prayer and personal sanctity; social involvement of any kind not specifically spiritual was to be eschewed. The Jansenism against which Jesuits fought had influenced them more than they realized, and a spirituality of the will, mathematical and readily controllable, became a central part of Jesuit training. Inevitably, the absolute obedience upon which Ignatius insisted and which enabled him to deploy his men throughout the world, wherever their maximum effectiveness might be, now became not a liberating force but a restrictive one, a kind of personal trap which could be opened only by the word of the superior. Creativity in theology, philosophy, poetry, and art gradually withered. Tradition, with its safety and its aura of respectability, embalmed the restored Society of Jesus.

What had happened is what almost always happens when men try to revive lost institutions. In the attempt to get back to original ideals, they look to principles and structures, to the external formalities of lawbooks and censures, and the society they create is in imitation of a pure ideal which is unattainable and which never existed in the first place. This is what happened to Judaism after the Babylonian exile, and it is what happened to the Jesuits after suppression. The spirit was crushed beneath mountains of legislation, and the Jesuits became a group of dedicated and harmless school-teachers for the sons of the upper middle class.

When a few years ago change finally came to the Jesuits, it came with a rapidity and a violence for which neither they nor the Church was prepared. In 1957 the Superior General summoned a Congregation in Rome to enact, so it was whispered, "sweeping legislation." Whatever the General's supposed intentions, the Congregation came to nothing. Almost before the delegates could meet, they were told by Pope Pius XII that "either they remain as they are or they cease to exist," and aware of their desire for change, he gave them some: he told them to stop smoking. That was in 1957. Before ten years had elapsed Latin had disappeared from the Jesuit seminary classroom, Jesuit theologates had formed consortiums with Jewish and Protestant theological schools, a Jesuit was chairman of Harvard's Near Eastern language and literature department and another was chairman of the music department at Brown. Further, Jesuits were in trouble with shadowy undesignated people for fighting slumlords in Chicago, in trouble with chanceries throughout the country for advocating birth control; they were silenced for defying the redoubtable Cardinal O'Boyle, and were jailed for defying the United States government.

What had happened during those ten years is typified by Woodstock College, where in fact many of the changes actually began. The Jesuits' largest and most prestigious theological school, Woodstock in the 1960s boasted a faculty headed by such men as Avery Dulles, Gustave Weigel, John Courtney Murray, Joseph Fitzmyer, Walter Burghardt. Its student body, men engaged in the four-year study of theology required of candidates for the priesthood, was the envy of any graduate school: 85 to 90 per cent had at least one M.A., many had two, and some 20 per cent had completed work for a Ph.D. Many had published books, all had taught school, some were already distinguished members of the artistic and literary world. Some two hundred and seventy of these men lived together at Woodstock in an immense stone fortress far outside the city of Baltimore.

Woodstock was the penultimate stage in the Jesuit course of training, which was a fifteen-year affair. Two years of novitiate, working and praying and becoming familiar with the principles of the spiritual life, brought the novice to vows of poverty, chastity, and obedience which marked the beginning of his properly Jesuit life. There followed two years of classical studies, three years of philosophy, three years of practical experience called Regency (usually spent teaching in a Jesuit school, though sometimes spent in getting an advanced degree), and three years of theology, after which the Jesuit was ordained a priest. Ordination was followed by another year of theology and a third and final year of novitiate. Today this lengthy course has been modified to something nearer ten years, although it varies with individuals.

In 1959 Woodstock was a fairly typical school of theology, though better staffed and far more liberal than most. Classes were still being conducted in Latin, lectures were dutifully delivered and just as dutifully transcribed and redelivered at exams (also conducted in Latin), courses were the same as they had been ninety years earlier when Woodstock was founded. Most oppressive was the enormous number of lectures required for each course, a number determined by Rome at a time when books were an expensive rarity and the learning process was rooted in the functions of memory. Canon law and moral theology were presented as eternally fixed bodies of truth; speculative theology was a precise science whose definitions preserved one safe from heresy. Liturgy was inflexible. Theology had nothing whatsoever to do with society or, for that matter, with living.

Given the student body and the generally high caliber of the faculty, change was inevitable. Professors were as much irked as students at the teaching strictures imposed by the Curia. But to annoy Rome was to invite reprimand, as Father Murray discovered when he published articles on Church-state relations and was forbidden to publish anything further on the topic. Though the fear of Rome's disapproval was great, pressure from the Woodstock student body and their own discontent finally obliged the faculty to abandon Latin. And after Latin, the deluge.

Students began to form committees to assess their theological training and to make recommendations regarding course content, number of lectures, new approaches to theologizing. They began to assign relative values: they questioned the significance of canon law, the validity of much of moral theology, the relevance of speculative theology to their own lives.

It was the mass defections, rising to fifteen in one year, and the almost universal unrest of the students that finally brought change. The president was removed from office in 1964. Class boycotts and sit-outs forced radical curriculum changes. Certain professors, brilliant in their field but unwilling or unable to change, stormed out in anger, vowing never to return to the theologate. For a year or more the men at Woodstock fought bitterly among themselves, forgave one another reluctantly and sometimes not at all; but what emerged from the chaos was a modern democratic religious institution in which, Rome and Jesuit history notwithstanding, students have a determining voice in their education and in their life-style.

Why all this began at Woodstock is unclear, though partial explanation can be found in the generally liberal cast of professors and the theological sophistication of most of the students. Another explanation is the presence of Weigel and Murray at the Vatican Council and their evident disappointment in the vacillations of Pope Paul. Perhaps the most basic explanation lies in Pope John, who, more than any other single influence, gave student Jesuits hope that sweeping change was not only good but immediately realizable; at his death these same Jesuits began to feel that if change were ever to come about, it would have to begin with their own efforts. These, of course, are external explanations. Fundamental to an understanding of the radical changes in the Jesuits—and in religious orders throughout the Church—is a realization of the sense of repression and frustration so many religious were experiencing. Legalistic evasions of the rules and the occult compensations of private pleasures did nothing to mask widespread discontent with the religious life. It was inevitable that in an age of unparalleled social and psychological freedom, the mind-bending rhetoric of the religious life would be challenged; and though the Woodstock reform was many years in the making, it is only within the past three years that all religious orders have found themselves under open attack from within their own structures.

The way in which change came about at Woodstock is the way in which it is only now coming about in the secular colleges of this country. There were no building take-overs—few theology schools have resident chapters of the SDS—and the violence was merely verbal. But the pattern is the same. It is, presumably, the way change will come about in the Church at large: men will determine their own actions in a way radically different from traditional Church teaching, an existential situation will be presented to the hierarchical Church of Rome, Rome will authenticate that situation by recognizing it—whether it be the practice of birth control, the marriage of priests, the validity of divorce.

Life at Woodstock is not paradisal any more than life in the Church will ever be paradisal. But the changes brought about by the insistence of the young Jesuits and the inspired leadership of the school's president, Felix Cardegna, have fostered a new kind of American Jesuit. He is a man intensely involved in the world around him; he demands a theology which is relevant to the problems of people rather than to the ancient and uninteresting debates of Scholasticism; he asks evidence of dynamic spiritual leadership in the men who are making decisions about his life and the life of his friends; he seeks a style of living consonant with the two most significant facts of his life—that he is a vowed religious, that he has only one life to live and it must be lived productively.

This is the positive side of the new Jesuit. There is another. He is also a man who admits to being profoundly uncertain about what being a Jesuit means and about what the religious life is or ought to become. His uncertainty often makes his commitment a tenuous one. His vows do not awe him as they did his predecessors, and he is aware that the stigma of the married priest exists no longer. In the more extreme cases he is likely to feel that, having given over ten years of his life to the Jesuits and with no pressing arguments to persuade him otherwise, he will go ahead with ordination to the priesthood; later, if it doesn't work out well, he will leave. "You follow the Spirit, keeping in mind that you're a very limited man."

This new kind of Jesuit has emerged from religious situations other than that of the seminary in revolt. In all age brackets, in all occupations, Jesuits have re-examined their motives and their ideals and have arrived at questions rather than solutions. Men in their fifties, painfully aware of the irrelevance of the theology they were taught, have returned to school to study the new theology. Others have suddenly broken out of a fifteen-year position on a Jesuit campus to work in a struggling Negro college in the South. And many, finding their priestly lives not so much open-ended as dead ends, have left the priesthood to marry. Regardless of age or background, the new Jesuits have a common experience. They are invariably men who have questioned all existing authority and found it wanting; and at the same time have found no adequate substitute for it. They are men who, in faith, are waiting.

What this new uncertain Jesuit takes most for granted is his freedom. He works hard. He is constantly involved with lay people. He very often has an active apostolate that keeps him out of the Jesuit community for a large part of the day or night. He is doing what he has chosen to do, for Christ he hopes, but in any case it is something that must be done and he intends to do it—whether it be living in the slums or arguing law cases for those who cannot afford legal aid or invading Dow Chemical to expose and then destroy its records. Similarly he celebrates Mass in homes without authorization from Chancery, he preaches against the Vietnam War or, more dangerous for him, against the misapplication of the Pope's statement on birth control, he experiments with the liturgy to discover the most effective way of making Mass a meaningful event for his congregation. The question of obedience or disobedience never arises: these men are acting in conscience, and most of them have traveled so far from the authority issue that they have forgotten that for a great many others it still exists as a problem.

The freedom, the activity, the uncertainty of the new Jesuits seem to have grown out of three basic issues: the failure of the rhetoric of spirituality, a lack of spiritual leadership in the men who are making decisions, and an uncertainty about what religious life is or should be, about what the priesthood means.

The rhetoric of spirituality began to sound hollow on the day a Master of Novices explained that on the altar of obedience we make our lives a holocaust to God, and the novice asked if it wouldn't make more sense to use them in God's service instead. Once the questioning of the spiritual canards began, they collapsed altogether, and when the rhetoric collapsed, many of the practices it canonized, or at least justified, collapsed with it. The daily breviary, a collection of psalms and readings obligatory on all priests under pain of mortal sin, was largely abandoned as irrelevant to an active priesthood. The hour meditation and two fifteen-minute examinations of conscience were at first modified to something simpler and less time-consuming and finally abandoned in favor of prayer with other Jesuits—not communal recitation of printed prayers but a personal prayer shared with others. The annual eight-day retreat spent in silent contemplation has been for many supplanted by group retreats spent in discussion. Failure of the rhetoric of spirituality brought with it a distrust for all Church rhetoric, something which explains in part the new Jesuit indifference to Pope Paul's periodic laments about dissident priests and schism in the Church. "That's just Curialese," one Jesuit remarked at Easter. "What the Pope means is that, by God, we'd better all knuckle under to the thinking of a few conservative Roman cardinals. What he fails to appreciate is that the Church of Christ if far more extensive than the merely hierarchical Church, and if I have to choose one or the other, I'm afraid my allegiance is with Christ."

The new Jesuit, however he may appear in statements like the preceding, insists that he is profoundly dedicated to the spiritual; what he has no regard for is a spirituality sanctified by tradition alone—"because we've always done it, it must be right." And what he finds most lacking among the Jesuit hierarchy is spiritual leadership in the men who are making decisions. The new Jesuit is not ready to say what spiritual leadership is or to propose ways to come by it, but he is certain that it is lacking. He points to decisions about Jesuit presence in a given geographical area—whether that presence involves retreat work or the construction of a university—and indicates that decisions about what to do and how to do it have more often than not been made pragmatically by men of limited vision and of limited concern for the men who are their subjects and for the people those men will serve. High schools have been opened, universities founded, missions undertaken without prior consultation with the men who will staff them, with the result that the new Jesuit feels his order is shackled by these institutions. Further, shackled or not, he questions their validity and their viability, asking how they differ from purely secular institutions, asking why so many highly trained Jesuits should be engaged in work that laymen do as well or better.

Some definite type of spiritual leadership, he feels, would emancipate the Jesuits from their schools and leave them free to engage in the kind of life Ignatius supposedly envisioned when he founded the order: an active priestly involvement in the social, political, religious issues of the present day. Seeing the nonimplementation of Vatican II, he has come to disbelieve in the likelihood and sometimes even in the possibility of change originating from the hierarchy. He suspects his highest superiors of clinging to the old ideas while talking glibly about the new. What actually is being done, he asks, to create programs for the poor, the Negro, the victims of the slumlords and the military-industrial complex? He asks, realizing he must create the programs himself, somehow coaxing the heavy machinery of the Jesuits into working order. Sometimes he shrugs and continues his work outside the order.

Finally, in his attitude toward the vows, the new Jesuit insists upon a positive orientation; he rejects altogether the idea of the vows as deprivation.

To a vow of poverty he prefers a firm commitment to use money and goods for others. He proposes a small community of Jesuits living together, pooling their incomes, using whatever is left over for communal projects which have something specific to do with involvement in a Christian community—rather than purchasing a fleet of cars or wall-to-wall carpet for the house. What he proposes, then, is a far more strict adherence to the essential spirit of poverty than now obtains in large Jesuit communities; it is more like the poverty of the early Society of Jesus. As traditionally lived, the new Jesuit complains, the vow of poverty does not focus on doing for others but rather on renunciation of money in such a way that formalism is its norm. If a man has his superior's permission for whatever he spends, he is legally observing his vow. This has led invariably to a situation in which individual religious consume a great share of this world's goods without ever actually owning any of them. The new Jesuit feels that the vow of poverty is a comfortable double standard which allows men to profess virtue without being inconvenienced by it.

Chastity is little problem for him. The sex issue has long since been solved; it takes only a year or so for him to discover whether or not sex is going to make the living of a chaste life impossible. He is aware that the sex drive is lifelong, and he does not expect it suddenly to disappear. Celibacy is quite another matter. The new Jesuit fears that not to marry may in some important way stunt his personal development, that he will be less the man he ought to be. And yet he realizes from the example of men who have preceded him that an effective life is not only consonant with a vow of chastity but is even necessary to sustain it. And love need not inevitably lead to sin or to marriage. By his vow of chastity, the religious is obliged to love—not all men and women, but individual ones, without demanding or even expecting a return of love from them. He hopes for it, of course, but he cannot count on it. The new Jesuit expects his assurance of love, of acceptance, to come from the religious community itself, and therefore that community must be small, open, warm, and generous. Unless it is these things, it cannot be a viable religious community, and his vow of chastity becomes an intolerable burden. But most new Jesuits do not concern themselves excessively with celibacy; they expect that within five years it will no longer be required for the priesthood.

Obedience, or the question of authority, has ceased to be the important issue it was only two or three years ago. The Jesuit is now encouraged to become the kind of person his talents and his shortcomings indicate he ought to be. When he has chosen what he will do with his life, how he will use it within the apostolates of his order or to create a new apostolate, then the superior ratifies the man's choice. In that ratification lies the subject's obedience.

Less well thought out is the problem of what the priesthood should mean to contemporary Jesuits. For most of them it means a life of service to others, not necessarily in social reform, although that is where their major efforts are concentrated, but in a life which is inspired by the Gospel message of Christ and which manifests that message. It implies a large degree of selflessness, a tendency toward revolutionary thought, an impatience with a religion which tends to justify its divine claims rather than reveal the compassion of Christ. The priesthood for these men is not the safe harbor of salvation it was for another generation.

The new Jesuits are found not only among the young; they include college presidents, lawyers, theologians, scientists, and one luminous philosopher-and-superior who is seventy-six years old. At the other extreme of the new Jesuits are the not-new, who find those alarming men a stumbling block and sometimes a scandal. Having invested their lives in an immovable institution whose laws were their consciences and whose rhetoric was their deepest thought, they feel threatened and betrayed by what they see happening around them. They agonize, they condemn sometimes, but mostly they are sad. It seems to them that they are indeed on a doomed *Titanic*.

In the middle stand the large numbers of Jesuits who are neither new nor not-new. They applaud the work of the younger men, their involvement in politics and in social reform, and they see in them the realization of a Jesuit ideal. But their training has been conservative and rationalistic, and their willingness to shatter categories of thought or action is limited. They worry and they pray. They place great hope in the possibilities of reform by a natural process of evolution, and they center these hopes in the innumerable Jesuit congresses working for renewal. For these men the rest of their lives depends upon what will happen in the next few years.

In short the Jesuits today are a society in flux. It is as impossible to define a Jesuit as it is to define a Jew. Throughout the United States consulting agencies have been hired to advise the Jesuit hierarchy on restructuring the entire American organization—phasing out schools, redistributing manpower, turning colleges over to lay trustees. Major superiors are showing greater concern than ever before about the public face of their institutions and, simultaneously, greater concern for the spiritual and intellectual welfare of the individual Jesuit. They are prepared to do anything—abandon any outdated project, begin any new and valuable one—to make the Jesuits the dynamic Christian force they were at their inception.

But the new American Jesuit wonders if change has perhaps come too late. The giant overhauling of a vast and powerful religious organization is possible, he knows, but how long will it take and what will be the concrete results? Meanwhile, far from the machinery and the task forces and the immense outlay of Christian zeal being expended in his interest, he meets with his friends who are Jesuits and asks what their corporate identity is. Because the new American Jesuit is certain that whether or not change comes from above, the Society of Jesus is going to be what he decides to make it.

COMMUNICATION

12 / THE AMERICAN MEDIA BARONIES

Editors of *The Atlantic Monthly*

It is, or should be, of more than casual concern who owns any city's newspaper, radio, and television facilities. In more cities than most people have realized, a significant proportion of these communications outlets are owned by one man or one company; or a major paper or broadcast facility, or perhaps both, are subsidiaries of a large national business, often one with its own other interests to serve. Ownership of media for fun, profit, and significant power is increasingly characterized by Very Big Business.

Last year, the *Atlantic* published an article by Federal Communications Commissioner Nicholas Johnson ("The Media Barons and the Public Interest," June, 1968) warning of the dangers of diminished competition in "the marketplace of ideas," and examining the "impact of *ownership* upon the control of media." As previously promised, we present the *Atlantic's* atlas of the men, families, and combines who dominate the newspapers, radio, TV, and other media in this country, and trace some of the developments in slowly awakening Washington since Commissioner Johnson's article appeared.

The problem of who owns what facilities for telling us what is going on, and what to think about it, takes a variety of forms. Broadly, there are five types of baronies. However, one baron may be an example of more than one sort of communication power. What follows is a description of each type, with examples. Strange as it may seem, there is no single government agency in Washington which has made it its business to assemble all of the data on the reaches of this country's most powerful communicators in usable form. Only now, and still on an *ad hoc* basis, has there begun to be even any serious interest in the question.

THE LOCAL MONOPOLY

One owner may dominate a city's media. For example, one man, Donald W. Reynolds, owns the two newspapers in Fort Smith, Arkansas and its only television station. Reynolds is also an example of one man having great impact on entire regions through concentrated ownership of newspapers and/or broadcast properties in Arkansas and Oklahoma and Nevada. In Niles, Michigan, the Plym family owns the only daily newspaper, the only AM radio station, and the only FM station. There is no local television outlet. According to the information supplied by the FCC to the Senate Antitrust and Monopoly Subcommittee, as of late 1967 there were seventy-three communities where one person or company owned or controlled all of the local newspaper and broadcast outlets.

REGIONAL CONCENTRATION

There are a striking number of areas of the country where one media baron may not have a pure monopoly, but can have an equivalent impact through his preponderant interests. A branch of the Booth family, for instance, owns a string of newspapers in Michigan and contiguous areas, as well as an important interest in the company which owns and operates the Detroit *News* and the NBC TV and radio outlets in that city. Another branch owns several radio and CATV interests in the same region. There are separate companies involved, and the Booth family contends that they are controlled by separate and unfriendly branches of the family tree, and the FCC has accepted this rationale, but not unanimously. The owner of major news facilities in the most important city of a given state usually speaks to the state as a whole, and can constitute an enormous power in the state's affairs. The Mormon Church may be the most extraordinary example of regional power. Through an affiliate, the Bonneville International, the Church of the Latter Day Saints not only has extensive broadcast interests of its own but has negotiated a set of alliances with other Salt Lake City media owners, giving the combined group a mighty voice throughout the mountain states of the West. (The Mormons' interests are not at all confined to broadcasting. They are also reported to have holdings in a beet sugar company, a Salt Lake City department store, two Salt Lake City hotels, life and fire insurance companies, a bookstore, some six hundred farms, a real estate management company, a trucking company, sugar and pineapple plantations, three large Canadian ranches, forty mills, factories, and salvage stores, and substantial land in Florida.)

Relieved of the burdens of running the country, Lyndon B. Johnson has now had time to devote more attention to the family broadcasting collection, accumulated during Mr. Johnson's years in politics. (It was always argued that Lady Bird was the brains behind the whole thing.) The Johnsons own an AM and FM radio station and a TV station in Austin, as well as half a cable television company in that city. They also own 29 percent of a Waco, Texas, AM radio and TV station, which in turn owns a majority of the stock of a number of other radio and television stations in Texas. The former President's media baronial appetites are said to be whetted, not sated.

MULTIPLE OWNERSHIP

Anyone who owns more than one of a given kind of medium is, at least, an absentee owner, and at most, a national power. Gannett, Ridder, and Newhouse may not be household words everywhere in the nation, but they are in political circles in Washington, and of course in the many cities throughout the country where each owns frequently the only newspaper. Flourishing publishers are often considered by Presidents to be the sorts of people who ought to be the United States ambassadors abroad. This has been more true recently of Republicans than Democrats; John F. Kennedy showed more affinity for lowly journalists in ambassadorial posts. But mighty publishers have substantial access to the White House. Mr. Nixon recently appointed Walter Annenberg to the American Embassy in London. Annenberg is the owner of two Philadelphia newspapers, and television stations in Philadelphia, Altoona-Johnstown, and Lancaster-Lebanon, Pennsylvania; Binghamton, New York; Hartford-New Haven, Connecticut; and Fresno, California. He also is the proprietor of such variegated magazine properties as *Seventeen, TV Guide*, and the *Morning Telegraph*, a racing daily. Queried on whether Mr. Annenberg had to divest himself of his communications holdings now that he was an official servant of the State Department, a Department spokesman said that there were no rules requiring such action and was surprised that the question should even arise.

The "Big Six"—NBC, CBS, ABC, RKO, Westinghouse, and Metromedia—are the most striking examples of multiple broadcasting power. Each of the networks, beyond their vast national impact through their hundreds of affiliated stations, owns television stations in several major cities, including the three most important television markets, New York, Los Angeles, and Chicago. There are, as Commissioner Johnson pointed out, "many implications of their power. Groups of stations are able to bargain with networks, advertisers, and talent in ways that put lesser stations at substantial economic disadvantage. Group ownership means, by definition, that few stations in major markets will be locally owned. . . . But the basic point is simply that the national political power involved in ownership of a group of major VHF television stations in, say, New York, Los Angeles, Philadelphia, and Washington, D.C., is greater than a democracy should unthinkingly repose in one man or corporation."

MULTIMEDIA OWNERSHIP

Men or companies which have collected more than one kind of communications outlet—broadcasting and newspapers and/or magazines—can show up in different sorts of baronies: one with a local monopoly; one with regional concentration; a large company with great competitive advantages and a variety of interests to be served, the public interest being of unknown rank. RCA, for example, is a single company containing subsidiary companies which own a book-publishing company (Random House), radio stations, television stations, a radio and TV network (NBC), a record company, and a major manufacturer of television sets. Time Inc., the Washington *Post-Newsweek* complex, and the Cowles Communications and the Minneapolis Star and Tribune Company are all large and powerful publishing-broadcasting enterprises.

CBS is one of the more dazzling multimedia owners. Besides its network operations, it owns television stations in five major cities, a record company, musical-instrument manufacturing companies, a book-publishing house (Holt, Rinehart and Winston), educational film producers, CATV systems, Creative Playthings toys, and the New York Yankees.

CONGLOMERATES

RCA and CBS, of course, can also be termed conglomerates.

Conglomeration is a two-way street, and just as a number of communications media owners have used their enormous earnings to branch into other unrelated businesses, so have unrelated businesses increasingly eyed broadcasting properties as a means to enhanced power and earnings. (TV stations, on the average, earn nearly 100 percent return on tangible investment.) The worry here, as was brought out in the controversy over ITT's now abandoned attempt to wed ABC, is that there will be almost irresistible pressure and incentive to use the communications subsidiary to promote the corporate interests of the holding company. A conglomerate can be a community affair. Howard Hughes, aside from his other business interests, constitutes a conglomerate in Las Vegas alone: he owns land, hotels, casinos, an airport; and then acquired a television station there. (Having been warded off in his attempt in 1968 to purchase ABC, Hughes did acquire Sports Network, Inc., a significant occasional sports broadcasting network. The widespread assumption is that Hughes plans to build it into a rival television network. This is, by the way, an example of the frying-pan—fire syndrome of media ownership. While critics of the networks' power would welcome a rival, Hughes is not their idea of Lochinvar. On those rare occasions when a baron's holdings are challenged, it is frequently by another baron.)

CHALLENGES

There are, at last, some indications that official Washington has taken notice of what has been happening to the communications business and is concerned. No one anticipates that the situation will be radically different soon, but it is expected that the gobbling up of papers and channels by the baronies will at least proceed at a slower rate.

The Justice Department in 1967 became deeply concerned at the FCC's disinterest in the consequences of the proposed ABC-ITT merger; the result was the bizarre spectacle of the Department entering a case called "The United States versus the FCC" as an opponent of a regulatory agency. Ultimately, the proposed merger was dropped.

Thus aroused, the Department then proceeded to enter into a number of other FCC deliberations: a Beaumont, Texas, newspaper owner tried to acquire a TV station in the city. Justice filed a pleading with the FCC saying that it did not believe the purchase should be approved, and asking the FCC to hold a hearing—incredibly enough, not necessarily an FCC practice in such a case—so that it could participate. After the FCC told the applicant that it intended to hold a hearing, the application was dropped. On another occasion, too, Justice felt that it had to prod the FCC into holding a hearing on a case of license renewal (usually a rubber-stamp procedure for the guardians of the public's airwaves). In this instance, the renewal was sought by Frontier Broadcasting, in Cheyenne, Wyoming, which owned the town's only two daily newspapers, its only television station, and its only CATV system. Justice further suggested to the FCC that the company should be ordered to divest some of these properties. The case is still before the agency. In 1963, the Gannett group bought a television station in Rockford, Illinois; in 1967, it bought the two newspapers. At the end of 1967, the FCC, as usual, renewed the TV license. Justice was so disturbed that one year later it obtained a consent decree in which Gannett agreed to divest itself of one or the other of its Rockford properties.

Despite these and other actions, the Justice Department under the Democratic Administration was less than breathtakingly vigorous in its antitrust pursuits. The new group at Justice has already shown that it would do more, in particular against the rampant conglomerates. At this writing, a major conglomerate merger involving extensive communications holdings is pending at Justice; Metromedia with Transamerica, a $3 billion financial and real estate conglomerate. Conglomerates are unpopular in Washington these days; they have now come under the critical scrutiny of not only the Justice Department but also the Congress, the Federal Trade Commission, the Securities and Exchange Commission, and even the FCC.

The FCC's signs of life in the question of media ownership have been caused by a variety of stimulants: the Justice challenges to it to do its job, the criticism of outsiders, court rulings, and the persistent efforts of Commissioners Johnson and Kenneth Cox, and some of the Commission staff. As a result, if there is follow-through, it has taken some initial steps which could be of long-range significance. Also of critical importance will be Mr. Nixon's choice of a successor to Commission Chairman Rosel Hyde, whose term runs out this June 30, and who is expected to retire.

In perhaps its most significant move—and the first of its kind—the Commission on January 23, 1969, voted to take Channel 5 in Boston away from the Boston *Herald-Traveler*, which also has CATV interests, and give it to an independent group which filed for the license. Since then, competing applications have been filed in the cases of a few other renewals.

In March, 1968, the Commission proposed a new rule to prohibit in the future any single entity from having an interest in more than one broadcasting property in a single community. In August, the Justice Department proposed that the rule be broadened to include consideration of ownership of a newspaper and broadcasting property in the same community, and asked the FCC to consider ordering divestiture of excessive interests when the broadcast license came up for renewal, as all do every three years. The ruling is now only under consideration, and it can take the FCC years to decide whether to issue such a policy, and then of course it can get overturned by Congress. Sometimes the Commission does not wait for Congress to vote to prevent its issuing a new rule; mere sounds of displeasure from important congressmen can be sufficient to persuade the Commission to retreat. As of now, comments on the new rule have been filed, and it is up to the Commission to act.

In late March, the Commission ordered hearings—that is, withheld routine approval—on the renewal application for TV stations owned by the Chronicle Publishing Company in San Francisco, and by Midwest Radio-Television, Inc., in Minneapolis, controlled in turn by two supposedly rival newspaper publishing groups, Cowles and Ridder. In San Francisco, there were questions of concentration of control raised before the Commission, but also charges that the television had "managed" news programs for the larger corporate benefit, in particular the coverage of newspaper strikes and consolidation of the newspaper business. In Minneapolis, in addition to owner concentration, there was a charge to the Commission that the station had used its newspaper connections to secure radio broadcasting rights for professional sporting events in the area. At the same time, the Commission proposed a new rule which would make it substantially more difficult for the public to participate in license-renewal proceedings.

In 1967 and 1968, the Senate Antitrust and Monopoly Subcommitee, headed by Senator Philip A. Hart (Democrat, Michigan), held extensive hearings into the interlocking ownerships of the communications media, and its seven-volume transcript provides ample ammunition for opponents of the media barons. The takeoff point for the hearings was legislation introduced in Congress, the so-called "failing newspaper" bill, to permit joint operating agreements between a city's newspapers, one of which is deemed to be "failing." Under such agreements, the newspapers' owners might agree to fix advertising prices, and pool profits, and agree not to compete any further for circulation.

Hart's hearings were effective in killing off such legislation last year. In March of this year, the United States Supreme Court sustained an antitrust judgment against two Tucson, Arizona, newspapers which had established such "failing newspaper" joint operating agreements. The Court ruled that the "failing newspaper" doctrine could serve as a defense only if it could be shown that the paper was about to go out of business, and there was no other purchaser available. Forty-four newspapers in twenty-two other cities have joint operating agreements, a number of which could now be covered by the new decision. However, several congressmen rushed to introduce new bills to overturn that decision.

UNIT C / ISSUES FOR CONSIDERATION

1. What are the effects of changes in the typical size of the American family on the role of the male in the family?
2. Using the example of education, describe how difficult it is for institutional patterns to change in order to take advantage of technological advances such as television.
3. How does the heterogeneity of American society affect the strategy that must be used to accomplish political changes?
4. List some of the norms of the educational institution that you are involved in as a student. Distinguish between those norms that take the form of folkways and those that are mores.
5. Starting with the powerful owners of the media, list the position holders within the communication complex in our society whose roles you are familiar with. Include all those whose positions are oriented around the transmission of information within society, from the owners to the paperboy and TV repairman.

UNIT D SOCIAL GROUPS

As patterns of interpersonal relationships develop over a period of time, the individuals involved begin to see themselves as belonging together; they come to expect certain reactions from the others and realize that the others expect certain things of them. This collection of two or more persons who interact, share common norms, and have interlocking roles makes up what we call a *social group*. Note the three criteria—*interaction, shared norms,* and *interlocking roles.* Does your class in sociology fit the definition of a group? The answer, of course, is yes. Even in the largest, most formal setting, the teacher lecturing and the students responding by taking notes would be classed as interaction. You all share common norms as to when the class should start, where it should meet, what the topic should be, and so on. Finally, in the simplest analysis of your group there are at least two roles—students and teacher. The roles are interlocking in that the expectations for both dictate their relationship with the other. The teacher cannot teach unless there are students to learn.

The selections in this section describe two quite different types of groups. Bronfenbrenner's article, "The Split-Level American Family," talks about the influence on the individual of two groups—his family and his age-mates, or peers. These groups are called *primary groups* in that they are intimate, face-to-face groups which are influential in the socialization of their members. The article points out how in our society the patterns developed in the family, combined with our formal educational system, have placed the child's peer group in a most important position in determining the way he will behave and what he will believe.

Large groups tend to become formal; the role-expectations are likely to specify rigidly the relationships among the various positions in the group. An organization chart is a formal diagram depicting the structure of the type of large group that characterizes American industry. Winks makes fun of this tendency to formalize by pointing out some of the ways of beating the chart. The student can learn a great deal by carefully studying his insights.

As you read, think of how you would describe the indicators of interaction, shared norms, and interlocking roles that exist in the family and in American industry.

13 / THE SPLIT-LEVEL AMERICAN FAMILY

Urie Bronfenbrenner

Children used to be brought up by their parents.

It may seem presumptuous to put that statement in the past tense. Yet it belongs to the past. Why? Because *de facto* responsibility for upbringing has shifted away from the family to other settings in the society, where the task is not always recognized or accepted. While the family still has the primary moral and legal responsibility for developing character in children, the power or opportunity to do the job is often lacking in the home, primarily because parents and children no longer spend enough time together in those situations in which such training is possible. This is not because parents don't want to spend time with their children. It is simply that conditions of life have changed.

To begin with, families used to be bigger—not in terms of more children so much as more adults—grandparents, uncles, aunts, cousins.

Those relatives who didn't live with you lived nearby. You often went to their houses. They came as often to yours, and stayed for dinner. You knew them all—the old folks, the middle-aged, the older cousins. And they knew you. This had its good side and its bad side.

On the good side, some of these relatives were interesting people, or so you thought at the time. Uncle Charlie had been to China. Aunt Sue made the best penuche fudge on the block. Cousin Bill could read people's minds (according to him). And all these relatives gave you Christmas presents.

But there was the other side. You had to give Christmas presents to all your relatives. And they all minded your business throughout the years. They wanted to know where you had been, where you were going, and why. If they didn't like your answers, they said so (particularly if you had told them the truth).

Not just your relatives minded your business. Everybody in the neighborhood did. Again this had its two sides.

If you walked on the railroad trestle, the phone would ring at your house. Your parents would know what you had done before you got back home. People on the street would tell you to button your jacket, and ask why you weren't in church last Sunday.

But you also had the run of the neighborhood. You were allowed to play in the park. You could go into any store, whether you bought anything or not. They would let you go back of the store to watch them unpack the cartons and to hope that a carton would break. At the lumber yard, they let you pick up good scraps of wood. At the newspaper office, you could punch the linotype and burn your hand on the slugs of hot lead. And at the railroad station (they had railroad stations then), you could press the telegraph key and know that the telegraphers heard your dit-dah-dah all the way to Chicago.

These memories of a gone boyhood have been documented systematically in the research of Professor Herbert Wright and his associates at the University of Kansas. The Midwestern investigators have compared the daily life of children growing up in a small town with the lives of children living in a modern city or suburb. The contrast is sobering. Children in a small town get to know well a substantially greater number of adults in different walks of life and, in contrast to their urban and suburban agemates, are more likely to be active participants in the adult settings that they enter.

As the stable world of the small town has become absorbed into an ever-shifting suburbia, children are growing up in a different kind of environment. Urbanization has reduced the extended family to a nuclear one with only two adults, and the functioning neighborhood—where it has not decayed into an urban or rural slum—has withered to a small circle of friends, most of them accessible only by motor car or telephone. Whereas the world in which the child lived before consisted of a diversity of people in a diversity of settings, now for millions of American children the neighborhood is nothing but row upon row of buildings inhabited by strangers. One house, or apartment, is much like another, and so are the people. They all have about the same income, and the same way of life. And the child doesn't even see much of that, for all the adults in the neighborhood do is come home, have a drink, eat dinner, mow the lawn, watch TV, and sleep. Increasingly often, today's housing projects have no stores, no shops, no services, no adults at work or play. This is the sterile world in which many of our children grow, the "urban renewal" we offer to the families we would rescue from the slums.

Neighborhood experiences available to children are extremely limited nowadays. To do anything at all—go to a movie, get an ice cream cone, go swimming, or play ball—they have to travel by bus or private car. Rarely can a child watch adults working at their trades. Mechanics, tailors, or shopkeepers are either out of sight or unapproachable. A child cannot listen to gossip at the post office as he once did. And there are no abandoned houses, barns, or attics to break into. From a young point of view, it's a dull world.

Hardly any of this really matters, for children aren't home much, anyway. A child leaves the house early in the day, on a schoolbound bus, and it's almost suppertime when he gets back. There may not be anybody home when he get there. If his mother isn't working, at least part-time (more than a third of all mothers are), she's out a lot—because of social obligations, not just friends—doing things for the community. The child's father leaves home in the morning before the child does. It takes the father an hour and a half to get to work. He's often away weekends, not to mention absences during the week.

If a child is not with his parents or other adults, with whom does he spend his time? With other kids, of course—in school, after school, over weekends, on holidays. In these relationships, he is further restricted to children of his own age and the same socioeconomic background. The pattern was set when the old neighborhood school was abandoned as inefficient. Consolidated schools brought homogeneous grouping by age, and the homogenizing process more recently has been extended to segregate children by levels of ability; consequently, from the preschool years onward the child is dealing principally with replicas of the stamp of his own environment. Whereas social invitations used to be extended to entire families on a neighborhood basis, the cocktail party of nowadays has its segregated equivalent for every age group down to the toddlers.

It doesn't take the children very long to learn the lesson adults teach: Latch onto your peers. But to latch he must contend with a practical problem. He must hitch a ride. Anyone going in the right direction can take him. But if no one is going in that direction just then, the child can't get there.

The child who can't go somewhere else stays home, and does what everybody else does at home. He watches TV. Studies indicate that American youngsters see more TV than children in any other country do. By the late 1950s, the TV-watching figure had risen to two hours a day for the average five-year-old, three hours a day during the watching peak age period of twelve to fourteen years.

In short, whereas American children used to spend much of their time with parents and other grownups, more and more waking hours are now lived in the world of peers and of the television screen.

What do we know about the influence of the peer group, or of television, on the lives of young children? Not much.

The prevailing view in American society (indeed in the West generally) holds that the child's psychological development, to the extent that it is susceptible to environmental influence, is determined almost entirely by the parents and within the first six years of life. Scientific investigators—who are, of course, products of their own culture, imbued with its tacit assumptions about human nature—have acted accordingly. Western studies of influences on personality development in childhood overwhelmingly take the form of research on parent-child relations, with the peer group, or other extraparental influences, scarcely being considered.

In other cultures, this is not always so. A year ago, at the International Congress of Psychology in Moscow, it was my privilege to chair a symposium on "Social Factors in Personality Development." Of a score of papers presented, about half were from the West (mostly American) and half from the Socialist countries (mostly Russian). Virtually without exception, the Western reports dealt with parent-child relationships; those from the Soviet Union and other East European countries focused equally exclusively on the influence of the peer group, or, as they call it, the children's collective.

Some relevant studies have been carried out in our own society. For example, I, with others, have done research on a sample of American adolescents from middle-class families. We have found that children who reported their parents away from home for long periods of time rated significantly lower on such characteristics as responsibility and leadership. Perhaps because it was more pronounced, absence of the father was more critical than that of the mother, particularly in its effect on boys. Similar results have been reported in studies of the effects of father absence among soldiers' families during World War II, in homes of Norwegian sailors and whalers, and in Negro households with missing fathers, both in the West Indies and the United States. In general, father absence contributes to low motivation for achievement, inability to defer immediate for later gratification, low self-esteem, susceptibility to group influence, and juvenile delinquency. All of these effects are much more marked for boys than for girls.

The fact that father-absence increases susceptibility to group influence leads us directly to the question of the impact of the peer group on the child's attitudes and behavior. The first—and as yet the only—comprehensive research on this question was carried out by two University of North Carolina sociologists, Charles Bowerman and John Kinch, in 1959. Working with a sample of several hundred students from the fourth to the tenth grades in the Seattle school system, these investigators studied age trends in the tendency of children to turn to parents versus peers for opinion, advice, or company in various activities. In general, there was a turning point at about the seventh grade. Before that, the majority looked mainly to their parents as models, companions, and guides to behavior; thereafter, the children's peers had equal or greater influence.

Though I can cite no documentation from similar investigations since then, I suspect the shift comes earlier now, and is more pronounced.

In the early 1960s, the power of the peer group was documented even more dramatically by James Coleman in his book *The Adolescent Society*. Coleman investigated the values and behaviors of teen-agers in eight large American high schools. He reported that the aspirations and actions of American adolescents were primarily determined by the "leading crowd" in the school society. For boys in this leading crowd, the hallmark of success was glory in athletics; for girls, it was the popular date.

Intellectual achievement was, at best, a secondary value. The most intellectually able students were not those getting the best grades. The classroom wasn't where the action was. The students who did well were "not really those of highest intelligence, but only the ones who were willing to work hard at a relatively unrewarded activity."

The most comprehensive study relevant to the subject of our concern here was completed only a year ago by the same James Coleman. The data were obtained from more than 600,000 children in grades one to twelve in 4,000 schools carefully selected as representative of public education in the United States. An attempt was made to assess the relative contribution to the child's intellectual development (as measured by standardized intelligence and achievement tests) of the following factors: 1) family background (e.g., parents' education, family size, presence in the home of reading materials, records, etc.); 2) school characteristics (e.g., per pupil expenditure, classroom size, laboratory and library facilities, etc.); 3) teacher characteristics (e.g., background, training, years of experience, verbal skills, etc.); and 4) characteristics of other children in the same school (e.g., their background, academic achievement, career plans, etc.).

Of the many findings of the study, two were particularly impressive; the first was entirely expected, the second somewhat surprising. The expected finding was that home background was the most important element in determining how well the child did at school, more important than any of all aspects of the school which the child attended. This generalization, while especially true for Northern whites, applied to a lesser degree to Southern whites and Northern Negroes, and was actually reversed for Southern Negroes, for whom the characteristics of the school were more important than those of the home. The child apparently drew sustenance from wherever sustenance was most available. Where the home had most to offer, the home was the most determining; but where the school could provide more stimulation than the home, the school was the more influential factor.

The second major conclusion concerned the aspects of the school environment which contributed most to the child's intellectual achievement. Surprisingly enough, such items as per pupil expenditure, number of children per class, laboratory space, number of volumes in the school library, and the presence or absence of ability grouping were of negligible significance. Teacher qualifications accounted for some of the child's achievement. But by far the most important factor was the pattern of characteristics of the other children attending the same school. Specifically, if a lower-class child had schoolmates who came from advantaged homes, he did reasonably well; but if all the other children also came from deprived backgrounds, he did poorly.

What about the other side of the story? What happens to a middle-class child in a predominantly lower-class school? Is he pulled down by his classmates? According to Coleman's data, the answer is no; the performance of the advantaged children remains unaffected. It is as though good home background had immunized them against the possibility of contagion.

This is the picture so far as academic achievement is concerned. How about other aspects of psychological development? Specifically, how about social behavior—such qualities as responsibility, consideration for others, or, at the opposite pole, aggressiveness or delinquent behavior? How are these affected by the child's peer group?

The Coleman study obtained no data on this score. Some light has been shed on the problem, however, by an experiment which my Cornell colleagues and I recently carried out with school children in the United

States and in the Soviet Union. Working with a sample of more than 150 sixth-graders (from six classrooms) in each country, we placed the children in situations in which we could test their readiness to engage in morally disapproved behavior such as cheating on a test, denying responsibility for property damage, etc. The results indicated that American children were far more ready to take part in such actions.

The effect of the peer group (friends in school) was quite different in the two societies. When told that their friends would know of their actions, American children were even more willing to engage in misconduct. Soviet youngsters showed just the opposite tendency. In their case, the peer group operated to support the values of the adult society, at least at their age level.

We believe these contrasting results are explained in part by the differing role of the peer group in the two societies. In the Soviet Union, *vospitanie*, or character development, is regarded as an integral part of the process of education, and its principal agent—even more important than the family—is the child's collective in school and out. A major goal of the Soviet educational process, beginning in the nursery, is "to forge a healthy, self-sufficient collective" which, in turn, has the task of developing the child into a responsible, altruistic, and loyal member of a socialist society. In contrast, in the United States, the peer group is often an autonomous agent relatively free from adult control and uncommitted—if not outrightly opposed—to the values and codes of conduct approved by society at large. Witness the new phenomenon of American middle-class vandalism and juvenile delinquency, with crime rates increasing rapidly not only for teen-agers but for younger children as well.

14 / READING AN ORGANIZATION CHART FOR FUN AND SURVIVAL

Donald Winks

Although there are many kinds of organizations, the same type of organization chart is used to describe them all. This is the familiar pyramid of lines and boxes arranged in ascending order of importance. Astute management people find this standard Orgchart wholly satisfying, but it remains an enigma to those most directly concerned. This is because few executives have pursued the sort of analytic study necessary to understand the variable semantics of the Orgchart.

On the surface, all Orgcharts look alike. There at the apex is the board chairman, just atop the president. Below, vice presidents, general managers, and assorted staff minions are ranked in rows like pinstriped cherubim and seraphim. Each is represented by a box labeled with his title and area of responsibility, and each box is linked by a solid black line to the box of his superior. The visual effect is of an upside-down family tree. Each vice president, in turn, has an Orgchart for his own area—in which he occupies the top box. Similarly his division and department heads have *theirs*. Indeed, the Orgcharts of any large corporation fill a fat manual, but the principle is the same whether the company is General Motors or Gaîté Brassieres. The lines and boxes tell you who is who, who is responsible for what, and how the Org is organized. That is the theory, anyway.

Unfortunately, it seldom works out so neatly. For one thing, corporations today are constantly expanding, diversifying, acquiring other corporations, and merging. This often makes it necessary to issue revised charts every quarter or even every month. Consequently, charts are ever more complex, and there are more of them. But this is the lesser problem. The real difficulty lies in the fact that it is not organizations but people that are being reorganized; and the sensitivity of executives to their position on the chart defies belief.

For example, in one major financial institution all its top executives insisted on having their boxes appear to the right of the president. The problem was resolved only by promising all the left-hand people that they would be moved to the right on the next chart. The size and shape of the box, the thickness of the line linking one to another, and even the typeface cause keen concern to those involved. All executives abhor dotted lines since they indicate less than absolute authority. An unobservant manager recently transferred to a new district was sacked not long ago for firing four salesmen. Headquarters informed him afterward that they did not report to him. He had not noticed that the lines were dotted, but then neither had the men who were fired.

The true purpose of the Orgchart today is a reversal of the Bauhaus *obiter dictum* that form follows function; it is designed and distributed to induce function to follow form, being—in itself—an instrument of change. If this were not so, it would be no more worthy of study than the corporate telephone directory.

In fact, the Orgchart is commonly used to deal with promotions and demotions, transfers of authority, personality clashes, and even dehiring—that is, showing an unwanted executive the door without actually throwing him out of it. An Orgplanner for a large chemical company who chooses to remain anonymous revealed how this can happen.

"We had a top vice president who had been with the company for many years, but who simply didn't fit in any more," he said. "It was impossible to fire him, and he didn't want to retire. So we moved him off the chart. As each new chart appeared his box moved higher up, closer and closer to the president, and at the same time further and further to the left of the page. He didn't suspect a thing; in fact, he was flattered. But one day, just as his box reached the edge of the page, he got the idea. By then it was too late to do anything but quietly resign."

Though this is an extreme case, the knowledgeable executive scans each new chart with the avidity of a race tout studying the morning line. It tells him whether his own position has changed and, if so, in what direction. He can also get a reading on how well or badly his rivals are doing. Has a straight line been replaced by one with an angle to it? Or worse has it become dotted? Does Bill now report directly to J. B. instead of to Harry? Is product development under sales now instead of, as formerly, manufacturing?

If you know how to find them, the answers are in the chart. In fact, the Orgchart—properly studied—will disclose much that you did not know before, including things top management does not want you to know. Such information can be helpful in planning a career—or a dignified exit.

Unfortunately, at the present time no university or executive development program offers a practical course in Orgchart reading. This may be because either (a) the subject is not considered worthy of serious academic attention; or (b) management is reluctant to have attention drawn to its true significance. Research suggests the latter to be the case. This essay is a modest first step toward an understanding in depth of the science and semantics of the Orgchart.

Most organization charts are drawn by a clerk or a draftsman on loan from the engineering section. Like Saint Matthew with the angel hovering nearby to dictate the Gospel, he merely records what has come down from a higher source, but these days this exalted being is seldom the company president. In the last few years organization planning has become a full-fledged management speciality whose members have evolved their own language, their own theory, and their own hierarchy. Most large corporations harbor at least one Orgplanner, and some have an entire department devoted to analyzing the needs of the enterprise and devising suitable organizational structures. Necessarily, the Orgplanner works closely with the president in a sort of doctor-patient relationship. He helps the chief executive diagnose organizational ills and prescribe the proper remedies, including amputation where necessary. C. A. Efferson, an Orgplanner of national renown, has lucidly described the genesis of an Orgchart:

"First," he said, "you study the work to be done, the functions, the long-range goals, and then draw the ideal organizational structure, forgetting personalities. The next step is to take the ideal structure to top management and determine what compromises have to be made—mainly because of personalities. However, the ideal structure is not thrown away when the official chart is published. It is kept and continually updated so that future planning does not run counter to the ideal structure, compounding mistakes and necessitating further compromises."

Knowing that the chart is essentially a compromise from the moment of publication, the really astute executive keeps a copy of his company's Orgchart in his desk drawer. Then he keeps modifying it as he finds out whom you actually have to see to get things done. This is the real—or, in Orgplanner's language, "shadow"—organization, as opposed to the official version on the wall, and chances are it bears more than a passing resemblance to the ideal chart in the Orgplanner's office.

In recent years, as companies have grown more gigantic and less comprehensible, Orgplanners have tried to refine their methods and develop new techniques. They argue about whether boxes should be square, in keeping with historical precedent, or oblong, to accommodate in full names like Feinmanhartsberger or Smythe-Forthingay. Should color codes be used to identify line and staff functions? Should staff assistants be shown in the same box as their superior? Prickly though these questions are, they are less controversial than one current theory which holds that the ideal chart should be circular. Supporters of this theory are mainly academicians, who object to the hierarchic rigidity of the conventional squares and oblongs. They want lines of authority and communication to have "a functional and dynamic flow" freeing all members of the organization from artificial restraints. While circular charts do exist, there is no practical purpose to be served in trying to understand them because they cannot be understood. They can only be described.

It is an axiom of Orgplanning that the mere preparation of an accurate chart will reveal unsuspected organizational weaknesses—as, for example, whether there are "too many levels of authority," "overextended spans of control," "unclear lines of accountability," and "duplication of function." These phrases conceal such commonsensical notions as not letting too many cooks spoil the broth, giving each chief only as many Indians as he can keep an eye on, letting the Indians know who their chiefs *are,* and avoiding situations in which ten people—or divisions of departments—are assigned the same task.

A number of corporations resolutely refuse to issue Orgcharts at all on the grounds that they are "artificially restricting." This is roughly equivalent to the belief of certain primitive tribes that snapping a photograph is tantamount to stealing the subject's soul. Other corporations prepare charts but do not circulate them outside of top management—to whom, presumably, the information comes as no surprise and for whom it can have little practical value. Still others circulate charts on which positions but not individuals are named. Professor Chris Argyris of Yale, a leading theorist in Orgplanning and a sworn enemy of the pyramidal chart, found the practice of one large company especially interesting. Several executives were moved up but were instructed not to tell anyone they had been promoted until the news could be diplomatically broken to the old-timers they were replacing. As a result the Orgchart showed clearly who was who, except he wasn't.

This is not a unique situation. Some companies deliberately issue charts designed to keep the peace rather than picture reality. Even those that try to keep their charts reasonably up-to-date are plagued by ambiguity. Often a corporation may decide on some management changes, but postpone issuing a new Orgchart out of a peculiar sense of delicacy. Thus although everyone knows Bill has been promoted to vice president, they are spared the painful sight of their former peer alone at the apex with everyone reporting to him. Or, an executive being politely demoted is given a fancier title but the new Orgchart does not appear for a few months when the *de facto* situation has established itself and he can face the reality of his true level in the hierarchy.

The nation's top Orgplanners all belong to the Council on Organization Planning of the National Industrial Conference Board, which meets twice annually to discuss broad policy questions such as "Centralization or

Decentralization," "Relationships Between Line and Staff," and "Automation: Its Effects." At these gatherings they also exchange information on what each other's Orgcharts *really* mean. The broad policy questions are amply reported in the publications of the NICB. But to find out what was actually said at a Council meeting—including how to read a specific Orgchart—is next to impossible.

This is because the Council—whose members represent such corporate giants as U.S. Steel, Alcoa, RCA, Kaiser Aluminum & Chemical, Chase Manhattan Bank, IBM, Union Carbide, and General Electric—holds its meetings under security restrictions that would do credit to the CIA. Only members are admitted, no transcript of the proceedings is made, no guests are permitted at any time; and when professors from university business schools are invited to give papers, they are invited to leave before the regular session resumes. "Our group is so tightly knit," one member said confidentially, "that I can call another member and he will tell me details of his corporation's organization planning that he would not dare reveal to a high-ranking insider."

It should by now be plain that the only infallible way to read an Orgchart is in the company of the executive who designed it. And at each doubtful point you should demand what the hell he meant by *that*. Unfortunately, Council membership is restricted to twenty-seven Orgplanners, all of them sworn to secrecy.

However, the average executive should not despair. Imprecise, ambiguous, equivocal or even downright misleading though they are, Orgcharts can—if properly understood—cast much light on what is really transpiring within a large organization. In addition to the general guidelines implicit in what has gone before, there are seven rules which will help you to chart your way safely through the Orgchart. Success will come, not from memorizing the rules but from applying them wisely to your specific situation.

Rule 1—There is absolutely no point in studying any chart but your own. Time spent poring over manuals of organization charts or attending classes in organization planning is time wasted. All you can learn from an alien organization chart is the name of someone to phone to ask what it really means. This is exactly what Orgplanners do when they are not exchanging such information directly in secret conclave.

Rule 2—The present chart must not be studied *in vacuo*; it takes on meaning only in the context of previous charts. Gather all the charts issued over the past few years and study them. In other words, chart the charts. Trace how things came to be the way they are, develop a knowledge of your organization's structural and verbal euphemisms. Here, as elsewhere, the past illuminates the present.

Rule 3—The ideal organization tends to become real before it is officially charted. As we have seen, the chart is a compromise from the moment of publication. However, since both president and planner are agreed on an ideal structure—a master Orgplan—each new chart will logically prefigure future changes. By carefully plotting changes as they appear on new charts, the alert student can often divine the shape of things to come, thereby getting the jump on his corporate peers.

Rule 4—Do not put much trust in titles: study positions on the chart and who reports to whom. For example, if a vice president suddenly appears as "assistant to" a loftier official, often for "special projects," see if he is still in the same spot on the chart. If so, this is a legitimate assignment. But if he has moved up, down, or sideways, the odds are he will keep on moving right off the chart and out of the company. Conversely, when an executive from *outside* the company is brought in as "assistant to" one of the big brass, he is almost certainly his replacement.

Rule 5—Count the horizontal lines on the chart. If there are more than seven levels of authority between the president and the operating managers, give the chart up as a hopeless case; and, ideally, the job too. Too many levels bespeak a self-perpetuating top management and opportunities for promotion will dwindle as inefficiencies mount. Keep in mind that General Motors has only four levels of authority. Is your company bigger?

Rule 6—Study not only the headquarters chart, but also those of all divisions and departments, and keep a keen eye out for disappearing boxes. When one or more vanishes from your chart, don't assume that the hapless occupants have been thrown out on their ears. They may well crop up on another chart. *If this trend continues, the company is decentralizing, and before long all you chaps at headquarters will be regarded as overhead.*

Rule 7—In addition to the official chart on your wall, keep working on another copy. Draw new lines, cross out boxes, add and delete names on the basis of your personal observation. When you have perfected a chart of the shadow organization, throw it away. A new official chart will be along momentarily.

UNIT D / ISSUES FOR CONSIDERATION

1. What are some of the consequences of a child's spending more of his time in his peer group than in his family group?
2. Describe the indicators of interaction, shared norms, and interlocking roles that exist in an American industrial corporation.
3. Distinguish between the informal norms of the corporation and the formal norms reflected on its organizational chart.

4. Apply the sociological concepts of norms and roles to show the similarities between small informal groups like the family and large formal organizations like a corporation.
5. Why is an understanding of the types of groups with which a person is confronted throughout his lifetime important in understanding his behavior?

UNIT E
CULTURE

By "culture" we mean those ways of behaving and believing which result from contact with other human beings that characterize a given society. This contrasts with any aspect of the individual's behavior that might be inherited genetically. One might well argue that this entire book is a description of the culture of American society. The ways man behaves and believes are reflected in his language, his norms, his institutions, the differentiations he makes, and his reactions to change. Too frequently when the sociologist and anthropologist discuss the concept of culture they use as their only examples unusual societies—primitive tribes, small isolated communities. These are useful since we are apt to become so accustomed to our "ways of behaving" that they appear as a natural part of our existence and it is difficult to conceive of them as culturally transmitted. Here, the student is encouraged to think of his own way of life as an example of the concept of culture.

Both articles for this section provide examples of what we might call sub-cultures or cultures within a culture. Yet they are very different. The first article, by the famed anthropologist and writer Oscar Lewis, describes a culture that emerges within a larger society. Here the features of the larger culture are such as to lead certain persons within the society (the very poor) to form their own style of life which differs from that of the general society. This separate culture provides them with the set of solutions necessary for coping with their problems.

The Wahrhaftig and Thomas article about the Cherokee describes a culture that did not emerge from the larger society. However, the attitudes and values that the larger society holds toward the way of life of these people tends to preserve the Indian culture even though it is completely surrounded by the dominant society.

Can you describe norms in each of these sub-cultures that reflect the influence of the larger society?

15 / THE CULTURE OF POVERTY

Oscar Lewis

Poverty and the so-called war against it provide a principal theme for the domestic program of the present Administration. In the midst of a population that enjoys unexampled material well-being—with the average annual family income exceeding $7,000—it is officially acknowledged that some 18 million families, numbering more than 50 million individuals, live below the $3,000 "poverty line." Toward the improvement of the lot of these people some $1,600 million of Federal funds are directly allocated through the Office of Economic Opportunity, and many hundreds of millions of additional dollars flow indirectly through expanded Federal expenditures in the fields of health, education, welfare and urban affairs.

Along with the increase in activity on behalf of the poor indicated by these figures there has come a parallel expansion of publication in the social sciences on the subject of poverty. The new writings advance the same two opposed evaluations of the poor that are to be found in literature, in proverbs and in popular sayings throughout recorded history. Just as the poor have been pronounced blessed, virtuous, upright, serene, independent, honest, kind and happy, so contemporary students stress their great and neglected capacity for self-help, leadership and community

---

organization. Conversely, as the poor have been characterized as shiftless, mean, sordid, violent, evil and criminal, so other students point to the irreversibly destructive effects of poverty on individual character and emphasize the corresponding need to keep guidance and control of poverty projects in the hands of duly constituted authorities. This clash of viewpoints reflects in part the infighting for political control of the program between Federal and local officials. The confusion results also from the tendency to focus study and attention on the personality of the individual victim of poverty rather than on the slum community and family and from the consequent failure to distinguish between poverty and what I have called the culture of poverty.

The phrase is a catchy one and is used and misused with some frequency in the current literature. In my writings it is the label for a specific conceptual model that describes in positive terms a subculture of Western society with its own structure and rationale, a way of life handed on from generation to generation along family lines. The culture of poverty is not just a matter of deprivation or disorganization, a term signifying the absence of something. It is a culture in the traditional anthropological sense in that it provides human beings with a design for living, with a ready-made set of solutions for human problems, and so serves a significant adaptive function. This style of life transcends national boundaries and regional and rural-urban differences within nations. Wherever it occurs, its practitioners exhibit remarkable similarity in the structure of their families, in interpersonal relations, in spending habits, in their value systems and in their orientation in time.

Not nearly enough is known about this important complex of human behavior. My own concept of it has evolved as my work has progressed and remains subject to amendment by my own further work and that of others. The scarcity of literature on the culture of poverty is a measure of the gap in communication that exists between the very poor and the middle-class personnel—social scientists, social workers, teachers, physicians, priests and others—who bear the major responsibility for carrying out the antipoverty programs. Much of the behavior accepted in the culture of poverty goes counter to cherished ideals of the larger society. In writing about "multiproblem" families social scientists thus often stress their instability, their lack of order, direction and organization. Yet, as I have observed them, their behavior seems clearly patterned and reasonably predictable. I am more often struck by the inexorable repetitiousness and the iron entrenchment of their lifeways.

The concept of the culture of poverty may help to correct misapprehensions that have ascribed some behavior patterns of ethnic, national or regional groups as distinctive characteristics. For example, a high incidence of commonlaw marriage and of households headed by women has been thought to be distinctive of Negro family life in this country and has been attributed to the Negro's historical experience of slavery. In actuality it turns out that such households express essential traits of the culture of poverty and are found among diverse peoples in many parts of the world and among peoples that have had no history of slavery. Although it is now possible to assert such generalizations, there is still much to be learned about this difficult and affecting subject. The absence of intensive anthropological studies of poor families in a wide variety of national contexts—particularly the lack of such studies in socialist countries—remains a serious handicap to the formulation of dependable cross-cultural constants of the culture of poverty.

My studies of poverty and family life have centered largely in Mexico. On occasion some of my Mexican friends have suggested delicately that I turn to a study of poverty in my own country. As a first step in this direction I am currently engaged in a study of Puerto Rican families. Over the past three years my staff and I have been assembling data on 100 representative families in four slums of Greater San Juan and some 50 families of their relatives in New York City.

Our methods combine the traditional techniques of sociology, anthropology and psychology. This includes a battery of 19 questionnaires, the administration of which requires 12 hours per informant. They cover the residence and employment history of each adult; family relations; income and expenditure; complete inventory of household and personal possessions; friendship patterns, particularly the *compadrazgo*, or godparent, relationship that serves as a kind of informal social security for the children of these families and establishes special obligations among the adults; recreational patterns; health and medical history; politics; religion; world view and "cosmopolitanism." Open-end interviews and psychological tests (such as the thematic apperception test, the Rorschach test and the sentence-completion test) are administered to a sampling of this population.

All this work serves to establish the context for close-range study of a selected few families. Because the family is a small social system, it lends itself to the holistic approach of anthropology. Whole-family studies bridge the gap between the conceptual extremes of the culture at one pole and of the individual at the other, making possible observation of both culture and personality as they are interrelated in real life. In a large metropolis such as San Juan or New York the family is the natural unit of study.

Ideally our objective is the naturalistic observation of the life of "our" families, with a minimum of intervention. Such intensive study, however, necessarily involves the establishment of deep personal ties. My assistants include two Mexicans whose families I had studied; their "Mexican's-eye view" of the Puerto Rican slum has helped to point up the similarities and differences between the Mexican and Puerto Rican subcultures. We have spent many hours attending family parties, wakes and baptisms, responding to emergency calls, taking people to the hospital, getting them out of jail, filling out applications for them, hunting apartments with them, helping them to get jobs or to get on relief. With each member of these families we conduct tape-recorded interviews, taking down their life stories and their answers to questions on a wide variety of topics. For the ordering of our material we undertake to reconstruct, by close interrogation, the history of a week or more of consecutive days in the lives of each family, and we observe and record complete days as they unfold. The first volume to issue from this study is entitled *La Vida, a Puerto Rican Family in the Culture of Poverty—San Juan and New York* (Random House).

There are many poor people in the world. Indeed, the poverty of the two-thirds of the world's population who live in the underdeveloped countries has been rightly called "the problem of problems." But not all of them by any means live in the culture of poverty. For this way of life to come into being and flourish it seems clear that certain preconditions must be met.

The setting is a cash economy, with wage labor and production for profit and with a persistently high rate of unemployment and underemployment, at low wages, for unskilled labor. The society fails to provide social, political and economic organization, on either a voluntary basis or by government imposition, for the low-income population. There is a bilateral kinship system centered on the nuclear progenitive family, as distinguished from the unilateral extended kinship system of lineage and clan. The dominant class asserts a set of values that prizes thrift and the accumulation of wealth and property, stresses the possibility of upward mobility and explains low economic status as the result of individual personal inadequacy and inferiority.

Where these conditions prevail the way of life that develops among some of the poor is the culture of poverty. That is why I have described it as a subculture of the Western social order. It is both an adaptation and a reaction of the poor to their marginal position in a class-stratified, highly individuated, capitalistic society. It represents an effort to cope with feelings of hopelessness and despair that arise from the realization by the members of the marginal communities in these societies of the improbability of their achieving success in terms of the prevailing values and goals. Many of the traits of the culture of poverty can be viewed as local, spontaneous attempts to meet needs not served in the case of the poor by the institutions and agencies of the larger society because the poor are not eligible for such service, cannot afford it or are ignorant and suspicious.

Once the culture of poverty has come into existence it tends to perpetuate itself. By the time slum children are six or seven they have usually absorbed the basic attitudes and values of their subculture. Thereafter they are psychologically unready to take full advantage of changing conditions or improving opportunities that may develop in their lifetime.

My studies have identified some 70 traits that characterize the culture of poverty. The principal ones may be described in four dimensions of the system: the relationship between the subculture and the larger society; the nature of the slum community; the nature of the family, and the attitudes, values and character structure of the individual.

The disengagement, the nonintegration, of the poor with respect to the major institutions of society is a crucial element in the culture of poverty. It reflects the combined effect of a variety of factors including poverty, to begin with, but also segregation and discrimination, fear, suspicion and apathy and the development of alternative institutions and procedures in the slum community. The people do not belong to labor unions or political parties and make little use of banks, hospitals, department stores or museums. Such involvement as there is in the institutions of the large society—in the jails, the army and the public welfare system—does little to suppress the traits of the culture of poverty. A relief system that barely keeps people alive perpetuates rather than eliminates poverty and the pervading sense of hopelessness.

People in a culture of poverty produce little wealth and receive little in return. Chronic unemployment and underemployment, low wages, lack of property, lack of savings, absence of food reserves in the home and chronic shortage of cash imprison the family and the individual in a vicious circle. Thus for lack of cash the slum householder makes frequent purchases of small quantities of food at higher prices. The slum economy turns inward; it shows a high incidence of pawning of personal goods, borrowing at usurious rates of interest, informal credit arrangements among neighbors, use of secondhand clothing and furniture.

There is awareness of middle-class values. People talk about them and even claim some of them as their own. On the whole, however, they do not live by them. They will declare that marriage by law, by the church or by both is the ideal form of marriage, but few will marry. For men who have no steady jobs, no property and no prospect of wealth to pass on to their children, who live in the present without expectations of the future, who want to avoid the expense and legal difficulties involved in marriage and divorce, a free union or consensual marriage makes good sense. The women, for their part, will turn down offers of marriage from men who are likely to be immature, punishing and generally unreliable. They feel that a consensual union gives them some of the freedom and flexibility men have. By not giving the fathers of their children legal status as husbands, the women have a stronger claim on the children. They also maintain exclusive rights to their own property.

Along with disengagement from the larger society, there is a hostility to the basic institutions of what are regarded as the dominant classes. There is hatred of the police, mistrust of government and of those in high positions and a cynicism that extends to the church. The culture of poverty thus holds a certain potential for protest and for entrainment in political movements aimed against the existing order.

With its poor housing and overcrowding, the community of the culture of poverty is high in gregariousness, but it has a minimum of organization beyond the nuclear and extended family. Occasionally slum dwellers come together in temporary informal groupings; neighborhood gangs that cut across slum settlements represent a considerable advance beyond the zero point of the continuum I have in mind. It is the low level of organization that gives the culture of poverty its marginal and anomalous quality in our highly organized society. Most primitive peoples have achieved a higher degree of sociocultural organization than contemporary urban slum dwellers. This is not to say that there may not be a sense of community and *esprit de corps* in a slum neighborhood. In fact, where slums are isolated from their surroundings by enclosing walls or other physical barriers, where rents are low and residence is stable and where the population constitutes a distinct ethnic, racial or language group, the sense of community may approach that of a village. In Mexico City and San Juan such territoriality is engendered by the scarcity of low-cost housing outside of established slum areas. In South Africa it is actively enforced by the *apartheid* that confines rural migrants to prescribed locations.

The family in the culture of poverty does not cherish childhood as a specially prolonged and protected stage in the life cycle. Initiation into sex comes early. With the instability of consensual marriage the family tends to be mother-centered and tied more closely to the mother's extended family. The female head of the house is given to authoritarian rule. In spite of much verbal emphasis on family solidarity, sibling rivalry for the limited supply of goods and maternal affection is intense. There is little privacy.

The individual who grows up in this culture has a strong feeling of fatalism, helplessness, dependence and inferiority. These traits, so often remarked in the current literature as characteristic of the American Negro, I found equally strong in slum dwellers of Mexico City and San Juan, who are not segregated or discriminated against as a distinct ethnic or racial group. Other traits include a high incidence of weak ego structure, orality and confusion of sexual identification, all reflecting maternal deprivation; a strong present-time orientation with relatively little disposition to defer gratification and plan for the future, and a high tolerance for psychological pathology of all kinds. There is widespread belief in male superiority and among the men a strong preoccupation with *machismo*, their masculinity.

Provincial and local in outlook, with little sense of history, these people know only their own neighborhood and their own way of life. Usually they do not have the knowledge, the vision or the ideology to see the similarities between their troubles and those of their counterparts elsewhere in the world. They are not class-conscious, although they are sensitive indeed to symbols of status.

The distinction between poverty and the culture of poverty is basic to the model described here. There are numerous examples of poor people whose way of life I would not characterize as belonging to this subculture. Many primitive and preliterate peoples that have been studied by anthropologists suffer dire poverty attributable to low technology or thin resources or both. Yet even the simplest of these peoples have a high degree of social organization and a relatively integrated, satisfying and self-sufficient culture.

In India the destitute lower-caste peoples—such as the Chamars, the leatherworkers, and the Bhangis, the sweepers—remain integrated in the larger society and have their own panchayat institutions of self-government. Their panchayats and their extended unilateral kinship systems, or clans, cut across village lines, giving them a strong sense of identity and continuity. In my studies of these peoples I found no culture of poverty to go with their poverty.

The Jews of eastern Europe were a poor urban people, often confined to ghettos. Yet they did not have many traits of the culture of poverty. They had a tradition of literacy that placed great value on learning; they formed many voluntary associations and adhered with devotion to the central community organization around the rabbi, and they had a religion that taught them they were the chosen people.

I would cite also a fourth, somewhat speculative example of poverty dissociated from the culture of poverty. On the basis of limited direct observation in one country—Cuba—and from indirect evidence, I am inclined to believe the culture of poverty does not exist in socialist countries. In 1947 I undertook a study of a slum in Havana. Recently I had an opportunity to revisit the same slum and some of the same families. The physical aspect of the place had changed little, except for a beautiful new nursery school. The people were as poor as before, but I was impressed to find much less of the feelings of despair and apathy, so symptomatic of the culture of poverty in the urban slums of the U.S. The slum was now highly organized, with block committees, educational committees, party committees. The people had found a new sense of power and importance in a doctrine that glorified the lower class as the hope of humanity, and they were armed. I was told by one Cuban official that the Castro government had practically eliminated delinquency by giving arms to the delinquents!

Evidently the Castro regime—revising Marx and Engels—did not write off the so-called *lumpenproletariat* as an inherently reactionary and antirevolutionary force but rather found in them a revolutionary potential and utilized it. Frantz Fanon, in his book *The Wretched of the Earth,* makes a similar evaluation of their role in the Algerian revolution: "It is within this mass of humanity, this people of the shantytowns, at the core of the *lumpenproletariat,* that the rebellion will find its urban spearhead. For the *lumpenproletariat,* that horde of starving men, uprooted from their tribe and from their clan, constitutes one of the most spontaneous and most radically revolutionary forces of a colonized people."

It is true that I have found little revolutionary spirit or radical ideology among low-income Puerto Ricans. Most of the families I studied were politically conservative, about half of them favoring the Statehood Republican Party, which provides opposition on the right to the Popular Democratic Party that dominates the politics of the commonwealth. It seems to me, therefore, that disposition for protest among people living in the culture of poverty will vary considerably according to the national context and historical circumstances. In contrast to Algeria, the independence movement in Puerto Rico has found little popular support. In Mexico, where the cause of independence carried long ago, there is no longer any such movement to stir the dwellers in the new and old slums of the capital city.

Yet it would seem that any movement—be it religious, pacifist or revolutionary—that organizes and gives hope to the poor and effectively promotes a sense of solidarity with larger groups must effectively destroy the psychological and social core of the culture of poverty. In this connection, I suspect that the civil rights movement among American Negroes has of itself done more to improve their self-image and self-respect than such economic gains as it has won although, without doubt, the two kinds of progress are mutually reinforcing. In the culture of poverty of the American Negro the additional disadvantage of racial discrimination has generated a potential for revolutionary protest and organization that is absent in the slums of San Juan and Mexico City and, for that matter, among the poor whites in the South.

If it is true, as I suspect, that the culture of poverty flourishes and is endemic to the free-enterprise, pre-welfare-state stage of capitalism, then it is also endemic in colonial societies. The most likely candidates for the culture of poverty would be the people who come from the lower strata of a rapidly changing society and who are already partially alienated from it. Accordingly the subculture is likely to be found where imperial conquest has smashed the native social and economic structure and held the natives, perhaps for generations, in servile status, or where feudalism is yielding to capitalism in the later evolution of a colonial economy. Landless rural workers who migrate to the cities, as in Latin America, can be expected to fall into this way of life more readily than migrants from stable peasant villages with a well-organized traditional culture, as in India. It remains to be seen, however, whether the culture of poverty has not already begun to develop in the slums of Bombay and Calcutta. Compared with Latin America also, the strong corporate nature of many African tribal societies may tend to inhibit or delay the formation of a full-blown culture of poverty in the new towns and cities of that continent. In South Africa the institutionalization of repression and discrimination under *apartheid* may also have begun to promote an immunizing sense of identity and group consciousness among the African Negroes.

One must therefore keep the dynamic aspects of human institutions forward in observing and assessing the evidence for the presence, the waxing or the waning of this subculture. Measured on the dimension of relationship to the larger society, some slum dwellers may have a warmer identification with their national tradition even though they suffer deeper poverty than members of a similar community in another country. In Mexico City a high percentage of our respondents, including those with little or no formal schooling, knew of Cuauhtémoc, Hidalgo, Father Morelos, Juárez, Díaz, Zapata, Carranza and Cárdenas. In San Juan the names of Rámon Power, José de Diego, Baldorioty de Castro, Rámon Betances, Nemesio Canales, Lloréns Torres rang no bell; a few could tell about the late Albizu Campos. For the lower-income Puerto Rican, however, history begins with Muñoz Rivera and ends with his son Muñoz Marín.

The national context can make a big difference in the play of the crucial traits of fatalism and hopelessness. Given the advanced technology, the high level of literacy, the all-pervasive reach of the media of mass communications and the relatively high aspirations of all sectors of the population, even the poorest and most marginal communities of the U.S. must aspire to a larger future than the slum dwellers of Ecuador and Peru, where the actual possibilities are more limited and where an authoritarian social order persists in city and country. Among the 50 million U.S. citizens now more or less officially certified as poor, I would guess that about 20 percent live in a culture of poverty. The largest numbers in this group are made up of Negroes, Puerto Ricans, Mexicans, American Indians and Southern poor whites. In these figures there is some reassurance for those concerned, because it is much more difficult to undo the culture of poverty than to cure poverty itself.

Middle-class people—this would certainly include most social scientists—tend to concentrate on the negative aspects of the culture of poverty. They attach a minus sign to such traits as present-time orientation and readiness to indulge impulses. I do not intend to idealize or romanticize the culture of poverty—"it is easier to praise poverty than to live in it." Yet the positive aspects of these traits must not be overlooked. Living in the present may develop a capacity for spontaneity, for the enjoyment of the sensual, which is often blunted in the middle-class, future-oriented man. Indeed, I am often struck by the analogies that can be drawn between the mores of the very rich—of the "jet set" and "café society"—and the culture of the very poor. Yet it is, on the whole, a comparatively superficial culture. There is in it much pathos, suffering and emptiness. It does not provide much support or satisfaction; its pervading mistrust magnifies individual helplessness and isolation. Indeed, poverty of culture is one of the crucial traits of the culture of poverty.

The concept of the culture of poverty provides a generalization that may help to unify and explain a number of phenomena hitherto viewed as peculiar to certain racial, national or regional groups. Problems we think of as being distinctively our own or distinctively Negro (or as typifying any other ethnic group) prove to be endemic in countries where there are no segregated ethnic minority groups. If it follows that the elimination of physical poverty may not by itself eliminate the culture of poverty, then an understanding of the sub-culture may contribute to the design of measures specific to that purpose.

What is the future of the culture of poverty? In considering this question one must distinguish between those countries in which it represents a relatively small segment of the population and those in which it constitutes a large one. In the U.S. the major solution proposed by social workers dealing with the "hard core" poor has been slowly to raise their level of living and incorporate them in the middle class. Wherever possible psychiatric treatment is prescribed.

In underdeveloped countries where great masses of people live in the culture of poverty, such a social-work solution does not seem feasible. The local psychiatrists have all they can do to care for their own growing middle class. In those countries the people with a culture of poverty may seek a more revolutionary solution. By creating basic structural changes in society, by redistributing wealth, by organizing the poor and giving them a sense of belonging, of power and of leadership, revolutions frequently succeed in abolishing some of the basic characteristics of the culture of poverty even when they do not succeed in curing poverty itself.

16 / RENAISSANCE AND REPRESSION: THE OKLAHOMA CHEROKEE

Albert L. Wahrhaftig and Robert K. Thomas

A week in eastern Oklahoma demonstrates to most outsiders that the Cherokee Indians are a populous and lively community: Indians *par excellence.* Still, whites in eastern Oklahoma unanimously declare the Cherokees to be a vanishing breed. Prominent whites say with pride, "we're all a little bit Indian here." They maintain that real Cherokees are about "bred out." Few Cherokees are left who can speak their native tongue, whites insist, and fewer still are learning their language. In twenty years, according to white myth, the Cherokee language and with it the separate and distinctive community that speaks it will fade into memory.

Astonishingly, this pervasive social fiction disguises the presence of one of the largest and most traditional tribes of American Indians. Six rural counties in northeastern Oklahoma contain more than fifty Cherokee settlements with a population of more than 9,500. An additional 2,000 Cherokees live in Indian enclaves in towns and small cities. Anthropologists visiting us in the field, men who thought their previous studies had taught them what a conservative tribe is like, were astonished by Cherokees. Seldom had they seen people who speak so little English, who are so unshakably traditional in outlook.

How can native whites overlook this very identifiable Indian community? The answers, we believe, will give us not only an intriguing insight into the nature of Oklahoma society, but also some general conclusions about the position of other ethnic groups in American society.

This myth of Cherokee assimilation gives sanction to the social system of which Cherokees are a part, and to the position Cherokees have within that system. This image of the vanishing Cherokee in some ways is reminiscent both of the conservative Southern mythology which asserts that "our colored folk are a contented and carefree lot," and of the liberal Northern mythology, which asserts that "Negroes are just like whites except for the color of their skins." The fiction serves to keep Cherokees in place as a docile and exploitable minority population; it gives an official rationale to an existing, historic social system; and it implies that

From *Trans-action,* February 1969.

when the Indian Territory, the last Indian refuge, was dissolved, no Indian was betrayed, but all were absorbed into the mainstream.

The roots of modern eastern Oklahoma are in the rural South. Cherokees, and whites, came from the South; Cherokees from Georgia and Tennessee; and whites from Tennessee, Kentucky, Arkansas and southern Illinois.

In the years immediately preceding 1840, Cherokees, forced out of their sacred homelands in Georgia and Tennessee, marched over an infamous "Trail of Tears," and relocated in a new Cherokee Nation in what is now the state of Oklahoma. They created an international wonder: an autonomous Cherokee Nation with its own national constitution, legislature, judiciary, school system, publishing house, international bilingual newspaper, and many other trappings of a prosperous Republic. The Cherokees, who as a people accomplished all this, along with their neighbors, the Creeks, Choctaws, Chicasaws and Seminoles, who followed similar paths, were called the five civilized tribes.

Promising as the Cherokee Nation's future might have seemed, it was plagued by internal controversy from birth. Bitterness between the traditional Ross Party and the Treaty Party was intense. The Ross Party resisted demands for relocating from the South until its followers were finally corralled by the Army; the Treaty Party believed cooperation with the United States Government was the more prudent course for all Cherokees.

The sons and daughters of the Ross Party kept their ancient villages together. They reestablished these in the hollows and rough "Ozark" country of the Indian territory. Hewing new log cabins and planting new garden spots, they hoped to live unmolested by their opponents. They are today's "fullbloods," that is, traditional and Cherokee speaking Cherokees. On the other hand, descendants of the Treaty Party, who concentrated in the flat bottomlands and prairies they preferred for farming, are now assimilated and functionally white Americans, though fiercely proud of their Cherokee blood.

The Ross Party was the core of the Cherokee tribes. It was an institution which emerged from the experience of people who lived communally in settlements of kinsmen. The Treaty Party was a composite of individuals splintered from the tribal body. There were of course great differences in life style among nineteenth century Cherokee citizens. The Ross men, often well-educated, directed the Cherokee legislators from backwoods settlements. Treaty Party men were more often plantation owners, merchants, entrepreneurs, and professionals—conventional southern gentlemen. The overriding difference between the two factions, however, was between men who lived for their community and men who lived for themselves.

During the 1880s this difference came to be associated not with party but with blood. Geographically separated and ostracized by Ross men, members of the Treaty Party perforce married among the growing population of opportunistic whites who squatted on Indian land, defying U.S. and Cherokee law. The Treaty Party became known as the "mixed blood" faction of the tribe; the Ross Party as "full bloods." These terms imply that miscegenation caused a change of life style, a reversal of the historic events.

By 1907 when the Cherokee Nation was dissolved by Congressional fiat and the State of Oklahoma was created, the mixed bloods were already socially if not politically, part of the white population of the United States. The Ross Party settlements, now the whole of the functionally Cherokee population, are intact but surrounded by an assimilated population of mixed blood Cherokees integrated with white immigrants.

From the 1890s to 1920s, development of this area was astonishingly rapid. A flood of whites arrived. Land was populated by subsistence farmers, small town trade boomed, commercial farming expanded, railroads were built, timber exhausted, petroleum exploited and token industrialization established.

Already shorn of their nation, fullbloods were stunned and disadvantaged by the overnight expansion and growth. Change was rapid, the class system open. Future distinguished elders of small town society arrived as raggedy tots in the back of one-mule wagons. Not only was social mobility easy, few questions were asked about how the newly rich became rich. Incredible land swindles were commonplace. At the turn of the century, every square inch of eastern Oklahoma was allotted to Cherokees; by the 1930s little acreage remained in Indian possession.

The result of this explosive development was a remarkably stratified society, characterized by highly personal relationships, old time rural political machines, Protestant fundamentalism, reverence of free enterprise, and unscrupulous exploitation; in short, a system typical of the rural south.

Superficially, this society appears to be one with the most resourceful at the top, and the unworthy, who let opportunity slip by, at the bottom. In reality, however, the system consists of ranked ethnic groups, rather than classes. The successful old mixed-blood families, now functionally "white," whose self-identification as "Cherokee" is taken as a claim to the venerable status of "original settlers," dominate. Below them are the prosperous whites who "made something of themselves," and at the bottom, beneath the poor country whites, Cherokee "full bloods."

In primitive tribes, myth is a sacred explanation of the creation of the tribe and of its subsequent history. Myth specifies the holy design within which man was set to live. The fiction of Cherokee assimilation illustrates that modern man still uses myth, though differently. For in Oklahoma, the myth of Cherokee assimilation validates the social conditions men themselves have created, justifying the rightness and inevitability of what was done. As Oklahomans see it, the demise of the Cherokee as a people was tragic, albeit necessary. For only thus were individual Cherokees able to share in the American dream. The Oklahoman conceives of his society as an aggregate of individuals ranked by class, with unlimited opportunity for mobility regardless of individual ancestry. The high class position of the old Cherokee mixed-bloods signifies to the Oklahoman that the job of building Oklahoma was well done. The "responsible" Indians made it. The Cherokees, as a single historic people, died without heirs, and rightfully all those who settled on their estate now share in the distribution of its assets. For the culturally Indian individuals remaining, Oklahoma can only hope that they will do better in the future.

Even as the mythology serves to sanctify their high rank position, it insulates whites from the recognition of the Cherokee as a viable but low ranked ethnic community with unique collective aims and interests. Where a real community exists, Oklahomans see only a residue of low status individuals. The myth, by altering perceptions, becomes self-perpetuating.

Paradoxically, the myth of Cherokee assimilation has also contributed to the survival of the Cherokee as a people. To the extent that Cherokees believed the myth, and many did, it was not only an explanation of how the tribe came into the present but a cohesive force. Since the end of a tribal movement led by Redbird Smith, a half century ago, in response to the final pressures for Oklahoma statehood, Cherokees have seemed inert, hardly a living people. Nevertheless, Cherokee communal life persisted, and is in a surprisingly healthy state. Cherokee settlements remain isolated, and if what goes on in them is not hidden, it is calculatedly inconspicuous. For the freedom from interference that it afforded, Cherokees willingly acceded to the notion that the Cherokees no longer exist.

In addition to sanctioning the form of Oklahoma society, the myth also gives credence to basic social and economic institutions. The economy of the area depends on Cherokees and country whites as an inexpensive and permanent labor market. Cherokees are expected to do low paying manual work without complaint. In 1963, Cherokee median per capita income, approximately $500, was less than half the per capita income of neighboring rural whites. In some areas, Cherokees live in virtual peonage; in others, straw bosses recruit Cherokee laborers for irregular work at low pay. Even though Cherokee communities are relatively hidden, Cherokee labor has become an indispensable part of the local economy. Apparently one would think that daily contact of white workers and bosses with these Cherokee laborers might expose the myth of the well-off assimilated Cherokee. On the contrary, the myth prevails because the humble occupations practiced by Cherokees are seen as evidence that Cherokee character is indeed that which the myth of assimilation predicts.

WHITE BLOOD MAKES GOOD INDIANS

Imbedded in the Oklahoma concept of assimilation, is a glaring racism. Typical is the introductory page of a book published in 1938 entitled *A Political History of the Cherokee Nation*, written by Morris Wardell, a professor at the University of Oklahoma.

A selection: "Traders, soldiers, and treaty-makers came among the Cherokees to trade, compel and negotiate. Some of these visitors married Indian women and lived in the Indian villages the remainder of their days. Children born to such unions preferred the open and free life and here grew to manhood and womanhood, never going to the white settlements. This mixture of blood helped to produce strategy and cleverness which made formidable diplomats of many of the Indian leaders."

To white genes go the credit for Sequoyah's genius and John Ross's astuteness, whereas the remaining Cherokee genes contribute qualities that are endearing but less productive. Thus, in a history of the Cherokees published only six years ago, the author, an Oklahoman, says of modern "fullbloods": "They supplement their small income from farms and subsidies from the government with wage work or seasonal jobs in nearby towns or on farms belonging to white men. . . . Paid fair wages, this type of worker usually spends his money as quickly as he makes it on whisky, and on cars, washing machines, and other items that, uncared for, soon fall into necessitous disuse."

Oklahomans divide the contemporary Cherokees into two categories: those who are progressive and those who are not. The page just quoted continues, "this progressive type of Indian will not long remain in the background of the growing and thriving, and comparatively new, State of Oklahoma." That a viable Indian tribe exists is apparently inconceivable. Either Cherokees are worthy, responsible and assimilating, or they are the dregs; irresponsible, deculturated and racially inferior.

Through mythology, the exploitation of Cherokee labor is redefined into benevolent paternalism. Some patrons have Cherokees deliver their welfare checks to them, deduct from these housing and groceries. Afterwards the remainder is handed over to Cherokee tenants. Unknown to the welfare department, these same Cherokees receive stingy wages for working land and orchards belonging to the patron or to his kin. Patrons consider that they are providing employment and a steady paternal hand for unfortunate people who they contend could never manage themselves. The same ethic enables whites in good conscience to direct vestigal

Cherokee tribal affairs; including the disbursement of well over two million dollars in funds left from a tribal land claim settlement.

POLITICIANS ARE VICTIMS OF OLD FEARS

It might seem odd that no one seeking to improve his position in the local establishment has ever tried to weaken these relationships. Why has no political figure taken cognizance of those thousands of Cherokee votes, and championed their cause? Instead politicians rely on the inefficient machinery of county patronage to collect Cherokee ballots. Unfortunately no one has yet dared, because fear binds the system. Older whites remember living in fear of a blood bath. The proposal to create Oklahoma meant a new state to whites; to Cherokees it meant the end of their own national existence. Their resistance to statehood was most desperate. Cherokees were a force to be contended with. They were feared as an ominously silent, chillingly mysterious people, unpredictable and violent. And Cherokees did organize into secret societies, much akin to the committees of twenty-five delegated in days past to murder collaborators who signed treaties. The reward of public office, politicians feel, does not justify the risk of rekindling that flame. To the extent that Oklahomans are aware of the numbers of Cherokees and the force they might generate, the myth of the assimilated Cherokee is a form of wishful thinking.

Finally, the myth protects the specific relationships of rank and power which determine the stability of the present eastern Oklahoma social system. It does this in the following ways: By preventing recognition by whites and Indians alike of the Cherokees as a permanent community of people whose demands and aspirations must be taken seriously, it allows whites to direct the affairs of the region as they see fit.

By causing Cherokee aspirations to be discounted as romantic and irrelevant, it prevents the emergence of a competitive Cherokee leadership and discourages Cherokees from taking action as a community. For example, by 1904 Cherokees were given what was thought of as an opportunity to develop individualism and responsibility. The U.S. Government divided their communally owned land and each Indian was given his own piece. Thus the efforts of the present day Cherokee Four Mothers Society to piece together individual land holdings, reestablish communal title, and develop cooperative productive enterprises, is smilingly dismissed as an atavistic retreat to "clannishness."

By fostering the notion that Cherokees are an aggregate of disoriented individuals, it allows whites to plan for Cherokees, to control Cherokee resources, and to reinforce their own power by directing programs devoted to Cherokee advancement.

By denying that there is a Cherokee community with which a Cherokee middle class could identify and to which a Cherokee middle class could be responsive, it draws off educated Cherokees into "white" society and leaves an educationally impoverished pool of Cherokees to perpetuate the image of Cherokee incompetence.

The myth prevents scholars, Indian interest organizations, and the like from becoming overly curious about the area. If Cherokees are assimilated and prosperous, as the myth implies, there is neither a problem nor a culture to study. For 40 years no social scientist has completed a major study of any of the five civilized tribes. For 40 years the spread of information which might cast doubt on the myth itself has been successfully impeded.

In all, the myth stabilizes and disguises the Oklahoma social system.

The stability of a local social system, such as that of eastern Oklahoma, is heavily influenced by events in the larger society. The past decade of civil rights activity shook Oklahoma. Gradually, Oklahomans are becoming aware that their society is not as virtuous, homogeneous, attractive, and open as they may have supposed. And Oklahomans will now have to deal with the old agrarian social system of Cherokees, hillbillies, mixed-blood Cherokees, and a new urban elite grafted onto the old.

Left behind in the rush of workers to industry and of power to industrialized areas, the Ozark east of Oklahoma is a shell, depopulated, and controlled by newly dominant cities, Tulsa and Oklahoma City. The area, quaint enough to attract tourists, is far too rustic for sophisticated Oklahoma urbanites to take seriously. Local politicians offer weak leadership. Beginning to suspect that the local establishment is no longer all powerful, Cherokees have begun to assert themselves as a tribal community. The Cherokees conceive of themselves as a civilized nation, waiting for the dark days of the foreigners' suppression and exploitation to end. Oklahomans regard Cherokees as an aggregate of disadvantaged people still in the background of an integrated state, a definition which Cherokees do not share. In fact, the Cherokees are flirting with political office and have entered the courts with a hunting rights case. In launching a "Five County Northeast Oklahoma Cherokee Organization," they are gaining recognition as a legitimate community with rights, aspirations, resources and competence.

Consequently, the reappearance of assimilated Cherokees threatens the newly emergent regional power structure. Cherokees and the local establishment have begun jousting on a field of honor extending from county welfare offices (where the welfare-sponsored jobs of suspect members of the "Five County Organizations" are in jeopardy) to annual conventions of the National Congress of American Indians. Besides threatening an already shaky white power structure, the militant Cherokees are challenging the self esteem of the elderly and powerful "assimilated." Curiously, many white Oklahomans do not appear to be alarmed, but pleased, apparently, to relieve the tension that has developed between conflicting images of pretended assimilation and the reality of a work-aday world.

The manner in which Oklahomans view their society is the manner in which American sociologists all too often view American society. Great emphasis is placed on class and on individual mobility. And, social description, in these terms, is seen very much as a product of the American ethos.

White Oklahomans consider themselves members of a class-stratified society in which any individual (Negroes excepted) has free access to any class. Descriptions of that system vary according to who is doing the describing. Generally, white Oklahomans conceive their society to be one in which the upper class is made up of prosperous whites and old Cherokee mixed-blood families, or their descendants; next in order is a layer of middle class whites and assimilated Cherokees; then, a lower class of poor, country whites, full-blood Cherokees and Negroes. Young liberals see a two-class system: A middle class of "decent" whites and Cherokees and a socially unacceptable class of poor, country whites, Cherokees and Negroes.

HOW MYTHICAL IS MOBILITY?

This latter classification suggests that younger people perceive a much more closed system than their elders. Everyone is viewed as part of the same *community*—a word Oklahomans are fond of using. Presumably all groups of people have an equal share in the life of the community. Nationality, the word Okalahomans use to denote ethnic origin, is a principal clue to class position. As evidence of how open their society is, eastern Oklahomans point to Cherokees and poor, country whites (although not yet to Negroes, to whom the system is closed) who occupy respected positions. These are store owners, bureaucrats, and entrepreneurs; Babbits of the 1960s, though born of traditional Cherokee parents. Always, however, these have been individuals who followed the only approved channel of mobility by scrupulously conforming to standards of behavior defined by those in control of the system.

The classic sociological studies on class in America, such as those by W. Lloyd Warner and Robert Lynd, are essentially static descriptions of the rank position of aggregates of individuals similar to the native Oklahoman's conception of his society. These studies reflect a peculiarly American bias. First, they examine the system that has formed rather than study how the system was formed. Americans are phenomenologists, more concerned with the things they have created than with the lengthy processes whereby these things have developed, more interested in ends than concerned with means.

Secondly, Americans do not stress ethnic considerations. In the American dream all individuals can "make it," regardless of nationality. For sociologists, class is a phenomenon in which individuals have social rank; ethnicity is treated as no more than an important clue in determining that rank. Thus, to be Irish was to be an outcast in nineteenth century Boston; not so today.

Thirdly, Americans, envisioning themselves as a nation of individualists, have assumed that social mobility for the most part rests on individual achievement. Immigrant groups are seen as having migrated into lower class positions in a relatively fixed class system through which individual immigrants rapidly became mobile. By contrast, Oklahoma's rapid entry into the formative American industrial economy caused a class-like structure to form on top of pre-existing ethnic communities.

A more balanced view shows that in the parts of the United States which industrialized earlier and more gradually, whole immigrant communities were successively imported into and butted one another through a social system which was in the process of formation and closure. The ways in which entire ethnic communities achieve mobility are overlooked.

Now it is becoming obvious that this mobility has slowed, even for those ethnic communities (like Poles) already "in the system." For communities which were brought into the system late (like Puerto Ricans) or at its territorial fringe (like Mexican-Americans in the Southwest) the situation is different.

Cherokees maintained technical independence as an autonomous nation until 1907, and in fact held America at arm's length until the 1890s. They provide an example of incorporation of an ethnic group into the industrial system in an area where no earlier group has paved the way. Thus, Cherokees are a "case type" which illustrated the modern dynamics of our system in pure form. Cherokees are now caught in our "historically mature" system of rank ethnic groups—a system which, for some, is rigid and closed, with little chance for individual and less for communal mobility. The total rank-structure of eastern Oklahoma is cemented by the mythology Americans use to obscure and rationalize their privileged position in a closed system.

In their conception of class, American sociologists are often as wedded to myth as are Oklahomans, and the resulting large areas of American social science they have created obediently subscribe to official fictions within the American world view.

Now, successive summers of violence have exploded some of the folk and scientific mythology shrouding the structure of our nation. The

Report of the National Advisory Commission on Civil Disorders declares: "What white Americans have never fully understood—but what the Negro can never forget—is that white society is deeply implicated in the ghetto. White institutions created it, white institutions maintain it, and white society condones it." Yet throughout this unusually clear report the phenomenon of white racism is barely alluded to, as though it were an "attitude" born by an uniformed populace and unrelated to the core of our national social system. That system, as we see it in operation in Oklahoma, beneath its mythology of assimilation, consists of a structure of ranked ethnic groups, euphemistically called "classes" by American sociologists; a structure which is growing more stable and more rigid. This kind of structure is general in America and, of course, implied in the above quote from the Kerner report. In Oklahoma such a system of relationships has enabled aggressive entrepreneurs to harness and utilize the resources of ethnic communities which are frozen into a low ranked position by the dominant community's contol over channels of mobility and by the insistence that the whole complex represents one single community differentiated only by personal capability. Thus, essentially "racist" perceptions and relationships are the "motor" driving the system and are embedded in the very day-to-day relationships of middle class Oklahoma.

UNIT E / ISSUES FOR CONSIDERATION

1. Distinguish between the characteristics of the family within American middle-class culture and within the culture of poverty.
2. How is being a Cherokee Indian in Oklahoma like being a Puerto Rican in the slums of New York City?
3. Why can American society be thought of as constituting a single culture?
4. How do the sociological concepts studied in this book help you to understand the transmission of the culture from one generation to another?

UNIT F COLLECTIVE BEHAVIOR

Collective behavior is a term that sociologists use to refer to behavior that does not reflect the expectations of the group or society, but rather reflects the individual's reaction to his close proximity to others. When people are physically close to each other, they are likely to affect one another in ways that cannot always be explained in terms of the concepts we discussed earlier. The suggestibility of the crowd and the emotional contagion of the mob are examples. The power that the aggregate has over the individual seems to be a function of the social and emotional conditions surrounding the encounter. Once the individual loses himself in the spell of the crowd he is likely to behave most unconventionally. The series of riots that hit the United States in 1967, when there were 41 different occasions of major disorder in 39 cities, illustrate this point. A thorough investigation of these riots was conducted by a national advisory commission on civil disorder. Its report, usually referred to as the Kerner Report, describes these regularities in the occasion studied: In each city there had accumulated a reservoir of grievances in the Negro community; there occurred a "precipitating" incident or incidents that could be related to these grievances; violence developed after its initial outbreak; and, finally, a series of control efforts, including official force, negotiation, and persuasion, emerged. In the section of the report that is presented here you will find the commission's description of what happened in one city, Newark, New Jersey. Can you find the elements listed above? Try to note instances in which an individual seemed to behave contrary to the norms as a result of being caught up in the crowd. Is this phenomenon limited to the ghetto dweller, or does it sometimes apply to those who are brought there to maintain order?

17 / PROFILE OF DISORDER: NEWARK, 1967

National Advisory Commission on Civil Disorder

NEWARK

The last outburst in Atlanta occurred on Tuesday night, June 20. That same night, in Newark, New Jersey, a tumultuous meeting of the Planning Board took place. Until 4 A.M., speaker after speaker from the Negro ghetto arose to denounce the city's intent to turn over 150 acres in the heart of the Central Ward as a site for the state's new medical and dental college.

The growing opposition to the city administration by vocal black residents had paralyzed both the Planning Board and the Board of Education. Tension had been rising so steadily throughout the northern New Jersey area that, in the first week of June, Colonel David Kelly, head of the state police, had met with municipal police chiefs to draw up plans for state police support of city police wherever a riot developed. Nowhere was the tension greater than in Newark.

Founded in 1666, the city, part of the Greater New York City port complex, rises from the salt marshes of the Passaic River. Although in 1967 Newark's population of 400,000 still ranked it thirtieth among American municipalities, for the past 20 years the white middle class had been deserting the city for the suburbs.

In the late 1950s the desertions had become a rout. Between 1960 and 1967, the city lost a net total of more than 70,000 white residents. Replacing them in vast areas of dilapidated housing where living conditions, ac-

---

From *The Report of The National Advisory Commission on Civil Disorder (The Kerner Report)*, Washington, D.C.: U.S. Printing Office, 1968.

cording to a prominent member of the County Bar Association, were so bad that "people would be kinder to their pets," were Negro migrants, Cubans and Puerto Ricans. In six years the city switched from 65 per cent white to 52 per cent Negro and 10 per cent Puerto Rican and Cuban.

The white population, nevertheless, retained political control of the city. On both the City Council and the Board of Education seven of nine members were white. On other key boards the disparity was equal or greater. In the Central Ward, where the medical college controversy raged, the Negro constituents and their white councilman found themselves on opposite sides of almost every crucial issue.

The municipal administration lacked the ability to respond quickly enough to navigate the swiftly changing currents. Even had it had great astuteness, it would have lacked the financial resources to affect significantly the course of events.

In 1962, seven-term Congressman Hugh Addonizio had forged an Italian-Negro coalition to overthrow long-time Irish control of the City Hall. A liberal in Congress, Addonizio, when he became mayor, had opened his door to all people. Negroes, who had been excluded from the previous administration, were brought into the government. The police department was integrated.

Nevertheless, progress was slow. As the Negro population increased, more and more of the politically oriented found the progress inadequate.

The Negro-Italian coalition began to develop strains over the issue of the police. The police were largely Italian, the persons they arrested largely Negro. Community leaders agreed that, as in many police forces, there was a small minority of officers who abused their responsibility. This gave credibility to the cries of "Brutality!" voiced periodically by ghetto Negroes.

In 1965 Mayor Addonizio, acknowledged that there was "a small group of misguided individuals" in the department, declared that "it is vital to establish once and for all, in the minds of the public, that charges of alleged police brutality will be thoroughly investigated and the appropriate legal or punitive action be taken if the charges are found to be substantiated."

Pulled one way by the Negro citizens who wanted a Police Review Board, and the other by the police, who adamantly opposed it, the mayor decided to transfer "the control and investigation of complaints of police brutality out of the hands of both the police and the public and into the hands of an agency that all can support—the Federal Bureau of Investigation;" and to send "a copy of any charge of police brutality . . . directly to the Prosecutor's office." However, the FBI could act only if there had been a violation of a person's federal civil rights. No complaint was ever heard of again.

Nor was there much redress for other complaints. The city has no money with which to redress them.

The city had already reached its legal bonding limit, yet expenditures continued to outstrip income. Health and welfare costs, per capita, were 20 times as great as for some of the surrounding communities. Cramped by its small land area of 23.6 square miles—one-third of which was taken up by the Newark Airport and unusable marshland—and surrounded by independent jurisdictions, the city had nowhere to expand.

Taxable property was contracting as land, cleared for urban renewal, lay fallow year after year. Property taxes had been increased, perhaps, to the point of diminishing return. By the fall of 1967 they were to reach $661.70 on a $10,000 house—double that of suburban communities.* As a result, people were refusing either to own or to renovate property in the city. Seventy-four percent of white and 87 percent of Negro families lived in rental housing. Whoever was able to move to the suburbs, moved. Many of these persons, as downtown areas were cleared and new office buildings were constructed, continued to work in the city. Among them were a large proportion of the people from whom a city normally draws its civic leaders, but who, after moving out, tended to cease involving themselves in the community's problems.

During the daytime Newark more than doubled its population—and was, therefore, forced to provide services for a large number of people who contributed nothing in property taxes. The city's per capita outlay for police, fire protection and other municipal services continued to increase. By 1967 it was twice that of the surrounding area.

Consequently, there was less money to spend on education. Newark's per capita outlay on schools was considerably less than that of surrounding communities. Yet within the city's school system were 78,000 children, 14,000 more than 10 years earlier.

Twenty thousand pupils were on double sessions. The dropout rate was estimated to be as high as 33 percent. Of 13,600 Negroes between the ages of 16 and 19, more than 6,000 were not in school. In 1960 over half of the adult Negro population had less than an eighth grade education.

The typical ghetto cycle of high unemployment, family breakup, and crime was present in all its elements. Approximately 12 percent of Negroes were without jobs. As estimated 40 percent of Negro children lived in

---

*The legal tax rate is $7.76 per $100 of market value. However, because of inflation, a guideline of 85.27 percent of market value is used in assessing, reducing the true tax rate to $6.617 per $100.

broken homes. Although Newark maintained proportionately the largest police force of any major city, its crime rate was among the highest in the nation. In narcotics violations it ranked fifth nationally. Almost 80 percent of the crimes were committed within two miles of the core of the city, where the Central Ward is located. A majority of the criminals were Negro. Most of the victims, likewise, were Negro. The Mafia was reputed to control much of the organized crime.

Under such conditions a major segment of the Negro population became increasingly militant. Largely excluded from positions of traditional political power, Negroes, tutored by a handful of militant social activists who had moved into the city in the early 1960's, made use of the anti-poverty program, in which poor people were guaranteed representation, as a political springboard. This led to friction between the United Community Corporation, the agency that administered the anti-poverty program, and the city administration.

When it became known that the secretary of the Board of Education intended to retire, the militants proposed for the position the city's budget director, a Negro with a master's degree in accounting. The mayor, however, had already nominated a white man. Since the white man had only a high school education, and at least 70 percent of the children in the school system were Negro, the issue of who was to obtain the secretaryship, an important and powerful position, quickly became a focal issue.

Joined with the issue of the 150-acre medical school site, the area of which had been expanded to triple the original request—an expansion regarded by the militants as an effort to dilute the black political power by moving out Negro residents—the Board of Education battle resulted in a confrontation between the mayor and the militants. Both sides refused to alter their positions.

Into this impasse stepped a Washington Negro named Albert Roy Osborne. A flamboyant, 42-year-old former wig salesman who called himself Colonel Hassan Jeru-Ahmed and wore a black beret, he presided over a mythical "Blackman's Volunteer Army of Liberation." Articulate and magnetic, the self-commissioned "Colonel" proved to be a one-man show. He brought Negro residents flocking to Board of Education and Planning Board meetings. The Colonel spoke in violent terms, and backed his words with violent action. At one meeting he tore the tape from the official stenographic recorder. After he was ejected, one of his captains threw a mapboard across the stage and smashed a tape recorder against the wall.

It became more and more evident to the militants that, though they might not be able to prevail, they could prevent the normal transaction of business. Filibustering began. A Negro former state assemblyman held the floor for more than four hours. One meeting of the Board of Education began at 5:00 P.M. and did not adjorn until 3:23 A.M. Throughout the months of May and June speaker after speaker warned that if the mayor persisted in naming a white man as Secretary to the Board of Education, and in moving ahead with plans for the medical school site, violence would ensue. The city administration played down the threats.

On June 27th, when a new secretary to the Board of Education was to be named, the state police set up a command post in the Newark armory.

The militants, led by the local CORE (Congress of Racial Equality) chapter, disrupted and took over the Board of Education meeting. The outcome was a stalemate. The incumbent secretary decided to stay on another year. No one was satisfied.

At the beginning of July there were 24,000 unemployed Negroes within the city limits. Their ranks were swelled by an estimated 20,000 teenagers, many of whom, with school out and the summer recreation program curtailed due to a lack of funds, had no place to go.

On July 8, Newark and East Orange Police attempted to disperse a group of Black Muslims. In the melee that followed, several police officers and Muslims suffered injuries necessitating medical treatment. The resulting charges and counter-charges heightened the tension between police and Negroes.

Early on the evening of July 12, a cab driver named John Smith began, according to police reports, tailgating a Newark police car. Smith was an unlikely candidate to set a riot in motion. Forty years old, a Georgian by birth, he had attended college for a year before entering the Army in 1950. In 1953 he had been honorably discharged with the rank of corporal. A chess-playing trumpet player, he had worked as a musician and a factory hand before, in 1963, becoming a cab driver.

As a cab driver, he appeared to be a hazard. Within a relatively short period of time he had eight or nine accidents. His license was revoked. When, with a woman passenger in his cab, he was stopped by the police, he was in violation of that revocation.

From the high-rise towers of the Reverend William P. Hayes Housing Project, the residents can look down on the orange-red brick facade of the Fourth Precinct Police Station and observe every movement. Shortly after 9:30 P.M., people saw Smith, who either refused or was unable to walk, being dragged out of a police car and into the front door of the station.

Within a few minutes at least two civil rights leaders received calls from a hysterical woman declaring a cab driver was being beaten by the police. When one of the persons at the station notified the cab company of Smith's arrest, cab drivers all over the city began learning of it over their cab radios.

A crowd formed on the grounds of the housing project across the narrow street from the station. As more and more people arrived, the description of the beating purportedly administered to Smith became more and more exaggerated. The descriptions were supported by other complaints of police malpractice that, over the years, had been submitted for investigation—but had never been heard of again.

Several Negro community leaders, telephoned by a civil rights worker and informed of the deteriorating situation, rushed to the scene. By 10:15 P.M. the atmosphere had become so potentially explosive that Kenneth Melchior, the senior police inspector on the night watch, was called. He arrived at approximately 10:30 P.M.

Met by a delegation of civil rights leaders and militants who requested the right to see and interview Smith, Inspector Melchior acceded to their request.

When the delegation was taken to Smith, Melchior agreed with their observations that, as a result of injuries Smith had suffered, he needed to be examined by a doctor. Arrangements were made to have a police car transport him to the hospital.

Both within and outside of the police station the atmosphere was electric with hostility. Carloads of police officers arriving for the 10:45 P.M. change of shifts were subjected to a gauntlet of catcalls, taunts and curses.

Joined by Oliver Lofton, administrative director of the Newark Legal Services Project, the Negro community leaders inside the station requested an interview with Inspector Melchior. As they were talking to the inspector about initiating an investigation to determine how Smith had been injured, the crowd outside became more and more unruly. Two of the Negro spokesmen went outside to attempt to pacify the people.

There was little reaction to the spokesmen's appeal that the people go home. The second of the two had just finished speaking from atop a car when several Molotov cocktails smashed against the wall of the police station.

With the call of "Fire!" most of those inside the station, police officers and civilians alike, rushed out of the front door. The Molotov cocktails had splattered to the ground; the fire was quickly extinguished.

Inspector Melchior had a squad of men form a line across the front of the station. The police officers and the Negroes on the other side of the street exchanged volleys of profanity.

Three of the Negro leaders, Timothy Still of the United Community Corporation, Robert Curvin of CORE, and Lofton, requested they be given another opportunity to disperse the crowd. Inspector Melchior agreed to let them try, and provided a bullhorn. It was apparent that the several hundred persons who had gathered in the street and on the grounds of the housing project were not going to disperse. Therefore, it was decided to attempt to channel the energies of the people into a nonviolent protest. While Lofton promised the crowd that a full investigation would be made of the Smith incident, the other Negro leaders urged those on the scene to form a line of march toward the city hall.

Some persons joined the line of march. Others milled about in the narrow street. From the dark grounds of the housing project came a barrage of rocks. Some of them fell among the crowd. Others hit persons in the line of march. Many smashed the windows of the police station. The rock throwing, it was believed, was the work of youngsters; approximately 2,500 children lived in the housing project.

Almost at the same time, an old car was set afire in a parking lot. The line of march began to disintegrate. The police, their heads protected by World War I-type helmets, sallied forth to disperse the crowd. A fire engine, arriving on the scene, was pelted with rocks. As police drove people away from the station, they scattered in all directions.

A few minutes later a nearby liquor store was broken into. Some persons, seeing a caravan of cabs appear at city hall to protest Smith's arrest, interpreted this as evidence that the disturbance had been organized, and generated rumors to that effect.

However, only a few stores were looted. Within a short period of time the disorder ran its course.

The next afternoon, Thursday, July 13, the mayor described it as an isolated incident. At a meeting with Negro leaders to discuss measures to defuse the situation, he agreed to appoint the first Negro police captain, and announced that he would set up a panel of citizens to investigate the Smith arrest. To one civil rights leader this sounded like "the playback of a record," and he walked out. Other observers reported that the mayor seemed unaware of the seriousness of the tensions.

The police were not. Unknown to the mayor, Dominick Spina, the director of police, had extended shifts from eight hours to 12, and was in the process of mobilizing half the strength of the department for that evening. The night before, Spina had arrived at the Fourth Precinct Police Station at approximately midnight, and had witnessed the latter half of the disturbance. Earlier in the evening he had held the regular weekly "open house" in his office. This was intended to give any person who wanted to talk to him an opportunity to do so. Not a single person had shown up.

As director of police, Spina had initiated many new programs: police-precinct councils, composed of the police precinct captain and business and civic leaders, who would meet once a month to discuss mutual problems; Junior Crime-fighters; a Boy Scout Explorer program for each precinct; mandatory human relations training for every officer; a Citizens' Observer Program, which permitted citizens to ride in police cars and observe activities in the stations; a Police Cadet program; and others.

Many of the programs initially had been received enthusiastically, but—as was the case with the "open house"—interest had fallen off. In general, the programs failed to reach the hard-core unemployed, the disaffected, the school dropouts—of whom Spina estimates there are 10,000 in Essex County—that constitute a major portion of the police problem.

Reports and rumors, including one that Smith had died, circulated through the Negro community. Tension continued to rise. Nowhere was the tension greater than at the Spirit House, the gathering place for Black Nationalists, Black Power advocates, and militants of every hue. Black Muslims, Orthodox Muslims, and members of the United Afro-American Association, a new and growing organization that follows, in general, the teachings of the late Malcolm X, came regularly to mingle and exchange views. Anti-white playwright LeRoi Jones held workshops. The two police-Negro clashes, coming one on top of the other, coupled with the unresolved political issues, had created a state of crisis.

On Thursday, inflammatory leaflets were circulated in the neighborhoods of the Fourth Precinct. A "Police Brutality Protest Rally" was announced for early evening in front of the Fourth Precinct Station. Several televison stations and newspapers sent news teams to interview people. Cameras were set up. A crowd gathered.

A picket line was formed to march in front of the police station. Between 7:00 and 7:30 P.M. James Threatt, Executive Director of the Newark Human Rights Commission, arrived to announce to the people the decision of the mayor to form a citizens group to investigate the Smith incident, and to elevate a Negro to the rank of captain.

The response from the loosely milling mass of people was derisive. One youngster shouted "Black Power!" Rocks were thrown at Threatt, a Negro. The barrage of missiles that followed placed the police station under siege.

After the barrage had continued for some minutes, police came out to disperse the crowd. According to witnesses, there was little restraint of language or action by either side. A number of police officers and Negroes were injured.

As on the night before, once the people had been dispersed, reports of looting began to come in. Soon the glow of the first fire was seen.

Without enough men to establish control, the police set up a perimeter around a two-mile stretch of Springfield Avenue, one of the principal business districts, where bands of youths roamed up and down smashing windows. Grocery and liquor stores, clothing and furniture stores, drug stores and cleaners, appliance stores and pawnshops were the principal targets. Periodically police officers would appear and fire their weapons over the heads of looters and rioters. Laden with stolen goods, people began returning to the housing projects.

Near midnight, activity appeared to taper off. The Mayor told reporters the city had turned the corner.

As news of the disturbance had spread, however, people had flocked into the streets. As they saw stores being broken into with impunity, many bowed to temptation and joined the looting.

Without the necessary personnel to make mass arrests, police were shooting into the air to clear stores. A Negro boy was wounded by a .22 caliber bullet said to have been fired by a white man riding in a car. Guns were reported stolen from a Sears Roebuck store. Looting, fires, and gunshots were reported from a widening area. Between 2:00 and 2:30 A.M. on Friday, July 14, the mayor decided to request Governor Richard J. Hughes to dispatch the state police, and National Guard troops. The first elements of the state police arrived with a sizeable contingent before dawn.

During the morning the governor and the mayor, together with police and National Guard officers, made a reconnaissance of the area. The police escort guarding the officials arrested looters as they went. By early afternoon the National Guard had set up 137 roadblocks, and state police and riot teams were beginning to achieve control. Command of anti-riot operations was taken over by the governor, who decreed a "hard line" in putting down the riot.

As a result of technical difficulties, such as the fact that the city and state police did not operate on the same radio wavelengths, the three-way command structure—city police, state police and National Guard—worked poorly.

At 3:30 P.M. that afternoon, the family of Mrs. D. J. was standing near the upstairs windows of their apartment, watching looters run in and out of a furniture store on Springfield Avenue. Three carloads of police rounded the corner. As the police yelled at the looters, they began running.

The police officers opened fire. A bullet smashed the kitchen window in Mrs. D. J.'s apartment. A moment later she heard a cry from the bedroom. Her 3-year old daughter, Debbie, came running into the room. Blood was streaming down the left side of her face: the bullet had entered her eye. The child spent the next two months in the hospital. She lost the sight of her left eye and the hearing in her left ear.

Simultaneously, on the street below, Horace W. Morris, an associate director of the Washington Urban League who had been visiting relatives in Newark, was about to enter a car for the drive to Newark Airport. With him were his two brothers and his 73-year old step-father, Isaac Harrison. About 60 persons had been on the street watching the looting. As the police arrived, three of the looters cut directly in front of the group of spectators. The police fired at the looters. Bullets plowed into the spectators. Everyone began running. As Harrison, followed by the family, headed toward the apartment building in which he lived, a bullet kicked his legs out from under him. Horace Morris lifted him to his feet. Again he fell. Mr. Morris' brother, Virgil, attempted to pick the old man up. As he was doing so, he was hit in the left leg and right forearm. Mr. Morris and his other brother managed to drag the two wounded men into the vestibule of the building, jammed with 60 to 70 frightened, angry Negroes.

Bullets continued to spatter against the walls of the buildings. Finally, as the firing died down, Morris—whose step-father died that evening—yelled to a sergeant that innocent people were being shot.

"Tell the black bastards to stop shooting at us," the sergeant, according to Morris, replied.

"They don't have guns; no one is shooting at you," Morris said.

"You shut up, there's a sniper on the roof," the sergeant yelled.

A short time later, at approximately 5:00 P.M., in the same vicinity a police detective was killed by a small caliber bullet. The origin of the shot could not be determined. Later during the riot a fireman was killed by a .30 caliber bullet. Snipers were blamed for the deaths of both.

At 5:30 P.M., on Beacon Street, W. F. told J. S., whose 1959 Pontiac he had taken to the station for inspection, that his front brake needed fixing. J. S., who had just returned from work, went to the car which was parked in the street, jacked up the front end, took the wheel off and got under the car.

The street was quiet. More than a dozen persons were sitting on porches, walking about, or shopping. None heard any shots. Suddenly several state troopers appeared at the corner of Springfield and Beacon. J. S. was startled by a shot clanging into the side of the garbage can next to his car. As he looked up he saw a state trooper with his rifle pointed at him. The next shot struck him in the right side.

At almost the same instant, K. G., standing on a porch, was struck in the right eye by a bullet. Both he and J. S. were critically injured.

At 8:00 P.M., Mrs. L. M. bundled her husband, her husband's brother, and her four sons into the family car to drive to a restaurant for dinner. On the return trip her husband, who was driving, panicked as he approached a National Guard roadblock. He slowed the car, then quickly swerved around. A shot rang out. When the family reached home, everyone began piling out of the car. Ten-year-old Eddie failed to move. Shot through the head, he was dead.

Although, by nightfall, most of the looting and burning had ended, reports of sniper fire increased. The fire was, according to New Jersey National Guard reports, "deliberately or otherwise inaccurate." Major General James F. Cantwell, Chief of Staff of the New Jersey National

Guard, testified before an Armed Services Subcommittee of the House of Representatives that "there was too much firing initially against snipers" because of "confusion when we were finally called on for help and our thinking of it as a military action."

"As a matter of fact," Director of Police Spina told the Commission, "down in the Springfield Avenue area it was so bad that, in my opinion, Guardsmen were firing upon police and police were firing back at them . . . I really don't believe there was as much sniping as we thought . . . We have since compiled statistics indicating that there were 79 specified instances of sniping."

Several problems contributed to the misconceptions regarding snipers: the lack of communications; the fact that one shot might be reported half a dozen times by half a dozen different persons as it caromed and reverberated a mile or more through the city; the fact that the National Guard troops lacked riot training. They were, said a police official, "young and very scared," and had had little contact with Negroes.

Within the Guard itself contact with Negroes had certainly been limited. Although, in 1949, out of a force of 12,529 men there had been 1,183 Negroes, following the integration of the Guard in the 1950's the number had declined until, by July of 1967, there were 303 Negroes in a force of 17,529 men.

On Saturday, July 15, Spina received a report of snipers in a housing project. When he arrived he saw approximately 100 National Guardsmen and police officers crouching behind vehicles, hiding in corners and lying on the ground around the edge of the courtyard.

Since everything appeared quiet and it was broad daylight, Spina walked directly down the middle of the street. Nothing happened. As he came to the last building of the complex, he heard a shot. All around him the troopers jumped, believing themselves to be under sniper fire. A moment later a young Guardsman ran from behind a building.

The director of police went over and asked him if he had fired the shot. The soldier said yes, he had fired to scare a man away from a window; that his orders were to keep everyone away from windows.

Spina said he told the soldier: "Do you know what you just did? You have now created a state of hysteria. Every Guardsman up and down this street and every State Policeman and every city policeman that is present thinks that somebody just fired a shot and that it is probably a sniper."

A short time later more "gunshots" were heard. Investigating, Spina came upon a Puerto Rican sitting on a wall. In reply to a question as to whether he knew "where the firing is coming from?" the man said:

"That's no firing. That's fireworks. If you look up to the fourth floor, you will see the people who are throwing down these cherry bombs."

By this time four truckloads of National Guardsmen had arrived and troopers and policemen were again crouched everywhere, looking for a sniper. The director of police remained at the scene for three hours, and the only shot fired was the one by the Guardsman.

Nevertheless, at six o'clock that evening two columns of National Guardsmen and state troopers were directing mass fire at the Hayes Housing Project in response to what they believed were snipers.

On the tenth floor, Eloise Spellman, the mother of several children, fell, a bullet through her neck.

Across the street a number of persons, standing in an apartment window, were watching the firing directed at the housing project. Suddenly several troopers whirled and began firing in the general direction of the spectators. Mrs. Hattie Gainer, a grandmother, sank to the floor.

A block away Rebecca Brown's 2-year old daughter was standing at the window. Mrs. Brown rushed to drag her to safety. As Mrs. Brown was, momentarily, framed in the window, a bullet spun into her back.

All three women died.

A number of eye witnesses, at varying times and places, reported seeing bottles thrown from upper story windows. As these would land at the feet of an officer he would turn and fire. Thereupon, other officers and Guardsmen up and down the street would join in.

In order to protect his property, B. W. W., the owner of a Chinese laundry, had placed a sign saying "Soul Brother" in his window. Between 1:00 and 1:30 A.M., on Sunday, July 16, he, his mother, wife, and brother, were watching television in the back room. The neighborhood had been quiet. Suddenly B. W. W. heard the sound of jeeps, then shots.

Going to an upstairs window he was able to look out into the street. There he observed several jeeps, from which soldiers and state troopers were firing into stores that had "Soul Brother" signs in the windows. During the course of three nights, according to dozens of eye witness reports, law enforcement officers shot into and smashed windows of businesses that contained signs indicating they were Negro owned.

At 11:00 P.M., on Sunday, July 16th, Mrs. Lucille Pugh looked out of the window to see if the streets were clear. She then asked her 11-year-old son, Michael, to take the garbage out. As he reached the street and was illuminated by a street light, a shot rang out. He died.

By Monday afternoon, July 17, state police and National Guard forces were withdrawn. That evening, a Catholic priest saw two Negro men walking down the street. They were carrying a case of soda and two bags of groceries. An unmarked car with five police officers pulled up beside them. Two white officers got out of the car. Accusing the Negro men of looting, the officers made them put the groceries on the sidewalk, then kicked the bags open, scattering their contents all over the street.

Telling the men, "Get out of here," the officers drove off. The Catholic priest went across the street to help gather up the groceries. One of the men turned to him: "I've just been back from Vietnam two days," he said, "and this is what I get. I feel like going home and getting a rifle and shooting the cops."

Of the 250 fire alarms, many had been false, and 13 were considered by the city to have been "serious." Of the $10,251,000 damage total, four-fifths was due to stock loss. Damage to buildings and fixtures was less than $2 million.

Twenty-three persons were killed—a white detective, a white fireman, and 21 Negroes. One was 73-year-old Isaac Harrison. Six were women. Two were children.

UNIT F / ISSUES FOR CONSIDERATION

1. There were four common elements in all occasions investigated by the Kerner Commission. Can you find where these elements, listed in the introduction to this section, occurred in Newark, New Jersey?
2. Describe the behavior of an individual as discussed in the Newark report that probably could not be explained by that individual's conformity to the norms of his groups but rather to the excitement and tensions of the situation in which he found himself.
3. Describe other instances with which you are familiar in which ordinarily law-abiding persons acted in violation of the law and customs because they were caught up in the emotional contagion and excitement of a crowd. Are there other happenings in our current society that follow the patterns that the Kerner Commission describes?

PART TWO
SOCIAL DIFFERENTIATION

There are almost an infinite number of ways that a human being can be classified: tall or short, intelligent or ignorant, etc. A clear perception of the standard ways used to classify persons will give significant insights into the nature of the society. There was a time in America's history when the first thing a person wanted to know about a stranger was where he was from; somehow if he knew the newcomer was from Big Sandy, Montana, he felt he knew more about him than if he knew he was rich or poor, Italian or Spanish. That particular differentiation has faded in most areas of America, although there are still some places where "where you are from" is very important. This process of dividing persons into categories is what we mean by *social differentiation.*

It is our aim in the second half of this book to consider some of the more important of these differentiations in our complex society—social class, race, residence, age, sex, and deviance. However, before we consider them individually it will be helpful to look at the abstract nature of each of the categories. Can you note something that race, age, and sex have in common that differentiates them from class, residence, and deviance? The first set of characteristics cannot be changed. Some blacks pass as white, and a handful of persons have had operations to change their sex, and many persons try to stay young, but it is fair to say for most of us that once we are born there is nothing we can do to change these factors. This is not to suggest that it is particularly easy to become rich or for a nonconformist to become straight, but these blocks in the way of change are largely social in nature, not biological.

The sociologist, when considering the topic of social differentiation, is also very interested in the values that the society places on the various categories. We can clarify this by comparing the social class dimension with the sex variable. Social class by its social definition implies a value hierarchy. We use the labels upper, middle, and lower; we talk about rising out of the lower class. The old adage that America is the place where anyone can rise from "rags to riches" probably says more about the negative values that Americans place on being poor than about the nature of opportunities in our society. Thus we conclude that it is bad to be poor, and good to be rich. This, of course, is an oversimplification, but it makes our point. Let us now consider the two categories of sex. Few in our society go around claiming it is good to be female and bad to be male or vice versa, but no one would deny that there is a difference. Note that this differentiation is more along the line of a social role which we covered earlier; that is, there are quite different expectations for men than there are for women. Now consider the values that society places on being black or white, urban, suburban or rural, young or old, conformist or nonconformist.

Another dimension that interests the sociologist with regard to social differentiation is the nature of the relationship of the persons within the categories. Note that we have not used the word group or sub-culture in discussing the abstract nature of differentiation. This is because some of the categories do not fit the notions of groups or sub-cultures while others do. Again, let us compare class and sex. Being poor, as we saw in the section on culture, is not just a matter of a lack of money. It is a way of life. The poor are likely to live among other poor and have only a superficial relationship with the non-poor. They form a true culture. But the female's way of life is deeply integrated into that of the male; even though she may have a few all-female associations and may feel a certain identity with all others of her sex, the category takes the form of a role, not of a sub-culture or group.

One might well ask at this point why the sociologist with his years of study and all his abstract concepts still prefers to use society's classification schemes rather than ones of his own. One answer to this is that his observations of the schemes used by society in classifying its members provides him with very important social facts that aid in his analysis of the structure of social organization. He recognizes that that which is perceived by members of society as important to them is going to be important in its consequences. This does not mean that the perceptions of society are always accurate. The notions that women are inferior or that Negroes are lazy will not hold up under careful objective analysis, but the fact that a large portion of society believes these notions is going to have serious consequences for both those evaluated and those doing the evaluation.

Of course, the student should not be lead to believe that the sociologist relies solely on society's differentiations. The categories chosen for this part of the book were selected because they seemed to be significant for both the members of American society and for sociological analysis.

The selections that follow try to accomplish several things. Some are chosen to try to provide the student with a clear picture of the differences between people in our society and to belie some of the stereotypes you may have developed. Others were selected because they portray society's attitude toward a particular category or division, while still others discuss ways of breaking out of society's classification. As in Part One, many of the selections deal with the effects of social change on the meanings and significance of the categories.

UNIT G
SOCIAL CLASS: THE RICH AND THE POOR

As you are probably aware by now, in its attempt to be systematic about its approach to man and society sociology runs into problems with words. *Social class* is a prime example. The term has been used to differentiate persons according to power, prestige, associations, ways of life, income, education, occupations, and various combinations of these and other factors. The terms upper class, middle class, and lower class are a part of the vocabulary of almost every American. A look into a study of persons' self-placement into class categories is instructive. When asked to classify themselves as members of the upper, middle, or lower class, a large sample of Americans overwhelmingly replied that they felt they were middle class, but when a similar sample was asked to indicate if they were upper, middle, or working class, almost as many said they were working class as indicated they were middle class. Note the different connotations of the words "working" and "lower." The latter definitely implies a stratum: lower class is at the bottom, upper class at the top. When sociologists have used this perspective they usually use the concept *social stratification.* It happens that our society is stratified along the lines of income, education, and occupation. If one were to compare members of the various strata, or levels, of American society it would be obvious that they differ in the amount of money available to them, the formal education they have, and the type of work they do. Of course they will vary in other ways as well.

Other sociologists prefer to use the notion of social class to refer to differences in ways of life. Oscar Lewis' article in the section on culture showed how the very poor formed a culture or way of life, of their own.

The readings in this section are designed to familiarize the student with the differences that exist among classes in American society. Note the differences in the style of life of the family described in Lewis' article in this section and of the types of people described in Zimmerman's review of *The Right People*. As you read Schrag's article, which describes the plight of the forgotten American in the middle, note how class differences go much deeper than money, schooling, and jobs. The perceptive reader will realize that the social class system in American society is more complex than the simplistic divisions into lower, middle, and upper. What we wish to portray here is the heterogeneity and complexity that result from society's tendency to differentiate its members according to social class. Could a person be completely without material wealth, have no job and little education, and still not be lower class?

18 / EVEN THE SAINTS CRY

Oscar Lewis

This article describes the experiences of a young Puerto Rican mother, Cruz Rios, who moved from La Esmeralda—one of the oldest slums in San Juan only a short distance from the governor's palace—about four miles east to Villa Hermosa, a new government housing project in a middle-class section of Rio Piedras. Cruz' story illustrates the difficult problems of adjustment in her new environment and helps us understand why, in spite of the efforts of well-intentioned governments and the spending of huge sums of money on public housing, the positive effects hoped for by social planners are not always forthcoming.

When I began my study of Cruz in 1963, she was just 17 and living alone on relief with her two children. She lived in a small, dark, one-room apartment for which she paid a rental of eight dollars a month.

Her kitchen was a tiny corner alcove equipped with a three-burner kerosene stove and a water faucet jutting out from the wall. She shared a run-down hall toilet with two other families and paid a neighbor $1.50 a month for the privilege of an extension cord which supplied her with electricity.

Cruz, a crippled, mulatto girl with reddish brown kinky hair and a pretty face, was lame since early childhood. She left school after the fifth grade, set up house with her sweetheart at 14 and gave birth to her first child at 15. Two years later, before the birth of her second child, she separated from her husband, Emilio, who refused to recognize the baby as his own.

Part I gives the reader a glimpse of living conditions in the slum; part II, recorded five months after Cruz had moved, gives her reactions to the housing project. (Names of all places and people in this tape-recorded narrative have been changed to guarantee the anonymity of the narrator.)

Here in La Esmeralda, the only thing that disturbs me are the rats. Lice, bedbugs, and rats have always been a problem in my room. When I moved in here a year ago, the first thing I found were little baby rats. "Kill them!" my friend Gloria said. "*Ay Bendito!* I can't do it. Poor little things—they look like children," I said, and I left them there in a hole. The next day they were gone. I didn't kill them, they just disappeared. I cleaned up the house and about a month later they were going back and forth through the room from one hole to another, with me just looking at them.

When Alejandro was living with me, more rats came because there was a hen with eggs under the house. A rat had given birth and had eaten some of the chicks. The owner took the hen and 29 chicks out of there because there were baby rats underneath the hen too. The man threw them out but a week later they came back and were all over the place, even getting into the pan with the baby's milk and eating up whatever I left around.

One Sunday my *mamá* said, "Let's buy a rat trap and see if we can't get rid of some of them." Well, we tried it and that day between us and the next-door neighbor we caught 29 little rats. After a while, more came. Anita used to chase them across the room to see if she could catch them, and the boys who came to the house would say, "Look, a rat."

I would tell them, "Let it be, it's one of the family. They keep me company, now that I'm all by myself. I'm raising them for soup."

So I left them alone, but before I knew it, there were great big rats here. One Sunday I said to Catín, who had just eaten a breaded cutlet, "Catín, you'd better go bathe or the rats will eat you up." Then I forgot about it and she lay down. Later I took a bath and went to bed. About midnight, Catín screamed, "*Ay, ay, ay,* it bit me!" The first thing that came to my mind was that it was a snake or a scorpion. "What bit you?" I asked and when I turned on the light, she said, "Look, look!" and I could see a rat running away.

She had been bitten on the arm and I could see the little teeth marks. I squeezed out the blood and smeared urine and bay rum on it.

Then I said, "Catín, you'd better come into my bed with me. God knows whether it was because the crib is dirty or you are dirty." I was wearing only panties, Chuito and Anita were naked, but Catín was wearing a jacket and pants. Well, later that same rat came and bit her again on the other arm. I sprinkled bay rum all over the bed where she was sleeping and rubbed it on her and nothing else happened that night.

The next day I went to the church and told the Sister that the girl had been bitten by a rat. She told me that if Catín didn't start running a fever, to leave her alone, and if she did, to take her to the hospital. Then I said to Catín, "You see? That's what happens when you don't bathe." She took a bath every day after that.

At the end of the year, Anita got a rat bite on the lip. I squeezed it out for her and it dried up and she didn't get a fever or anything. A few days after that, I was sitting in a chair with my arm hanging down when a rat came and *pra!* it tried to take off my finger. It wanted human flesh. I lifted my hand, and the rat ran to a hole and disappeared.

Then I said to myself, "These rats have to be finished off. I can't live like this with so many blessed rats. There are more rats than people." And I bought a trap from the man next door. I fixed the bacon myself and put it in the trap. First I caught a real big rat, then another, and another. Three in all that same night. But there were still more left.

The next morning, I heard screams coming from Rosa Maria's room up above. I said, "Rosa, what's wrong?" Her little boy was crying and shaking his hand, with a rat hanging from it. "Kill it," I said, but he answered, "I can't. Its teeth are stuck in my finger." Finally he got it off by dragging it along the floor. Rosa Maria attended him but the next day the child had a fever which kept going up. The doctor said that the boy was getting tetanus and had to go to the hospital.

The people upstairs leave a lot of rotting clothes piled there, and cans of food and rice. If they don't get rid of that filth, the rats won't leave. I asked the landlord to cover the holes because the rats keep coming in and out as if they were in a bus terminal. He said he didn't live here and I should do it myself.

There are lots of cockroaches in my room too. And new fleas have come in, I don't know from where, except probably from the rats themselves. There are also crickets and lizards. These houses are hollow underneath, and below the floor there's a lot of old boards and filth and all kinds of garbage that has accumulated, and at night the animals come crawling up.

I've noticed that it's on Thursday nights that the rats give us the most trouble. Every other Thursday, before the social worker comes, I clean my house from top to bottom so there are no crumbs on the floor for the rats to eat and no dirty dishes for them to clean. I've learned that unless I leave something for them, the rats come closer and closer to us. When the house is clean, we are in more danger of getting bitten.

The social worker told me it would be a good idea to get the children out of La Esmeralda because there's so much delinquency there. My moving to the housing project was practically her idea; she insisted and insisted. Finally one day she came to me and said, "Tomorrow you have to move to the *caserío* in Villa Hermosa." I didn't want to upset her because she's been good to me, so I said okay.

You should have seen this place when I moved in. It was bursting with garbage and smelling of shit, pure shit. Imagine, when the social worker opened the door that first day, a breeze happened to blow her way. She stepped back and said, "Wait, I can't go in. This is barbarous." I had to go outside with her. I tell you, the people who lived here before me were dirtier than the dirtiest pig. When I moved out of my little room in La Esmeralda, I scrubbed it so clean you could have eaten off the floor. Whoever moved in could see that a decent person had lived there. And then I came here and found this pig-sty, and the place looked so big I felt too little and weak to get it clean. So, fool that I am, instead of sending out for a mop and getting right down to work, I just stood in a corner and cried. I locked the door and stayed in all day, weeping. I cried floods.

And this place isn't like La Esmeralda, you know, where there's so much liveliness and noise and something is always going on. Here you never see any movement on the street, not one little domino or card game or anything. The place is dead. People act as if they're angry or in mourning. Either they don't know how to live or they're afraid to. And yet it's full of shameless good-for-nothings. It's true what the proverb says, "May God deliver me from quiet places; I can defend myself in the wild ones."

Everything was so strange to me when I first moved here that I was scared to death. I hated to go out because it's hard to find your way back to this place even if you know the address. The first couple of times I got lost, and I didn't dare ask anybody the way for fear they would fall on me and beat me. If anyone knocked on my door I thought four times before deciding to open it. Then when I did, I took a knife along. But I'm not like that any more. I've made my decision: if someone wants to kill me, let him. I can't live shut in like that. And if anybody interferes with me it will be the worse for them. I have a couple of tricks up my sleeve and can really fuck things up for anybody when I want to.

After a few days, I finally started cleaning up the place. I scrubbed the floors and put everything in order. I even painted the whole apartment, although I had to fight tooth and nail with the man in charge of the buildings in order to get the paint. The old man wanted to get something from me in return, but I wouldn't give it to him. I never have been attracted to old men.

The apartment is a good one. I have a living room, bedroom, kitchen, porch and my own private bathroom. That's something I never had in La Esmeralda. I clean it every morning and when the children use it I go and pull the chain right away.

I never had a kitchen sink in La Esmeralda either, and here I have a brand new one. It's easy to wash the dishes in these double sinks because they're so wide and comfortable. The only trouble is the water, because sometimes it goes off and the electricity, too—three times since I've been here.

I still don't have an ice-box or refrigerator but the stove here is the first electric one I've ever had in my life. I didn't know how to light it the day I moved in. I tried everything I could think of, backward and forward. Luckily, the social worker came and she lit it for me, but even so I didn't learn and Nanda had to show me again that afternoon. She has worked for rich people so long that she knows all those things. I really miss my own little kerosene stove, but Nanda wanted it, so what could I do? She's my *mamá* and if she hankered after a star I would climb up to heaven to get it for her if I could.

The main advantage of the electric stove is that when I have a lot of work to do and it gets to be ten or eleven o'clock, I just connect the stove and have lunch ready in no time. In La Esmeralda I had to wait for the kerosene to light up well before I could even start to cook. And this stove doesn't smoke and leave soot all over the place, either. Still, if the power fails again or is cut off because I don't pay my bill, the kids will just have to go hungry. I won't even be able to heat a cup of milk for them. In La Esmeralda, whenever I didn't have a quarter to buy a full gallon of kerosene, I got ten cents worth. But who's going to sell you five or ten cents worth of electricity?

I haven't seen any rats here, just one tiny little mouse. It doesn't bother me much because it lives down below, in a hole at the bottom of the stairs. There's no lack of company anywhere, I guess—rats in La Esmeralda and lots of little cockroaches here.

This apartment is so big that I don't have to knock myself out keeping it in order. There's plenty of room for my junk. I even have closets here, and lots of shelves. I have so many shelves and so few dishes that I have to put a dish here and a dish there just to keep each shelf from being completely empty. All the counters and things are no use at all to me, because I just cook a bit of oatmeal for the children and let them sit anywhere to eat it since I have no dishes with which to set a table. Half of my plates broke on the way from La Esmeralda. I guess they wanted to stay back there where they weren't so lonely.

Here even my saints cry! They look so sad. They think I am punishing them. This house is so big I had to separate the saints and hang them up in different places just to cover the empty walls. In La Esmeralda I kept them all together to form a little altar, and I lit candles for them. In La Esmeralda they helped me, but here I ask until I'm tired of asking and they don't help me at all. They are punishing me.

In La Esmeralda I never seemed to need as many things as here. I think it is because we all had about the same, so we didn't need any more. But here, when you go to other people's apartment and see all their things . . . It's not that I'm jealous. God forbid! I don't want anyone to have less than they have. It's only that I would like to have things of my own too.

What does bother me is the way people here come into my apartment and furnish the place with their mouths. They start saying, "Oh, here's where the set of furniture should go; you need a TV set in that corner and this one is just right for a record-player." And so on. I bite my tongue to keep from swearing at them because, damn it, I have good taste too. I know a TV set would look fine in that corner, but if I don't have the money to buy one, how can I put it there? That's what I like about La Esmeralda—if people there could help someone, they did; if not, they kept their mouths shut.

I really would like a TV though, because they don't have public sets here, the way they do in La Esmeralda. I filled in some blanks for that program, Queen for a Day, to see if I can get one as a gift. It was Nanda's idea and she's so lucky that maybe I will get it. If I do, then at least I could spend the holidays looking at TV. And the children might stay home instead of wandering around the neighborhood so much.

The traffic here really scares me. That's the main reason I don't like this place. Cars scud by like clouds in a high wind and, I'm telling you, I'm always afraid a car will hit the children. If something should happen to my little penguins, I'd go mad, I swear I would. My kids are little devils, and when I bring them in through the front door, they slip out again by climbing over the porch railing. Back in La Esmeralda, where our house was so small, they had to play out in the street whenever people came over, but here there is plenty of room to run around indoors.

Maybe I was better off in La Esmeralda. You certainly have to pay for the comforts you have here! Listen, I'm jittery, really nervous, because if you fail to pay the rent even once here, the following month you're thrown out. I hardly ever got behind on my payments in La Esmeralda, but if I did, I knew that they wouldn't put me out on the street. It's true that my rent is only $6.50 a month here while I paid $11.50 in La Esmeralda, but there I didn't have a water bill and I paid only $1.50 a month for electricity. Here I have already had to pay $3.50 for electricity and if I use more than the minimum they allow in water, I'll have to pay for that too. And I do so much washing!

It's a fact that as long as I lived in La Esmeralda I could always scare up some money, but here I'm always broke. I've gone as much as two days without eating. I don't play the races at El Comandante any more. I can't afford to. And I can't sell *bolita* numbers here because several cops live in this *caserío* and the place is full of detectives. Only the other day I almost sold a number to one of them, but luckily I was warned in time. I don't want to be arrested for anything in the world, not because I'm scared of being in jail but because of the children.

Since I can't sell numbers here, I sell Avon cosmetics. I like the pretty sets of china they give away, and I'm trying to sell a lot so that they'll give me one. But there's hardly any profit in it for me.

In La Esmeralda I could get an old man now and then to give me five dollars for sleeping with him. But here I haven't found anything like that at all. The truth is, if a man comes here and tries to strike up a conversation I usually slam the door in his face. So, well, I have this beautiful, clean apartment, but what good does it do me? Where am I to get money? I can't dig for it.

In La Esmeralda we used to buy things cheap from thieves. They stole from people who lived far away and then they came to La Esmeralda through one of the side entrances to sell. And who the hell is going to go looking for his things down there? Not a chance! You hardly ever saw a rich person in La Esmeralda. We didn't like them, and we scared them off. But so far as I can tell, these dopes around here always steal from the *blanquitos*, the rich people, nearby. Suppose one of them took it into his head to come here to look for the missing stuff? What then?

Since I've moved I'm worse off than I have ever been before, because now I realize all the things I lack and, besides, the rich people around here are always wanting everything for themselves. In La Esmeralda you can bum a nickel from any one. But with these people, the more they have, the more they want. It's everything for themselves. If you ask them for work, they'll find something for you to do fast enough, but when it's time to pay you'd think it hurt them to pull a dollar out of their pocket.

Listen, to get a few beans from some people who live in a house near here I had to help pick and shell them. People here are real hard and stingy. What's worse, they take advantage of you. The other day I ironed all day long for a woman and all I got for it was two dollars and my dinner. I felt like throwing the money in her face but I just calmly took it. I would have been paid six dollars at the very least for a whole day's ironing in La Esmeralda. At another lady's house near here I cooked, washed the dishes, even scrubbed the floor, and for all that she just gave me one of her old dresses, which I can't even wear because it's too big for me.

Right now, I don't have a cent. The lady next door lets me charge the food for breakfast at her husband's *kiosko*. She's become so fond of me, you can't imagine. Her husband won't sell on credit to anybody, but there's nothing impossible for the person who is really interested in helping you out. She trusts me, so she lets me write down what I take and keep the account myself.

I buy most of my food at the Villa Hermosa grocery. It's a long way from here and I have to walk it on foot every time I need something, like rice or tomato sauce. It's a supermarket, so they don't give credit, but everything is cheaper there, much cheaper. A can of tomato sauce costs seven cents there and 10 cents in La Esmeralda. Ten pounds of rice costs $1.25 in La Esmeralda and 99 cents here. The small bottles of King Pine that cost 15 cents each in La Esmeralda are two for a quarter here.

Sometimes Public Welfare gives me food, but not always, and I don't like most of the things they give. That long-grained rice doesn't taste like anything. It's like eating hay. The meat they give has fat on top and it comes in a can and it's real dark. They say it's corned beef but I don't know. The same goes for that powdered milk. Who could drink the stuff? In La Esmeralda I saved it until I was really hard up and then I sold it to anybody who was willing to shell out a quarter for it to feed it to their animals or something. But I don't dare do that here because it's federal government food, and it's against the law to sell it. I could get into trouble that way in a place like this, where I don't know anybody. I might try to sell that stuff to a detective without realizing who he was and I'd land in jail.

I haven't been to La Esmeralda often since I moved here, because I can't afford it. Every trip costs 40 cents, 20 cents each way. I want to pay off all my debts in La Esmeralda so that I can hold my head high and proud when I go there. I want people to think I've bettered myself because one can't be screwed all one's life. Even now when I visit, still owing money as I do, I put on my best clothes and always try to carry a little cash. I do this so Minerva, Emilio's aunt, won't get the idea I'm starving or anything like that. She really suffers when she sees me in La Esmeralda, and I do all that just to bother her. I dress up the kids real nice and take them to call on everybody except her.

When I first moved out of La Esmeralda, nobody knew that I was leaving, in the first place because it made me sad and in the second place because that old Minerva had gone around telling everybody she hoped I'd clear out. She even said it to my face. I'd yell back at her, "What right do you have to say that? Did you buy La Esmeralda or something?"

Another reason why I hardly ever go to La Esmeralda is because Emilio spies on me. He has come after me in the *caserío* just the way he did in La Esmeralda, though not as often. He likes to use the shower in my new apartment when he comes. When I start home after visiting La Esmeralda, he gets into his car and drives along behind me, offering to give me a lift. But, listen, I wouldn't get into that car even if I had to walk all the way from San Juan to Villa Hermosa. I put a curse on that car, such a tremendous curse that I'm just waiting to see it strike. I did it one day when Anita had asthma and I had no money to take her to the hospital. I happened to glance out of the window and I saw Emilio stretched out in his car, relaxed as could be, as if he deserved nothing but the best. I let go and yelled with all the breath in my chest, "I hope to God someday you'll wear that car as a hat. I hope it turns to dust with you all fucked up inside." Now I can't ride in the car, because I'm afraid the curse will come true some time when both of us are in it.

You can't imagine how lonely I feel here. I have friends, but they're sort of artificial, pasted-on friends. I couldn't confide in them at all. For example, I got pregnant a little while ago, and I had to have an abortion. I nearly went crazy thinking about it. Having a baby is nothing, it's the burden you have to take on afterwards, especially with a cowardly husband like mine who takes the easiest way out, denying that the child is his. So there I was, pregnant and, you know, I was ashamed. I was already out of La Esmeralda, see? Well, I know that my womb is weak, so I took two doses of Epsom salts with quinine and out came the kid. You can't imagine how unpleasant that is. In La Esmeralda you can tell everybody about it, and that sort of eases your heart. But here I didn't tell anybody. These girls I know here are *señoritas*, mere children, and something like that . . . *ay, bendito!*

But, to tell you the truth, I don't know what they call a *señorita* here in Villa Hermosa. The way it is in La Esmeralda, a girl and boy fall in love. For a few months they control themselves. Then they can't any more, and the boy does what he has to do to the girl. The hole is bigger than the full moon and that's that. They tell everybody and become husband and wife in the eyes of all the world. There's no trying to hide it. But here you see girls, who by rights should already have had a couple of kids, trying to keep from being found out. They'll go to a hotel with their sweethearts and let them stick their pricks into every hole in their body except the right one. And then they're so brazen as to come out of that hotel claiming they're still *señoritas*. It's plain shameless.

There are some policemen here who make love like this to some girls I know. Well, the policeman who did it to my friend Mimi came and told me that if I loaned him my bed for a little while he would give me three pesos. As that money wouldn't be bad at all and as he wasn't going to do it to me, I rented him the bed and grabbed the three pesos. Let them go screw! They locked themselves in the bedroom for a little while and then they went away. It was none of my business. If they didn't do it here, they would go do it somewhere else. And she didn't lose her virginity or anything here. So my hands are clean.

Sometimes I want to go back to La Esmeralda to live and other times I don't. It's not that I miss my family so much. On the contrary, relatives can be very bothersome. But you do need them in case you get sick because then you can dump the children on them. Sometimes I cry for loneliness here. Sometimes I'm bored to death. There's more neighborliness in La Esmeralda. I was used to having good friends stop by my house all the time. I haven't seen much of this neighborhood because I never go out. There's a Catholic church nearby but I've never been there. And I haven't been to the movies once since I've been living here. In La Esmeralda I used to go now and then. And in La Esmeralda, when nothing else was going on, you could at least hear the sea.

In La Esmeralda nobody ever made fun of my lameness. On the contrary, it was an advantage because everyone went out of his way to help me: "Let me help the lame girl. Let me buy *bolita* numbers from Lame Crucita, because cripples bring luck." But it isn't like that here, where people just laugh. That's why I'd like to live in La Esmeralda again or have Nanda move in here with me.

The social worker told me that I could go to the hospital and have an operation to fix my back. But who could I leave my little baby crows with? And suppose what they do is take my guts out in order to make me look right? Still, now that I live in a place like Villa Hermosa, I would like to have an operation to make me straight.

19 / THE UPPER CRUST: REVIEW OF STEPHEN BIRMINGHAM'S *THE RIGHT PEOPLE*

Paul D. Zimmerman

Having anatomized America's Jewish elite in his best seller, "Our Crowd," free-lance writer Stephen Birmingham now turns a jaundiced, sometimes unsteady eye upon "Real Society." "In America," he explains, "there is Society. Then there is Real Society. Real Society is part of Society—the upper part. Everybody who is in Society knows who the the people in Real Society are. But the people in Real Society do not necessarily know who the other Society people are."

Nor, Birmingham adds, do they really care. The denizens of Real Society—the Auchinclosses, the Morgans, the Spreckelses, the Saltonstalls, the Peabodys—carry impeccable credentials and need only know who is in, not who is out. Perhaps, once upon a time, they were parvenus but their money is "old money" now, their antecedents have been respectable for at least several generations and, most important, their sense of their rightful place in the social stratosphere is secure enough to relieve them of the chore of following the ups and downs of social climbers beneath them.

Members of Real Society, Birmingham contends, have a "look" about them, a simple style of dressing that never falls from fashion, an accent all their own that mixes the flat A of New England with a patina of Brooklynese and soupçon of Southern drawl, a particular way of thinking, and even, according to one observer, a special smell of their own.

They are not so much special by birth as by breeding. The "right people" send their children to the "right schools." Boys prep at "St. Grottlesex"—a catchall name for St. Mark's, St. Paul's, St. George's, Groton, Middlesex. Choate and Hotchkiss are also permissible. Girls attend Foxcroft, Miss Porter's, Westover, Madeira, Dobbs, Ethel Walker or Chatham Hall. Boys go on to Princeton or Yale—not Harvard. "Princeton has a lot of style," writes Birmingham, voicing the view of Real Society, "but Yale is solider."

The girls continue their education at one of the Seven Sisters schools of which Barnard, oddly enough, is considered the toniest, or at equally regarded junior colleges like Bennett, Briarcliff and Colby. The girls will

---

play field hockey, whose social stock is rising. The boys will specialize in the "racquet sports"—tennis, squash and court tennis—which have supplanted football and crew as fit recreation. The girls, if they belong to Real Society in New York, will come out at private parties given by their parents or, failing that, the Grosvenor Ball at the Plaza, but not at the Waldorf-Astoria's Cotillion.

FOURSOME

Where they live does not matter so much as how they live. One can even belong to Real Society in San Francisco, despite its inferiority complex vis-à-vis the East, *if* one has Style. Mrs. Adolph Spreckels, grande dame of San Francisco, entertains where she pleases—in her bedroom or in one of her 25 spacious bathrooms, each decked out with a bridge table in in case a foursome materializes. She is fond of visiting her chief philanthropy, the California Palace of the Legion of Honor, clad in mink and night-gown. When she invites friends to her pool, the 82-year-old dowager occasionally adds, "Of course, I swim in the raw hope you don't mind, pet." Once, when her daughter sent her a picture of the Duke of Windsor with a note, "Look who I'm sitting with," Mrs. Spreckels replied: "Well, I give up. Who is it?"

To those who say Society is dead, Birmingham offers proof that it is alive and well in Newport, Boston, Philadelphia and New York. Many of his judgments are open to dispute, but, right or wrong, he takes the smallest social difference seriously. "When a person says . . . Real Society is dead and gone, it is reasonably safe to assume that that person is not a member. People in Real Society know that their world is very much alive. But they don't think it is quite polite to say so."

20 / THE FORGOTTEN AMERICAN

Peter Schrag

There is hardly a language to describe him, or even a set of social statistics. Just names: racist-bigot-redneck-ethnic-Irish-Italian-Pole-Hunkie-Yahoo. The lower middle class. A blank. The man under whose hat lies the great American desert. Who watches the tube, plays the horses, and keeps the niggers out of his union and his neighborhood. Who might vote for Wallace (but didn't). Who cheers when the cops beat up on demonstrators. Who is free, white, and twenty-one, has a job, a home, a family, and is up to his eyeballs in credit. In the guise of the working class—or the American yeoman or John Smith—he was once the hero of the civics book, the man that Andrew Jackson called "the bone and sinew of the country." Now he is "the forgotten man," perhaps the most alienated person in America.

Nothing quite fits, except perhaps omission and semi-invisibility. America is supposed to be divided between affluence and poverty, between slums and suburbs. John Kenneth Galbraith begins the foreword to *The Affluent Society* with the phrase, "Since I sailed for Switzerland in the early summer 1955 to begin work on this book . . ." But *between* slums and suburbs, between Scarsdale and Harlem, between Wellesley and Roxbury, between Shaker Heights and Hough, there are some eighty million people (depending on how you count them) who didn't sail for Switzerland in the summer of 1955, or at any other time, and who never expect to. Between slums and suburbs: South Boston and South San Francisco, Bell and Parma, Astoria and Bay Ridge, Newark, Cicero, Downey, Daly City, Charlestown, Flatbush. Union halls, American Legion posts, neighborhood bars and bowling leagues, the Ukrainian Club and the Holy Name. Main Street. To try to describe all this is like trying to describe America itself. If you look for it, you find it everywhere: the rows of frame houses overlooking the belching steel mills in Bethlehem, Pennsylvania, two-family brick houses in Canarsie (where the most common slogan, even in the middle of a political campaign, is "curb your dog"); the Fords and Chevies with a decal American flag on the rear window (usually a cut-out from the *Reader's Digest,* and displayed in counter-protest against peaceniks and "those bastard who carry Vietcong flags in demonstrations"); the bunting on the porch rail with the inscription, "Welcome Home, Pete." The gold star in the window.

When he was Under Secretary of Housing and Urban Development, Robert C. Wood tried a definition. It is not good, but it's the best we have:

> He is a white employed male . . . earning between $5,000 and $10,000. He works regularly, steadily, dependably, wearing a blue collar or white collar. Yet the frontiers of his career expectations have been fixed since he reached the age of thirty-five, when he found that he had too many obligations, too much family, and too few skills to match opportunities with aspirations.
>
> This definition of the "working American" involves almost 23-million American families.
>
> The working American lives in the gray area fringes of a central city or in a close-in or very far-out cheaper suburban subdivision of a large metropolitan area. He is likely to own a home and a car, especially as his income begins to rise. Of those earning between $6,000 and $7,500, 70 per cent own their own homes and 94 per cent drive their own cars.
>
> 94 per cent have no education beyond high school and 43 per cent have only completed the eighth grade.

He does all the right things, obeys the law, goes to church and insists—usually—that his kids get a better education than he had. But the right things don't seem to be paying off. While he is making more than he ever made—perhaps more than he'd ever dreamed—he's still struggling while a lot of others—"them" (on welfare, in demonstrations, in the ghettos) are getting most of the attention. "I'm working my ass off," a guy tells you on a stoop in South Boston. "My kids don't have a place to swim, my parks are full of glass, and I'm supposed to bleed for a bunch of people on relief." In New York a man who drives a Post Office trailer truck at night (4:00 P.M. to midnight) and a cab during the day (7:00 A.M. to 2:00 P.M.), and who hustles radios for his Post Office buddies on the side, is ready, as he says, to "knock somebody's ass." "The colored guys work when they feel like it. Sometimes they show up and sometimes they don't. One guy tore up all the time cards. I'd like to see a white guy do that and get away with it."

WHAT COUNTS

Nobody knows how many people in America moonlight (half of the eighteen million families in the $5,000 to $10,000 bracket have two or more wage earners) or how many have to hustle on the side. "I don't think anybody has a single job anymore," said Nicholas Kisburg, the research director for a Teamsters Union Council in New York. "All the cops are moonlighting, and the teachers; and there's a million guys who are hustling, guys with phony social-security numbers who are hiding part of what they make so they don't get kicked out of a housing project, or guys who work as guards at sports events and get free meals that they don't want to pay taxes on. Every one of them is cheating. They are underground people—*Untermenschen*. . . . We really have no systematic data on any of this. We have no ideas of the attitudes of the white worker. (We've been too busy studying the black worker.) And yet he's the source of most of the reaction in this country."

The reaction is directed at almost every visible target: at integration and welfare, taxes and sex education, at the rich and the poor, the foundations and students, at the "smart people in the suburbs." In New York State the legislature cuts the welfare budget; in Los Angeles, the voters reelect Yorty after a whispered racial campaign against the Negro favorite. In Minneapolis a police detective named Charles Stenvig, promising "to take the handcuffs off the police," wins by a margin stunning even to his supporters: in Massachusetts the voters mail tea bags to their representatives in protest against new taxes, and in state after state legislatures are passing bills to punish student demonstrators. ("We keep talking about permissiveness in training kids," said a Los Angeles labor official, "but we forget that these are our kids.")

And yet all these things are side manifestations of a malaise that lacks a language. Whatever law and order means, for example, to a man who feels his wife is unsafe on the street after dark or in the park at any time, or whose kids get shaken down in the school yard, it also means something like normality—the demand that everybody play it by the book, that cultural and social standards be somehow restored to their civics-book simplicity, that things shouldn't be as they are but as they were supposed to be. If there is a revolution in this country—a revolt in manners, standards of dress and obscenity, and, more importantly, in our official sense of what America is—there is also a counter-revolt. Sometimes it is inarticulate, and sometimes (perhaps most of the time) people are either too confused or apathetic—or simply too polite and too decent—to declare themselves. In Astoria, Queens, a white working-class district of New York, people who make $7,000 or $8,000 a year (sometimes in two jobs) call themselves affluent, even though the Bureau of Labor Statistics regards an income of less than $9,500 in New York inadequate to a moderate standard of living. And in a similar neighborhood in Brooklyn a truck driver who earns $151 a week tells you he's doing well, living in a two-story frame house separated by a narrow driveway from similar houses, thousands of them in block after block. This year, for the first time, he will go on a cruise—he and his wife and two other couples—two weeks in the Caribbean. He went to work after World War II ($57 a week) and he has lived in the same house for twenty years, accumulating two television sets, wall-to-wall carpeting in a small living room, and a basement that he recently remodeled into a recreation room with the help of two moonlighting firemen. "We get fairly good salaries, and this is a good neighborhood, one of the few good ones left. We have no smoked Irishmen around."

Stability is what counts, stability in job and home and neighborhood, stability in the church and in friends. At night you watch television and sometimes on a weekend you go to a nice place—maybe a downtown hotel—for dinner with another couple. (Or maybe your sister, or maybe bowling, or maybe, if you're defeated, a night at the track.) The wife has the necessary appliances, often still being paid off, and the money you save goes for your daughter's orthodontist, and later for her wedding. The smoked Irishmen—the colored (no one says black; few even say Negro)—represent change and instability, kids who cause trouble in school, who get treatment that your kids never got, that you never got. ("Those fucking kids," they tell you in South Boston, "raising hell, and not one of 'em paying his own way. Their fucking mothers are all on welfare.") The black kids mean a change in the rules, a double standard in grades and discipline, and—vaguely—a challenge to all you believed right. Law and order is the stability and predictability of established ways. Law and order is equal treatment—in school, in jobs, in the courts—even if you're cheating a little yourself. The Forgotten Man is Jackson's man. He is the vestigial American democrat of 1840: "They all know that their success depends upon their own industry and economy and that they must not expect to become suddenly rich by the fruits of their toil." He is also Franklin Roosevelt's man—the man whose vote (or whose father's vote) sustained the New Deal.

There are other considerations, other styles, other problems. A postman in a Charlestown (Boston) housing project: eight children and a ninth on the way. Last year, by working overtime, his income went over $7,000. This year, because he reported it, the Housing Authority is raising his rent from $78 to $106 a month, a catastrophe for a family that pays $2.20 a day for milk, has never had a vacation, and for which an excursion is "going out for ice cream." "You try and save for something better; we hope to get out of here to someplace where the kids can play, where there's no broken glass, and then something always comes along that knocks you right back. It's like being at the bottom of the well waiting for a guy to throw you a rope." The description becomes almost

Chaplinesque. Life is humble but not simple; the terrors of insolent bureaucracies and contemptuous officials produce a demonology that loses little of its horror for being partly misunderstood. You want to get a sink fixed but don't want to offend the manager; want to get an eye operation that may (or may not) have been necessitated by a military injury five years earlier, "but the Veterans Administration says I signed away my benefits"; want to complain to someone about the teen-agers who run around breaking windows and harassing women but get no response either from the management or the police. "You're afraid to complain because if they don't get you during the day they'll get you at night." Automobiles, windows, children, all become hostages to the vague terrors of everyday life; everything is vulnerable. Liabilities that began long ago cannot possibly be liquidated: "I never learned anything in that school except how to fight. I got tired of being caned by the teachers so at sixteen I quit and joined the Marines. I still don't know anything."

AT THE BOTTOM OF THE WELL

American culture? Wealth is visible, and so, now, is poverty. Both have become intimidating clichés. But the rest? A vast, complex, and disregarded world that was once—in belief, and in fact—the American middle: Greyhound and Trailways bus terminals in little cities at midnight, each of them with its neon lights and its cardboard hamburgers; acres of tar-paper beach bungalows in places like Revere and Rockaway; the hair curlers in the supermarket on Saturday, and the little girls in the communion dresses the next morning; pinball machines and the *Daily News*, the *Reader's Digest* and Ed Sullivan; houses with tiny front lawns (or even large ones) adorned with statues of the Virgin or of Sambo welcomin' de folks home; Clint Eastwood or Julie Andrews at the Palace; the trotting tracks and the dog tracks—Aurora Downs, Connaught Park, Roosevelt, Yonkers, Rockingham, and forty others—where gray men come not for sport and beauty, but to read numbers, to study and dope. (If you win you have figured something, have in a small way controlled your world, have surmounted your impotence. If you lose, bad luck, shit. "I'll break his goddamned head.") Baseball is not the national pastime; racing is. For every man who goes to a major-league baseball game there are four who go to the track and probably four more who go to the candy store or the barbershop to make their bets. (Total track attendance in 1965: 62 million plus another 10 million who went to the dogs.)

There are places, and styles, and attitudes. If there are neighborhoods of aspiration, suburban enclaves for the mobile young executive and the aspiring worker, there are also places of limited expectation and dead-end districts where mobility is finished. But even there you can often find, however vestigial, a sense of place, the roots of old ethnic loyalties, and a passionate, if often futile, battle against intrusion and change. "Everybody around here," you are told, "pays his own way." In this world the problems are not the ABM or air pollution (have they heard of Biafra?) or the international population crisis; the problem is to get your street cleaned, your garbage collected, to get your husband home from Vietnam alive; to negotiate installment payments and to keep the schools orderly. Ask anyone in Scarsdale or Winnetka about the schools and they'll tell you about new programs, or about how many are getting into Harvard, or about the teachers; ask in Oakland or the North Side of Chicago, and they'll tell you that they have (or haven't) had trouble. Somewhere in his gut the man in those communities knows that mobility and choice in this society are limited. He cannot imagine any major change for the better; but he can imagine change for the worse. And yet for a decade he is the one who has been asked to carry the burden of social reform, to integrate his schools and his neighborhood, has been asked by comfortable people to pay the social debts due to the poor and the black. In Boston, in San Francisco, in Chicago (not to mention Newark or Oakland) he has been telling the reformers to go to hell. The Jewish school-teachers of New York and the Irish parents of Dorchester have asked the same question: "What the hell did Lindsay (or the Beacon Hill Establishment) ever do for us?"

The ambiguities and changes in American life that occupy discussions in university seminars and policy debates in Washington, and that form the backbone of contemporary popular sociology, become increasingly the conditions of trauma and frustration in the middle. Although the New Frontier and Great Society contained some programs for those not already on the rolls of social pathology—federal aid for higher education, for example—the public priorities and the rhetoric contained little. The emphasis, properly, was on the poor, on the inner cities (*e.g.*, Negroes) and the unemployed. But in Chicago a widow with three children who earns $7,000 a year can't get them college loans because she makes too much; the money is reserved for people on relief. New schools are built in the ghetto but not in the white working-class neighborhoods where they are just as dilapidated. In Newark the head of a white vigilante group (now a city councilman) runs, among other things, on a platform opposing pro-Negro discrimination. "When pools are being built in the Central Ward—don't they think white kids have got frustration? The white can't get a job; we have to hire Negroes first." The middle class, said Congressman Roman Pucinski of Illinois, who represents a lot of it, "is in revolt. Everyone has been generous in supporting anti-poverty. Now the middle-class American is disqualified from most of the programs."

UNIT G / ISSUES FOR CONSIDERATION

1. What are some areas in which the norms of our society vary according to one's social class?
2. Because of her impoverished condition, the woman in Lewis's article spent a great deal of her time with health problems. Describe how the time required of the lower-class person in dealing with the necessities of life makes his life different from the life of the middle- or upper-class person?
3. To be rich in America and accepted as part of the upper-class takes more than money. What else does it take?
4. Why do the middle Americans in Schrag's article place such importance on law and order?
5. What are some of the problems a person from a lower-class family would have in adjusting to the expectations of a middle-class position?

UNIT H
RACE:
BLACK AND WHITE

It is certainly true that in American society the color of an individual's skin is for many of prime importance in "understanding" that individual. When there is a widespread notion that all persons with a particular racial background have certain characteristics in common, e.g. "all Negroes are lazy," we have what we call a *stereotype*. White liberals went through a long period of moralizing about the evils of stereotyping, suggesting that under the skin every man is alike, regardless of his race. It is true that when a stereotype has no foundation and is used to degrade and deprive a person of his individuality, it is not good. However, the second part of the liberals' message, that we are all alike, is poor sociology. It would lead us to the conclusion that years of slavery, followed by more than a hundred years of oppression of the black man in America, have had no effect on him "under his skin." If we accept the premise that the norms and values that make up a culture have an impact on the members of society, and the further premise that in American society we differentiate members according to race, we must conclude that there are differences among races. Members of minorities seemed to realize this before the white liberals. In the mid-1960's the goals of integration were discarded to a great extent in the black movement in America and replaced by an attitude of "black is beautiful." Integration said we are all alike, while "black is beautiful" says that we are different and can be proud of our differences.

One of the results of the new attitudes of minorities is a reminder that the majority are members of a race themselves. Eldridge Cleaver, a writer and Minister of Information of the Black Panther Party, brings home that message in his article on the white race. The selection on the black athlete gives a picture of what it is like to be black in the sports world. The series of articles and book from which this selection is drawn have gone a long way toward destroying the myth that sports have made a major contribution to the improvement of race relations.

Can you apply the notions of a social institution to athletics in American society? If so, how does this affect the problems of the individual athlete?

21 / THE WHITE RACE AND ITS HEROES

Eldridge Cleaver

White people cannot, in the generality, be taken as models of how to live. Rather, the white man is himself in sore need of new standards, which will release him from his confusion and place him once again in fruitful communion with the depths of his own being.

James Baldwin,
—*The Fire Next Time*

Right from the go, let me make one thing absolutely clear: I am not now, nor have I ever been, a white man. Nor, I hasten to add, am I now a Black Muslim—although I used to be. But I *am* an Ofay Watcher, a member of that unchartered, amorphous league which has members on all continents and the islands of the seas. Ofay Watchers Anonymous, we might be called, because we exist concealed in the shadows wherever colored people have known oppression by whites, by white enslavers, colonizers, imperialists, and neo-colonialists.

Did it irritate you, compatriot, for me to string those epithets out like that? Tolerate me. My intention was not necessarily to sprinkle salt over anyone's wounds. I did it primarily to relieve a certain pressure on my brain. Do you cop that? If not, then we're in trouble, because we Ofay Watchers have a pronounced tendency to slip into that mood. If it is bothersome to you, it is quite a task for me because not too long ago it was my way of life to preach, as ardently as I could, that the white race is a race of devils, created by their maker to do evil, and make evil appear as good; that the white race is the natural, unchangeable enemy of the black man, who is the original man, owner, maker, cream of the planet Earth; that the white race was soon to be destroyed by Allah, and that the black man would then inherit the earth, which has always, in fact, been his.

I have, so to speak, washed my hands in the blood of the martyr, Malcolm X, whose retreat from the precipice of madness created new room for others to turn about in, and I am now caught up in that tiny space, attempting a maneuver of my own. Having renounced the teachings of Elijah Muhammad, I find that a rebirth does not follow automatically, of its own accord, that a void is left in one's vision, and this void seeks constantly to obliterate itself by pulling one back to one's former outlook. I have tried a tentative compromise by adopting a select vocabulary, so that now when I see the whites of *their* eyes, instead of saying "devil" or "beast" I say "imperialist" or "colonialist," and everyone seems to be happier.

In silence, we have spent our years watching the ofays, trying to understand them, on the principle that you have a better chance coping with the known that with the unknown. Some of us have been, and some still are, interested in learning whether it is *ultimately* possible to live in the same territory with people who seem so disagreeable to live with; still others want to get as far away from ofays as possible. What we share in common is the desire to break the ofays' power over us.

At times of fundamental social change, such as the era in which we live, it is easy to be deceived by the onrush of events, beguiled by the craving for social stability into mistaking transitory phenomena for enduring reality. The strength and permanence of "white backlash" in America is just such an illusion. However much this rearguard action might seem to grow in strength, the initiative, and the future, rest with those whites and blacks who have liberated themselves from the master/slave syndrome. And these are to be found mainly among the youth.

Over the past twelve years there has surfaced a political conflict between the generations that is deeper, even, than the struggle between the races. Its first dramatic manifestation was within the ranks of the Negro people, when college students in the South, fed up with Uncle

Tom's hat-in-hand approach to revolution, threw off the yoke of the NAACP. When these students initiated the first sit-ins, their spirit spread like a raging fire across the nation, and the technique of nonviolent direct action, constantly refined and honed into a sharp cutting tool, swiftly matured. The older Negro "leaders," who are now all die-hard advocates of this tactic, scolded the students for sitting-in. The students rained down contempt upon their hoary heads. In the pre-sit-in days, these conservative leaders had always succeeded in putting down insurgent elements among the Negro people. (A measure of their power, prior to the students' rebellion, is shown by their success in isolating such great black men as the late W. E. B. DuBois and Paul Robeson, when these stalwarts, refusing to bite their tongues, lost favor with the U.S. government by their unstinting efforts to link up the Negro revolution with national liberation movements around the world.)

The "Negro leaders," and the whites who depended upon them to control their people, were outraged by the impudence of the students. Calling for a moratorium on student initiative, they were greeted instead by an encore of sit-ins, and retired to their ivory towers to contemplate the new phenomenon. Others, less prudent because held on a tighter leash by the whites, had their careers brought to an abrupt end because they thought they could lead a black/white backlash against the students, only to find themselves in a kind of Bay of Pigs. Negro college presidents, who expelled students from all-Negro colleges in an attempt to quash the demonstrations, ended up losing their jobs; the victorious students would no longer allow them to preside over the campuses. The spontaneous protests on southern campuses over the repressive measures of their college administrations were an earnest of the Free Speech upheaval which years later was to shake the UC campus at Berkeley. In countless ways, the rebellion of the black students served as catalyst for the brewing revolt of the whites.

What has suddenly happened is that the white race has lost its heroes. Worse, its heroes have been revealed as villains and its greatest heroes as the arch-villains. The new generations of whites, appalled by the sanguine and despicable record carved over the face of the globe by their race in the last five hundred years, are rejecting the panoply of white heroes, whose heroism consisted in erecting the inglorious edifice of colonialism and imperialism; heroes whose careers rested on a system of foreign and domestic exploitation, rooted in the myth of white supremacy and the manifest destiny of the white race. The emerging shape of a new world order, and the requisites for survival in such a world, are fostering in young whites a new outlook. They recoil in shame from the spectacle of cowboys and pioneers—their heroic forefathers whose exploits filled earlier generations with pride—galloping across a movie screen shooting down Indians like Coke bottles. Even Winston Churchill, who is looked upon by older whites as perhaps the greatest hero of the twentieth century—even he, because of the system of which he was a creature and which he served, is an arch-villain in the eyes of the young white rebels.

At the close of World War II, national liberation movements in the colonized world picked up new momentum and audacity, seeking to cash in on the democratic promises made by the Allies during the war. The Atlantic Charter, signed by President Roosevelt and Prime Minister Churchill in 1941, affirming "the right of all people to choose the form of government under which they may live," established the principle, although it took years of postwar struggle to give this piece of rhetoric even the appearance of reality. And just as world revolution has prompted the oppressed to re-evaluate their self-image in terms of the changing conditions, to slough off the servile attitudes inculcated by long years of subordination, the same dynamics of change have prompted the white people of the world to re-evaluate their self-image as well, to disabuse themselves of the Master Race psychology developed over centuries of imperial hegemony.

It is among the white youth of the world that the greatest change is taking place. It is they who are experiencing the great psychic pain of waking into consciousness to find their inherited heroes turned by events into villains. Communication and understanding between the older and younger generations of whites has entered a crisis. The elders, who, in the tradition of privileged classes or races, genuinely do not understand the youth, trapped by old ways of thinking and blind to the future, have only just begun to be vexed—because the youth have only just begun to rebel. So thoroughgoing is the revolution in the psyches of white youth that the traditional tolerance which every older generation has found it necessary to display is quickly exhausted, leaving a gulf of fear, hostility, mutual misunderstanding, and contempt.

The rebellion of the oppressed peoples of the world, along with the Negro revolution in America, have opened the way to a new evaluation of history, a re-examination of the role played by the white race since the beginning of European expansion. The positive achievements are also there in the record, and future generations will applaud them. But there can be no applause now, not while the master still holds the whip in his hand! Not even the master's own children can find it possible to applaud him—he cannot even applaud himself! The negative rings too loudly. Slavecatchers, slaveowners, murderers, butchers, invaders, oppressors—the white heroes have acquired new names. The great white statesmen whom school children are taught to revere are revealed as the architects of systems of human exploitation and slavery. Religious leaders are exposed as condoners and justifiers of all these evil deeds. Schoolteachers and college professors are seen as a clique of brainwashers and white-washers.

The white youth of today are coming to see, intuitively, that to escape the onus of the history their fathers made they must face and admit the moral truth concerning the works of their fathers. That such venerated figures as George Washington and Thomas Jefferson owned hundreds of black slaves, that all of the Presidents up to Lincoln presided over a slave state, and that every President since Lincoln connived politically and cynically with the issues affecting the human rights and general welfare of the broad masses of the American people—these facts weigh heavily upon the hearts of these young people.

The elders do not like to give these youngsters credit for being able to understand what is going on and what has gone on. When speaking of juvenile delinquency, or the rebellious attitude of today's youth, the elders employ a glib rhetoric. They speak of the "alienation of youth," the desire of the young to be independent, the problems of "the father image" and "the mother image" and their effect upon growing children who lack sound models upon which to pattern themselves. But they consider it bad form to connect the problems of the youth with the central events of our era—the national liberation movements abroad and the Negro revolution at home. The foundations of authority have been blasted to bits in America because the whole society has been indicted, tried, and convicted of injustice. To the youth, the elders are Ugly Americans; to the elders, the youth have gone mad.

The rebellion of the white youth has gone through four broadly discernible stages. First there was an initial recoiling away, a rejection of the conformity which America expected, and had always received, sooner or later, from its youth. The disaffected youth were refusing to participate in the system, having discovered that America, far from helping the underdog, was up to its ears in the mud trying to hold the dog down. Because of the publicity and self-advertisements of the more vocal rebels, this period has come to be known as the beatnik era, although not all of the youth affected by these changes thought of themselves as beatniks. The howl of the beatniks and their scathing, outraged denunciation of the system—characterized by Ginsberg as Moloch, a bloodthirsty Semitic deity to which the ancient tribes sacrificed their firstborn children—was a serious, irrevocable declaration of war. It is revealing that the elders looked upon the beatniks as mere obscene misfits who were too lazy to take baths and too stingy to buy a haircut. The elders had eyes but couldn't see, ears but couldn't hear—not even when the message came through as clearly as in this remarkable passage from Jack Kerouac's *On the Road*:

> At lilac evening I walked with every muscle aching among the lights of 27th and Welton in the Denver colored section, wishing I were a Negro, feeling that the best the white world had offered was not enough ecstasy for me, not enough life, joy, kicks, darkness, music, not enough night. I wished I were a Denver Mexican, or even a poor overworked Jap, anything but what I so drearily was, a "white man" disillusioned. All my life I'd had white ambitions . . . I passed the dark porches of Mexican and Negro homes, soft voices were there, occasionally the dusky knee of some mysterious sensuous gal; the dark faces of the men behind rose arbors. Little children sat like sages in ancient rocking chairs.

The second stage arrived when these young people, having decided emphatically that the world, and particularly the U.S.A., was unacceptable to them in its present form, began an active search for roles they could play in changing the society. If many of these young people were content to lay up in their cool beat pads, smoking pot and listening to jazz in a perpetual orgy of esoteric bliss, there were others, less crushed by the system, who recognized the need for positive action. Moloch could not ask for anything more than to have its disaffected victims withdraw into safe, passive, apolitical little nonparticipatory islands, in an economy less and less able to provide jobs for the growing pool of unemployed. If all the unemployed had followed the lead of the beatniks, Moloch would gladly have legalized the use of euphoric drugs and marijuana, passed out free jazz albums and sleeping bags, to all those willing to sign affidavits promising to remain "beat." The non-beat disenchanted white youth were attracted magnetically to the Negro revolution, which had begun to take on a mass, insurrectionary tone. But they had difficulty understanding their relationship to the Negro, and what role "whites" could play in a "Negro revolution." For the time being they watched the Negro activists from afar.

The third stage, which is rapidly drawing to a close, emerged when white youth started joining Negro demonstrations in large numbers. The presence of whites among the demonstrators emboldened the Negro leaders and allowed them to use tactics they never would have been able to employ with all-black troops. The racist conscience of America is such that murder does not register as murder, really, unless the victim is white. And it was only when the newspapers and magazines started carrying pictures and stories of white demonstrators being beaten and maimed by mobs and police that the public began to protest. Negroes have become so used to this double standard that they, too, react differently to the death of a white. When white freedom riders were brutalized along with blacks, a sigh of relief went up from the black masses, because the blacks knew that white blood is the coin of freedom in a land where for four hundred years black blood has been shed unremarked and with impunity. America has never truly been outraged by the murder of a black man, woman, or child. White politicians may, if Negroes are aroused by a particular murder, say with their lips what they know with their minds they should feel with their hearts—but don't.

It is a measure of what the Negro feels that when the two white and one black civil rights workers were murdered in Mississippi in 1964, the event was welcomed by Negroes on a level of understanding beyond and deeper than the grief they felt for the victims and their families. This welcoming of violence and death to whites can almost be heard—in the inevitable words, oft repeated by Negroes, that those whites, and blacks, do not die in vain. So it was with Mrs. Viola Liuzzo. And much of the anger which Negroes felt toward Martin Luther King during the Battle of Selma stemmed from the fact that he denied history a great moment, never to be recaptured, when he turned tail on the Edmund Pettus Bridge and refused to all those whites behind him what they had traveled thousands of miles to receive. If the police had turned them back by force, all those nuns, priests, rabbis, preachers, and distinguished ladies and gentlemen old and young—as they had done the Negroes a week earlier—the violence and brutality of the system would have been ruthlessly exposed. Or if, seeing King determined to lead them on to Montgomery, the troopers had stepped aside to avoid precisely the confrontation that Washington would not have tolerated, it would have signaled the capitulation of the militant white South. As it turned out, the march on Montgomery was a show of somewhat dim luster, stage-managed by the Establishment. But by this time the young whites were already active participants in the Negro revolution. In fact they had begun to transform it into something broader, with the potential of encompassing the whole of America in a radical reordering of Society.

The fourth stage, now in its infancy, sees these white youth taking the initiative, using techniques learned in the Negro struggle to attack problems in the general society. The classic example of this new energy in action was the student battle on the UC campus at Berkeley, California—the Free Speech Movement. Leading the revolt were veterans of the civil rights movement, some of whom spent time on the firing line in the wilderness of Mississippi/Alabama. Flowing from the same momentum were student demonstrations against U.S. interference in the internal affairs of Vietnam, Cuba, the Dominican Republic, and the Congo and U.S. aid to apartheid in South Africa. The students even aroused the intellectual community to actions and positions unthinkable a few years ago: witness the teach-ins. But their revolt is deeper than single-issue protest. The characteristics of the white rebels which most alarm their elders—the long hair, the new dances, their love for Negro music, their use of marijuana, their mystical attitude toward sex—are all tools of their rebellion. They have turned these tools against the totalitarian fabric of American society—and they mean to change it.

From the beginning, America has been a schizophrenic nation. Its two conflicting images of itself were never reconciled, because never before has the survival of its most cherished myths made a reconciliation mandatory. Once before, during the bitter struggle between North and South climaxed by the Civil War, the two images of America came into conflict, although whites North and South scarcely understood it. The image of America held by its most alienated citizens was advanced neither by the North nor by the South; it was perhaps best expressed by Frederick Douglass, who was born into slavery in 1817, escaped to the North, and became the greatest leader-spokesman for the blacks of his era. In words that can still, years later, arouse an audience of black Americans, Frederick Douglass delivered, in 1852, a scorching indictment in his Fourth of July oration in Rochester:

> What to the American slave is your Fourth of July? I answer: a day that reveals to him, more than all other days in the year, the gross injustice and cruelty to which he is the constant victim. To him your celebration is a sham; your boasted liberty, an unholy licence; your national greatness, swelling vanity; your sounds of rejoicing are empty and heartless; your denunciation of tyrants, brass-fronted impudence; your shouts of liberty and equality, hollow mockery; your prayers and hymns, your sermons and thanksgiving, with all your religious parade and solemnity, are, to him, more bombast, fraud, deception, impiety and hypocrisy—a thin veil to cover up crimes which would disgrace a nation of savages. . . .
>
> You boast of your love of liberty, your superior civilization, and your pure Christianity, while the whole political power of the nation (as embodied in the two great political parties) is solemnly pledged to support and perpetuate the enslavement of three millions of your countrymen. You hurl your anathemas at all the crown-headed tyrants of Russia and Austria and pride yourselves on your democratic institutions, while you yourselves consent to be the mere *tools* and *bodyguards* of the tyrants of Virginia and Carolina.
>
> You invite to your shores fugitives of oppression from abroad, honor them with banquets, greet them with ovations, cheer them, toast them, salute them, protect them, and pour out your money to them like water; but the fugitive from your own land you advertise, hunt, arrest, shoot, and kill. You glory in your refinement and your universal

> education; yet you maintain a system as barbarous and dreadful as ever stained the character of a nation—a system begun in avarice, supported in pride, and perpetuated in cruelty.
>
> You shed tears over fallen Hungary, and make the sad story of her wrongs the theme of your poets, statesmen and orators, till your gallant sons are ready to fly to arms to vindicate her cause against the oppressor; but, in regard to the ten thousand wrongs of the American slave, you would enforce the strictest silence, and would hail him as an enemy of the nation who dares to make these wrongs the subject of public discourse!

This most alienated view of America was preached by the Abolitionists, and by Harriet Beecher Stowe in her *Uncle Tom's Cabin*. But such a view of America was too distasteful to receive wide attention, and serious debate about America's image and her reality was engaged in only on the fringes of society. Even when confronted with overwhelming evidence to the contrary, most white Americans have found it possible, after steadying their rattled nerves, to settle comfortably back into their vaunted belief that America is dedicated to the proposition that all men are created equal and endowed by their Creator with certain inalienable rights—life, liberty and the pursuit of happiness. With the Constitution for a rudder and the Declaration of Independence as its guiding star, the ship of state is sailing always toward a brighter vision of freedom and justice for all.

Because there is no common ground between these two contradictory images of America, they had to be kept apart. But the moment the blacks were let into the white world—let out of the voiceless and faceless cages of their ghettos, singing, walking, talking, dancing, writing, and orating *their* image of America and of Americans—the white world was suddenly challenged to match its practice to its preachments. And this is why those whites who abandon the *white* image of America and adopt the *black* are greeted with such unmitigated hostility by their elders.

For all these years whites have been taught to believe in the myth they preached, while Negroes have had to face the bitter reality of what America practiced. But without the lies and distortions, white Americans would not have been able to do the things they have done. When whites are forced to look honestly upon the objective proof of their deeds, the cement of mendacity holding white society together swiftly disintegrates. On the other hand, the core of the black world's vision remains intact, and in fact begins to expand and spread into the psychological territory vacated by the non-viable white lies, i.e., into the minds of young whites. It is remarkable how the system worked for so many years, how the majority of whites remained effectively unaware of any contradiction between their view of the world and that world itself. The mechanism by which this was rendered possible requires examination at this point.

Let us recall that the white man, in order to justify slavery and, later on, to justify segregation, elaborated a complex, all-pervasive myth which at one time classified the black man as a sub-human beast of burden. The myth was progressively modified, gradually elevating the blacks on the scale of evolution, following their slowly changing status, until the plateau of separate-but-equal was reached at the close of the nineteenth century. During slavery, the black was seen as a mindless Supermasculine Menial. Forced to do the back-breaking work, he was conceived in terms of his ability to do such work—"field niggers," etc. The white man administered the plantation, doing all the thinking, exercising omnipotent power over the slaves. He had little difficulty dissociating himself from the black slaves, and he could not conceive of their positions being reversed or even reversible.

Blacks and whites being conceived as mutually exclusive types, those attributes imputed to the blacks could not also be imputed to the whites—at least not in equal degree—without blurring the line separating the races. These images were based upon the social function of the two races, the work they performed. The ideal white man was one who knew how to use his head, who knew how to manage and control things and get things done. Those whites who were not in a position to perform these functions nevertheless aspired to them. The ideal black man was one who did exactly as he was told, and did it efficiently and cheerfully. "Slaves," said Frederick Douglass, "are generally expected to sing as well as to work." As the black man's position and function became more varied, the images of white and black, having become stereotypes, lagged behind.

The separate-but-equal doctrine was promulgated by the Supreme Court in 1896. It had the same purpose domestically as the Open Door Policy toward China in the international arena: to stabilize a situation and subordinate a non-white population so that racist exploiters could manipulate those people according to their own selfish interests. These doctrines were foisted off as *the epitome of enlightened justice, the highest expression of morality*. Sanctified by religion, justified by philosophy and legalized by the Supreme Court, separate-but-equal was enforced by day by agencies of the law, and by the KKK & Co. under cover of night. Booker T. Washington, the Martin Luther King of his day, accepted separate-but-equal in the name of all Negroes. W.E.B. DuBois denounced it.

Separate-but-equal marked the last stage of the white man's flight into cultural neurosis, and the beginning of the black man's frantic striving to assert his humanity and equalize his position with the white. Blacks ventured into all fields of endeavor to which they could gain entrance. Their goal was to present in all fields a performance that would equal or surpass that of the whites. It was long axiomatic among blacks that a black had to be twice as competent as a white in any field in order to win grudging recognition from the whites. This produced a pathological motivation in the blacks to equal or surpass the whites, and a pathological motivation in the whites to maintain a distance from the blacks. This is the rack on which black and white Americans received their delicious torture! At first there was the color bar, flatly denying the blacks entrance to certain spheres of activity. When this no longer worked, and blacks invaded sector after sector of American life and economy, the whites evolved other methods of keeping their distance. The illusion of the Negro's inferior nature had to be maintained.

One device evolved by the whites was to tab whatever the blacks did with the prefix "Negro." We had *Negro* literature, *Negro* athletes, *Negro* music, *Negro* doctors, *Negro* politicians, *Negro* workers. The malignant ingeniousness of this device is that although it accurately describes an objective biological fact—or, at least, a sociological fact in America—it concealed the paramount psychological fact: that to the white mind, prefixing anything with "Negro" automatically consigned it to an inferior category. A well-known example of the white necessity to deny due credit to blacks is in the realm of music. White musicians were famous for going to Harlem and other Negro cultural centers literally to steal the black man's music, carrying it back across the color line into the Great White World and passing off the watered-down loot as their own original creations. Blacks, meanwhile, were ridiculed as *Negro* musicians playing inferior coon music.

The Negro revolution at home and national liberation movements abroad have unceremoniously shattered the world of fantasy in which the whites have been living. It is painful that many do not yet see that their fantasy world has been rendered uninhabitable in the last half of the twentieth century. But it is away from this world that the white youth of today are turning. The "paper tiger" hero, James Bond, offering the whites a triumphant image of themselves, is saying what many whites want desperately to hear reaffirmed: *I am still the White Man, lord of the land, licensed to kill, and the world is still an empire at my feet.* James Bond feeds on that secret little anxiety, the psychological white backlash, felt in some degree by most whites alive. It is exasperating to see little brown men and little yellow men from the mysterious Orient, and the opaque black men of Africa (to say nothing of these impudent American Negroes!) who come to the UN and talk smart to us, who are scurrying all over *our* globe in their strange modes of dress—much as if they were new, unpleasant arrivals from another planet. Many whites believe in their ulcers that it is only a matter of time before the Marines get the signal to round up these truants and put them back securely in their cages. But it is away from this fantasy world that the white youth of today are turning.

In the world revolution now under way, the initiative rests with people of color. That growing numbers of white youth are repudiating their heritage of blood and taking people of color as their heroes and models is a tribute not only to their insight but to the resilience of the human spirit. For today the heroes of the initiative are people not usually thought of as white: Fidel Castro, Che Guevara, Kwame Nkrumah, Mao Tse-tung, Gamal Abdel Nasser, Robert F. Williams, Malcom X, Ben Bella, John Lewis, Martin Luther King, Jr., Robert Parris Moses, Ho Chi Minh, Stokely Carmichael, W. E. B. DuBois, James Forman, Chou En-lai.

The white youth of today have begun to react to the fact that the "American Way of Life" is a fossil of history. What do they care if their old baldheaded and crew-cut elders don't dig their caveman mops? They couldn't care less about the old stiffassed honkies who don't like their new dances: Frug, Monkey, Jerk, Swim, Watusi. All they know is that it feels good to swing to wayout body-rhythms instead of dragassing across the dance floor like zombies to the dead beat of mind-smothered Mickey Mouse music. Is it any wonder that the youth have lost all respect for their elders, for law and order, when for as long as they can remember all they've witnessed is a monumental bickering over the Negro's place in American society and the right of people around the world to be left alone by outside powers? They have witnessed the law, both domestic and international, being spat upon by those who do not like its terms. Is it any wonder, then, that they feel justified, by sitting-in and freedom riding, in breaking laws made by lawless men? Old funny-styled, zipper-mouthed political night riders know nothing but to haul out an investigating committee *to look into the disturbance* to find the cause of the unrest among the youth. Look into a mirror! The cause is you, Mr. and Mrs. Yesterday, you with your forked tongues.

A young white today cannot help but recoil from the base deeds of his people. On every side, on every continent, he sees racial arrogance, savage brutality toward the conquered and subjugated people, genocide; he sees the human cargo of the slave trade; he sees the systematic extermination of American Indians; he sees the civilized nations of Europe fighting in imperial depravity over the lands of other people—and over possession of the very people themselves. There seems to be no end to the ghastly deeds of which his people are guilty. *GUILTY*. The slaughter of the Jews by the Germans, the dropping of atomic bombs on the Japanese people—these deeds weigh heavily upon the prostrate souls and tumultuous consciences of the white youth. The white heroes, their hands dripping with blood, are dead.

The young whites know that the colored people of the world, Afro-Americans included, do not seek revenge for their suffering. They seek the same things the white rebel wants: an end to war and exploitation.

Black and white, the young rebels are free people, free in a way that Americans have never been before in the history of their country. And they are outraged.

There is in America today a generation of white youth that is truly worthy of a black man's respect, and this is a rare event in the foul annals of American history. From the beginning of the contact between blacks and whites, there has been very little reason for a black man to respect a white, with such exceptions as John Brown and others lesser known. But respect commands itself and it can neither be given nor withheld when it is due. If a man like Malcolm X could change and repudiate racism, if I myself and other former Muslims can change, if young whites can change, then there is hope for America. It was certainly strange to find myself, while steeped in the doctrine that all whites were devils by nature, commanded by the heart to applaud and acknowledge respect for these young whites—despite the fact that they are descendants of the masters and I the descendant of slave. The sins of the fathers are visited upon the heads of the children—but only if the children continue in the evil deeds of the fathers.

22 / THE UNKNOWN PRICE OF SUCCESS

Jack Olsen

What is happening today amounts to a revolt by the black athlete against the framework and attitudes of American sport. To the white sports follower this upheaval has come as a surprise; the man in the grandstand, comfortable in his feeling that sports is his own pet province, accustomed to regarding the Negro athlete as a symbol of integration, has failed to see the disillusion beneath the surface. He knows nothing about the blacks whom he professes to understand, for a wall of misapprehension

---

and apathy cuts the white off from the realities of the black athlete's background and hopes.

For three years Elvin Hayes was the hero of Houston, admired and respected by black and white alike. He was always the last Cougar to be introduced over the P.A. system before each home game, and by the time the second or third man had been introduced, the chant of "E . . . E . . . E" had become so loud that the other players' names were lost. When Elvin would finally detach his long body from the bench, throw down the polka-dot towel that was a team trademark and amble out on the floor in his size 16s, the cheering made the needles on the volume-indicator meters in the radio booth jump across the red line.

Then Elvin used up his last semester of eligibility. He ignored the local professional basketball team, the Houston Mavericks of the ABA and signed for an estimated $440,000 with the NBA's San Diego Rockets. The folks who used to chant "E . . . E . . . E" took a new view of him. Letters to the editors began mentioning how ungrateful Elvin had become. Fans would call radio programs and air their objections to the way their former hero had ignored the offers of the Houston Mavericks. The street corner conversations were more to the point. "I used to think he knew his place," a cab driver said, "but now he's acting like one of your smart-ass Northern jigs." A Houston reporter summed up the attitude of the townsfolk: "When Elvin was representing the University of Houston on the court, he was called 'a credit to his race.' But when he signed with the San Diego team, he became another 'smart nigger.' Houston's attitude about him turned just like that." And once again that familiar cry was heard in the land: "Sports has been good to him. He should be more grateful to the people who made him." One is reminded of a remark made long ago by the heavyweight champion of the rational world. "Who made me is *me*," said Cassius Clay with authority. Who made Elvin Hayes of Rayville, Louisiana, is Elvin Hayes.

Rayville is a town in northeast Louisiana about 60 miles upcountry from Waterproof, four miles from Bee Bayou, just down the road from Alto and Holly Ridge. Its 5,000 residents, divided about 50-50 racially, work in small businesses, cotton gins, a clothing mill or two. The farms around Rayville are tilled by machines nowadays; hundreds of former field hands, Negroes almost to the last man, have gone away to places like Dallas and Los Angeles and Chicago seeking work. In 1969 one of the local schools will drop agriculture as a course; "Ag" used to be the mainstay of the curriculum. Signs on the post-office bulletin board advise young residents that the U.S. Army is "a wise choice," and others say, "Go Air Force." These are two labor markets that are still hiring. Now that cotton has ended a way of life, the Negro youth of Rayville have a tendency to rattle around in meaningless pursuits.

Racially, Rayville is relaxed, as Southern towns go. The big midtown high school has been integrated for several years, although hardly any Negroes elect to attend. The malt and sundae stand on the corner of Madeline and Louisa Streets has one takeout window for whites and and a separate one for Negroes, but no one gets upset about it. "You have to expect that in a Southern town," says Elvin Hayes's sister, Bunnatine. "It doesn't bother us. We go elsewhere. You have to make up your mind about things like that." For the most part, the two races mind their own business in Rayville.

Now that Elvin Hayes is a famous All-America basketball player, everyone in Rayville professes to be his dear friend, his old acquaintance. "Ah've known Elving all his laff," says a white man at the Rayville Motel, at the west end of town. "Fan boy, fan family." Later, someone passes the remark along to James P. Smith, principal of the all-black Eula D. Britton school, where Elvin attended class. James Smith explodes in a big laugh and says, "That white man doesn't know Elvin or anybody else on this side of town. This is a different world."

The "different world" is the east part of Rayville, literally the other side of the tracks, where black families live in homes ranging from shacks to a few fairly comfortable family dwellings. The Hayes family is better off than most. You walk across a few wooden boards that span a gully and you are on the front steps of the rectangular frame house at 603 Texas Street. There are no sidewalks. The Hayes house is not fancy; the ceiling sags, and now and then a leak has to be patched, but there is space and order and warmth and a matriarch who runs the show. Mrs. Savannah Hayes, mother of Elvin and five others, sits in a stiff-backed chair in the living room and explains how and why she and her late husband sent their six children to college: "I been in the fields. Raised on a farm. My daddy worked another man's land. I chopped cotton and I picked cotton. Before I was married I always said, 'if I ever own a family, I want them to have a better chance than I have.' Well, I married a man who felt the same way. Chris Hayes. A powerful man. He had a fourth-grade education, but he'd traveled all around the world as a fireman on a ship, and he'd learned a few things. We settled here, and he began firing the boilers at the Union [cotton] Compress, and when the children came along, he'd tell'em: 'I'll wear overalls for you if you'll go to school, but if *you* won't, I won't!' And what he wasn't telling them, I was. I'd say, 'Look, if you go to school I'll be with you all the way, but if you don't go to school, you'll have to go out on your own—because I'm not going to take care of you so you can run in the streets.' So we started sending our children off to college one by one, and my husband worked two jobs to pay for it. Sometimes three jobs. Some days I'd put on overalls and fire them boilers myself—I can do it as good as anybody else, and

I have did it many times! Even after my husband had a heart attack, you couldn't stop him. And when he lay on his death bed, he said to me, 'Don't feel like everything gonna be done when I'm gone. Keep them children in school! The Lawd's gonna make a way for you to do it.' Well, the Lawd did. Four of our children were either in or through college, and that left Bunnatine and Elvin. Bunnatine got a full academic scholarship to Southern University and Elvin got a full athletic scholarship to Houston, and that made it six out of six."

Elvin was the baby of the family, and by the time he entered the Eula D. Britton school a few blocks from his home, the Hayes pattern of academic excellence had been firmly established. For a while, the tradition worked against the gangly boy. At seven, he had told an aunt that his ambition was to be "a noble man."

"You're not gonna be anything," the aunt chided the boy. "Look at you, all arms and elbows."

"Yes, I am," Elvin insisted. "Someday I'm gonna be a noble man."

But in school he was deeply troubled by the idea that too much was expected of him, that he would be judged by the records of his five older brothers and sisters and found wanting.

Mrs. Savannah Hayes well remembers the device Elvin put up to help him retreat from the troubling reality around him. "Oh, how I *do* remember!" Mrs. Hayes says. "He put up a bucket with a hole in the bottom, right on a beautiful water elm I had in the back of the house, and he threw a rubber ball into that bucket and stomped around that tree and dried the ground out till he killed it. Killed my beautiful water elm! Then he hung the bucket on the side of the house and kept right on throwing the ball into it."

"Well, a kid in my neighborhood had to play outside or not at all," Elvin recalls. "We didn't have the facilities that other kids have. No concrete to play on. No baskets to shoot at. I cut the bottom out of this old bucket. My basketball was one of those five-and-ten-cent-store rubber balls about the size of a softball. I lallygagged around with balls like that right through high school. People say, 'Wouldn't that ruin your game, throwing the wrong kind of ball at the wrong kind of basket?' But no, it didn't. If you could dribble that little ball across that uneven dirt, you'd never have trouble on a basketball court."

In the eighth grade, Elvin was still playing the role of the child who wanted to be different from his brothers and sisters, and he had started running with a bad crowd. "I became tough, and they had to put me in a special section of my class. But while I was running with that crowd I learned a lot about kids that they called bad. Nobody understood those kids. Nobody took the time. A lot of them had no other way to be noticed. They were poor; they had no books in their house; they had bad backgrounds. The only way they could be noticed in the world and get any attention at all was to be bad, to do mischievous things. They had no interest in school, because school offered them nothing. Like, maybe some of them would have liked to study automobile body work, but there was no automobile bodies in school to work on."

Elvin had not been in with the "bad" crowd for long when he came under the influence of the Reverend Dr. John Calvin, a former dean of men at Grambling College in Grambling, Louisiana. "Dr. Calvin showed me that someone understood me, and he made me realize that someone was willing to give me their hand and help me. He told me it was fine for me to want to be a basketball player but I couldn't if I didn't study. He told me that the two things went together. This was the eighth grade. This was the turning point. From then on I started bearing down. From then on it was nothing but study and practice, study and practice."

At first, Elvin was too gawky and clumsy to count for much in the free ebb and flow of a basketball game. "They used him on a neighborhood team just so they'd have the full five men," his sister Christine says, chortling at the memory. "He'd fall all over himself when the ball came to him. We were so embarassed! Every time they threw the ball to Elvin, he'd miss it." He was cut from the freshman team and he spent that whole summer shooting baskets. He shot 11 hours a day. Eleven. He is sure, because it is not the kind of thing you forget. "That boy worked," says Melvin Rogers.

"When I finally made the high-school team," Elvin recalls, "the fans would holler, 'Take him out! Take him out!' I was growing fast and I had coordination problems. And I didn't have the money for the right equipment. One time I started a game with two right shoes—my own had fallen apart and these were all I could find lying around."

"He finally pulled himself together in the eleventh grade," says Melvin Rogers, known to everyone in black Rayville as "Cawch." "Understand, he was no ball of fire. He was like any big tall boy who doesn't know his hands from his feet. He used to stumble over the center line! And Bill Russell was always in his mind. His thinking skipped college. In his thinking he saw himself playing against Russell right away. College was just a means to that. That's why I knew this year that there wasn't a chance that Elvin would sign with the Houston Mavericks. There's no Bill Russell in that league!"

Louisiana maintains the segregation of the races by having white high-school teams play in one grouping and black in another, and Eula D. Britton High School won the black championship behind its superstar Elvin Hayes in his senior year. The University of Houston offered him a full athletic scholarship, and Elvin went into a world that flabbergasted him. "I walked around the Houston campus without saying a word, because I had a speech problem. My speech problem was that I talked like a small-town Southern Negro. I mumbled my words and strung them together, and certain words like 'individual' and 'computer' I couldn't say at all. I still have trouble with those words. I spoke the way the kids of Rayville spoke, not the way English was spoken in my home. I mean, my sister the English teacher, she would speak perfect English around the house, but then I would go out and listen to the other kids on the street and that sounded good to me, jiving around with them. And then I couldn't get rid of it in college. So I decided to major in speech education, for two reasons. One was to help myself. The other was to try to help other kids with the same problem."

At first Elvin could not accustom himself to the attitude of the big city crowds. In Louisiana he had played before mostly Negro audiences, and they had viewed him as both athlete and human being. But in Houston the crowd seemed to expect him to be all athlete, to approach perfection. Elvin and Don "Duck" Chaney of Baton Rouge, Louisiana, were the first Negroes ever to play basketball for a University of Houston team, and they were cheered and praised and patted when the game went well. "But if we had a little off night, the crowds would get on us more than the other players," Elvin says. "Duck and I could be hurt or sick or just off our game and the people would cut loose on us. They expected us to be terrific every minute."

Off the court, Elvin's size and his personal dignity held racial incidents to a minimum, though one of his teammates forgot himself one night after a game and muttered the word "nigger."

"We sat right down and talked about it," Elvin says. "He explained that it was just something he had in his vocabulary and it slipped out. It's not something you can break overnight. So we discussed why he said it, where it came from, what it meant to the whites and what it meant to the Negroes. That talk went on for a long time, and I think it changed that guy's mind. I think he became a different person."

Four years at the University of Houston crystallized Elvin Hayes's own thinking about race, caste, delinquency and the problems of poverty. He married Erna Livingston as a junior and became a father as a senior ("We call ourselves the triple E: me, Erna and little Elvin"), and except for his appearances in class and on the court, he seldom was seen about the campus. "People would ask me where I was keeping myself, and I'd just shrug and say, 'Around.'"

Elvin was keeping himself in Houston's black ghetto, jiving around with the poor boys of grammar- and high-school age. "It's like this," he says. "Before I got into basketball in high school, nobody noticed me, nobody cared anything about me. Then you play on a team, and they get to know you, and then everybody wants to be with you. And then they start saying to you, 'Why are you running with those bad guys, those bums from the poor neighborhood? You should look over those guys!' But that's why they're bad guys! Because everybody looked over them! The only way they can be seen is by fights or troublemaking, and then people say, 'Oh, he's bad!' So I go down there and try to correspond to those kids, to show them that somebody cares for them like Reverend Calvin cared for me, to show them that they have a place in life just like everybody else.

"But when I first started doing this in Houston, the better-off people would ask me what I was doing hanging around the poor. They'd say, 'Why do you do that? Those people are below your class.' Well, I feel that you have no class. Now I can go anywhere I want, but I prefer the poor people. You should see the change that comes over these kids when they find out you care. They come up to me and they say, 'I can't believe you'd talk to me. Why do you talk to me?' And I say, 'I talk to you because I'm no different than you are.' And that's what people can do nowadays. That's what whites can do too. Just go around caring about people and instilling some truth into the younger heads. Tell them from birth why discrimination is wrong, how the world can be better. Put out their hands. Trouble is, nowadays when some of the Negroes put out their hands, they get 'em slapped, and then they're ready to resort to violence. A man gets tired of being pushed around. But the violence isn't for me. It's not my way. All I'm trying to do is be a good man myself and just wait and see what happens."

In his determination to work among the Negro poor, to unlock the tongues of mumbly-jumbly black children in the South, Elvin Hayes is perfectly typical of the new Negro athlete, whose commitments extend far beyond a lime-washed goal line or an outfield fence 356 feet away. But in other respects, the Elvin Hayes story can be misleading. It can be employed, in fact, to buttress certain theories that have been used to keep the Negro in bondage since the Emancipation Proclamation. A white traveling salesman in Tupelo, Mississippi, makes the case on behalf of millions of racists: "Look at that Elvin Hayes. Started with nothing. Family had nothing. Came from the deep South, where we're supposed to be mistreating the Nigras. And look what happens? He gets a college education and then gets a four-hundred-and-forty-thousand-dollar deal. It just goes to show you: a Nigra *can* get ahead if he tries. Trouble is, most of them would rather sit around collecting welfare checks."

It is perfectly true that the Negro "can get ahead if he tries"—if the Negro is a highly gifted athlete like Elvin Hayes, if he has an iron-willed mother like Savannah Hayes and a hard-working father like the late Chris Hayes, if he sprouts to 80 inches in height and has a fanatical determination to shoot baskets, if he has a patient coach like Melvin Rogers and an inspiration like the Reverend Dr. John Calvin, if he gets enough to eat, if he is not weakened by pellagra or worms, if he does not fall from rheumatic fever or pneumonia or any of the other diseases that seem to concentrate on Negro children, and a dozen or so other ifs. If the chain of ifs is not broken at any point, an Elvin Hayes may be produced. The yawning gulf that separates whites from blacks may be crossed.

UNIT H / ISSUES FOR CONSIDERATION

1. In what ways has the Negro revolution caused the white man to recognize, for the first time, that he too is a member of a race?
2. Describe the ways that the statement "Look what sports has done for the Negro" is a myth of American society.
3. Is it possible to find parallels between the experiences of the blacks in the sports world and the Jews in the business world?
4. As society grows more complex does racial differentiation tend to increase or decrease? Explain why.
5. What are some of the similarities between racial differentiation and social class differentiation?

UNIT I
RESIDENCE: THE CITY AND THE COUNTRY

Among the many factors that differentiate man in modern society, his residence is of considerable significance. Not in quite the same way as his race or his sex, which are visible to all those around him, but in other ways his physical environment is of profound importance to our understanding of him. It does not take a sociologist to tell us that we are becoming an urban society and that more and more people are living in larger and larger cities. However, the sociologist can tell us a great deal about the effects of this phenomenon on the lives of people. In Gans' articles we get some idea of the importance of politics to life in the city. The student should note particularly the relationships among the various conditions that exist in the city. How does the suburbanite, who works in the city but lives in the suburbs, influence the lives of the "out-voted minorities"? Why does the political procedure (majority rule) have such important bearing on city problems like smog, minority tensions, crime, and transportation?

Our concern over the city should not lead us to forget that many Americans still live in towns and on farms. Towns like Mason City, so well described in Schrag's article, contain millions of Americans. As both Gans and Schrag make clear, these small-town Americans are no more immune to the changes in American society than are city dwellers. Both have to contend with the complexities of mass society. Considering public attitude and physical arrangements, what different sorts of factors would you be confronted with if you were black (or a young male with long hair) and living in Mason City as compared with living in New York City?

23 / WE WON'T END THE URBAN CRISIS UNTIL WE END MAJORITY RULE

Herbert J. Gans

In 1962, a group of us, planners and social scientists, assembled a book of essays about the city, and we called it "The Urban Condition." Had the book been published only a couple of years later, it would probably have been entitled "The Urban Problem," and today it would surely come out as "The Urban Crisis." But these catch phrases are misleading, for they divert attention from the real issues. Although American cities are in deep trouble, the real crisis is not urban but national, and stems in large part from short-comings in American democracy, particularly the dependence on majority rule.

The troubles of the city have been catalogued in long and by now familiar lists, but I would argue that, in reality, they boil down to three: *poverty and segregation,* with all their consequences for both their victims and other urban residents; and *municipal decay,* the low quality of public services and the declining tax revenues which are rapidly leading to municipal bankruptcy. Moreover, the first two problems are actually the major cause of the third, for the inability of the poor to pay their share of keeping up the city, as well as the crime and other pathology stimulated by poverty and segregation have brought about much of the municipal decay. In addition, the fear of the ghetto poor has recently accelerated the middle-class exodus, thus depriving cities of an important source of taxes at the very moment their expenditures have been increased by the needs of the poor. Consequently, the elimination of urban poverty and segregation would go far toward relieving the other problems of the city.

Neither poverty and segregation nor municipal decay are unique to the city, however; indeed, they are often more prevalent in rural areas. More important, all three problems are caused by nationwide conditions. Poverty is to a considerable extent a by-product of the American economy, which is today growing only in the industries and services that employ the skilled, semi-professional and professional worker, and, in fact, many of the unskilled now living in urban slums were driven out of rural areas where the demand for their labor had dried up even earlier than in the cities. Municipal decay is similarly national in cause, for small communities can also no longer collect enough in taxes to provide the needed public services, and their populations, too, are becoming increasingly poor and black as the nationwide suburbanization of the middle class proceeds.

In short, the so-called urban crisis is actually an American crisis, brought on largely by our failure to deal with the twin evils of poverty and segregation. This failure has often been ascribed to a lack of national will, as if the country were an individual who could pull himself together if he only wanted to, but even the miraculous emergence of a national consensus would not be sufficient, for the sources of our failure are built into our most important economic and political institutions.

One major source of failure is the corporate economy, which has not realized, or been made to realize, that the rural and urban unskilled workers it has cast aside are part of the same economic process which has created affluence or near-affluence for most Americans. As a result, private enterprise has been able to improve productivity and profit without having to charge against its profit the third of the population which must live in poverty or near-poverty. Instead, government has been left the responsibility for this by-product of the economic process, just as it has often been given the task of removing the waste materials that are a by-product of the production process.

But government has not been able or willing to require private enterprise—and its own public agencies—to incorporate the employable poor into the economy. Not only is there as yet little recognition among the general public or most of our leaders of the extent to which urban and rural poverty result from the structure of the economy, but private enterprise is powerful enough to persuade most people that government should take care of the poor or subsidize industry to create jobs for them.

However, government—whether Federal, state or local—has not been able or willing to absorb responsibility for the poor either, and for several important political reasons.

First, most voters—and the politicians that represent them—are not inclined to give the cities the funds and powers to deal with poverty, or segregation. This disinclination is by no means as arbitrary as it may seem, for the plight of the urban poor, the anger of the rebellious, and the bankruptcy of the municipal treasury have not yet hurt or even seriously inconvenienced the vast majority of Americans.

Rural and small-town America make little use of the city anyway, except for occasional tourist forays, and the city financial institutions which play an influential part in their economies are not impaired in their functioning by the urban condition. Suburbanites may complain about the dirt, crime and traffic congestion when they commute to city jobs, but they can still get downtown without difficulty, and, besides, many of their employers are also moving out to the suburbs.

But even the city-dwellers who are neither poor nor black can pursue their daily routines unchanged, for most of them never need to enter the slum areas and ghettos. Only the urbanites who work in these areas or live near them are directly touched by the urban condition—and they are a small minority of America's voters.

Second, many Americans, regardless of where they live, are opposed to significant governmental activity on behalf of the poor and black—or, for that matter, to further governmental participation in the economy. Not only do they consider taxes an imposition on their ability to spend their earnings, but they view governmental expenditure as economic waste, whereas private enterprise expenditures are proudly counted in the Gross National Product. The average American taxpayer is generous in paying for the defense of the country and for projects that increase American power and prestige in the world, be it a war in Vietnam or a moon shot, but he is often opposed to governmental activities that help anyone other than himself. The very corporations and workers whose incomes depend on government contracts often fight against Federal support of other activities and groups—and without ever becoming aware of the contradiction.

Consequently, many taxpayers and voters refuse to see the extent to which governmental activities create jobs and provide incomes, and how much government subsidizes some sectors of American life but not others. By and large, these subsidies go to people who need them less: there are tax exemptions for home-owners, Federal highway programs and mortgage insurance for suburbanites; direct subsidies to airlines, merchant shipping, large farms, colleges and college students; and, of course, the depletion allowance for oil producers. Grants to the poor are fewer and smaller; the most significant one is public welfare, and it is called a handout, not a subsidy.

Subsidies are generally provided not on the basis of merit but power, and this is a *third* reason for the lack of action in the cities. Even though many Americans live in the city, urban areas and their political representatives have relatively little power, and the poor, of course, yet less. The poor are powerless because they are a minority of the population, are often difficult to organize, and are not even a homogeneous group with similar interests that could be organized into an effective pressure group.

The cities are relatively powerless because of the long-time gerrymandering of American state and Federal governments in favor of rural and small-town areas. As a result, rural-dominated state legislatures can use the tax receipts of the cities to subsidize their own areas, and Congressmen from these areas have been able to outvote the representatives of urban constituencies. The Supreme Court's requirement of one man-one vote is now bringing about reapportionment, but it may be too late for the cities. As more and more Americans leave for the suburbs it appears that the cities will not be able to increase their power, for voters and politicians from rural and suburban areas who share a common interest in not helping the cities can unite against them.

In effect, then, the cities and the poor and the black are politically outnumbered. This state of affairs suggests the *fourth* and perhaps most important reason for the national failure to act: the structure of American democracy and majority rule.

America, more so than other democratic nations in the world, runs its political structure on the basis of majority rule. A majority vote in our various political institutions determines who will be nominated and elected to office, what legislation will be passed and funded, and who will be appointed to run the administering and administrative agencies. Of course, the candidates, laws and budgets which are subject to the vote of the majority are almost always determined by minorities; the only men who can run for office these days are either affluent or financed by the affluent groups who donate the campaign funds, and the legislation these men vote on is often suggested or even drafted by campaign-fund donors or other small groups with specific interests in government action. Properly speaking then, American democracy allows affluent minorities to propose, and the majority to dispose.

There is nothing intrinsically conspiratorial about this phenomenon, for it follows from the nature of American political participation. Although every citizen is urged to be active in the affairs of his community and nation, in actual practice participation is almost entirely limited to organized interest groups or lobbies who want something from government.

As a result, legislation tends to favor the interests of the organized: of businessmen, not consumers, even though the latter are a vast majority; of landlords, not tenants; doctors, not patients. Unorganized citizens may gripe about the lack of consumer legislation or even the defense budget, but only when their interests are similar and immediately threatened so that they can organize or be organized are they able to affect governmental affairs.

This is not to say that many governmental decisions often violate the wishes of a majority of Americans, for, by and large, that majority is usually happy—or at least not too unhappy—with the decisions of its governments. The almost $100-billion spent annually for defense and space exploration are appropriated because, until recently, the majority of the voters wanted a victory in Vietnam and a man on the moon before the Russians. There is no Federal mass-transit program because the majority of Americans, even in the cities, prefer to use their cars; and Congress can pay more attention to a small number of tobacco farmers and producers than to the danger of cigarette smoking because the majority is not sufficiently concerned about this danger, and, as a recent study showed, many heavy smokers do not even believe that smoking leads to cancer or heart disease.

But while the American political structure often satisfies the majority, it also creates *outvoted minorities* who can be tyrannized and repressed by majority rule, such as the poor and the black, students, migrant workers and many others. In the past, such minorities have had to rely on the good-will of the majority, hoping that it would act morally, but it generally offered them only charity, if that much. For example, the majority has granted the poor miserly welfare payments, and then added dehumanizing regulations for obtaining and spending the funds.

Today, many outvoted minorities have tired of waiting for an upturn in public altruism and are exerting political pressure on the majority. Thus, the poor and the black have been organizing their own pressure groups, forming coalitions with more powerful minorities (like the progressive wing of the labor movement) and getting support from liberals, other advocates of social justice and guilty whites. Indeed, such methods enabled the poor and the black to achieve the civil rights and antipoverty programs of the nineteen-sixties.

Even so, these gains, however much of an improvement they represent over the past, remain fairly small, and have not significantly improved the living conditions of large numbers in the slums and ghettos. Moreover, the activities of ghetto demonstrators and rioters have cooled some of the ardor of white liberals and trade unionists, and it is questionable whether many other groups would derive much benefit from coalition with poor or black organizations. Like all outvoted minorities, they can offer little to a coalition except the moral urgency of their cause.

Consequently, the poor and the black are caught in an almost hopeless political bind, for any programs that would produce significant gains, such as a massive antipoverty effort, an effective assault on segregation or even a workable community control scheme, are likely to be voted down by the majority, or the coalitions of minorities that make up majorities in American political life. *Moreover, since the poor and the black will probably always be outvoted by the majority, they are thus doomed to be permanently outvoted minorities.*

But if I am correct in arguing that the urban condition cannot be improved until poverty and segregation are eliminated or sharply reduced, it is likely that *under the present structure of American government there cannot be and will not be a real solution to the problem of the cities.*

The only other source of power left to outvoted minorities is *disruption*, upsetting the orderly processes of government and of daily life so as to inconvenience or threaten more powerful groups. This explains why the ghettos have rebelled, why young people sometimes resort to what adults consider to be meaningless delinquency, or students to occupations of school buildings, or working-class people to occasionally violent forms of white backlash.

Although disruption is bitterly attacked as antisocial by defenders of the existing social order, strikes were also once considered antisocial, but are now so legitimate that they are no longer even thought of as a form of disruption. The disrupters of today do not strike, but their methods have not been so unproductive as their opponents would have us believe. The ghetto rebellions have been responsible for stimulating private enterprise to find jobs for the so-called hard-core unemployed; the sit-ins—as well as the organizational activity—of the Welfare Rights movement have won higher grants for welfare recipients in some cities and have helped to arouse the interest of the Nixon Administration in re-examining the Federal welfare program; and the uprisings by college and high school students have been effective in winning them a voice in their schools.

Needless to say, disruption also has disadvantages: the possibility that it will be accompanied by violence and that it will be followed by counter-disruption—for example, police or vigilante violence—and by political efforts of more powerful groups to wipe out the gains achieved through disruption. Thus, the backlash generated by the ghetto rebellions has been partly responsible for the cutback in antipoverty and civil-rights efforts, and the disruptions by welfare recipients and college students are now producing repressive legislation against both groups. But disruption also creates serious costs for the rest of society, particularly in terms of the polarization of opposing groups, the hardening of attitudes among other citizens, and the hysterical atmosphere which then results in more repressive legislation. Clearly, disruption is not the ideal way for outvoted minorities to achieve their demands.

Nevertheless, disruption has become an accepted political technique, and may be used more widely in the nineteen-seventies, as other groups who feel they are being short-changed by American democracy begin to voice their demands. Consequently, perhaps the most important domestic issue before the country today is whether outvoted minorities—in the cities and elsewhere—must resort to further disruption, or whether more peaceful and productive ways of meeting their needs can be found.

If the outvoted minorities are to be properly represented in the political structure, two kinds of changes are necessary. First, they must be counted fairly, so that they are actually consulted in the decision-making process, and are not overpowered by other minorities who would be outvoted were they not affluent enough to shape the political agenda. But since even a fairer counting of the voters would still leave the outvoted minorities with little influence, ways of restricting majority rule must be found when that rule is always deaf to their demands.

Majority rule is, of course, one of the unquestioned traditions of American political life, for the first axiom of democracy has always been that the majority should decide. But democracy is not inviolably equivalent to majority rule, for government of the people, by the people and for the people need not mean that a majority is "the people." Indeed, despite its traditional usage in democracies, majority rule is little more than an easily applied quantitative formula for solving the knotty problems of how the wishes of the people are to be determined. Moreover, traditions deserve to be re-examined from time to time, particularly if society has changed since they came into being.

And American society has changed since its government was created. What might be called *majoritarian democracy* was adopted when America was a small and primarily agrarian nation, with a great degree of economic and cultural homogeneity, few conflicting interest groups, and a since-rejected tradition that the propertyless should have fewer rights than the propertied. As a result, there were few serious disputes between majorities and minorities, at least until the Civil War, and majoritarian democracy could be said to have worked. Today, however, America is a highly heterogeneous and pluralistic nation, a society of minority groups, so to speak, and every important political decision requires an intense amount of negotiation and compromise so that enough minorities can be found to create a majority coalition. And even then, America is so pluralistic that not all minorities can be accommodated and must suffer all the consequences of being outvoted.

America has been a pluralistic society for almost a century, but the shortcomings of majority rule have not become a public issue before, mainly because previous generations of outvoted groups had other forms of redress. The outvoted of the past were concentrated among poor ethnic and racial minorities, as they are today, but in earlier years the economy needed their unskilled labor, so that they had less incentive to confront the majority, except to fight for the establishment of labor unions. Moreover, they had little reason even to think about majority rule, for government played a smaller role in the economy and in their lives.

Now all this has changed. When governmental policies and appropriations very nearly decide the fate of the poor, the black, draft-age college students, disadvantaged high school students, and not so affluent blue-collar workers, such groups must deal with government; and more often than not, their demands are frustrated by the workings of majority rule.

Thus, it becomes quite pertinent to ask whether majoritarian democracy is still viable, and whether the tradition of majority rule should not be re-examined. If three-fourths of the voters or of a legislative body are agreed on a course of action, it is perhaps hard to argue against majority rule, but what if that rule seriously deprives the other fourth and drives it to disruption? And what if the majority is no more than 55 per cent, and consists only of an uneasy and temporary coalition of minorities? Or if the remaining 45 per cent are unable to obtain compromises from the slender majority?

I believe that the time has come to modernize American democracy and adapt it to the needs of a pluralistic society; in short, to create a *pluralistic democracy.* A pluralistic form of democracy would not do away with majority rule, but would require systems of proposing and disposing which take the needs of minorities into consideration, so that when majority rule has serious negative consequences, outvoted minorities would be able to achieve their most important demands, and not be forced to accept tokenism, or resort to despair or disruption.

Pluralistic democracy would allow the innumerable minorities of which America is made up to live together and share the country's resources more equitably, with full recognition of their various diversities. Legislation and appropriations would be based on the principle of "live and let live," with different programs of action for different groups whenever consensus is impossible. Groups of minorities could still coalesce into a majority, but other minorities would be able to choose their own ways of using public power and funds without being punished for it by a majority.

It would take a book to describe how the American political system might be restructured to create a pluralistic democracy, but I can suggest some specific proposals toward this goal. They fall into two categories: those that incorporate outvoted minorities into the political structure by increasing the responsiveness of governments to the diversity of citizen interests—and to all citizens; and those which restrict majority rule so as to prevent the tyrannization of minorities. Many of my proposals have drawbacks, and some are outright utopian, but I suggest them more to illustrate what has to be done than to provide immediate feasible solutions.

The responsiveness of governments can be increased in several ways.

First, the one man-one vote principle must be extended to all levels of government and the political parties. County and municipal bodies need to be reapportioned to eliminate gerrymandering of the poor and the black; party leaders, high and low, should be elected by party members, and party candidates should be nominated by primaries, rather than by conventions or closed meetings of party leaders.

Second, the seniority system must be abolished in all legislatures, so that politicians can no longer obtain undue power simply because their own districts re-elect them time after time. The power of committee chairmen who may represent only a small number of voters to block legislation wanted by a larger number must also be eliminated.

Third, the administrative agencies and their bureaucracies must become more accountable, perhaps by replacing appointive officers with elective ones, or by requiring such bodies to be run by elected boards of directors.

Fourth, all election campaigns should be funded by government, to discourage the near-monopoly that wealthy individuals now have in becoming candidates, and to prevent affluent interest groups from making demands on candidates as a price for financing their campaigns. If equal amounts—and plenty of free television time—were given to all candidates, even from third, fourth and fifth parties, the diversity of the population would be better represented in the electoral process. This might lead to election by plurality rather than majority, although in a highly diverse community or state such an outcome might not be undesirable, and run-offs can always be required to produce a final majority vote.

Fifth, methods by which the citizenry communicates with its elected representatives ought to be improved. Today, legislators tend to hear only from lobbyists, people in their own social circles, and the writers of letters and newspaper editorialists—a highly biased sample of their constituencies. Indeed, the only way an ordinary citizen can communicate is by organizing or writing letters. Of course, such methods make sure that a legislator hears only from deeply interested citizens, protecting him from being overwhelmed by too much feedback, but they also discriminate against equally interested people who cannot organize or write.

One possible solution is for governments to make postage-free forms available for people who want to write letters to their representatives, to be picked up in banks, post offices, stores and taverns. Another solution is for governments to finance the establishment of regular but independently run public-opinion polls on every major issue, so that government officials can obtain adequate feedback from a random sample of their constituents, and not only on the few issues a handful of private pollsters today decide are worth polling about.

Yet another solution is for governments to encourage people to organize politically, by allowing them to claim as tax deductions the dues and contributions to lobbying organizations (other than political parties). Limits on the size of such deductions would have to be set to prevent affluent minorities from using their funds to gain extra power; and organizations of the poor, whose members cannot afford to pay dues and do not benefit from tax deductions, could be given government grants if they could prove that two-thirds of their members were poor.

Feasible methods for increasing the power of minorities at the expense of majority rule are more difficult to formulate. One approach is to enhance the power of existing institutions that represent minority interests—for example, the courts and Cabinet departments. If constitutional amendments to establish an economic and racial bill of rights could be passed, for instance, a provision giving every American citizen the right to a job or an income above the poverty-line, the power of the poor would be increased somewhat.

Cabinet departments also represent minority interests, particularly at the Federal and state levels, although more often than not they speak for affluent minorities. Nevertheless, if the Office of Economic Opportunity were raised to full Cabinet status and a Department of Minorities established in Washington, at least some new legislation and higher appropriations for the poor and the black would result. In other Cabinet departments, new bureaus should be set up to represent the interests of outvoted minorities; in Housing and Urban Development (now dominated by builders and mayors), to look after the needs of slum dwellers; in Health, Education and Welfare, to deal with the concerns of patients, students and welfare recipients, respectively. Moreover, the policy-making boards that I suggested earlier to oversee Cabinet departments and other administrative agencies should include their clients. Thus, all school boards should include some students; welfare departments, some welfare recipients; and housing agencies, some residents of public housing and F.H.A.-supported projects.

The financial power of poor minorities could be increased by extending the principles of the progressive income tax and of school-equalization payments to all governmental expenditures. Funding of government programs could be based in part on the incomes of eventual recipients, so that the lower their income, the higher the government grant. Poorer communities would thus obtain more Federal money per capita for all public services, and subsidies for mass transit programs would automatically be higher than for expressways to suburbia.

In addition, changes in the electoral system would be needed. One solution would be election by proportional representation. P.R. has not been popular in America, partly because it wreaks havoc with the two-party system, but it is not at all clear whether a pluralistic society is best served by a two-party system to begin with. Proportional representation by race or income would go against the American grain, but as long as racial and economic integration seems to be unachievable in the near future, this solution might be more desirable than forcing the poor or the black to resort to disruption.

Actually, proportional representation is already practiced informally in many places; in New York City, election slates have always been "balanced" to include candidates from the major ethnic and religious groups.

Perhaps we should even think about proportional representation by occupational groups, for job concerns are often uppermost in the voters' choices. After all, many pro-Wallace factory workers voted for Humphrey at the last minute, realizing that their job interests were more important than their fear of black militancy.

Another approach would restrict majority rule directly, by making all elections and voting procedures inlegislative branches of government go through a two-step process, with majority rule applying only to the final step. This system, somewhat like the runoff used in some state and municipal elections, would require that if any legislative proposal or appropriation obtains at least 25 per cent of the total vote, it must be revised and voted on again until it is either approved by a majority or rejected by 76 per cent of the voting body. In the meantime, compromises would have to be made, either watering down the initial proposal so that a majority could accept it, or satisfying other demands of the minority through the time-honored practice of log-rolling so that they would allow 76 per cent of the voting body to reject the original proposal.

For example, if at least a quarter of a Congressional committee supported a strong negative income tax, it is likely that the second vote would produce at least a weaker version of the tax that the majority could live with. Of course, such a system would work only if outvoted minority groups were able to elect representatives in the first place. (Also, it is always possible that legislators who favoured a highly regressive income tax or segregationist policies would be able to obtain legislation for *their* minorities, but if an economic and racial bill of rights were added to the Constitution, such legislation would be thrown out by the courts.)

Outvoted minorities can also achieve greater political power by the alteration of existing political boundaries and powers so that they could even become majorities in their own bailiwicks. Current proposals for decentralization and community control are boundary-altering schemes with just this political consequence, and some of the disadvantages of these schemes today could be alleviated by my previous proposal for progressive methods of government funding to provide more money to poorer communities.

But the concept of redrawing boundaries ought to be applied more broadly, for many existing political subdivisions are anachronistic. For example, it is difficult to justify the existence of many of the states as political units today, and it might be useful to think about creating smaller and more homogeneous units in highly urbanized parts of the country, perhaps of county size, particularly in order to reduce the number of outvoted minorities (Norman Mailer has suggested just that in proposing statehood for New York City.)

Along the same line, the old idea of replacing geographical political units by groupings along economic and other interests deserves reexamination. For instance, the welfare recipient's lot would probably be improved if he or she became part of a regional governmental body of welfare recipients which could determine how the welfare system ought to be run.

Sometimes, outvoted minorities are tyrannized because their demands are diametrically opposed to the majority's. When this happens within a school or other institution, the minority should have the right to secede, establishing its own institution without being financially punished by the majority. If some parents want a Summerhill education for their children, they should be given tax money to start their own school, just as determined black nationalists should be free to build their own community if and when public aid for new towns becomes available. In a pluralistic nation, all impulses for diversity that do not clearly harm the rest of society should be encouraged.

Finally, changes in the rules of the political system must be supplemented by changes in the economic system, for ultimately it is the major obstacle to improving the lot of many outvoted minorities—and even of the unorganized majority. Some of my earlier proposals are equally applicable here.

The one-man, one-vote principle might be extended to stockholders who elect corporate boards of directors; a Cabinet department to represent consumers and other corporate customers should be set up; feedback from stockholders and customers to the corporate "legislature" should be improved, and they, as well as workers, should sit on corporate boards. In an era when many firms are subsidized by government contracts and tax credits, it is certainly possible to argue that at least such firms should become more democratic.

Most of the proposals for a pluralistic democracy are purposely intended to enhance the power of poor and black minorities; for, as I noted earlier, this seems to me the only way of solving the problems of the cities. But such a democracy is needed by all minorities who stand in danger of being outvoted by a majority, whatever their income or color. As the current demands of more people for greater equality and more control over their lives accelerate, and the role of government in society continues to mount at the same time, the need for more political pluralism will become increasingly urgent. What we so inaccurately describe as the urban crisis is in reality the beginning of a national political crisis. But it is also an opportunity for Americans to develop new ways of living together.

24 / IS MAIN STREET STILL THERE?

Peter Schrag

Mason City, Iowa. Pop. 32,642. Meat packing, Portland cement, brick and tile, beet sugar, dairy products, commercial feeds, soybean oil and meal, thermopane windows and mobile homes. At the intersection of Highways 18 and 65, 135 miles south of Minneapolis, 125 miles north of Des Moines. Three major railroads. Ozark Airlines. Daily newspaper, one local television station. Library, art museum.

It is hard to stay in any small American town for more than a few days and remain an outsider. There seems to be a common feeling that anyone—even a writer from New York—is, somewhere in his heart, a small-town boy come home. The light but unceasing stream of traffic that moves through Main Street—Federal Avenue in Mason City—north to Minneapolis and beyond, south to Des Moines, reinforces the belief that this flat, open place is part of a great American continuity extending through other Main Streets, across the fields of corn and beets, past tractor depots and filling stations, past grain elevators and loading pens to the very limits of the national imagination. Such a belief must make it difficult to conceive of anyone as a total stranger, for being here—local pride notwithstanding—cannot seem very different from being anywhere else.

They take you in, absorb you, soak you up; they know where you've been, whom you've seen, what you've done. In Mississippi hamlets, the sheriff follows you around; here it is The Word. *Small towns co-opt* (you tell yourself), *and nice small towns co-opt absolutely.* But it is not just them, it's you. The things that you bring with you—your sense of yourself as a friendly sort, the wish to believe that the claims of small-town virtue are valid, your particular kind of chauvinism—all these things make you a willing collaborator. So maybe they're right. *Maybe we're all just small-town boys come home.* Yes, you're willing to come to dinner, to visit the Club, to suspend the suspicion that all this is some sort of do-it-yourself Chamber of Commerce trick. Later perhaps (says the Inner Voice of Reason) you will be

---

able to sort things out, to distinguish Main Street from the fantasies that you and a lot of other people from New York have invented for it. Later.

You have come here to see what is happening to the heart of this country, to ask how the great flat democracy responds to Vietnam and Black Power, to marijuana and SDS, to see how it is taking technology and the Bomb—all the things that overwhelm the visible spectrum of public concern. Is there something here that can survive in New York and Chicago? Is there an Americanism that will endure, or will it perish with the farm and the small town? What, you ask, is happening to Main Street? Later. For the moment you are simply in it, listening to them worry about a proposed civic center, about the construction of a mall, about taxes and industrial development, and about something they call "the traffic problem," which seems, by even the more placid standards of New York, more imagined than real.

There are ghosts in this country—local ghosts, and ghosts that you bring with you, that refuse to stay behind: shades of brawling railroad workers and dispossessed farmers; frontiersmen and Babbitts; the old remembered tales of reaction and America First, of capital "R" Republicanism and the Ku Klux Klan; the romance of Jefferson and Frederick Jackson Turner, the yeoman farmer and the self-made man. As a place of literary irony, Middle America is celebrating its golden anniversary. "Main Street," wrote Sinclair Lewis in 1920, "is the climax of civilization. That this Ford car might stand in front of the Bon Ton Store, Hannibal invaded Rome and Erasmus wrote in Oxford cloisters. What Ole Jensen the grocer says to Ezra Stowbody the banker is the new law for London, Prague, and the unprofitable isles of the sea; whatsoever Ezra does not know and sanction, that thing is heresy, worthless for knowing and wicked to consider." But such irony, too, may be a ghost—now as much myth, perhaps, as the self-flattering cultural propositions invented to answer it. ("Right here in Mason City," someone tells you, "we sell 300 tickets each year for the Metropolitan Opera tour performances in Minneapolis.") The life of Babbittry, you tell yourself, follows the life (and art) of others. But the models are no longer clear. Main Street once insisted on rising from Perfection (rural) to Progress (urban): Sauk Centre and Zenith were trying to do Chicago's "thing," but what does Chicago have to offer now? The Main Street boosters are still there, hanging signs across the road proclaiming "A Community on the March," but their days are numbered. How would Lewis have portrayed the three hundred marchers of the Vietnam Moratorium in Mason City? How would he deal with the growing number of long-haired, pot-smoking kids? Here, too, Mason City follows New York and Chicago. (The Mafia, you are told, controls the floating dice games that occasionally rumble through the back rooms of a local saloon.) The certainty of Lewis's kind of irony was directed to the provincial insularity that war, technology, and television are rendering obsolete. Main Street lives modern not in its dishwashers and combines—not even in Huntley-Brinkley and Walter Cronkite—but in its growing ambivalence about the America that creates them, the America that crosses the seas of beets and corn, and therefore about Main Street itself.

It is not a simple place, and perhaps never was. You see what you expect, and then begin to see (or imagine) what you did not. Standard America, yes: the Civil War monument in the square; the First National Bank; Osco's Self-Service Drugs; the shoe store and movie theaters; Damon's and Younkers' ("Satisfaction Always"); Maizes' and Penney's; Sears and Monkey Ward. Middle America the way it was supposed to be: the farmers coming to shop on Saturday afternoon; the hunting and fishing; the high school football game Friday night; the swimming and sailing at Clear Lake, a small resort nine miles to the west. You cannot pass through town without being told that Mason City is a good place to raise a family, without hearing praise for the schools, and without incessant reminders that Meredith Willson's musical play *The Music Man* was *about* Mason City, that Willson was born here, and that the town was almost renamed River City because of it. (There *is* a river, the Winnebago, which makes itself known only at times of flood.) Mr. Toot, the figure of a trombone-blowing bandsman (says a man at the Chamber of Commerce) is now the town symbol. "We hope," says the man, "that we can make our band festival into a major event." Someday, you imagine, this could be the band capital of the nation, the world, and maybe the whole wicked universe.

Mason City, they tell you, is a stable community: steady population, little unemployment, no race problem (there are, at most, 300 Negroes in town), clean water, and—with some huffy qualifications (dust from one of the cement plants, odor from the packing house)—clean air. A cliché. In the *Globe Gazette*, the editor, Bob Spiegel, suggests that the problems and resources of the large cities be dispersed to all the Mason Cities in America. A Jeffersonian, Mr. Spiegel, and a nice guy: "The smaller communities need the plants and the people that are polluting the urban centers—not in large doses, but steadily, surely. . . . The small communities are geared up. They have comprehensive plans. They know they can't stand still or they will be passed by." Stable, perhaps, but what is stable in a relativistic universe? The very thing that Spiegel proposes seems to be happening in reverse. The community is becoming less pluralistic: it has fewer Negroes, fewer Jews, and fewer members of other minorities than it had twenty years ago. "After the war," said Nate Levinson, an attorney, who is president of the synagogue, "we had eighty Jewish families. Now we have forty. We can't afford a rabbi anymore." On the few occasions that Mason City has tried to attract Negro professionals, they refused to come or to stay.

There is nobody to keep them company, and the subtle forms of discrimination—in housing and employment—are pervasive enough to discourage pioneers. ("My maid says if she hears any more about Black Power she'll scream. . . . I wouldn't mind one living next door, if he mowed the grass and kept the place neat.") The brighter kids—black and white—move away, off to college, off to the cities, and beneath that migration one can sense the fear that the city's declining agricultural base will not be replaced by enough industrial jobs to maintain even the stability that now exists.

Mason City is not a depressed town, although in its stagnating downtown shopping area it often looks like one. (Shopping centers are thriving on the periphery; the farmers come in to shop, but not all the way.) The city shares many of the attributes of other small Middle Western communities, competing with them for industry, counting, each week, another farm family that is selling out or giving up, counting the abandoned houses around the county, counting the number of acres (now exceeding 200) required for an efficient agricultural operation. An acre of land costs $500, a four-row combine $24,000. If you stop in such places as Plymouth, a town of 400, nine miles from Mason City, you hear the cadences of compromise and decline: men who have become part-time farmers and make ends meet, at $2.25 an hour, by working in the sugar mill in Mason City. Independence becomes, ever more, a hopeful illusion belied by abandoned shops and boarded windows, and by tales of success set in other places—an engineer in California, a chemist in Detroit, a teacher in Oregon.

Iowa, you realize, not just from statistics, but from faces, is a state of old people: "What do the kids here want to do? What do the kids in Mason City want to do? What do the kids in Iowa want to do? They want to get out. I'd get out, go to California if I could." There is a double migration, from farms into towns, from towns into cities, and out of the state. More than 10 per cent of Mason City's work force is employed at the Decker packing plant on the north side of town. (The plant is a division of Armour and Company.) At the moment the plant is prosperous; it pays good wages. (A hamboner—who does piece work—can make $6 to $7 an hour). But what would happen, asked one of the city's corporate managers, if the place should succumb to the increasing efficiency of newer plants? "What'll we do the day—and don't quote me—when the place has to shut down?"

It is the fashion to worry slow, worry with a drawl. Urgency and crisis are not the style. Through most of its history, Mason City was dominated by a few families, and to some extent it still is—not because they are so powerful, but because Federal Avenue once thought they were. Small towns create their own patriarchs, tall men who look even taller against the flatness of history, producing—inevitably—a belief that civic motion and inertia are the subtle work of Big Men: bankers, real estate operators, and corporate managers. Mason City still talks about the General, Hanford MacNider (banking, cement, real estate), who was an Assistant Secretary of War under Coolidge, ambassador to Canada, an aspirant for the 1940 Republican nomination for President, and, for a time, a supporter of America First. (In Mason City, MacNider was *Secretary* of War and barely missed becoming President.) The MacNiders gave the city land for parks, for the public library, and for a museum. (The General was also a founder of the Euchre and Cycle Club, a lunch-and-dinner club—all the best people—which still has no Jewish members, and he is remembered, among other things, as the man who did not lower his flag for thirty days after John F. Kennedy was killed.) "My father," said Jack MacNider, now president of the Northwestern States Portland Cement Company, "was quite a guy. Some people thought he was tough. To some he was a patron saint. You should have known him."

The General's shadow has survived him, and there are still people who are persuaded that nothing of major consequence can be accomplished in Mason City against the opposition of the MacNider family. Is that true, you ask Jack, sitting in his second-story office overlooking Federal Avenue. (There is a picture of the General, in full uniform, behind Jack's desk.) "I'm flattered," he answers, not defensively, but with some amusement, saying more between the lines than on the record, telling you—you imagine—that the MacNiders take the rap for a lot of small-town inertia they can't control, and that they suffer (or enjoy) a visibility for which they haven't asked. At this very moment, a young lawyer named Tom Jolas, a second generation Greek, is challenging the Establishment (such as it is) in his campaign for mayor; you both know that Jolas is likely to win (on November 4 he did win, handily) and that the city's style and mood are now determined as much by younger businesmen and professionals—and by hundreds of packing house workers and cement workers—as they are by the old families. "This must be a fish bowl for the MacNiders," you say, and Jack offers no argument. And when you speak about prejudice in Mason City, Jack agrees—yes, there is—but you can't be sure whether he means only against Catholics, Jews, and Negroes (or Greeks, and Chicanos), or also against the MacNiders. The shadow is still there, but the General is dead.

Mason City's traditional style of politics and political behavior was nicely represented by sixty-five-year-old George Mendon, who was mayor for sixteen years until Jolas beat him. Small towns always create the illusion of responsiveness—you can call any public official, any corporate manager, with little interference from secretaries who ask your business, your name, and your pedigree—and you thus can walk into Mendon's office unannounced and receive an audience. But you are never sure that, once in, you have really arrived anywhere. The action must be someplace else. The room is almost bare, the desk virtually clean, the man without visible passion. Yes, jobs and industrial development are a problem, and Mason City has done pretty well, but there are 20,000 other towns trying to attract industry, and, you know, these things take time. Yes, they would like to hire some Negroes for the police force, but none has qualified. Yes, the MacNiders had been good to the city—all that land they'd given (and all those tax deductions?) but. . . . When Mendon was challenged during the campaign about operating an underpaid and undertrained police force, he answered that the city had the most modern equipment, including riot guns, Mace, and bulletproof vests. What are they for, you ask, and Mendon, rattling the change in his pocket, identifies himself. "Our colored population is peaceful," he said. "They wouldn't riot. But you never know when people from the outside might come in and try to start something." Mason City is prepared for Watts and Newark, and somewhere in its open heart there lurks an edge of apprehension that the fire next time might burn even here. But when Mendon spoke about his riot guns at an open meeting, the general response was tempered by considerable facetious amusement, and the people who were amused went out to vote against him, and beat him.

There is no single current running against the old style of politics, or against the Mendons and the Establishment they are supposed to represent. In 1968, Mason City voted for Nixon, for the conservative Congressman, H. R. Gross, and for Harold Hughes, a liberal Democrat, for the U.S. Senate. ("We helped elect Gross the first time he ran," said a union official, "and we've been sorry ever since.") Sociology and political calculations don't help much. "The issue here," said Bud Stewart, who runs a music store and worked for Jolas, "is generational," implying that whatever was young and progressive supported the challenger against the older Establishment. Jolas campaigned under the slogan "Time for a Change," including, among other things, concern for public housing (which the city does not have, but desperately needs), more attention to the problems of youth, and the creation of a modern police force that could meet what he called the rising rate of crime. (And which meant, I was told, getting rid of the reactionary police chief who had bought all the riot junk). But what Jolas said was clearly not as important as what he is: young, energetic, and, beneath it all, ambiguously liberal, and unambiguously decent. "I had my hair long and wore sideburns," he tells you (two years ago, he managed a teen-age rock band), "but my friends said I couldn't win with it; so I cut it short. But maybe after the election I might get a notion and let it grow again."

Jolas's great political achievement before he ran for mayor was to force the state to reroute a projected interstate highway so that it would pass within a few miles of Mason City, but it was undoubtedly personality rather than politics that elected him. ("You know what they're saying about me?" he mused one day toward the end of the campaign. "They're saying that, if I'm elected, the Greeks and the niggers are going to take over Mason City. I even had someone charge that I belong to the Mafia—the Greek Mafia.") More than anything else, Jolas seems to have a sense of concern about youth—not a program—but an awakening awareness of how kids are shortchanged by schools, by politicians, by adults. ("He knows," I wrote in my notes, "that the world screws kids.")

What Jolas can achieve is doubtful. He will not have a sympathetic city council nor perhaps even a sympathetic community, and his commitment to a downtown civic center and mall as a means of restoring the vitality of the central business area may be more the token of modernism than the substance of progress; yet it is clear that Jolas received the support, and represented the aspirations, of whatever liberalism (black, labor, professional) the city could muster. If you sit in his storefront headquarters long enough, you learn how far Main Street has come from Babbittry. You meet Marie Dresser, the recently widowed wife of a physician, who, as president of the Iowa League of Women Voters, carried a reapportionment fight through the legislature and who speaks of how, when their son decided to grow a mustache, she and her husband decided to back him against the school authorities and how, eventually, they won; Jean Beatty, the wife of a psychologist, answering phone calls and stuffing Jolas campaign envelopes, and shuttling between meetings of the league and the local branch of the NAACP, knowing that the organization should be run by black people, but knowing also that its precariously weak membership cannot sustain it without help; or Jim Shannon, the county Democratic chairman, who has worked for the Milwaukee Railroad all his life, and who has gone back to the local community college (working nights, studying economics during the day), speaking in his soft, laconic, infinitely American cadences about the campaign for Bobby Kennedy in 1968, about a decade of legislative fights, reminding you, without meaning to, or even mentioning it, that liberalism wasn't invented in New York, that the Phil Harts, the Frank Churches, the Fred Harrises, and the George McGoverns weren't elected by professors.

If that were all—if one could merely say that Mason City and Middle America are going modern—it would be easy, but it is not. (What, after all, is modern—uniquely modern—after technology has been dispensed with?) The national culture is there—mass cult, high, middle, and low, mod and trad: Bud Stewart in the Edwardian double-breasted suits that he orders from advertisements through the local stores; the elite trooping off to Minneapolis to hear the Met when it comes on tour, or to Ames to catch the New York Philharmonic (mostly, say the cynics, to be conspicuous, not for love of music); the rock on the radio and in the jukes (the Fifth Dimension, Blood, Sweat and Tears, new Dylan and old Baez, plus some leavening from the likes of Johnny Cash); the long hair and the short skirts, the drugs and the booze. (At the same time, beer, rather than pot, seems still to be the preponderant, though not the exclusive, form of adolescent sin.) But somehow what Mason City receives through the box and the tube—and from trips to Minneapolis and Des Moines, where some of the ladies do almost weekly shopping—Mason City seems to shape and reshape into its own forms. There is a tendency to mute the decibels of public controversy and social friction, perhaps because people are more tolerant and relaxed, perhaps because they are simply less crowded. There is talk about crime and violence, but the most common examples seem usually to involve the theft of bicycles and the destruction of Halloween pumpkins. (Another way of staking a claim on the modern?) If you ask long enough, you can get some of the blue-collar workers to speak about their resentment against welfare, taxes, and student demonstrators (not at Harvard, mind you, but at the State University of Iowa), but it is commonly only television and the newspapers that produce the talk. And so it tends to be dispassionate, distant, and somewhat abstract. Bumper stickers and decals are scarce; American flags are rarely seen on the rear windows of automobiles because, one might assume, there aren't many people at whom to wave them, not many devils to exorcise. The silent majority here is an abstraction, a collage of minorities, except when it comes to the normalcy of the ladies' study clubs and bridge clubs, the football, the hunting and fishing, and the trip to the lake. And every two years they go back, most of them, and vote for H. R. Gross.

What you see most of all (see is not a good word; feel, maybe) is a faith in the capacity of people and institutions to be responsive, the belief that, finally, things are pretty much what they seem, that Things Work. "This is just a big farm town," said a Mason City businessman. "You don't check people's credit here. You just assume they'll pay their bills. In Waterloo, which is really an industrial city, even though it isn't very big, you check everybody out." The answer to an economic problem is to work harder, to take a second job, or to send your wife to work, usually as a clerk or a waitress. (Wages for women are extremely low.) On the radio, *Junior Achievement* makes its peace with modernism by setting its jingle to "Get With It" to a rock beat, but the message of adolescent enterprise (Babbittry?) is the same, and around the lunch tables at the Green Mill Restaurant or the bar at Tom MacNider's Chart House it is difficult to convince anyone that sometimes even people with the normal quota of ambition can't make it.

The advantages of that faith are obvious, but the price is high. "This is a nice town as long as you don't rock the boat," said Willis Haddix, a meat packer, who is president of the struggling Mason City chapter of NAACP. "What's wrong here is in the secret places": in subtle discrimination in housing and jobs; in the out-of-sight, dilapidated frame houses at the north and south ends of town, buildings surrounded with little piles of lumber, rusting metal chairs, decaying junk cars once slated for repair; in the lingering aroma of personal defeat; and in the cross between arrogance and apathy that declares "there are no poor people in this area." On Sundays, while most people are packing their campers for the trip home, or making the transition between church and television football, the old, who have little to do, wander into the Park Inn for lunch—hot roast beef sandwiches for $1.25—and to talk about Medicare. And against theirs you hear other voices: Murray Lawson, for example, a civilized, compassionate man, who represents Mason City in the legislature, saying, "We've been generous with education, but not so generous with the old. We've had a rough time with nursing homes"; Jim Shannon, who supports his wife and seven children on the salary of a railroad clerk and janitor, describing the effects of a regressive sales tax that victimizes the small man but makes little impact on the rich; the official of the local OEO poverty agency talking about the county's third welfare generation and reflecting that "an admission of poverty is an admission of failure, and people here don't do that"; Tom Jolas describing Mason City's enthusiasm for the New York Mets when they won the World Series after a ninth place finish in 1968, because "people believe in coming off the bottom."

And then you learn something else—about yourself, and about the phenomenon you choose to call Main Street. You hear them complain about Eastern, urban provincialism, about those people who cannot believe that Mason City has television ("You must get it from the West Coast"), let alone an art museum, a decent library, or a couple of go-go joints (or that you can buy Philip Roth, Malcolm X, and Henry Miller in the bookstore), and you begin to understand, almost by suggestion, what the barriers of comprehension are all about. Is it really surprising that Main Street cannot fully comprehend talk about police brutality, police rigidity, or social disillusionment? If the system works here, why doesn't it work everywhere else? Main Street's uniquely provincial vice lies in its excessive, unquestioning belief (in the Protestant ethic, hard work, honesty, and conventional politics); New York's in the conviction that most of the time nothing may make much difference, that institutions and public life are by their very nature unresponsive. And if New York has come to doubt the values and the beliefs of tradition, it still hasn't invented anything to replace them. The anger of the blue-collar worker—at welfare, students, Negroes—is rooted in the frustrated ethic of Main Street, frustrated in not only its encounters with urban problems and technology, but in the growing doubt of the Best people—Wallace's pointy heads, Agnew's effete impudent snobs—that it still has merit. Among the characteristic excesses of rural populism (whether expressed by William Jennings Bryan, Joe McCarthy, or Spiro Agnew) was a paranoia about Them: the bankers, the railroads, the Communists in government, the Eastern Establishment. But paranoia is surely also one of the characteristic defenses of almost every other inhabitant of New York. (If you try to explain the vicissitudes of dealing with Con Edison or the New York Telephone Company, most people in Mason City stare at you in disbelief; if you speak about rents and housing, they're certain you've gone mad.) Every rural or small-town vote against some proposal for the alleviation of a problem in New York or Chicago or Cleveland is not merely an act of self-interest (keeping taxes low, protecting the farmers) but a gesture of disbelief that Main Street's ethic and tactics—if they were really applied—would be ineffective in the Big City.

At the end, sitting in the waiting room at the Municipal Airport (all flights from Chicago, naturally, are late), you detach yourself. You hear, still, one of the Federal Avenue lawyers saying, "This town is solid. It's solid as a commercial center, and as a medical and cultural center for a large region." You see his nearly bare office, the brown wood furniture, the linoleum floors, and the fluorescent lights, see his partner in a sleeveless, gray pullover walking through the outer office (Clarence Darrow?), and hear the trucks stopping for the red light at the intersection below. You hear Jack MacNider speaking about the gradual movement of the "iron triangle"—the Midwestern industrial region—into north central Iowa, speaking about the ultimate industrialization of the area around the city. You see the high school homecoming queen, fragile and uncomfortable in the back of an open convertible in the wind-chilled stadium; see the wide residential streets with their maples and time-threatened elms, the section of magnificent houses by Prairie School architects (one of them by Frank Lloyd Wright) and the crumbling streets at the south end, near the Brick and Tile; and you hear, in that same neighborhood, two NAACP ladies, one white, one Negro, discussing the phrasing of a letter to the school board politely protesting the use of *Little Black Sambo* in the elementary grades. And then, finally, you hear again all those people speaking about how good Mason City is for raising a family, and you wonder what kind of society it is that must separate growing up and the rearing of children from the places where most of its business is transacted, its ideas discussed, and its policies determined. And then you wonder, too, what would happen if something ever came seriously to disturb Main Street's normalcy, if direct demands were ever made, if the letters ceased being polite, if the dark places—the discrimination and disregard—were probed and, for the first time, tested. Small towns do co-opt, you think, not by what they do, not by their hospitality, but by what we wish they were—because all of us, big city boys and small, *want* to believe. And yet, when Ozark 974 rises from the runway, off to Dubuque, over the corn and beets, over the Mississippi, off to Chicago, you know that you can't go home again, that the world is elsewhere, and that every moment the distances grow not smaller but greater. Main Street is far away.

UNIT I / ISSUES FOR CONSIDERATION

1. How does the place where one lives affect the relative importance of his vote?
2. Is it true that the typical small town in the United States has not been affected by changes that are taking place in the larger society?
3. What are some of the consequences of having large numbers of persons who live one place (in the suburbs) but work somewhere else (in the city)?
4. How does increased urbanization affect the functioning of the educational institution? What about the family? The church?
5. If you were Chinese, what would be some of the different problems you would confront in San Francisco as compared with Mason City, Iowa?

UNIT J
SEX AND AGE: MAN AND WOMAN, YOUNG AND OLD

In this section we bring together two differentiating factors that have some characteristics in common and yet in other ways are very different. Age and sex are both "visible" in the sense that one carries with him visible indicators of his age and sex which he cannot easily put aside. In addition, these characteristics provide the individual with what some sociologists have called ascribed statuses. There is little one can do about changing these characteristics. With the exception of a few transexuals, if you are born a male you stay a male all your life. Although your age-status is continually changing, the changes are inevitable, despite vigorous attempts by some to stay young.

What is most important from the frame of reference that we have been using in this part of the book is the fact that society places great emphasis on these factors. Weisstein's article on women in the first part of the book clearly pointed this out. It is not significant that some people are young and some old, some female and others male. What is significant for our understanding of the behavior of these individuals is the *meaning*, the *expectations*, and the *values* that society places on these attributes. Hentoff's analysis of current books on the role of women reflects the attention being placed on this topic at the present time.

It is a valuable exercise to consider each of these differentiating factors in relation to the institutions that were studied in Part One of this text. Rockefeller does this in his article on youth. Can you see differences in the function of the educational institution for men and women? What about the family? What does Burger's article reveal regarding the relationship between age and the economy?

25 / THE CURSE

Margot Hentoff

Up From the Pedestal, edited by Aileen S. Kraditor. Quadrangle Books, 372 pp., $8.95.

Thinking About Women, by Mary Ellmann. Harcourt, Brace & World, 240 pp., $4.95.

Born Female, by Caroline Bird, with Sara Welles Briller. McKay, 288 pp., $5.95.

"One does not like to be told that one is naturally the inferior of a little man . . . who breathes hard, wears a ready-made tie, and has not shaved this fortnight."

Virginia Woolf,
A Room of One's Own

It is not good luck to be born a woman. Given the choice in advance, who would elect it? It is disagreeable to be part of a lesser class unless that class is both militant and rising. But women, as a class, have their fortunes inextricably bound up with those of their oppressors. They, says Aileen Kraditor, "have been the only subordinated group that has belonged to the same families as its rulers."

Still, we make the best of it. "I have not," writes Mary Ellmann, "heard of women who have killed themselves simply and entirely because they were women." For a depressed majority, we are rather cheerful; enjoying the benefits of a kind of culture of poverty in which lowered expectations allow us to be successful even when we have not really achieved anything. The wife of a president—so long as she does not fall down drunk in public—will invariably appear on a list of most admired women.

This notion of the existence of women's spheres in which it is possible to be both best-of-class and still inferior to half the population has come down intact from the past. Only the definition of woman's territory changes as conditions change. Activities tend to fall within her boundaries after having slipped from the highest status levels. One suspects that women doctors became emotionally acceptable at about the time pure science leaped into prominence as the field for the best minds.

From *The New York Review of Books*, Jan. 16, 1969. Reprinted with permission from

Yet women are not too much disturbed by their condition. Except for brief periods of heightened interest—most notably during those times when society threatens to come apart—women have been largely indifferent to feminism. In fact, they tend to be embarrassed by it. One has only to complain publicly of sex-based inequities to elicit a protesting letter from, let us say, a mother who writes that carving wooden birds for her children is more creative than taking a job—which is doubtless true, jobs being what they are, but has nothing to do with equity.

Anti-feminists have always maintained that women were privileged not to be forced into the dreary day-to-day work of the world, a slippery concept responsive to a feminist movement of middle-class women of leisure. During this century, however, women increasingly do the dreary work outside their homes, and then go home and do it inside.

"Women don't want to be plant managers," we are told. "They have other concerns." Or, Mary Ellmann writes: "I read that only nineteen American women became orthodontists in 1962. I am humiliated .... It's days before I think to be glad that so few *wanted* to be orthodontists."

Yes—but then one thinks of the women who have grown old as assistants to plant managers and orthodontists and wonders if, being stuck with the machines and the teeth anyway, they might not as well enjoy the money and the fun.

But they do not really think about it, women. And, can they be expected to? Acquiescence in one's oppression is the mark of oppression. One of the quandaries of early feminism was that if it were acknowledged that women had been impaired by subjugation, how could equal rights be demanded for an inferior caste? If, however, women had not been damaged, what then was wrong with the system? In any case, thinking about women is disheartening. As is reading about them. After a while, one begins to imagine that if all events had been utterly changed, if wars and revolutions had ended differently, if history had not happened, the status of women would still be what it is. We are a class outside history.

Aileen Kraditor, the author of *The Ideas of the Woman Suffrage Movement* has now, in *Up From the Pedestal,* edited and commented on an impressive selection of 300 years of writing about women. Here is Anne Bradstreet in 1642:

> *For such despight they cast on female wits:*
> *If what I doe prove well, it wo'nt advance,*
> *They'l say its stolne, or else, it was by chance.*

And "Constantia," writing in the *Massachusetts Magazine* in 1790 of the differences in nurturing the sexes:

> ... the one is taught to aspire, and the other is early confined and limited.... She experiences a mortifying consciousness of inferiority, which embitters every enjoyment.

Here are puffy men dwelling on the analogy of the female vine clinging to the sturdy masculine oak; the feminist response that if they will look at the oak about which the ivy twines, they will see that it is dead at the top. And those awesone nineteenth-century feminists, the Grimké sisters, Elizabeth Cady Stanton, Susan B. Anthony, and the others who vigorously proclaimed the legitimacy of women—even their superiority—demanded female autonomy, challenged man and the Bible, rummaged in the past for evidence of ancient matriarchates which, like those vanished African civilizations of black history, were always golden. Later, there were new names and more politic approaches as the high-minded abolitionist morality faded into the turn-of-the-century pragmatism of the next generation of suffragists.

The last document in the book is the 1966 *Statement of Purpose* marking the inception of the National Organization for Women, which was formed to "bring women into full participation in the mainstream of American society now ... [believing] the time has come to move beyond the abstract argument, discussion, and symposia over the status and special nature of women...."

It would seem that, over so long a period of time, every possible argument against the full political, economic, and social equality of women would have been beaten into the ground. The issue should be done with by now. It is a bore. Yet, Caroline Bird's *Born Female*, which is useful for its documentation of discrimination against women, tells us with facts and statistics what we all already know: women today do not have political, economic, and social rights equal to men. Even the addition of the category "sex" to that section of the Civil Rights Bill of 1964 which prohibited discrimination in employment was introduced by a Southern Congressman in order to embarrass and annoy the Northern liberals. We are, in victory too, it seems, a joke.

Thinking About Women is the twist of the knife; a witty, rueful essay by Mary Ellmann on attitudes toward women—literary and other. Norman Mailer is much in evidence, as is fitting for America's pre-eminent male colonialist. Here is Mailer in the *Presidential Papers*:

> The fact of the matter is that the prime responsibility of a woman probably is to be on earth long enough to find the best mate possible for herself, and conceive children who will improve the species.

And Freud who, resenting John Stuart Mill's conception of intellectual freedom for women, wrote about his fiancée:

> Am I to think of my delicate sweet girl as a competitor . . . I will make every effort to get her out of the competitive role into the quiet, undisturbed activity of my home.

Mrs. Ellmann is sharp and funny in the sections on sexual analogy (the ovum has a lonely existential journey while the sperm travels like a mass of jostling commuters), phallic criticism, and feminine stereotypes. Her writing is mordant and dry—perhaps to avoid embodying what she sees as a fundamental male concept of females: that they are wet. They are also shrill, hysterical, formless, irrational, and deciduous. Soft, too. One cannot argue with her statement that "The male body lends credence to assertions, while the female takes it away." In this context, only imagine Johnson, Nixon, or Humphrey as women. Who would have put up with any of them. for an instant?

When one reads about women, it becomes clear why so few women, anywhere in the world, are in positions of real power and authority: people do not think much of them.

What, if anything, is to be done? Feminist thinking on the subject has shifted as each specific victory on a list of demands failed to bring total victory: higher education, access to professions, the vote. At one time, the socialist answer was the abolition of private property. Engels found the elemental instance of class oppression in monogamy: male using female as his means of production of legitimate heirs so that his property could be preserved intact. But where are the female leaders in the socialist states?

There has been, in the past few years, a resurgence of American feminist activity—most recently in response to the discovery by some women in the new radical movements that they had once again become a ladies' auxiliary. Even while "restructuring" the society, women were still most useful as typists and cooks. Simultaneously, militant black women were encouraged to subordinate their own drive for equality to black men's assertion of their rightful masculine role.

Among the new women's liberation groups, WITCH (Women's International Terrorist Conspiracy from Hell) has the most arresting name, but its activities so far have been more guerrilla theater than IRA—not nearly so terrorist as Mrs. Pankhurst's British suffragettes who poured acid in mailboxes and blew things up until the First World War threw them back into the service of Man.

Of course, it is easier to fight unjust laws than an ambiance; difficult to unite women against an attitude. So the new feminists again look for a focus in the law: abortion law reform, state-supported day care centers, the end of protective legislation. But many of them have concluded that it is the family structure which is the root cause of difficulty. The most radical insist it is the fundamental fact that only females reproduce. To be a mother is to be the eternal footman. Nothing short of the destruction of the family system *and* the end of internal reproduction will do.

This future is made at least faintly plausible by projected advances in biology which deal with the artifical production of life. Add to this the increasing need to limit population growth and you have the possibility of eliminating women *qua* women altogether.

But that is at least a generation away. In the meantime, there will be more books.

26 / WHO CARES FOR THE AGED?

Robert E. Burger

Approximately one of every ten Americans is over sixty-five, and the proportion is increasing every year. Two-thirds of these Americans suffer from some chronic condition—high blood pressure, arthritis, diabetes, or other afflictions. Yet there are only about 30,000 institutions of all kinds designed to take care of them—with enough beds to handle only one out of fifty. The majority of the aged, in addition, do not qualify for either Medicare or Medicaid. The *median* annual income for the single person over sixty-five is $1,055, and 30 per cent—single or married—live in poverty. Their families, therefore, must be able to pay what amounts to half of a normal take-home wage per month for even the most limited care.

The financial dilemma posed by nursing homes reflects a more fundamental question. What is the place of the aged in America? Most Americans have accepted the assumption that the aged are better off by themselves. We seem to believe that their medical needs are different, and that they can be treated more efficiently as a group; that their interests and their sensibilities are protected when they are among others of their own age; and that they live longer, happier lives away from the pressures of the competitive, youthful world. All of these assumptions are fundamentally incorrect, but the pressures leading to them are easy to understand. We have not been able to face the basic medical need of the aged—rehabilitation. A definitive study in 1966 of 2,000 public-welfare patients of New York nursing homes concluded that, "extensive rehabilitation of aged residents in nursing homes is neither practical nor socially productive.... Maximum rehabilitation efforts should be applied earlier, and in other sites than nursing homes." We have habitually viewed the nursing home not as a place for rehabilitation at all, but as "the last resort" for a "difficult" older person. Thus, the basic technique of rehabilitation—keeping the patient active—has been systematically precluded by the way such homes are filled and financed. Bedridden patients receive a higher welfare payment, require less attention, and seldom leave.

The rapid industrialization of America has also stripped our aged of the responsibilities and functions they possessed in an agrarian society. Unproductive, they soon feel unwanted. And so the pressures for separation from society grow on both sides, a tendency that seems to have psychological validity among younger and younger age groups. The executive "retires early" because his fifty-ish age level has put him out of contention for a promotion. The blue collar worker buys a condominium in a "retirement village" (minimum age, once fifty-three, is now down to forty-five), because his grown children have no real contact with him.

These psychological pressures, working to widen the gap between the old and young, have received unexpected impetus from another source. The miracle that has made old age possible for many more Americans has also made it more frustrating. Modern medicine has increased the life expectancy for American men from forty-nine years in 1900 to almost seventy years today. Yet the life expectancy for men at the age of sixty-five is fourteen additional years, compared to thirteen in 1900. We have prolonged life in general, thereby creating a larger group of the aged; but we have not prolonged the life of the aged. Worse, we have not made the life of the aged meaningful or in any sense self-sufficient. Instead, we have placed most of the burdens of health care on the shoulders of the aged and their families.

The American "solution"—nursing homes, homes for the aged, rest homes, retirement villages—begs the question of whether the aged are better off away from society. We have been able to hide the problem of the impossible demands of medical attention for the aged only by putting the aged who are ill out of public sight.

The latest fad in the stock market, according to financial columnist

Sylvia Porter, is the nursing home business. Even before Medicare was voted in, such firms as Holiday Inn and Sheraton Hotels were planning nursing home chains. At least seven chains are now publicly owned and, according to *Business Week* "most have become high fliers." Federally financed programs are obviously behind this boomlet, as they are responsible for the construction of housing for the aged in low-income redevelopment projects. Tax laws have also made church-sponsored old-age apartment complexes financially feasible. It would seem that, although the cost to the individual family may still be high, care for the aged is catching up with the medical and environmental problem.

A basic misconception, however, clouds the issue. Medicare covers only a small minority of the aged—those who require post-hospital care for a maximum of 100 days. In the language of the bill, Title XVIII of the Social Security Act of 1967, a Medicare patient is one who needs "extended care" in a "medically oriented" facility. "Extended" means extended from a hospital, not extended in time or extensive in nature. The idea of Medicare was to take old people out of hospitals when they could be treated adequately in a nursing home near a hospital before going home. Medicare pays $16 a day for room, board, and medical care to the nursing home, for each qualified patient. It is not intended to provide a solution for old people who wish to retire from society.

The nursing home chains touted in financial circles have been developed merely for the specialized need of providing hospital-related, short-term care. It is a sad commentary on the standards of nursing homes prior to Medicare that such a wide-open market exists for facilities that meet even the nominal requirements of Title XVIII. To qualify under Medicare, a home must have a physician and a registered nurse "on call" around the clock—and, since the home must be affiliated with a hospital in the first place, this presents no problem. The physical-therapy specialists required by Medicare would also be only a matter of cost, not availability.

In the strictest sense of the phrase these Medicare facilities are nursing homes. Yet the expression has been used so loosely in the past that a new nomenclature has been felt necessary. Such homes are officially referred to as "medically oriented nursing homes."

Non-medically oriented nursing homes, a contradiction in terms, make up the market for long-term or terminal care of the aged. Such facilities, as well as the more aptly described rest homes and homes for the aged, benefit from another provision of the 1967 Social Security Act, Title XIX. Dubbed "Medicaid" but usually confused with Medicare, this legislation is far broader in application and depends on matching programs established state by state. The Medicaid program is really nothing new as far as the aged are concerned, nor, in many cases, does it increase the level of care for the aged offered in state welfare programs. Institutions are paid about the same amounts under Medicaid as they were under previous programs (a basic rate of about $300 a month per patient), but more of the money now comes from Washington. Medicaid simply provides a financial base for medical assistance to citizens of all ages who fall in certain income categories. Residents of New York State are familiar with the comprehensive program initiated by Governor Rockefeller under the Medicaid program, which directly affects about one out of ten people in New York City. Besides dramatizing the skyrocketing costs of providing adequate medical care for the general public, Medicaid initially gave promise of establishing some kind of uniformity and enforceable standards among participating doctors and institutions.

Yet Medicaid has proved to be toothless in regulating the institutions that are subsidized by this law to care for the aged. "Welfare" or "MAA" (Medical Assistance to the Aged) patients and the homes that will take them are still the responsibility of *state* licensing agencies. This was assured by powerful lobbying by nursing home associations in writing key provisions of Medicaid. For years, state authorities have grappled with the problem of how to regulate substandard homes for the aged when strict enforcement would bring only further hardship on their patients. When threatened with being closed up for persistent violations, operators of ragtag homes shrug, "What do you want us to do—throw them out in the street?"

Of the roughly 30,000 institutions offering long-term care for the aged, more than half make no pretense of offering adequate nursing care. The law in most states requires a registered nurse or a licensed practical nurse to be in attendance eight hours a day at homes that care for MAA patients. But the standards for a "practical nurse" hardly measure up to the demands of aged patients with both psychological and medical problems. The shortage of registered nurses for good paying jobs in hospitals suggests the quality of care offered by registered nurses in nursing homes—whose average salary breaks down to $2.40 an hour. Practical nurses average $1.65, and the national average for all employees in nursing homes is less than $1.25. "Nurse's Aide" has become almost a meaningless designation in the trade, yet it is constantly used by nursing home operators to rationalize their fees. If a licensing agency finds that a home is ignoring the requirement of having a professional nurse on duty, a "grace period" is extended until the situation can be remedied. Some homes have been in "grace periods" for a year at a time. The Oregon Board of Health only expressed the common dilemma when it stated, "It is a hoax on the public to call these institutions for old people 'nursing homes' when there is no nursing service."

The hoax is perpetuated by individual states, however, in refusing to reorganize their agencies which regulate the field. And the $300 or more per month paid by the state for each welfare patient subsidizies substandard homes and spawns new ones.

At the other end of the medical profession, an equally destructive masquerade goes on. This is the practice of doctors setting up or sponsoring a nursing home to which they refer patients without disclosing their interest. Several years ago, Consumers Union termed this a "festering scandal that warrants prompt attention by the American Medical Association." The AMA, however, lobbies side by side with the American Nursing Home Association. Far from being attended to, this problem of conflict of interest has been openly dismissed by the new nursing home promoters. (Four Seasons Nursing Centers of America, Inc., is one of many developers who finance their homes by selling interests to physicians. Four Seasons reports that 50 per cent of its beds are often filled by referrals from their doctor-owners.)

Potentially more dangerous than conflict of interest is the moral and financial weight that the medical profession is throwing behind nursing homes as *the* solution to the problems of the aged. Rehabilitation is simply not a profitable field for investment.

It can be argued that at least these new physician-sponsored homes are correcting the abuses that have plagued the industry for the last thirty years. Yet, for every new home with private rooms, a beauty parlor, a cocktail hour, and physical therapists (at $600–$900 a month), there are a dozen that exist by cutting all possible corners to make a $300 a month subsidy from the state profitable.

According to the National Fire Prevention Association, the most dangerous place to be in America, with respect to fire, is in a nursing home. Nursing home fires are especially terrifying because of the helplessness of their victims. The NFPA has stated that deaths resulting from these fires could be greatly reduced or eliminated if sprinkler systems were universally required. But in many states, such a regulation has been systematically opposed by nursing-home or homes-for-the-aged groups on the grounds that it would put many homes out of business. In the most disastrous fire in Ohio's history, a modern, concrete-block structure became a funeral pyre for sixty-three aged patients in 1963—yet the state association successfully blocked a sprinkler ordinance that might have made such a fire impossible.

A second abuse is the threat to health in general. Gerontologists tell us that one of the most dangerous treatments for non-psychotic seniles is enforced inactivity. Under the pressure of Medicaid payments (and other "welfare" payments before Medicaid), patients are confined to bed more often than necessary, to earn a $3 to $5 additional subsidy. They are also easier to deal with, pose less of an insurance hazard from falls, and are more permanent guests.

Mere confinement to a bed, moreover, is only the beginning of the health hazard to the patient. In the typically understaffed home, the patient is not turned in his bed often enough to prevent the dreaded decubitus ulcer (euphemistically, a bedsore), an open wound which is as painful as it is difficult to arrest. The misuse of drugs, either to control patients or to cut expenses, is widespread and leads to irreversible medical problems that untrained help cannot be expected to handle. A less publicized abuse is the deprivation of those small conveniences and human activities that make up the stuff of life and, in many cases, are all that make life worth living. Food, for example, is a constant problem in the substandard home. In the states with admittedly the best nursing homes, the average spent per patient per day for food is 94 cents—and this is according to the homes' own figures supplied to justify the highest possible welfare rate. The patient's sense of purpose, or even the mere feeling of accomplishing something is absent—and this void is exploited by unscrupulous nursing home operators to cow the patients, to prevent exposure of other abuses, or to magnify their own importance. One of the most common complaints from visitors to nursing homes is the disregard for the privacy of patients. Operators often conduct an inspection tour for the benefit of prospective customers without the faintest apology to the dumbfounded patients on exhibition.

Perhaps the basic abuse is the insult to the patient as a person. Sometimes this occurs by intention. The notorious "life-care contract," for instance, amounts to an insurance policy, paid in advance by the patient or his family in a lump sum, and guarantees a bed as long as the patient lives. Whether he lives or dies, however, the money is in the hands of the person who stands to benefit from the patient's early demise. By stripping the patient of his will to live—through daily sniping, snubs, and slurs—a nursing home can kill a man. Even where life-care contracts are simply a reasonable bet by both parties, the unconscious resentment of a guest who is "overdue" cannot fail to have its effect.

In spite of numerous newspaper exposés, voluminous testimony at Congressional hearings, and an endless recitation of personal experiences by nurses, patients, and their relatives, the official stance of the industry is first to deny the existence of a problem, and second to blame any documented abuses on government red tape. When the Attorney General of California recently issued a report charging an $8-million "bilking" of MediCal by doctors, pharmacies, hospitals, and nursing homes, spokesmen for these groups called the accusation "unfounded." "Only a small minority" always seems to be the culprit. Yet the state, which pays an average of $140,000 a year to each home under MediCal, claims that *most* of these homes are guilty of double billing, over-servicing, padding, or all three.

The Department of Health, Education, and Welfare has promised a nationwide review of Medicare and Medicaid as a result of the California scandal. This review could well be the opportunity for a look into the social and medical aspects of our old-age institutions as well as their financial meanderings.

Hopefully legislators and government agencies will examine the obvious alternatives to institutional care of the aged. In the parallel field of the mentally handicapped, "de-institutionalization" has already begun. Three-fourths of the population of the village of Botton, England, consist of mentally handicapped adults who have achieved a degree of isolation consistent with their malady but have, at the same time, avoided the hospital atmosphere and psychological imprisonment of an institution. At recent conferences in the United States, specialists in this field have called for an end to the "bounty" that government agencies confer on institutions for each handicapped inmate, thereby frustrating any other form of care.

Among the alternatives to institutional care of the aged are two general courses of action: greater stress on rehabilitation, and assistance to the aged as persons rather than as patients. Rehabilitation, socially and psychologically as well as physically, will have to be made as profitable as "terminal care" for any chance of success on a large scale. Medicare, with its higher medical standards and limitation to short-term care, is a step in this direction. Unfortunately, its impetus has been all but smothered in the far broader and less selective provisions of Medicaid.

Perhaps the most direct method of encouraging rehabilitation is simply to offer Medicare and Medicaid benefits to the person rather than to the institution that claims him as a patient. Payments could be made to the family for medical treatments under the supervision of their doctor and for nursing care when no adult relatives are at home. If this seems a less efficient method than mass-care in an institution, consider the success of Homemakers, Inc. This profit-minded operation now has franchises in some fifteen major cities, offering in-home nursing or attendant care at well under the cost of a nursing or rest home. Similar services are offered in some metropolitan areas by non-profit groups.

The point is that Medicare provides only for emergency in-home care, and Medicaid offers a maximum of four hours a day. Far too many old people who desperately require some sort of personal care therefore find themselves caught in a trap between the regulations of federal and state programs—simply because these programs are built on institutional requirements other than the variety of personal needs. HEW officials are now exploring an "intermediate" form of Medicare that would recognize more general medical needs of old people other than post-hospital recuperation. Given our commitment to institutions, this at least offers a measure of relief for the present.

Amendments to Medicaid, to become effective in 1969, indicate that Congress is not unaware of the drawbacks of the present system. Although state agencies must still police the program, benefits are to be broadened beyond institutional care, and higher standards will be required—such as disclosure of ownership of nursing homes, accounting for drugs, and a level of health services similar to that of Medicare. By December 31, 1969, national fire safety regulations will go into effect for Medicaid facilities.

Strict enforcement of Medicaid provisions at the state level will have to come before the stranglehold of substandard institutions can be broken. Nursing home associations must realize that such enforcement and such exposés as the Attorney General's report in California can only help them, not hurt them. The need for good nursing homes will remain for a long time to come in a competitive, profit-motivated society. At the same time, the more basic need for a just, human, and respectful treatment of 20,000,000 aged Americans cannot remain unfulfilled.

Charles Boucher, senior medical officer in the British Ministry of Health, says: "our philosophy is that old people want to remain at home, in their own houses, surrounded by their own possessions, their own memories. We don't mind whether it is a good home, a bad home, a tiny home. That's where we believe they should be . . . where they feel secure, where they've got confidence. It's tempting to think that it's a matter of institutions and that sort of thing. I think it is rather like condemning old cars to the scrap heap."

27 / IN PRAISE OF YOUNG REVOLUTIONARIES

John D. Rockefeller III

For some months, I have been engaged in the adventure of trying to understand a problem which, for want of a better term, has been called the "Youth Revolution." I found that young people will talk to an older person—even though they may regard him as a member of the Establishment—but only if they feel he is genuinely interested in them.

Every generation has had its gap. But it seems unmistakably clear to me that we are experiencing something much more than the age-old rebelliousness of youth. The ferment of today is deep and intense. Although the activists are a minority of young people, it is a larger and more vocal minority than ever before. The youth revolt is a world-wide phenomenon, occurring not only in the United States, but in a dozen other countries such as France, Mexico, Japan, and Czechoslovakia. There is a tenacity that was lacking in the past. Young people do not seem to be merely getting something out of their systems. Perhaps it is too early to tell, but I do not believe they will slip easily into the comforts of suburbia and the career, leaving behind their idealism and impulse for change.

How do we explain this phenomenon as it is occurring in the United States? There are many theories and no entirely satisfactory answers. The young people of today were born after the Depression and under a nuclear shadow. In an age of affluence and potential Armageddon, they are less concerned about material security and more concerned about basic human values. They feel that time is running out on the great problems—war, racial injustice, poverty. They dislike the impersonalism of large organizations and rapid technological change. Because of the influence of the mass media and the freedoms of our society, young people today learn faster and mature earlier. They become quickly aware—and deeply resentful—of the differences between what older people say and what they do. In short, the very accomplishments of our generation—in technology, communications, affluence—have served to focus the attention of the young on what we have failed to accomplish.

From *Saturday Review*, Dec. 14, 1968. Based on remarks by John D. Rockefeller 3rd upon receiving the annual award of the Society for the Family of Man on Oct. 23, 1968 in New York City.

I want to confess frankly that when I started my inquiry I was biased. My instincts told me that very much of what young people are doing and saying today basically makes sense and is good. I found this to be even more true than I had thought.

At the same time, I do not ignore the disturbing elements of the youth revolution. There are the far-left extremists who say that present society must be destroyed. Their challenge must be met. There are the truly alienated, the loners, and dropouts. They must be helped. There is the use of dangerous drugs. This must be stopped. Too often, while fighting for their beliefs, young people disregard the basic human values and rights which they are espousing. They frequently lack compassion. They are often contemptuous of those who do not fully agree with them. While crying out to be heard, they will shout down a speaker.

There is much to irritate and disturb the older generation. But I submit that we have let ourselves be distracted by the colorful fringes to the point where we miss the central meaning of today's youthful protest. I am convinced that not only is there tremendous vitality here, but that there is also great potential for good if we can only understand and respond positively. I believe this becomes evident if we examine how the youth revolution is manifested in three of the basic institutions of our society.

There is, first of all, the legal framework of society and its attendant issues of violence, social protest, justice, and respect for the law. A major factor distinguishing the current revolt from the past is the skill of young people in the tactics of social protest. They act in ways that would have been hard to imagine for the rebels of my generation. They have learned well from the civil rights movement of the 1950s and the Vietnam protests of the 1960s.

Yet, for the most part, young people attempt to work within normal channels to present their grievances and establish a dialogue. They have tried to work through the political system, their support of Senator McCarthy being the best example. It is they who have made the Peace Corps, VISTA, and the Teacher's Corps more than slogans. Many young people are preparing for long-term efforts to change society. For example, the law students of today are concerned less about trusts and estates and corporate law and more about how just the laws are, how poor people and black people can get a better break before the law.

But even as the majority of young people work constructively for change, it remains a fact that severe provocation and even violence have increased as forms of social protest. The protesters are fired by their sense of moral righteousness. They feel that they have learned from experience that it is necessary to be loud and demonstrative to get results. It is this behavior that compels attention and strikes fear for the very stability of American society.

The nature of our response is crucial, for it has everything to do with whether there will continue to be violence and whether violence will pay. We must understand that social protest has an honorable history and has a rightful place in any enlightened society. We must remember that it was social protest that brought this nation into being.

At the same time, we must recognize that respect for law and the maintenance of order are essential for the protection of everyone in our society. Young people—anyone—who break the law as a form of protest must be prepared to pay the penalty and hope for ultimate vindication. But if we stop here we will have failed. The concept of law and order is meaningless without justice. We must be ready to re-examine our assumptions—and our laws. To do so, we must open channels of communication. We must have dialogue. If we do not—if we think the only answer is to suppress dissent—then the responsibility for violence hangs as heavily on us as it does on those who protest.

Many persons feel today that another of our fundamental institutions—the family—is in trouble. Much has been written and said about the permissive nature of the American family, which allegedly is responsible for many of the ills of today's youth. Yet criticism of American parents' "overpermissiveness" has been part of our society since the seventeenth-century Puritans. In his penetrating study of our country early in the nineteenth century, de Tocqueville commented about the domination of youth and their lack of respect for their elders. Even the authoritarian Victorian age was beset with youthful rebellion.

The family provides a framework and a set of guidelines for a child's growth and development toward adulthood. It is the parents' responsibility to give the child love, freely and warmly shared, and discipline, fairly but firmly administered, which in turn means time, attention, and interest devoted to the child. In this way, family life plays a major role in determining the stability of the child and the depth and solidarity of his values.

I cannot stress too strongly my belief that children learn much more from what their parents do than from what they say. Many young people state that while their parents talk about love, integrity, freedom, and fair play, their actions are heavily oriented toward materialistic security, comfort, and status. They repeatedly point out that they are not rejecting their parents themselves, but rather what they see as the hypocrisy of their parents' double-standard approach to important social values.

Again, it seems to me that the nature of our response is crucial. If I am right that the ferment of youth is potentially of enormous benefit to society, then we might ask: Would we really rather have apathetic and obedient copies of ourselves? More importantly, we might take the criticisms of young people seriously and re-examine some of our basic assumptions. This, of course is not easy. We are used to having our children listen to us, rather than our listening to them. Everyone likes to think that he has done reasonably well in life; it comes as a shock to find that our children believe differently. Change can be very difficult and threatening, especially when the pressure comes from the young. The temptation is to tune them out; it takes much more courage to listen.

When we turn to the third of our basic institutions—the church—we encounter a deep irony. Young people today are committed to values of love, human dignity, individual rights, and trust in one's fellowman. These are precisely the values of our Judeo-Christian heritage. The church has been the proponent of these values for centuries. Yet no institution in our society today suffers more from the sheer indifference of the young. By and large, they have dismissed the church as archaic, ineffective, and irrelevant. One young man told me: "There's a genuine religious revival going on, but the church is missing out on it." Another said: "The church could fill a great need in our society, if it would focus less on the divine and more on how to apply Christian teaching to today's world."

The problem again is that the young people perceive hypocrisy. They know the values that the church upholds, but they see too little in the way of action and results. Religion to many of them is Sunday-morning tedium instead of a guiding force and an inspiration. The older generation must examine its own behavior. The church is not an impersonal edifice, although all too often it seems that way. The church is what we have made it. Its dilemma is that while its mission should be the righting of wrongs and the active pursuit of the great Judeo-Christian values, we have instead made it for the most part a force for the status quo.

By and large, we are much more conservative as elders of the church than we are as parents. The minister who would remain a minister all too often must please a conservative laity, those who support the church financially. The result is that the church loses some of the finest members of the younger generation. If we have made this situation, we can also change it. Any dramatic reversal seems improbable. But the young people will come back gradually if the church becomes a place for searching inquiry, for social action; if more of the clergy become involved in today's problems and if the laity support them—and become involved, too.

There are common threads that run through all of these basic institutions of our society. The problem is not in our legal system, or the family, or the church. The problem lies in ourselves as people. The crucial issue is not the revolt of youth but the nature of our response to it. Broadly speaking, there are three possible responses. One is backlash and suppression. We caught frightening glimpses of what this would be like in

Chicago and Mexico City. If we choose this route, the only victors will be the small fringe of extremists who want to see our society destroyed. They are playing one of the oldest of political games, that of provocateurs. They want a backlash because they know that repression starts a vicious circle that inevitably leads to greater and greater explosions. If we are foolish enough to fall into this trap, then we will deserve what happens to us.

A much more likely response is apathy or muted hostility. We are resentful over the ingratitude and brashness of the young. We think if we cover our eyes and stop our ears their noise and fervor will go away. They don't understand how really complex everything is, we say. Being older, we believe we are wiser. We know that idealism is tempered by time and that realism sets in. Soon the young activists will pass the magic age of thirty, and eventually they will be stepping into our vacant shoes. We secretly enjoy thinking about what a tough time they will have explaining to their children why they did not solve all the problems of the world.

This response, or lack of it, basically avoids the issue or yields grudgingly in a kind of tokenism. It is not working very well, and if I am right that the youth revolt of today is something much more than the normal rebelliousness of the young, then it will not work at all in the long run. We will find ourselves constantly pushed toward the brink of backlash.

The greater tragedy will be the opportunity we will have lost. For we know all too well that time is running out on the great problems the world faces. It seems to me that we have a choice. By suppression or apathy, we can make the youth revolution into yet another problem—in which case the burden will become crushing. Or we can respond in positive ways so that the energy and idealism of youth can be a constructive force in helping to solve the world's great problems. The third possible response, then, is simply to be responsive—to trust our young people, to listen to them, to understand them, to let them know that we care deeply about them.

Instead of worrying about how to suppress the youth revolution, we of the older generation should be worrying about how to sustain it. The student activists are in many ways the elite of our young people. They perform a service in shaking us out of our complacency. We badly need their ability and fervor in these troubled and difficult times. The key to sustaining the energy and idealism of youth is more direct and effective action on the problems about which young people are concerned—the problems of our cities, of our environment, of racial injustice, of irrelevant and outmoded teachings, of overpopulation, of poverty, of war.

To achieve such action, we of the older generation must re-examine our attitudes, our assumptions, and our goals. We must take as seriously as do the young the great Judeo-Christian values of our heritage. We must be as dedicated as they in fighting injustices and improving our laws. We must have a sense of responsibility, individually and collectively, for resolving the massive problems of our society. Secondly, we must revitalize our existing institutions whether they be in education, government, religion, business, or politics. They must be made more relevant to today's problems and have a greater sense of mission. At the same time, in support of the initiative of the young, new programs and institutions must be developed which can be effective in areas of pressing social need. Fresh approaches to meeting today's problems are essential.

A unique opportunity is before us to bring together our age and experience and money and organization with the energy and idealism and social consciousness of the young. Working together, almost anything is possible. If we follow this course, each of us will be involved personally and positively in the great drama of our times, rather than feeling like weary and impotent victims of imponderable forces. The antidote to despair is to be involved, to be imbued with the same spirit that fires the imagination and the efforts of the young. There is a VISTA slogan which captures this spirit: "If you're not part of the solution, you're part of the problem."

UNIT J / ISSUES FOR CONSIDERATION

1. How is the changing role of women in American society a function of changes in society's institutions?
2. Does all the concern that has been expressed about the role of the woman in American society suggest that the role of men is pretty well agreed upon and therefore requires little change? How will changes in one of these roles require changes in the other?
3. How do role changes that must take place at retirement lead to serious difficulties for some aged persons?
4. Explain what Rockefeller means when he says that the problem is not with the revolt of youth but with the nature of society's response to it.
5. Some societies make a clear distinction between the child and the adult. What are some of the consequences of the ambiguous status of the adolescent in our society?

UNIT K
DEVIANCE: THE GOOD AND THE BAD

Deviance, as seen by the sociologist, concerns not only the behavior of individuals, but also the *definitions* that society places on this behavior. The relationship between society and the deviant within society is the theme of Becker's article. The remaining three articles are designed to give the reader a feeling for the variation in the types of deviant behavior that might be found in our society and some notion of how society responds to these forms of behavior.

An important dimension of the study of deviant behavior is a concern for the process used by society to control the deviant. Since the deviant may be seen as a threat to the smooth functioning of society, its members are likely to take measures to restrict deviant forms of behavior. Perhaps it is a cultural trait of American society to react to undesirable behavior by creating laws and leaving control measures to the official institutions designed for that purpose. However, whereas some laws may be seen as a reflection of public opinion, many are not. For example, laws may be a reflection of one segment of society and directed against another. Brown's study of the persecution of the hippies is an example of this. New laws have been enacted and old laws revised in order for the dominate factions to deal with an undesirable minority: the hippies.

Public opinion is a dynamic thing, changing with the many other changes that take place in modern society. However, the law tends to be more static; with its formal institutionalized character, it changes more slowly. As a consequence, we may find instances in which the law which once reflected public opinion no longer does so. This may be the case with laws regarding marijuana. Although our society may not be willing at this point to completely legalize the use of marijuana, it is generally accepted that the punishment for possession of pot is far too severe. Fort's careful analysis of this problem should be enlightening to the reader.

We have tried to choose articles that will help the reader understand some of the relationships that exist among the law, public opinion, and the behavior of the deviant. Compare the hippies, the embezzler, and the pot smoker. The hippies show that behavior need not be against the law to be considered deviant and to lead to condemnation. The embezzler shows that perfectly "respectable" persons can engage in behavior that is clearly in violation of the law and, at least for a time, not think of themselves or be thought of by others as deviant. In the case of the pot smoker, we have a situation in which norms are in transition and it is difficult to know whether or not we wish to consider the smoker as a deviant. This last example is also instructive in studying the relationship between law and public opinion. No one would seriously argue that the laws against embezzlement should be done away with, but many feel this way about marijuana laws.

Is it possible to use our knowledge of deviant behavior to improve our understanding of the political institutions in our society?

28 / DEVIANCE AND DEVIATES

Howard S. Becker

What is interesting about deviance is not what it is, but what people think it is. To be sure, there are such things as drug addiction and homosexuality, and they pose interesting problems for the physiologist, the biochemist and the psychologist. But interesting scientific problems do

---

not create public concern. The still unexplained physiological mechanisms that produce heroin addiction do not generate newspaper headlines. What arouses the government, the press and the public is the crime attributed to addicts, the fear of attack by a drug-crazed kid on a lonely street, even though addicts engage mainly in shoplifting and other kinds of petty theft; the stories of high school students using marijuana, though there is no evidence that marijuana will harm them as much as the alcohol their parents allow them to drink; the fear even, for some, that the Chinese Communists are using narcotics to weaken the will of the American people.

Deviance, in general, as opposed to concrete forms of behavior like drug use or homosexuality, is a creation of the public imagination. The act of injecting heroin into a vein is not inherently deviant. If a nurse gives a patient drugs under a doctor's orders, it is perfectly proper. It is when it is done in a way that is not publicly defined as proper that it becomes deviant. The act's deviant character lies in the way it is defined in the public mind.

The public definition of an act as deviant has, of course, drastic consequences for the person who commits it. Under one definition, he may continue to live as an ordinary citizen. Under another definition, he may become a hounded criminal. A consideration of deviance in America over the last one hundred years must inevitably focus on what people have thought of deviance and how public thinking about it has changed, and must interpret what deviants do as a reaction to the way society reacts to them.

We have had drug addicts for a long time. Before the turn of the century, as a number of early studies show, many older people were addicted to patent medicines that were liberally laced with opium. Women helped themselves through menopause with the aid of opiates, and men and women alike alleviated their minor ills with such remedies. They came to depend on their "medicine" and were addicts without knowing it. We also had more self-conscious addicts: jockeys, gamblers, pimps, whores and others in the "sporting life," who smoked opium and became addicted.

Prostitution is, of course, the oldest profession. But prostitutes in earlier times were fallen women, fenced off (in red-light districts) from more respectable people.

Homosexuality is one of the oldest vices. Homosexual literature delights in naming the famous homosexuals of early times, from Nero to the present. But it seems likely that homosexual activity in an earlier day was usually practiced as a secret vice by those who lived in the conventional world.

The examples indicate the range of possibilities, in an earlier period, in the relations between respectable people and those they considered deviant. People who engaged in practices thought to be morally repellent either did not know that they were "doing wrong," like the patent medicine addicts; knew what they were doing, but did it secretly and despised themselves for it, as they would have been despised by others if their sin were known; or lived in a separate part of society, like the sporting world, segregated and isolated from the conventional society.

Have things changed? Yes and no. The same relationships can be observed today between some kinds of deviants and the rest of society. Large numbers of people are addicted to sleeping pills and tranquilizers; since the public has not yet been persuaded that these are dangerous drugs, they do not think of themselves, and are not thought of, as deviant. Yet the observation I heard attributed to a Kansas City tavern owner—"Everybody who doesn't drink takes pills"—becomes more true every day.

The practitioners of secret vices are still around, though the catalogue of vices involved has been enlarged. There are still secret addicts and "closet queens" who hide their homosexuality. There are, in addition, secret transvestites, secret devotees of sadomasochistic thrills, secret fetishists, and others whose kicks are mailed to them in plain brown envelopes with no return address.

But the analogue of the old red-light district, in which the deviant lived walled off from a society that might otherwise be contaminated by contact with him, is harder to find. Prostitutes inhabit most of the public places people go to for entertainment—bars, night clubs and hotels—at every level of society. Their way of life is not so different from that of other people as to mark them off as a special breed. It is difficult to think of any class of deviants so segregated and marked today.

Though some of the relations between deviants and respectable society characteristic of an earlier era can still be found, much has changed. Not only are deviants less segregated, but they have come, in increasing measure, to take a different view of themselves and of how they ought to be treated by others.

One component of the change is an increasing tolerance of deviance by respectable society. The deviant is no longer branded as a sinner whose consignment to hell is a foregone conclusion. Instead, ordinary people are willing to see extenuating circumstances that might account for the deviance, are willing to believe that deviants can be reformed, and are increasingly unwilling to take harsh punitive action toward deviants. Public beliefs have changed in this way, in part, because high court decisions have made it more difficult for the police to "roust" deviants in what used to be their customary fashion. Police habitually control deviance not by actually convicting people of crimes on the basis of evidence, but rather by harassing them with illegal and quasi-legal arrests that deviants are not disposed to fight because they cannot come into court with clean hands. But increasingly strict judicial interpretations of the search and seizure rule, and other decisions affecting civil rights in the area of vice and obscenity, have handcuffed the police so that these means are less available to them. (They have not, of course, given up completely; the nationwide harassment of Lenny Bruce, in clear contravention of Supreme Court decisions on obscenity, is a case in point.)

With the gradual lessening of police harassment, other influences have been at work. The rise of dimestore psychoanalysis—the easy explanation of deviant or odd behavior as the product of childhood traumas that might have happened to anyone—has helped the public to absolve deviants of responsibility for what they do. And, perhaps more important, it has helped deviants themselves to decide that what they do, right or wrong, is not their fault and, indeed, that it might not even be wrong. It is unlikely that any deviant believes this so completely that he never has a qualm about his deviant acts, but it provides the moral basis on which he can demand to be let alone.

Finally, various kinds of popular philosophical positions—the Eastern philosophies, psychological doctrines of self-development, and so on—have brought some people to see the means of salvation in what were formerly thought to be deviant practices. In particular, the use of drugs—both old-fashioned marijuana and heroin and such newer discoveries as peyote and LSD—has been seen as a way of expanding the consciousness and achieving higher levels of human experience. From this point of view, what ordinary people think deviant is not deviant at all; it is all a mistake and they need to be enlightened if they are capable of it and fought against if they attempt to interfere with one's own enlightenment.

In any case, for any or all of these reasons, deviants have become more self-conscious, more organized, more willing to fight with conventional society than ever before. They are more open in their deviance, prouder of what they are and less willing to be treated as others want to treat them without having some voice in the matter.

Homosexuals have organized what can only be called "defense groups," very much on the model of such ethnic defense organizations as the Anti-Defamation League or the NAACP. The Mattachine Society (for male homosexuals) and the Daughters of Bilitis (for Lesbians) have branches in several large cities and publish magazines (*The Mattachine Review* and *The Ladder*); they hold annual conventions at which panels of experts and members discuss the biological, psychological, sociological and legal problems of homosexuality. Their magazines are filled with discussions of famous homosexuals in history, of civil rights cases and decisions involving them or applicable to their problem, and other matters justifying their right to be homosexual.

When I addressed a Lesbian group not long ago, I was surprised (a sign of how much I accepted conventional stereotypes) at how much the group looked like a middle-class women's club having a meeting to decide how to run the next charity bazaar. Since they were conventionally dressed, not in the least "butchy," I found myself amused by the disparity between my conception of them and the reality. But I stopped smiling when I realized the aggressiveness and courage it took to identify oneself publicly as the officer of a Lesbian organization and the risk these women were taking in doing so.

Homosexual organizations have won support from "straight" scientists, psychologists, lawyers and, most recently, the clergy. A group of San Francisco clergymen sponsored a homosexual New Year's Eve dance, a gesture deliberately designed to make the affair publicly respectable. Though the police had not bothered a Halloween dance at the Hilton (to which the guests came "in drag," to the great delight of news photographers), they saw a threat in this legitimately sponsored affair and moved in, taking pictures of everyone there. Lawyers, on hand to protest such maneuvers, were the only ones arrested. But the police, undoubtedly motivated by a wish to "keep them in their place," will not prevent homosexual defense groups from winning further allies in the respectable world and pressing their fight for equal rights. The militancy of the homosexual organizations has provoked a frightened warning from a committee of the New York Academy of Medicine.

Another version of the new self-conscious deviant organization is found in Synanon, a self-help organization of heroin addicts now more or less permanently settled in several places around the country, from Santa Monica and Marin County in the West to Westport in the East. The characteristic feature of Synanon is not that it thinks addicts ought to be allowed to take drugs in peace, even though many experts feel this is the most efficient and humane solution to the drug problem, but that it thinks addicts ought to break the habit with the help of ex-addicts rather than being cured forcibly by police or psychiatrists. With merciless discipline, Synanon forces the addicts who join to toe the line or get out. Since no professional group has very much success curing addicts, Synanon (whose successes are not yet reliably measured, if indeed there is any reliable measure) stands on solid ground when it demands that its members be given the right to help themselves. It has, of course, provoked strong reactions from many professionals in the drug-cure field, who cannot believe that any good can come of ex-addicts associating with one another. On the other hand, it has won strong support from many legislators and a few of the professionals who have had an opportunity to inspect its establishments.

Synanon is a grim operation. Not so the short-lived International Foundation for Internal Freedom (IFIF), headed by Timothy Leary and Richard Alpert, the psychologists who left Harvard after an extended battle over whether their experimental use of LSD and other psychedelic (mind-expanding) drugs with students was a proper professional activity. IFIF, in contrast to Synanon and the homosexual groups, is a frankly utopian organization. It looks forward to a radically changed society, in which people will see through the games of life they now play in deadly earnest—the family game, the work game, etc.—and, freed by the use of LSD, live in happier forms of human association, realizing at last the as yet untapped resources of the human mind and spirit.

Leary and Alpert attempted to found a colony embodying these ideas in Zihuatanejo, but the Mexican government drove them out. They are now giving seminars and lectures designed to let others in on the good news, and Leary has just published a book, based on the *Tibetan Book of the Dead*, of ritual and instruction to be used to enhance the LSD experience. They have had a fair amount of success, most of it with well-educated people, including many engineers and "hard" scientists, who seem especially drawn by the appeal of new kinds of mystical experience. Their success has been clouded, however, by the hostility with which officialdom greets them everywhere from Massachusetts to Mexico.

The LSD movement (if it is really big enough to merit being called a movement) differs from the organizations of drug addicts and homosexuals in being composed of people who were not, prior to their involvement with LSD, deviant in any sense. But all three groups exemplify the increasing militancy, organization and self-consciousness of deviant worlds and their growing unwillingness to let respectable society have its own way with them unchallenged.

A sense of what this might lead to (if every group engaged in deviant practices became self-consciously aggressive) comes from the recent lighthearted attempt in San Francisco to have marijuana legalized. One man staged a "puff-in" at the Hall of Justice, lighting up a marijuana cigarette in front of police officers so that he could become a test case. A local attorney has become interested in testing the legality of the law. A group of forty or fifty paraded around Union Square every Sunday for a month (some of the paraders were mothers pushing baby carriages) carrying signs advocating legalization. And when President Johnson spoke, during the campaign, in front of St. Peter and Paul's Church in North Beach, scattered among the "LBJ All the Way" signs that greeted him were a few that said, "Make Marijuana Legal."

Perhaps more interesting than the organization of deviant groups, though much harder to document, is the possibility that practices and beliefs formerly labeled deviant have spread to broad segments of the "normal" population. This possibility first became known to the public, I think, with the publication of the Kinsey Report, which reported surprisingly high percentages of men who had engaged in various abnormal forms of sex behavior. Although substantial questions have been raised about Kinsey's sampling and techniques, the figures were so much higher than anyone had suspected that it is a worthwhile hypothesis that there is a lot more deviance around than meets the eye and that Americans, while not advertising the fact, are by no means as straitlaced as we had thought.

With the Kinsey findings to point the way, a good deal more evidence, most of it quite impressionistic, can be cited in favor of such conclusions. As a simple example, note the mammoth sales of works like *Candy, Fanny Hill* and the *Tropics,* which had been smuggled in from France as pornography only a few years ago. Once the legal restraints were removed, there turned out to be a good many pornography fans around.

Other evidence is not hard to come by. Not long ago, police discovered that some sixty high school students in Woodside, an affluent suburb of San Francisco, were smoking marijuana supplied by a recent graduate. Similar stories could no doubt be told about hundreds of other communities. Marijuana use is not confined to Negroes, Puerto Ricans, musicians and show people. I know of no profession which does not have at least a few members who are at least occasional marijuana users. As an example, far out enough to make the point, one user I know was first offered marijuana by a clergyman, who himself saw nothing wrong with it, though he made sure that his congregation did not find out his views. (Perhaps because I have studied marijuana use and published on the subject, similar cases are constantly brought to my attention.)

Somewhat less direct evidence comes from a survey recently conducted by Paul Verden and Harold Hodges in Santa Clara County. They asked people a number of questions designed to measure "cultural orthodoxy," the tendency to be conservative in areas ranging from political and economic attitudes to attitudes toward sex. The results are somewhat surprising. There are a great many more people who are culturally unorthodox than one might have expected. In addition, the unorthodox are scattered uniformly through all the social classes of the community. In other words, this kind of deviance—and let us grant that asking people whether or not they agree with a number of unorthodox statements is at best a weak measure of actual deviant practice—is not the monopoly of any group in the community. People of all kinds, rich and poor, feel restive under the constraints of our Victorian public morality.

Given the growing underground of practicing deviants and adherents to the culturally unorthodox, what can we make of our official morality? Why does it receive overwhelming public support, even though many, probably a growing number, no longer believe in it or allow it to restrain their activity? The most likely answer is, of course, that official morality—preached by leading public figures, embodied in laws and enforced sporadically by police—is a political product. Politicians make laws embodying its precepts, or refuse to repeal laws which embody them, because organized pressure groups make that a wise course. Those in favor of a more relaxed official morality seldom organize in a way that makes them politically effective, although ministers, physicians or lawyers may occasionally act on their behalf, as when a New York county medical society issued a report advocating less punitive narcotics laws.

Public morality must, of course, keep itself in some sort of relation to "the times," to the slow drift of opinion and practice in the country. If it gets too far out of step, it creates the kind of situation we had during Prohibition; and public leaders do not care for the widespread disrespect for law such a situation engenders and soon put an end to it. But as long as some sizable and politically influential group demands a particular official morality, state legislatures and others are likely to bow to the demand, even if the consequence is simply a public affirmation of a way of life many no longer follow. If the laws embodying the morality are not enforced too strictly and if deviants do not mind being somewhat secretive in their activities, an accommodation can be worked out more or less to everyone's satisfaction.

But our public morality may have gotten too far out of step. Recent reports on college students indicate that a vast number of college girls, whatever their private beliefs and whatever their practice, simply no longer believe in chastity, virginity and the sexual double standard that once was the American way. Whether they "do" or "don't" they do not feel that they can successfully argue—either with the boys who pursue them or with other girls—that premarital intercourse is wrong in and of itself. In the same way, it seems likely that the general public is now prepared to accept revisions of our extremely punitive laws on homosexuality and addiction.

It is hard to say what things will be like if the trend toward relaxation of older standards of morality continues. We can get a clue, perhaps, from a look at the "swingers" of Los Angeles. Los Angeles is probably the most unorganized city in the country. It has a vast number of new migrants every year, no well-organized elites to absorb and tame the newcomers (as does the San Francisco Bay Area, which also has a large in-migration), and nearly perpetual summer. With none of the constraints that might be imposed by tightly organized neighborhoods, the presence of extended families close by, or even by a seasonal change that would get people off the beach, new kinds of manners and morals seem to have grown up.

A long-time resident of the Los Angeles beach communities told me the following tale. When he moved into a house already inhabited by three other bachelors, one of them handed him a pack of calling cards that had just a phone number, the number of the house phone, printed on them. He was told to hand the cards out to likely girls wherever he met them—on the beach, in bars, in department stores, wherever—and wait for the response. And, just as he had been told, within a week the phone started ringing and never stopped. Girls who couldn't even remember who had given them the card, girls he had thought attractive but unlikely to be intrigued, old ones, young ones—they all called and they all wanted to go to bed. Neither he nor his housemates have ever wanted for companionship.

While few Angelenos are so enterprising as to have cards printed up, and while such a story is a slim basis for generalization, a community where such a gimmick will work must surely be something new in American life. Though no one has really done a thorough investigation of the matter, the casualness about sex indicated by the story is said to permeate large segments of Los Angeles society. (This in a town whose police harass Lenny Bruce as efficiently and conscientiously as those of more puritanical eastern cities!)

David Boroff has suggested that sex is the politics of the sixties, and I think he is right, though perhaps not in the sense he meant. Sex of the Los Angeles variety, drugs (both the hipster's marijuana and the more intellectual drugs like LSD), and other varieties of exotic behavior may well come to be thought of as inalienable rights, not to be interfered with by either the police or self-appointed censors of family, neighborhood or community. Whether proponents take the low road of quiet evasion of existing moralities (like the quiet coteries of marijuana users found everywhere) or the high road of principled defiance (best exemplified by Leary and Alpert's open conflict with their Harvard colleagues), they will contribute to a growing tension between themselves and those who are not ready to countenance the new ways.

The newly organized deviant groups are making use of the potential for revolutionary change contained in our cultural emphasis on egalitarianism and our legal emphasis on due process. Our institutions can, when they are spurred into action by determined men, protect minorities of whatever kind from the restraints of cultural tradition and local prejudice. The civil rights movement has shown that. The techniques, legal and extra-legal, used by opponents of racial segregation, will probably be used more and more frequently by deviant groups in the years ahead. Recent events in Berkeley have shown that political freedoms and less conventional freedoms go hand in hand; the same powers use the same means to stifle both. As the indivisible nature of freedom becomes clear, even those who do not engage in forbidden activities will be drawn into the battle, just as physicians, lawyers and ministers have already been drawn into the fight for more humane and rational treatment of addicts and homosexuals. The seeds of independence planted in 1776 will yet bear some strange fruit.

29 / THE CONDEMNATION AND PERSECUTION OF HIPPIES

Michael E. Brown

This article is about persecution and terror. It speaks of the Hippie and the temptations of intimacy that the myth of Hippie has made poignant, and it does this to discuss the institutionalization of repression in the United States.

When people are attacked as a group, they change. Individuals in the group may or may not change, but the organization and expression of their collective life will be transformed. When the members of a gathering believe that there is a grave danger imminent and that opportunities for escape are rapidly diminishing, the group loses its organizational quality. It becomes transformed in panic. This type of change can also occur outside a situation of strict urgency: When opportunities for mobility or access to needed resources are cut off, people may engage in desperate collective actions. In both cases, the conversion of social form occurs when members of a collectivity are about to be hopelessly locked into undesired and undesirable positions.

The process is not, however, automatic. The essential ingredient for conversion is social control exercised by external agents on the collectivity itself. The result can be benign, as a panic mob can be converted into a crowd that makes an orderly exit from danger. Or it can be cruel.

The transformation of groups under pressure is of general interest; but there are special cases that are morally critical to any epoch. Such critical cases occur when pressure is persecution, and transformation is destruction. The growth of repressive mechanisms and institutions is a key concern in this time of administrative cruelty. Such is the justification for the present study.

SOCIAL CONTROL AS TERROR

Four aspects of repressive social control such as that experienced by Hippies are important. First, the administration of control is suspicious. It projects a dangerous future and guards against it. It also refuses the risk of inadequate coverage by enlarging the controlled population to include all who might be active in any capacity. Control may or may not be administered with a heavy hand, but it is always a generalization applied to specific instances. It is a rule and thus ends by pulling many fringe innocents into its bailiwick; it creates as it destroys.

Second, the administration of control is a technical problem which, depending on its site and object, requires the bringing together of many different agencies that are ordinarily dissociated or mutually hostile. A conglomerate of educational, legal, social welfare, and police organizations is highly efficient. The German case demonstrates that. Even more important, it is virtually impossible to oppose control administered under the auspices of such a conglomerate since it includes the countervailing institutions ordinarily available. When this happens control is not only efficient and widespread, but also legitimate, commanding a practical, moral and ideological realm that is truly "one-dimensional."

Third, as time passes, control is applied to a wider and wider range of details, ultimately blanketing its objects' lives. At that point, as Hilberg suggests in his *The Destruction of the European Jews*, the extermination of the forms of lives leads easily to the extermination of the lives themselves. The line between persecution and terror is thin. For the oppressed, life is purged of personal style as every act becomes inexpressive, part of the struggle for survival. The options of a life-style are eliminated at the same time that its proponents are locked into it.

Fourth, control is relentless. It develops momentum as organization accumulates, as audiences develop, and as unofficial collaborators assume the definition of tasks, expression and ideology. This, according to W. A. Westley's "The Escalation of Violence Through Legitimation," is the culture of control. It not only limits the behaviors, styles, individuals and groups toward whom it is directed, it suppresses all unsanctioned efforts. As struggle itself is destroyed, motivation vanishes or is turned inward.

These are the effects of repressive control. We may contrast them with the criminal law, which merely prohibits the performance of specific acts (with the exception, of course, of the "crime without victims"—homosexuality, abortion, and drug use). Repression converts or destroys an entire social form, whether that form is embodied in a group, a style or an idea. In this sense, it is terror.

These general principles are especially relevant to our understanding of tendencies that are ripening in the United States day by day. Stated in terms that magnify it so that it can be seen despite ourselves, this is the persecution of the Hippies, a particularly vulnerable group of people who are the cultural wing of a way of life recently emerged from its quiet and individualistic quarters. Theodore Roszak, describing the Hippies in terms of their relationship to the culture and politics of dissent, notes that "the underlying unity of youthful dissent consists . . . in the effort of beat-hip bohemianism to work out the personality structure, the total life-style that follows from New Left social criticism." This life-style is currently bearing the brunt of the assault on what Roszak calls a "counter-culture"; it is an assault that is becoming more concentrated and savage every day. There are lessons for the American future to be drawn from this story.

PERSECUTION

Near Boulder, Colorado, a restaurant sign says "Hippies not served here." Large billboards in upstate New York carry slogans like "Keep America Clean: Take a Bath." and "Keep America Clean: Get a Haircut." These would be as amusing as ethnic jokes if they did not represent a more systematic repression.

The street sweeps so common in San Franciso and Berkeley in 1968 and 1969 were one of the first lines of attack. People were brutally scattered by club-wielding policemen who first closed exits from the assaulted area and then began systematically to beat and arrest those who were trapped. This form of place terror, like surveillance in Negro areas and defoliation in Vietnam, curbs freedom and forces people to fight or submit to minute inspection by hostile forces. There have also been one-shot neighborhood pogroms, such as the police assault on the Tompkins Square Park gathering in New York's Lower East Side on Memorial Day, 1967: "Sadistic glee was written on the faces of several officers," wrote the *East Village Other*. Some women became hysterical. The police slugged Frank Wise, and dragged him off, handcuffed and bloody, crying, "My God, my God, where is this happening? Is this America?" The police also plowed into a group of Hippies, Yippies, and straights at the April, 1968, "Yip-in" at Grand Central

Station. The brutality was as clear in this action as it had been in the Tompkins Square bust. In both cases, the major newspapers editorialized against the police tactics, and in the first the Mayor apologized for the "free wielding of nightsticks." But by the summer of 1968, street sweeps and busts and the continuous presence of New York's Tactical Police Force had given the Lower East Side an ominous atmosphere. Arrests were regularly accompanied by beatings and charges of "resistance to arrest." It became clear that arrests rather than subsequent procedures were the way in which control was to be exercised. The summer lost its street theaters, the relaxed circulation of people in the neighborhood and the easy park gatherings.

Official action legitimizes nonofficial action. Private citizens take up the cudgel of law and order newly freed from the boundaries of due process and respect. After Tompkins Square, rapes and assaults became common as local toughs assumed the role, with the police, of defender of the faith. In Cambridge, Massachusetts, following a virulent attack on Hippies by the Mayor, *Newsweek* reported that vigilantes attacked Hippie neighborhoods in force.

Ultimately more damaging are the attacks on centers of security. Police raids on "Hippie pads," crash pads, churches and movement centers have become daily occurrences in New York and California over the past two and a half years. The usual excuses for raids are drugs, runaways and housing violations, but many incidents of unlawful entry by police and the expressions of a more generalized hostility by the responsible officials suggests that something deeper is involved. The Chief of Police in San Francisco put it bluntly; quoted in *The New York Times* magazine in May, 1967, he said:

> Hippies are no asset to the community. These people do not have the courage to face the reality of life. They are trying to escape. Nobody should let their young children take part in this hippy thing.

The Director of Health for San Francisco gave teeth to this counsel when he sent a task force of inspectors on a door-to-door sweep of the Haight-Ashbury—"a two-day blitz" that ended with a strange result, again according to *The Times*: Very few of the Hippies were guilty of housing violations.

Harassment arrests and calculated degradation have been two of the most effective devices for introducing uncertainty to the day-to-day lives of the Hippies. Cambridge's Mayor's attack on the "hipbos" (the suffix stands for body odor) included, said *Newsweek* of Oct. 30, 1967, a raid on a "hippie pad" by the Mayor and "a platoon of television cameramen." They "seized a pile of diaries and personal letters and flushed a partially clad girl from the closet." In Wyoming, *The Times* reported that two "pacifists" were "jailed and shaved" for hitchhiking. This is a fairly common hazard, though Wyoming officials are perhaps more sadistic than most. A young couple whom I interviewed were also arrested in Wyoming during the summer of 1968. They were placed in solitary confinement for a week during which they were not permitted to place phone calls and were not told when or whether they would be charged or released. These are not exceptional cases. During the summer of 1968, I interviewed young hitchhikers throughout the country; most of them had similar stories to tell.

In the East Village of New York, one hears countless stories of apartment destruction by police (occasionally reported in the newspapers), insults from the police when rapes or robberies are reported, and cruel speeches and even crueler bails set by judges for arrested Hippies.

And what of the Hippies? They have come far since those balmy days of 1966–67, days of flowers, street-cleaning, free stores, decoration and love. Many have fled to the hills of Northern California to join their brethren who had set up camps there several years ago. Others have fled to communes outside the large cities and in the Middle West. After the Tompkins Square assault, many of the East Village Hippies refused to follow the lead of those who were more political. They refused to develop organizations of defense and to accept a hostile relationship with the police and neighborhood. Instead, they discussed at meeting after meeting, how they could show their attackers love. Many of those spirits have fled; others have been beaten or jailed too many times; and still others have modified their outlook in ways that reflect the struggle. Guerrilla theater, Up Against the Wall Mother Fucker, the Yippies, the urban communes; these are some of the more recent manifestations of the alternative culture. One could see these trends growing in the demonstrations mounted by Hippies against arrests of runaways or pot smokers, the community organizations, such as grew in Berkeley for self-defense and politics, and the beginnings of the will to fight back when trapped in street sweeps.

It is my impression that the Hippie culture is growing as it recedes from the eye of the media. As a consequence of the destruction of their urban places, there has been a redistribution of types. The flower people have left for the hills and become more communal; those who remained in the city were better adapted to terror, secretive or confrontative. The Hippie culture is one of the forms radicalism can take in this society. The youngsters, 5,000 of them, who came to Washington to counter-demonstrate against the Nixon inaugural showed the growing amalgamation of the New Left and its cultural wing. The Yippies who went to Chicago for guerrilla theater and learned about "pigs" were the multi-generational expression of the new wave. A UAWMF (Up Against the Wall Mother Fucker) drama, played at Lincoln Center during the New York City garbage strike—they carted garbage from the neglected Lower East Side and dumped it at the spic 'n' span cultural center—reflected another interpretation of the struggle, one that could include the politically militant as well as the culturally defiant. Many Hippies have gone underground—in an older sense of the word. They have shaved their beards, cut their hair, and taken straight jobs, like the secret Jews of Spain; but unlike those Jews, they are consciously an underground, a resistance.

What is most interesting and, I believe, a direct effect of the persecution, is the enormous divergence of forms that are still recognizable by the outsider as Hippie and are still experienced as a shared identity. "The Yippies," says Abbie Hoffman, "are like Hippies, only fiercer and more fun." The "hippie types" described in newspaper accounts of drug raids on colleges turn out, in many cases, to be New Leftists.

The dimensions by which these various forms are classified are quite conventional: religious-political, visible-secret, urban-hill, communal-individualistic. As their struggle intensifies, there will be more efforts for unity and more militant approaches to the society that gave birth to a real alternative only to turn against it with a mindless savagery.

Because the mass media have publicized the growth of a fairly well-articulated Hippie culture, it now bears the status of a social form. Variously identified as "counter-culture," "Hippie-dom," "Youth" or "Underground," the phenomenon centers on a philosophy of the present and takes the personal and public forms appropriate to that philosophy. Its values constitute a heresy in a society that consecrates the values of competition, social manipulation and functionalism, a society that defines ethical quality by long-range and general consequences, and that honors only those attitudes and institutions that affirm the primacy of the future and large-scale over the local and immediately present. It is a heresy in a society that eschews the primary value of intimacy for the sake of impersonal service to large and enduring organizations, a society that is essentialist rather than existentialist, a society that prizes biography over interactive quality. It is a heresy in a country whose President could be praised for crying, "Ask not what your country can do for you, but what you can do for your country!" Most important, however, it is heresy in a society whose official values, principles of operation and officials themselves are threatened domestically and abroad.

For these reasons the Hippie is available for persecution. When official authority is threatened, social and political deviants are readily conjured up as demons requiring collective exorcism and thus a reaffirmation of that authority. Where exorcism is the exclusive province of government, the government's power is reinforced by the adoption of a scapegoat. Deviant style and ideals make a group vulnerable to exploitation as a scapegoat, but it is official action which translates vulnerability into actionable heresy.

By contrast, recent political developments within black communities and the accommodations reached through bargaining with various official agencies have placed the blacks alongside the Viet Cong as an official enemy, but not as a scapegoat. As an enemy, the black is not a symbol but a source of society's troubles. It is a preferable position. The Hippie's threat lies in the lure of his way of life rather than in his political potential. His vulnerability as well as his proven capacity to develop a real alternative life permits his selection as scapegoat. A threatened officialdom is all too likely to take the final step that "brings on the judge." At the same time, by defining its attack as moderate, it reaffirms its moral superiority in the very field of hate it cultivates.

A PLAUSIBLE FORCE

We are speaking of that which claims the lives, totally or in part, of perhaps hundreds of thousands of people of all ages throughout the United States and elsewhere. The number is not inconsiderable.

The plausibility of the Hippie culture and its charisma can be argued on several grounds. Their outlook derives from a profound mobilizing idea: Quality resides in the present. Therefore, one seeks the local in all its social detail—not indulgently and alone, but openly and creatively. Vulnerability and improvisation are principles of action, repudiating the "rational" hierarchy of plans and stages that defines, for the grounded culture, all events as incidents of passage and means to an indefinitely postponable end—as transition. The allocation of reality to the past and the future is rejected in favor of the present, and a present that is known and felt immediately, not judged by external standards. The long run is the result rather than the goal of the present. "Psychical distance," the orientation of the insulated tourist to whom the environment is something forever foreign or of the administrator for whom the world is an object of administration, is repudiated as a relational principle. It is replaced by a principal of absorption. In this, relationships are more like play, dance or jazz. Intimacy derives from absorption, from spontaneous involvement, to use Erving Goffman's phrase, rather than from frequent contact or attraction, as social psychologists have long argued.

This vision of social reality makes assumptions about human nature. It sees man as only a part of a present that depends on all its parts. To be a "part" is not to play a stereotyped role or to plan one's behavior prior to entering the scene. It is to be a momentum. Collaboration, the overt manifestation of absorption, is critical to any social arrangement because the present, as experience, is essentially social. Love and charisma are the reflected properties of the plausible whole that results from mutual absorption. "To swing" or "to groove" is to be of the scene rather than simply at or in the scene. "Rapping," an improvised, expansive, and collaborative conversational form, is an active embodiment of the more general ethos. Its craft is humor, devotion, trust, openness to events in the process of formation, and the capacity to be relevant. Identity is neither strictly personal nor something to be maintained, but something always to be discovered. The individual body is the origin of sounds and motions, but behavior, ideas, images, and reflective thought stem from interaction itself. Development is not of personalities but of situations that include many bodies but, in effect, one mind. Various activities, such as smoking marijuana, are disciplines that serve the function of bringing people together and making them deeply interesting to each other.

The development of an authentic "counter-culture," or, better, "alternative culture," has some striking implications. For one, information and stress are processed through what amounts to a new conceptual system—a culture that replaces, in the committed, the intrapersonal structures that Western personality theories have assumed to account for intrapersonal order. For example, in 1966, young Hippies often turned against their friends and their experience after a bad acid trip. But that was the year during which "the Hippie thing" was merely one constructive expression of dissent. It was not, at that point, an alternative culture. As a result, the imagery cued in by the trauma was the imagery of the superego, the distant and punitive authority of the Western family and its macrocosmic social system. Guilt, self-hatred and the rejection of experience was the result. Many youngsters returned home filled with a humiliation that could be forgotten, or converted to a seedy and defensive hatred of the dangerously deviant. By 1968 the bad trip, while still an occasion for reconversion for some, had for others become something to be guarded against and coped with in a context of care and experienced guidance. The atmosphere of trust and new language of stress-inspired dependence rather than recoil as the initial stage of cure. One could "get high with a little help from friends." Conscience was purged of "authority."

Although the ethos depends on personal contact, it is carried by underground media (hundreds of newspapers claiming hundreds of thousands of readers), rock music, and collective activities, artistic and political, which deliver and duplicate the message; and it is processed through a generational flow. It is no longer simply a constructive expression of dissent and thus attractive because it is a vital answer to a system that destroys vitality; it is culture, and the young are growing up under the wisdom of its older generations. The ethos is realized most fully in the small communes that dot the American urbscape and constitute an important counter-institution of the Hippies.

This complex of population, culture, social form, and ideology is both a reinforcing environment for individuals and a context for the growth and elaboration of the complex itself. In it, life not only begins, it goes on; and, indeed, it must go on for those who are committed to it. Abbie Hoffman's *Revolution for the Hell of It* assumes the autonomy of this cultural frame of reference. It assumes that the individual has entered and has burned his bridges.

As the heresy takes an official definition and as the institutions of persecution form, a they-mentality emerges in the language which expresses the relationship between the oppressor and the oppressed. For the oppressed, it distinguishes life from nonlife so that living can go on. The they-mentality of the oppressed temporarily relieves them of the struggle by acknowledging the threat, identifying its agent, and compressing both into a quasi-poetic image, a cliche that can accommodate absurdity. One young man said, while coming down from an amphetamine high: "I'm simply going to continue to do what I want until they stop me."

But persecution is also structured by the they-mentality of the persecutors. This mentality draws lines around its objects as it fits them conceptually for full-scale social action. The particular uses of the term "hippie" in the mass media—like "Jew," "Communist," "Black Muslim," or "Black Panther"—cultivates not only disapproval and rejection but a climate of opinion capable of excluding Hippies from the moral order altogether. This is one phase of a subtle process that begins by locating and isolating a group, tying it to the criminal, sinful or obscene, developing and displaying referential symbols at a high level of abstraction which depersonalize and objectify the group, defining the stigmata by which members are to be known and placing the symbols in the context of ideology and readiness for action.

Once a life-style and its practices are declared illegal, its proponents are by definition criminal and subversive. On the one hand, the very dangers presupposed by the legal proscriptions immediately become clear and present. The illegal life-style becomes the living demonstration of its alleged dangers. The ragged vagabondage of the Hippie is proof that drugs and promiscuity are alienating, and the attempts to sleep in parks, gather and roam are the new "violence" of which we have been reading. Crime certainly is crime, and the Hippies commit crime by their very existence. The dangers are: (1) crime and the temptation to commit crime; (2) alienation and the temptation to drop out. The behaviors that, if unchecked, become imbedded in the personality of the suspectible are, among others, drug use (in particular marijuana), apparel deviance, dropping out (usually of school), sexual promiscuity, communal living, nudity, hair deviance, draft resistance, demonstrating against the feudal oligarchies in cities and colleges, gathering, roaming, doing strange art and being psychedelic. Many of these are defused by campaigns of definition; they become topical and in fashion. To wear bell-bottom pants, long sideburns, flowers on your car and beads, is, if done with taste and among the right people, stylish and eccentric rather than another step toward the brink or a way of lending aid and comfort to the enemy. The disintegration of a form by co-opting only its parts is a familiar phenomenon. It is tearing an argument apart by confronting each proposition as if it had no context, treating a message like an intellectual game.

Drugs, communalism, gathering, roaming, resisting and demonstrating, and certain styles of hair have not been defused. In fact, the drug scene is the site of the greatest concentration of justificatory energy and the banner under which the agencies of the control conglomerate unite. That their use is so widespread through the straight society indicates the role of drugs as temptation. That drugs have been pinned so clearly (despite the fact that many Hippies are nonusers) and so gladly to the Hippies, engages the institutions of persecution in the task of destroying the Hippie thing.

The assumption that society is held together by formal law and authority implies in principle that the habit of obedience must be reinforced. The details of the Hippie culture are, in relation to the grounded culture, disobedient. From that perspective, too, their values and ideology are also explicitly disobedient. The disobedience goes far beyond the forms of social organization and personal presentation to the conventional systems of healing, dietary practice and environmental use. There is virtually no system of authority that is not thrown into question. Methodologically, the situationalism of pornography, guerrilla theater and place conversion is not only profoundly subversive in itself; it turns the grounded culture around. By coating conventional behavioral norms with ridicule and obscenity, by tying radically different meanings to old routines, it challenges our sentiments. By raising the level of our self-consciousness it allows us to become moral in the areas we had allowed to degenerate into habit (apathy or gluttony). When the rock group, the Fugs, sings and dances "Group Grope" or any of their other songs devoted brutally to "love" and "taste," they pin our tender routines to a humiliating obscenity. We can no longer take our behavior and our intentions for granted. The confrontation enables us to disobey or to reconsider or to choose simply by forcing into consciousness the patterns of behavior and belief of which we have become victims. The confrontation is manly because it exposes both sides in an arena of conflict.

When questions are posed in ways that permit us to disengage ourselves from their meaning to our lives, we tolerate the questions as a moderate and decent form of dissent. And we congratulate ourselves for our tolerance. But when people refuse to know their place, and, what is worse, our place, and they insist on themselves openly and demand that we re-decide our own lives, we are willing to have them knocked down.

Consciousness permits disobedience. As a result, systems threatened from within often begin the work of reassertion by an attack on consciousness and chosen forms of life.

Youth, danger and disobedience define the heresy in terms that activate the host of agencies that, together, comprise the control conglomerate. Each agency, wrote Trevor-Roper, was ready: "The engine of persecution was set up before its future victims were legally subject to it." The conglomerate has its target. But it is a potential of the social system as much as it is an actor. Trevor-Roper comments further that:

> once we see the persecution of heresy as social intolerance, the intellectual difference between one heresy and another becomes less significant.

And the difference, one might add, between one persecutor and another becomes less significant. Someone, it does not matter who, tells Mr. Blue (in Tom Paxton's song): "What will it take to whip you into line?"

How have I ended here? The article is an analysis of the institutionalization of persecution and the relationship between the control conglomerate which is the advanced form of official persecution and the Hippies as an alternative culture, the target of control. But an analysis must work within a vision if it is to move beyond analysis into action. The tragedy of America may be that it completed the technology of control before it developed compassion and tolerance. It never learned to tolerate history, and now it is finally capable of ending history by ending the change that political sociologists and undergroups understand. The struggle has always gone on in the mind. Only now, for this society, is it going on in the open among people. Only now is it beginning to shape lives rather than simply shaping individuals. Whether it is too late or not will be worked out in the attempts to transcend the one-dimensionality that Marcuse described. That the alternative culture is here seems difficult to doubt. Whether it becomes revolutionary fast enough to supersede an officialdom bent on its destruction may be an important part of the story of America.

As an exercise in over-estimation, this essay proposes a methodological tool for going from analysis to action in areas which are too easily absorbed by a larger picture but which are at the same time too critical to be viewed outside the context of political action.

The analysis suggests several conclusions:

- Control usually transcends itself both in its selection of targets and in its organization.
- At some point in its development, control is readily institutionalized and finally institutional. The control conglomerate represents a new

stage in social organization and is an authentic change-inducing force for social systems.

- The hallmark of an advanced system of control (and the key to its beginning) is an ideology that unites otherwise highly differing agencies.
- Persecution and terror go in our society. The Hippies, as a genuine heresy, have engaged official opposition to a growing cultural-social-political tendency. The organization of control has both eliminated countervailing official forces and begun to place all deviance in the category of heresy. This pattern may soon become endemic to the society.

30 / THE RESPECTABLE CRIMINAL

Donald Cressy

Spring has returned, and with it two of the major themes of strategy in American life—how to win a baseball pennant and how to beat the income tax collector. Because as a sociologist I'm professionally interested in why people cheat, I'll leave theories about baseball to others.

As this time of year many of us toy with the idea of income tax evasion. Some succumb to the temptation. Those who do are not poor, culturally deprived slum dwellers. They do not like to think of themselves as "criminals." Tax evaders, along with people who pad their insurance claims, embezzle from their employers, or conspire with others to fix the price of goods usually have steady jobs and wear white collars to work. They are, nevertheless, committing what we call "respectable crimes." As recurrent newspaper headlines remind us, these are widespread forms of criminal behavior in our society. To develop a truly comprehensive theory of criminality we must learn more about why such men become violators of the law.

My own interest in "respectable crime" goes back to my days as a graduate student at Indiana University after World War II. My major professor, Edwin H. Sutherland, was conducting a study of the crimes committed by the 70 largest non-financial corporations in the U.S. He invented the concept of white-collar crime and encouraged criminologists, administrators of criminal justice, and laymen to re-examine the generalizations they had traditionally made about crime and criminals.

Sutherland's examination of the laws on certain kinds of business practices—such as restraint of trade, infringement of patents, false and misleading advertising, unfair labor practices—convinced him that these were indeed criminal laws. Violation of these laws is, accordingly, a crime; crimes of this sort must be included in any generalization about crimes and criminals. Sutherland found that the 70 largest corporations had about 980 decisions recorded against them for violation of four laws—an average of about 14 for each corporation. At the time of the study, the most popular criminological theories tended to link criminal behavior to social and personal pathologies of various kinds. Theoreticians emphasized poverty, poor education, broken homes, and psychological characteristics of criminals. The white-collar criminals that Sutherland had discovered, like the high officials of G. E. and Westinghouse who were convicted of conspiracy to fix prices in 1962, were persons of respectability and high social status who had committed crimes in connection with business. They did not fit the theoretical description. It followed that the theory would have to be revised to account for this type of criminality.

Sutherland's position was confused by the fact that he studied corporations, rather than individual white-collar criminals. I tried to correct this defect by making a study of embezzlers. It was my impression that embezzlers are white-collar criminals whose backgrounds are not likely to contain the social and personal pathologies which popular notions and traditional theory ascribe to criminals. Actually I doubt that these characteristics are in fact present in the background of *most* criminals. On the basis of my study, I *know* that they are almost never present in the background of embezzlers.

THE NATURAL HISTORY OF EMBEZZLING

When I turned, as a first step, to the existing literature for an explanation of embezzling, I found that there was a basic confusion about the nature of this crime. Most books about embezzling are written by accountants—guides to businessmen to help them avoid embezzling in their own firms. Their major thesis is that weak internal controls and poor auditing systems cause defalcations by failing to eliminate the possibility of committing the crime.

While I must agree that a detailed check on all business transactions would prevent defalcations, I doubt whether these crimes can be "explained" by the absence of such checks. In the first place, even the most "foolproof" accounting procedures can never eliminate cheating entirely. The versatility of embezzlers is astounding, and greatly underestimated. In the second place, modern society presupposes business transactions based upon a considerable amount of trust. No matter what accounting system is used, an element of trust remains. A brief review of the history of embezzlement as a crime will make this point clear.

When commerce was beginning to expand in the sixteenth century, the legal rule regarding financial relations between master, servants, and third persons was simply this: (a) property received from the master remained in his possession, the servant having "mere charge or custody" of it; but (b) property received from a third person for the master *was* in the *servant's* possession, and he was not guilty of a felony if he converted it for his own use. As business expanded and "servants" became in fact clerks and cashiers, the situations in which the master retained possession were expanded. It became the rule that if a clerk placed money in a cash drawer, it thereby came into the possession of the master; if the servant subsequently took the money from the cash drawer to keep, this act was larceny. But until 1799, if a clerk received money from one of his employer's customers and *put it directly into his own pocket,* he had committed no crime; the money had not yet come into his employer's possession. Later that same year the first general embezzlement statute was passed in England. The new law covered "servants" but it did not cover "agents"; when in 1812 a stockbroker took money given to him to invest and converted it for his own uses, the court held that the general embezzlement law did not cover this act. New legislation to cover brokers, agents, etc., was passed almost immediately. Clearly, the common law of fraud and larceny had been sufficient for a relatively simple economy where there was no need to trust servants with business transactions. But with the growth of business firms in the nineteenth century, embezzlement statutes had to be invented to cover the new offenses which arose with the new economic structure.

Dependence upon trusted employees, agents, brokers, and factors has increased steadily since the passage of these first statutes. To argue that criminal violation of financial trust can be prevented by rigid accounting methods is to overlook the pertinent point: if strict controls were imposed on all trusted persons, embezzlement could be prevented, but very little business could be conducted. To remove "the temptation, the opportunity, and even the suggestion to violate the solemn trust which has been placed in officers and employees," as one accountant-author suggests, would eliminate both "solemn trust" and large numbers of business transactions.

Writers who are not accountants have an alternative explanation of embezzling; they blame it on the weakness, moral depravity, natural dishonesty, weak moral fibre, etc., of the violator. The trouble with explanations of this sort is that they are always after-the-fact. Such hidden variables can be said to cause almost any kind of behavior. They usually become evident only after a person has proved that he is "bad" by stealing from his employer. The notion that an evil result must have something evil as a cause is a fallacy.

In my own attempt to explain this kind of crime, I spent about a year at the Illinois State Penitentiary at Joliet interviewing embezzlers. I then moved to California and talked to some more embezzlers in the California State Institution for Men at Chino. I was also able to gather a considerable number of cases from other studies. But I was disturbed because my sample of embezzlers included very few bankers; this was because bank embezzlement is a federal offense and most of my interviews had been conducted in state prisons. So I spent a summer working in the United States Penitentiary in Terre Haute, Indiana. From these interviews I developed a generalization which I think can be applied to all the embezzlers I talked to. I see no good reason to believe that it does not apply to all embezzlers, although I realize that one should not generalize beyond his data.

THE COMPLEAT CHEATER

What I came up with was the idea that embezzlement involves three essential kinds of psychological processes:

- the feeling that a personal financial problem is unshareable;
- the knowledge of how to solve the problem in secret, by violating a position of financial trust;
- the ability to find a formula which describes the act of embezzling in words which do not conflict with the image of oneself as a trusted person.

A man has an *unshareable financial problem* if it appears to him that he cannot turn to ordinary, legitimate sources for funds. To an outsider, the situation may not seem so dire; what matters is the psychological perspective of the potential embezzler. Recently I found an example of this state of mind in a newspaper letter to Ann Landers. The writer was a bookkeeper who had taken $75 from petty cash to pay some long-overdue personal bills. "I could have gone to my boss and received a loan for this amount with no trouble, but I had too much pride. My husband makes a small salary, and I was ashamed to admit we were having a difficult time financially." The writer, who signed herself "Ashamed," was paying the money back, but was terrified that she might succumb to the temptation again.

After I first formulated this unshareable problem notion, I tested it by asking a group of fifty embezzlers about an imaginary financial problem. I asked them to suppose that for some reason their fire insurance policy had lapsed and then, through no fault of their own, there was a short circuit in the wiring, or lightning struck, and their home burned down. The family lost everything they owned in the fire. My question was, "Do you think that in a situation like this you would have been tempted to embezzle to get the money you need?" Sixty percent of the cases indicated clearly that this situation did not seem to them unshareable, and that therefore they would not embezzle. The reasoning is clear in responses like these:

> Case 42. I don't believe I would. I think that in a case like that folks would have sympathized with me and helped me out. There would be outside aid. But in my own case, they didn't know about it and so they couldn't help.
>
> Case 57. Well, I don't doubt that I would if couldn't borrow the money or something of the sort. There are people or relatives that have money. I've never got along with them, but if it was a necessity like that I would go to them. I'd do anything to give my wife and children what they needed. (He indicated earlier that he had been too proud to go to his relatives for help at the time when he had embezzled.)

The second part of my generalization, the *realization* that the problem could be solved in secret by violating a trust, is a problem in the psychological perception of the opportunity to embezzle. Let me give just one statement, made by an embezzler (and former accountant), about the opportunity and techniques of embezzlement:

> In any case, I would have to say that I learned all of it in school and in my ordinary accounting experience. In school they teach you in your advanced years how to detect embezzlements, and you sort of absorb it. . . . It is just like a doctor performing abortions . . . I did not use any techniques which any ordinary accountant in my position could not have used; they are known by all accountants, just like the abortion technique is known by all doctors.

The third process in my generalization, *verbalization*, is the crux of the problem. I am convinced that the words that the potential embezzler uses in his conversation with himself are actually the most important elements in the process which gets him into trouble, or keeps him out of trouble. If he sees a possibility for embezzlement, it is because he has defined the relationship between the unshareable problem and an illegal solution in language that lets him look on trust violation as something other than trust violation. If he cannot do this, he does not become an embezzler.

To illustrate, let us suppose a man who is a pillar of the community, a respected, honest employee, a man with a background no more criminal than that of most of us. This man finds himself with an unshareable problem, and an objective opportunity to steal money from his company. The chances are very good that if in that situation I walked up to him and said, "Jack, steal the money from your boss," he would look at me in horror, as if I had suggested that he could solve his problem by going down and sticking a pistol into the face of the local cigar store owner. Honest and trusted men "just don't do such things." However, honest and trusted men do "borrow," and if he tells himself that he is borrowing the money he can continue to believe that he is an honest citizen, even as he is stealing the boss blind. Since he wants to remain an honest citizen, the "borrowing" verbalization becomes the key to his dishonest conduct.

I do not wish to overemphasize the idea of "borrowing." There are many verbalizations used, some of them quite complex. The "borrowing" verbalization is simply an example of a vocabulary that can adjust two contradictory roles—the role of an honest man and the role of a crook. I call the use of such a vocabulary a rationalization, which is different from the way psychoanalysts use the term. Let me give an illustration of rationalization that does *not* involve a dishonest role:

Suppose a Dean who is swamped with work in his university is invited to speak at a seminar of businessmen. He might at first feel he should decline the invitation, on the ground that he doesn't have the time, or he has to get the budget in, or he has to finish writing his book. But then suppose he says to himself, "A Dean should get out of the ivory tower now and then," or "Theoretical knowledge is no good unless it is passed on to practical men." *Now* he can accept the invitation, and does.

Vocabularies of motive are not something invented by embezzlers (or anyone else) on the spur of the moment. Before they can be taken over by an individual, these verbalizations exist as group definitions in which the behavior in question, even crime, is in a sense *appropriate*. There are any number of popular ideologies that sanction crime in our culture: "Honesty is the best policy, but business is business"; "It is all right to steal a loaf of bread when you are starving"; "All people steal when they get in a tight spot"; Once these verbalizations have been assimilated and internalized by individuals, they take a form such as: "I'm only going to use the money temporarily, so I am borrowing, not stealing," or "I have tried to live an honest life but I've had nothing but troubles, so to hell with it."

If my generalization about the psychological elements of embezzling is valid, it should have ramifications for crime prevention. Some change in prevention techniques is clearly necessary, for the embezzlement rate in the United States is on the rise. Increasingly complex business organizations need larger proportions of "trusted employees." Business procedures are becoming so involved that the whole fabric of an enterprise depends more and more upon men who have been given independent control over some segment of the enterprise. At the same time, studies of professional and technical workers indicate that many are dissatisfied with their jobs. These disgruntled employees are potential embezzlers.

It follows from my generalization that embezzling can be effectively blocked either at the unshareable problem point or at the verbalization point.

1. Trust violation rates might be reduced by eliminating some of the unshareable problems among employees. This means development of company programs so that employees have fewer financial problems and/or feel that they can share their financial problems with their employer. Wherever a company program solves a financial problem, or makes it shareable, embezzlement will not occur.

2. Companies could introduce educational programs that emphasize how trust violators commonly use verbalizations. These programs would make it increasingly difficult for trusted employees to think of themselves as "borrowers" rather than "thieves" when they take the boss's money. It is highly probable that our current practices in this regard actually encourage embezzlement. We tend to emphasize the notion that embezzlers are people who are the victims of "wine, women, and wagering." Because this lore is so popular, a person with an unshareable problem who is not gambling, drinking, or running around with women can easily think of himself as a nonembezzler who is simply "borrowing." What I am proposing is an educational program in which we say over and over again that a person who "pilfers" and "taps the till" or "borrows" or who is guilty of "defalcation," "peculation," or some other nice term is, in fact, a crook. And if the trusted employee rejects the notion of himself as a crook (and as a "respectable" type, he must), he will also reject the possibility of embezzling.

CRIME AS BUSINESS POLICY

The generalization I have developed here was made to fit only one crime—embezzling. But I suspect that the verbalization section of the generalization will fit other types of respectable crime as well. There is a study of crimes among New England shoe manufacturers that supports this notion. In the eight New England communities studied, there were wide variations in the number of shoe firms violating labor relations laws. In Haverhill, Massachusetts, for example, 7 percent of the shoe firms violated these laws, while in Auburn, Maine, 44 percent violated them. The author, Robert E. Lane, concluded that one of the reasons for the differences among the towns was differences in "attitudes toward the law, the government, and the morality of illegality." Those shoe manufacturers who associated with men whose attitudes favored violation were more likely to break the law; those manufacturers who were isolated from these attitudes were less likely to break the law. This influence on attitudes was evident even in the reading habits of these men; those who had violated the law had immersed themselves in a segment of the daily press so hostile to government that violation of the law seemed quite appropriate to them. Here, even the newspapers were providing verbalizations that made crime "all right." Lane predicted, on the basis of such observations, that managers of companies located in bigger cities, with a cosmopolitan press, diversified social life, and greater tolerance for heterodoxy, would accept legal restrictions on how they conducted their businesses more readily than would small town management. This prediction was borne out; firms located in small towns violated the laws much more frequently than did similar firms located in larger cities. The small town atmosphere provided a rationale to justify this particular crime; (government shouldn't tell a man how to run his business; "that man" in Washington is no good anyway; labor unions are corrupt). The bigger cities did not provide this justification. Another study, by Marshall B. Clinard, analyzed OPA violations during World War II and concluded that businessmen violated the regulations simply because they did not "believe in" them.

The G.E. and Westinghouse officials must have had a formula that made their conspiracy to fix the price of electrical equipment something other than a crime. Perhaps it was a generalized dislike of government regulation of business; perhaps they had convinced themselves that no one really abides by the Sherman Anti-trust Act anyway and that, like the prohibition amendment, it could be transgressed without any stigma of criminality. And surely all the income tax evaders do not see themselves as stealing money from the U.S. Treasury—to them the government may seem so rich that "they'll never miss it" or the intricate tax laws may seem a kind of game that allows an advantage to the shrewd player.

But whether the stakes are high or low, whether the financial game is played by an individual or a conspiring group, an aura of personal respectability does not erase (through it may temporarily obscure), the act of a criminal.

31 / POT: A RATIONAL APPROACH

Dr. Joel Fort

There are an estimated 10,000,000 Americans who smoke marijuana either regularly or occasionally, and they have very obvious reasons for wishing that pot were treated more sensibly by the law. As one of the 190,000,000 who have never smoked marijuana, I also favor the removal of grass from the criminal laws, but for less personal reasons. It is my considered opinion, after studying drug use and drug laws in 30 nations and dealing with drug-abuse problems professionally for 15 years, that the present marijuana statutes in America not only are bad laws for the offending minority but are bad for the vast majority of us who never have lit a marijuana cigarette and never will.

That some changes in these laws are coming in the near future is virtually certain, but it is not at all sure that the changes will be improvements.

On May 19, 1969, the U.S. Supreme Court, in an 8–0 vote, declared that the Marijuana Tax Act of 1937 was unconstitutional. This decision delighted the defendant, Timothy Leary, and was no surprise at all to lawyers who specialize in the fine points of constitutional law. It had long been recognized that the Marijuana Tax Act was "vulnerable"—a polite term meaning that the law had been hastily drawn, rashly considered and railroaded through Congress in a mood of old-maidish terror that spent no time on the niceties of the Bill of Rights, scientific fact or common sense.

Celebrations by marijuanaphiles and lamentations by marijuanaphobes, however, are both premature. The Court, while throwing out this one inept piece of legislation, specifically declared that Congress has the right to pass laws governing the use, sale and possession of this drug (provided these laws stay within the perimeter of the Constitution). And, of course, state laws against pot, which are often far harsher than the Federal law, still remain in effect.

There were two defects found by the Supreme Court in the Federal anti-marijuana law—a section that requires the suspect to pay a tax on the drug, thus incriminating himself, in violation of the Fifth Amendment;

---

and a section that assumes (rather than requiring proof) that a person with foreign-grown marijuana in his possession knows it is smuggled. These provisions were perversions of traditional American jurisprudence, no less than the remaining parts of the law that are bound to fall when challenged before the Supreme Court. These forthcoming decisions will, inevitably, affect the antimarijuana laws of the individual states as well. However, the striking down of the old laws does not guarantee that the new ones will be more enlightened; it merely invites more carefully drawn statutes that are less vulnerable to judicial review. In fact, in a message to Congress, President Nixon specifically demanded harsher penalties for marijuana convictions. But every sane and fair-minded person must be seriously concerned that the new laws are more just and more in harmony with known fact than the old ones. In my opinion, such new laws must treat marijuana no more harshly than alcohol is presently treated.

It is ironic that our present pot laws are upheld chiefly by the older generation, and flouted and condemned by the young; for it is the senior generation that should understand the issue most clearly, having lived through the era of alcohol prohibition. They saw with their own eyes that the entire nation—not just the drinkers and the sellers of liquor—suffered violent moral and mental harm from that particular outbreak of armed and rampant puritanism. They should certainly remember that attempts to legislate morality result only in widespread disrespect for law, new markets and new profits for gangsters, increased violence and such wholesale bribery and corruption that the Government itself becomes a greater object of contempt than the criminal class. Above all, they should be able to see the parallel between the lawless Twenties and the anarchic Sixties and realize that both were produced by bad laws—laws that had no right to exist in the first place.

"Bad law," it has been said, "is the worst form of tyranny." An open tyranny breeds open rebellion, and the issues are clear-cut; bad law, in an otherwise democratic nation, provokes a kind of cultural nihilism in which good and evil become hopelessly confused and the rebel, instead of formulating a single precise program, takes a perverse delight in anything and everything that will shock, startle, perplex, anger, baffle and offend the establishment. Thus it was during alcohol prohibition and thus it is under marijuana prohibition. The parallel is not obvious only because there were already millions of whiskey drinkers when the Volstead Act became law in 1919, leading to immediate flouting of "law and order" by vast hordes—whereas the use of marijuana did not become extensive until the early 1950s, more than 13 years after the Government banned pot in 1937. But the results, despite the delay, are the same: We have bred a generation of psychological rebels.

Banning marijuana not only perpetuates the rebelliousness of the young but it also establishes a frightening precedent, under which puritanical bias is more important to our legislators than experimentally determined fact—something every scientist must dread. Dr. Philip Handler, board chairman of the National Science Foundation, bluntly told a House subcommittee investigating drug laws, "It is our puritan ethics . . . rather than science" that say we should not smoke marijuana.

Consider the most recent study of the effects of marijuana, conducted under careful laboratory conditions and reported in *Science*. This is the research performed by Drs. Norman E. Zinberg and Andrew T. Weil at Boston University in 1968. This study was "double-blind"; that is, neither the subjects nor the researchers knew, during a given session, whether the product being smoked was real marijuana (from the female Cannabis plant) or an inactive placebo (from the male Cannabis plant). Thus, both suggestibility by the subjects and bias by the experimenters were kept to the scientific minimum. The results were:

1. Marijuana causes a moderate increase in heartbeat rate, some redness of the eyes and virtually no other physical effects. Contrary to the belief of both users and policemen, pot does not dilate the pupils—this myth apparently derives from the tradition of smoking Cannabis in a darkened room; it is the darkness that dilates the pupils.

2. Pot does not affect the blood-sugar level, as alcohol does, nor cause abnormal reactions of the involuntary muscles, as LSD often does, nor produce any effects likely to be somatically damaging. In the words of Zinberg and Weil, "The significance of this near absence of physical effects is twofold. First, it demonstrates once again the uniqueness of hemp among psychoactive drugs, most of which strongly affect the body as well as the mind. . . . Second, it makes it unlikely that marijuana has any seriously detrimental physical effects in either short-term or long-term usage."

3. As sociologist Howard Becker pointed out long ago, on the basis of interviews with users, the marijuana "high" is a learned experience. Subjects who had never had Cannabis before simply did not get a "buzz" and reported very minimal subjective reactions, even while physically "loaded" with very high doses, while experienced users were easily turned on.

4. The hypothesis about "set and setting" strongly influencing drug reactions was confirmed. The pharmacological properties of a psychoactive drug are only one factor in a subject's response: equally important—perhaps more important—are the set (his expectations and personality type) and the setting (the total emotional mood of the environment and persons in it).

5. Both inexperienced subjects and longtime users did equally well on some tests for concentration and mental stability, even while they were on very high doses. On tests requiring a higher ability to focus attention, the inexperienced users did show some temporary mental impairment, but the veterans sailed right on, as if they were not high at all. In short, experienced potheads do not have even a *temporary* lowering of the intelligence while they are high, much less a permanent mental impairment.

6. On some tests, the experienced users scored even higher while stoned than they did when tested without any drug.

7. Not only alcohol but even tobacco has more adverse effects on the body than marijuana does.

As Zinberg and Weil noted sardonically in a later article in *The New York Times Magazine*, there is a vicious circle operating in relation to marijuana: "Administrators of scientific and Government institutions feel that marijuana is dangerous. Because it is dangerous, they are reluctant to allow [research] to be done on it. Because no work is done, people continue to think of it as dangerous. We hope that our own study has significantly weakened this trend."

One slight sign that the trend may have been weakened was the appearance last June of a study by the Bureau of Motor Vehicles in the state of Washington concerning the effects of Cannabis on driving ability. Using driving-traffic simulators, not only did the study find that marijuana has less adverse effect on driving ability than alcohol—which many investigators have long suspected—but also, as in the Boston study, the evidence indicated that the only detrimental effect is on inexperienced users. Veteran potheads behave behind the wheel as if they were not drugged at all.

In short, we seem to have a drug here that makes many users very euphoric and happy—high—without doing any of the damage done by alcohol, narcotics, barbiturates, amphetamines or even tobacco.

Ever since there have been attempts to study marijuana scientifically, every major investigation has arrived at, substantially, the same conclusions, and these directly contradict the mythology of the Federal Bureau of Narcotics. In contrast with the above facts, consider the following advertisement, circulated before the passage of the 1937 Federal anti-marijuana law:

> *Beware!* Young and Old—People in All Walks of Life! This [picture of a marijuana cigarettte] may be handed you by the *friendly stranger*. It contains the Killer Drug "Marijuana"—a powerful narcotic in which lurks *Murder! Insanity! Death!*

Such propaganda was widely disseminated in the mid-1930s, and it was responsible for stampeding Congress into the passage of a law unique in all American history in the extent to which it is based on sheer ignorance and misinformation.

Few people realize how recent anti-marijuana legislation is. Pot was widely used as a folk medicine in the nineteenth century. Its recreational use in this country began in the early 1900s with Mexican laborers in the Southwest, spread to Mexican Americans and Negroes in the South and then the North, and then moved from rural to urban areas. In terms of public reaction and social policy, little attention was paid to pot until the mid-1930s (although some generally unenforced state laws existed before then). At that time, a group of former alcohol-prohibition agents headed by Harry J. Anslinger, who became head of the Federal Bureau of Narcotics, began issuing statements to the public (via a cooperative press) claiming that marijuana caused crime, violence, assassination, insanity, release of anti-social inhibitions, mental deterioration and numerous other onerous activities.

The present Federal laws impose a two-to-ten-year sentence for a first conviction for possessing even a small amount of marijuana, five to twenty years for a second conviction and ten to forty for a third. If Congress is not forced to recognize scientific fact and basic civil liberties, these penalties will be retained when the new Federal law is written without the sections declared invalid in the Leary case. The usual discretion that judges are given to grant probation or suspended sentences for real crimes is taken from them by this (and state) law as is the opportunity for parole. For sale or "dissemination," no matter how small the quantity of marijuana involved, and even if the dissemination is a gift between friends, the Federal penalty for first-offense conviction is five to twenty years; for a second offense, it's ten to forty.

The state laws, as I stated, are even hairier. Here are two real, and recent, cases: In Texas, Richard Dorsey, a shoeshine-stand operator in a bowling alley, sold a matchbox full of marijuana (considerably less than an ounce) to a Dallas undercover policeman, for five dollars. His sentence: 50 years.

In Michigan, for selling five dollars' worth of grass to another police agent, Larry Belcher was sentenced to 20 to 30 years in prison. This case is worth noting as an example of how the marijuana laws actually function in many instances. Belcher is the only individual in Grand Traverse County to receive this sentence in the past two years; 25 other marijuana arrestees were all placed on probation within that time. Belcher, it appears, was the author of a column called "Dope-O-Scope" in a local underground newspaper and had presented there some of the same scientific facts incorporated into this article. People who publicly oppose the marijuana laws and marijuana mythology of our narcotics police have an unusually high arrest record.

There is no consistency in these laws from state to state. Until 1968, South Dakota had the nation's lowest penalty for first-offense possession—90 days (it has since been raised to two to five years); however, if you crossed the state line to North Dakota, the picture changed abruptly. North Dakota had (and still has) the nation's highest penalty for first-offense possession—*99 years at hard labor.* In New York state, in spite of the revelatory work of the La Guardia commission, the penalties have increased since the Forties. Today, in that state, selling or transferring marijuana to anyone under 21 carries a penalty of one to 25 years, even if the transfer is by somebody who is also under 21 and is a gift to a friend. (The state legislature recently tried to raise this penalty to 15 years to life, but Governor Rockefeller vetoed the bill.) In Louisiana, a minor selling to a minor is subject to five to fifteen years' imprisonment, while an adult selling to a minor may receive the death penalty. Finally, in Georgia, the penalty for a first conviction for selling to a minor is life imprisonment. If the offender is parolled or his sentence suspended, and he is convicted again, he can be sentenced to death.

But the American marijuana tragedy is even worse than I have indicated. Like other crimes-without-victims, pot smoking is a private activity and involves no harm to anyone else. Remember: The police do not have to engage in cloak-and-dagger activities to find out if there have been any banks or grocery stores robbed lately—the bankers and store owners (the victims) call them immediately. But since there is no victim in the "crime" of smoking marijuana, nobody is going to call the police to report it—except, very rarely, a neighbor who finds the evidence. Hence, the entire apparatus of the police state comes into existence as soon as we attempt to enforce anti-grass legislation; and by the nature of such legislation, totalitarian results must ensue. We cannot police the private lives of the citizenry without invading their privacy; this is an axiom.

Consider, now, the actual social background in which this crusade against Cannabis is being waged. America is not the Victorian garden it pretends to be; we are, in fact, a drug-prone nation. Parents and others adults after whom children model their own behavior teach them that every time one relates to other human beings, whether at a wedding or at a funeral, and every time one has a pain, problem or trouble, it is necessary or desirable to pop a pill, drink a cocktail or smoke a cigarette. The alcohol, tobacco and over-the-counter pseudo-"sedative" industries jointly spend more than $2,000,000 a day in the United States alone to promote as much drug use as possible.

The average "straight" adult consumes three to five mind-altering drugs a day, beginning with the stimulant caffeine in coffee, tea or Coca-Cola, going on to include alcohol and nicotine, often a tranquilizer, not uncommonly a sleeping pill at night and sometimes an amphetamine the next morning to overcome the effects of the sedative taken the evening before.

We have 80,000,000 users of alcohol in this country, including 6,000,000 alcoholics; 50,000,000 users of tobacco cigarettes; 25,000,000 to 30,000,000 users of sedatives, stimulants and tranquilizers; and hundreds of thousands of users of consciousness alterers that range from heroin and LSD to cough syrup, glue, nutmeg and catnip—all in addition to marijuana use.

Drs. Manheimer and Mellinger, surveying California adults over 21, found that 51 percent had at some time used sedatives, stimulants or tranquilizers (17 percent had taken these drugs frequently) and 13 percent had at some time used marijuana.

Further underlining the extent of use of the prescription drugs is the estimate from the National Prescription Audit that 175,000,000 prescriptions for sedatives, stimulants and tranquilizers were filled in 1968. Also enough barbiturates (Nembutal, Seconal, phenobarbital) alone are manufactured to provide 25 to 30 average doses per year for every man, woman and child in this country.

In the light of this total drug picture, the persecution of potheads seems to be a species of what anthropologists call "scapegoatism"—the selection of one minority group to be punished for the sins of the whole population, whose guilt is vicariously extirpated in the punishment of the symbolic sacrificial victims.

Meanwhile, my criticisms—and those of increasing numbers of writers, scientific and popular—continue to bounce off the iron walls of prejudice that seem to surround Congress and state legislatures. It is quite possible that our new, post-Leary pot laws will be as bad as the old ones. If there is any improvement, it is likely to come, once again, from the courts.

A compelling medical, sociological and philosophical case exists for the full legalization of marijuana, particularly if legalization is the only alternative to the present criminalization of users. But an even more substantial case exists for ending all criminal penalties for possession or use of the drug, while still exercising some caution. I would recommend, for example, that to prevent the sale of dangerously adulterated forms of the drug, marijuana be produced under Federal supervision, as alcohol is. Furthermore, sellers of the drug should be licensed, and they should be prohibited from selling to minors. If there are infractions of these laws, the penalties should be directed at the seller, not the user. I would also strongly recommend that all advertising and promotion of marijuana be prohibited, and that packages of the drug carry the warning: CAUTION: MARIJUANA MAY BE HARMFUL TO YOUR HEALTH.

If marijuana were to be legalized, what would happen? According to the marijuanaphobes, the weed will spread into every American home; people will become lazy and sluggish, sit around all day in a drugged stupor and talk philosophy when they talk at all; we will sink into the "backward" state of the Near Eastern and Asian nations.

There are good, hard scientific reasons for doubting this gloomy prognostication.

1. Most Americans have already found their drug of choice—alcohol—and there is more conditioning involved in such preferences than most people realize. The average American heads straight for the bar when he feels the impulse to relax; a change in the laws will not change this conditioned reflex. When the Catholic Church allowed its members to eat meat on Friday, the majority went right on following the conditioned channel that told them, "Friday is fish day."

2. Of the small minority that will try pot (after it is legalized) in search of a new kick, most will be vastly disappointed, since (a) it doesn't live up to its sensational publicity, largely given to it by the Federal Narcotics Bureau; and (b) the "high" depends, as we have indicated, not only on set and setting but, unlike alcohol, on learning.

This involves conditioning and the relationship of the actual chemistry of the two drugs to the total *Gestalt* of our culture. What pot actually does—outside mythology—is produce a state midway between euphoria and drowsiness, like a mild alcohol high; accelerate and sharpen the thoughts (at least in the subjective impression of the user), like an amphetamine; and intensify sound and color perception, although not nearly as much as a true psychedelic. It can also enhance sexual experience, but not create it—contrary to Mr. Anslinger, pot is not an aphrodisiac. It is, in short, the drug of preference for creative and contemplative types—or, at least, people with a certain streak of that tendency in their personality. Alcohol, on the other hand, depresses the forebrain, relaxes inhibitions, produces euphoria and drowsiness and, while depleting some functions, such as speech and walking, does not draw one into the mixture of sensuality and introspection created by pot. It is the drug of preference for aggressive and extroverted types. Therefore, the picture of pot spreading everywhere and changing our culture is sociologically putting the cart before the horse; our society would first have to change basically before pot could spread everywhere.

3. Even if, against all likelihood, marijuana were to sweep the country, this would not have dire consequences. Marijuana has no specifically anti-machine property in it; it would not make our technology go away, like a

wave of an evil sorcerer's wand. Nor does it dull the mental faculties, as we have seen in reviewing the scientific evidence. (I might add, here, that the highest honor students at certain Ivy League colleges are frequently pot users, and one study at Yale found more marijuana smokers at the top of the class than at the bottom.)

4. Finally, the whole specter of America sinking into backwardness due to pot is based upon totally false anthropological concepts. The Near East is not tribal, preindustrial, superstitious, and so forth, merely because Mohammed banned alcohol in the Koran but forgot to exclude Cannabis drugs also; a whole complex of historical and cultural factors is involved, not the least of which is the continuous intervention of Western imperialism from the Crusades onward. Other factors are the rigid structure of the Islamic religion and the lack of a scientific minority that can effectively challenge these dogmas; the Western world was equally backward—please note—when the Christian religion was not open to scientific dissent and criticism. Backwardness is a relative concept, and, although pot has been used in the Arabic countries for millenniums, they have several times been ahead of the West in basic science (the most famous example being their invention of algebra). The populations of these nations are not "lazy" due to marijuana nor to any other cause; they are merely underemployed by a feudalistic economic system. The ones lucky enough to find work usually toil for longer hours, in a hotter sun, than most Americans would find bearable.

Thus, treating marijuana in a sane and rational way presents no threat to our society, whereas continuing the present hysteria will alienate increasing numbers of the young while accelerating the drift toward a police state. I take no pleasure in the spread of even so mild a drug as marijuana, and I am sure (personally, not scientifically) that in a truly open, libertarian and decent society, nobody would be inclined to any kind of drug use. While I agree with the psychedelic generation about the absurdity and injustice of our criminal laws relating to drugs, I am not an apostle of the "turn on, tune in, drop out" mystique. I recognize that drugs can be an evasion of responsibility, and that there is no simple chemical solution to all the psychic, social and political problems of our time. My own program would be: Turn on to the life around you, tune in to knowledge and feeling, and drop *in* to changing the world for the better. If that course could prevail, the adventurous young, no longer haunted by the anxiety and *anomie* of the present system, would probably discover that love, comradeship, music, the arts, sex, meaningful work, alertness, self-discipline, real education (which is a lifelong task), and plain hard thought are bigger, better and more permanent highs than any chemical can produce.

But, meanwhile, I must protest—I will continue to protest—against the bureaucrat who stands with cocktail in one hand and cigarette in the other and cries out that the innocent recreation of pot smoking is the major problem facing our society, one that can be solved only by raising the penalty to castration for the first offense and death for the second. He would be doing the young people—and all the rest of us—a true favor if he forgot about marijuana for a while and thought, a few minutes a day, about such real problems as racism, poverty, starvation, air pollution and our stumbling progress toward World War Three and the end of life on earth.

It is an irony of our time that our beloved George Washington would be a criminal today, for he grew hemp at Mount Vernon, and his diary entries, dealing specifically with separating the female plants from the male before pollination, show that he was not harvesting it for rope. The segregation of the plants by sex is only necessary if you intend to extract "the killer drug, marijuana" from the female plant.

Of course, we have no absolute evidence that George turned on. More likely, he was using marijuana as many Americans in that age used it: as a medicine for bronchitis, chest colds and other respiratory ailments. (Pot's euphoric qualities were not well known outside the East in those days.) But can you imagine General Washington trying to explain to an agent of the Federal Narcotics Bureau, "I was only smoking it to clear up my lumbago"? It would never work; he would land in prison, perhaps for as long as 40 years. He would be sharing the same cruel fate as several thousand other harmless Americans today. As it says in the book of *Job*, "From the dust the dying groan, and the souls of the wounded cry out."

UNIT K / ISSUES FOR CONSIDERATION

1. What do hippies, pot smokers, and embezzlers have in common which leads us to classify them as deviants?
2. Why is it more likely that the laws regarding marijuana will change than the laws regarding embezzlement?
3. As far as society is concerned, what are the differences between the criminal who commits burglary and the embezzler described in Cressey's article?
4. Why is it that scientific evidence is not more influential in affecting the establishment and changing our laws?
5. Give examples of how criminal behavior may take the form of conformity to group norms.

EPILOGUE SOCIAL CHANGE

Social change refers to differences over time in any aspect of the social order. It can take the form of the revision of long-fixed role expectations, as in the case of women's demands for new roles in our society, or of radical changes in an institution, as some see happening in our educational system in America. It may also take the form of a political revolution in which a new assertion of power succeeds the old processes of custom and tradition. Or it may take the form of a revolution in thought as society revises its patterns of differentiation.

Most of the readings in this book have dealt with social change. We started with a discussion of changes needed in our language, we will now end by dealing with changes in higher education.

In this last section, in which we deal specifically with social change, it is important to be aware of certain characteristics of change in our complex society. Perhaps the most important aspect of societal change is its *discontinuity.* That is, social change seldom occurs in a uniform predictable fashion; a chain-type process is usually going on in which one change demands another until the whole society is in a state of flux.

Change may be initiated from a number of sources. An invention, a disaster, a war, a treaty, or a plague may all prompt social change. However, once the change is started it may effect wide areas of the culture. A simple example of this is given in the first article in this section. Walls sees two events as initiating change in the tobacco industry, both most interesting from a sociological standpoint. The first is the introduction of technical and scientific changes in tobacco production which do away with the requirement for a large labor force and make it difficult for small farmers to compete with the larger companies. This pattern is quite familiar in industrial society. However, change in the tobacco industry is likely to come even faster because of a change in society's attitude toward smoking. Note the chain in these events: First, we have the scientific discovery that excessive smoking causes cancer. Then, slowly, society begins to decrease its use of tobacco. This change leads the big tobacco farmers to look for more efficient means of producing tobacco so that they can maintain themselves with a smaller gross sale. This in turn leads to an enormous lay-off of unskilled laborers who drift to the city in search of a means of surviving. We could go on, but from this point it is difficult to predict just what will happen, for our simple chain becomes so intertwined with other factors that it is impossible to tell just what cause is determining what effect. However, the interrelationship between the various dimensions of society that we have tried to illustrate throughout this book should help explain why a change in one aspect of society is going to cause changes in many other areas.

Our last two articles address themselves to questions of change in the future. Hurley wonders if science fiction might not have something to tell us about what to expect in the way of scientific development in the future. This type of change, which we like to call "progress," is one important dimension of social change, but, as we have seen, it is only one of many.

Jerome's article, which deals with changes needed in higher education, is concerned with quite a different process. Here is an institution changing in response to a changing society. It is not so much that the educational system has deteriorated to the point at which it can no longer do what it was originally intended to do; it is more that society has changed and is now asking higher education to do quite different things. On the first page of the Introduction we talked about a new type of student who wants his education to be relevant. Perhaps now we can explain something more about this student. In the past, college was for the elite few who could afford to pay high prices for their education. Over the years educational opportunities have grown considerably, so that now many feel that an affluent society such as ours ought to provide *free* higher education for everyone (or at least everyone who is qualified). How does this new value change the function of education? As you read the final selection of this book, you may realize that you have acquired a new perspective which will help you in understanding that student who demands that his education be related to his life. He could well be you.

32 / TOBACCO'S DOUBLE REVOLUTION

Dwayne E. Walls

The plant beds are lying idle now—little plastic bandages covering countless scratches in the dark, sandy soil of the Southeastern Coastal Plains. Through the winter nobody pays much attention to them except the Florida-bound tourists, to whom the beds and the strange-looking curing barns that dot the countryside are curiosities. Some time between mid-January and early March, depending on the location and the weather, the plant beds will be seeded and the plastic covering will be replaced by cheesecloth.

In early spring the shoots will be plucked gently from the plant beds and transplanted, carefully, symmetrically—42 inches between rows, 22 inches between plants—into the rich black loam of the region. By early summer, when the leaves begin to ripen, the rows of Bright Leaf tobacco will cover close to 600,000 acres of land from southside Virginia to northern Florida and into a tip of Alabama. Another 200,000 or so acres of Burley tobacco will stand ripening in the hills and bottom lands of Kentucky, Tennessee and the western portions of North Carolina and Virginia.

Altogether, more than half a million farm families in eight states will look to the 1970 tobacco crop as their major source—and in many cases only source—of income. But even now, before the seed is scattered down the plant beds, thousands of these tobacco farmers know that the 1970 crop will be their last. Thousands more wonder how much longer they will be able to hang on, to squeeze a meager living out of their annual crop.

Tobacco, agriculture's last great stronghold of hand labor, is in the early stage of a double revolution which might improve the nation's health and shore up its free enterprise, but which almost certainly will uproot the lives of several hundred thousand farm families who depend on tobacco for a living. These are the small landowners, the tenants and the sharecroppers who cannot possibly survive the changes. Already tens of thousands of them have been driven off the land, and they are only a fraction of those destined ultimately to lose or to change their livelihood.

In North Carolina alone, according to Dr. E. Walton Jones of the Coastal Plains Regional Commission, an estimated 100,000 farm

From *Nation* Magazine, February 2, 1970. Reprinted by permission of the publisher.

families will be surplus labor by 1975. These families, it should be noted, are mostly Negro and most of them live now in the tobacco-growing eastern portion of the state.

What is the double revolution in tobacco? Anyone who has watched television lately should be familiar with a small part of it. The health hazard in tobacco is amply advertised and no doubt accounts for the slight but steady decline in cigarette manufacture and consumption that began several years ago. It seems only a matter of time before the present voluntary ban on tobacco advertising, imposed piecemeal by some newspapers and radio and television stations, becomes mandatory for broadcasters. Worse yet, as the farmers see it. Congress' almost annual threat to drop the tobacco support program seems to pick up additional converts with each session.

But the greater part of the revolution in tobacco, the cause for most concern among the small landowners and the landless husbandmen, is sponsored not by the government and not by public or private health agencies but by the tobacco industry itself. The traditional, almost ritualistic methods by which tobacco has been grown, harvested and marketed can no longer prevail against recent technical and scientific developments. What science and technology did to the cotton fields of the Deep South and to the coal fields of the Southern Appalachians they are doing now to the tobacco fields of the Coastal Plains.

The most recent development was announced in mid-November by R. J. Reynolds Tobacco Co., the nation's largest manufacturer of tobacco products. The company has devised a process which expands the shredded leaf, increasing the volume of a given weight of tobacco 40 per cent to 50 per cent. Whatever its impact on the health factor in smoking, a point that is as yet unclear, the development of puffed tobacco seems to imply that the company eventually will need 40 per cent to 50 per cent less tonnage than it buys now.

A Reynolds spokesman has said that "tests conducted to date indicate that puffed tobacco would account for a relatively small percentage of the total tobacco blends used in Reynolds brands." But *The Wall Street Journal* seemed sure of its facts when it reported that Reynolds plans to switch to exclusive use of puffed tobacco in its cigarettes over the next two to three years. Other tobacco manufacturers and researchers at North Carolina State University in Raleigh are working on a freeze-drying process which would achieve the same 40 to 50 per cent increase in the tobacco's bulk.

Research, sponsored largely by tobacco manufacturers, has also developed cigarettes that look, taste and smell like the real thing but which contain not a shred of tobacco. Apparently the domestic manufacturers have no present plans to market the non-tobacco cigarettes because of problems with the shelf life of the product and lack of data on what effect the substitute material (cellulose in most of the experimental cigarettes) might have on the smoker's lungs. But part-tobacco cigarettes, identified as containing a substantial quantity of non-tobacco ingredients, are sold regularly in the United States by foreign manufacturers.

Any one of these development would be enough to create a tremor throughout the tobacco economy of the rural Coastal Plains. Together they have cast a pall over a region already troubled by problems of oversupply, labor shortage, rising costs and the beginning of a technological revolution in planting and harvesting.

Tobacco has always been a demanding crop, requiring large amounts of hand labor and some skill in its growing and curing. As one chronicler said of it more than half a century ago: "No sick child demands more constant and careful watching than a barn of golden leaf when it is being cured by the flue process."

From its modest beginning as a $10,950 crop out of Jamestown in 1618, tobacco rose to become the coin of the realm throughout Virginia and the Carolinas, justifying its title as the Golden Token. Vast fortunes were built on it. Merchants and even clergymen were paid in tobacco. And, significant to the region's later economic and political values, it created a class of small yeoman farmers—men whose tiny patch of tobacco gave them an essential freedom, if not the wealth, of the Virginia aristocrats and the Delta cotton planters. Even today the average tobacco allotment in North Carolina, the heartland of flue-cured leaf, is only about 3 acres.

Although the farmer may own considerably more acreage, he can, under the support program, plant only what he is allotted. He may buy or rent additional allotments from his neighbors, but he cannot transfer such allotments across county lines. Thus it is extremely difficult for the small farmer to enlarge his operation sufficiently to justify mechanization and equally difficult to operate at a profit without mechanization.

The old system survived because it had available the strong backs of hundreds of thousands of laborers—poor whites as well as Negroes—who were offered little more than bare survival in the near-feudal system. The relatively few big planters relied on tenants and sharecroppers to produce the crop. Small landowners and frequently tenants themselves have depended heavily on impoverished blacks, paid modest wages during the brief harvesting season but given little more than free housing the rest of the year.

This layered society has been shaken in recent years as blacks and poor whites moved out of the tobacco fields in increasing numbers. Some of them have been replaced by ever more advanced machinery rumbling into the fields. Others simply have left a labor vacuum.

Despite the difficulty of putting together large tobacco operations, the trend is in that direction. Mechanical harvesters already are operating on a few large farms. Once the demand for such machinery is sufficient to justify commercial production, the harvesters will sweep the small landowner and the tenant right out of farming. It requires no great imagination to foresee the day, maybe five years hence, when a relatively few large, corporate farms will grow all of the flue-cured tobacco the market demands.

Further, the corporate farms might grow it on contract to the manufacturers, largely without benefit of the present intricate system of marketing, warehousing and processing that supports much of the present tobacco economy.

For a great many tobacco farmers it does not really matter whether the upheaval comes in a single season or gradually over five seasons or a decade. The Negro tenants and sharecroppers have little hope of surviving on the land, no matter how gradually the revolution progresses. Thousands of them are leaving the tobacco fields every year, unable to survive on the tenant's share of a 5-acre patch or less. Their departure for the urban centers of the Northeast has created a labor shortage affecting larger tenants and small landowners, speeding up mechanization and thus creating more pressure on the marginal operators to get out or get bigger. Some larger farmers have resorted only recently to importing migratory labor. The state's first tobacco labor camp was built last year by a group of Wake County growers.

The prospects are little better for the small landowners, those who hold a 3-to-5-acre allotment. Some of them are selling out as tobacco farmers—sometimes to take industrial jobs that are beginning to open up in the region, but more often to remain on the land as truck farmers or chicken farmers. Still, diversification is slow to take hold because of tradition and the fear of breaking loose from a total dependence on the traditional crop. As one of the region's economists said not long ago: "Tobacco has been a damn good-looking woman to these farmers and they will stick with her to the end."

Each tobacco allotment carries with it a corresponding quota stipulating the maximum number of pounds of leaf that can be marketed. The poundage quota might range anywhere from 1,200 per acre to 2,000. Until two years ago, many farmers found that they could rent their allotments and clear almost as much profit as they could by farming the acreage themselves. The rental market has dropped sharply since 1967 because the high cost of production has cut down the price a farmer can expect in rental. In 1968, the latest year for which figures are available, 72,000 acres of tobacco were rented in North Carolina at an average price of about 14c per pound on an average quota of 1,800 pounds—or a return of about $250 per acre to the owner of the allotment.

The average rental price in 1967 was about 18c per pound. In 1969 it probably was about 12c, and the indications are that the price will fall to 10c for the 1970 crop. Increasingly, allotment owners by the thousands are learning that their allotments or portions of them are nearly worthless.

Again using the figures from North Carolina as a standard, it is probable that close to 10 per cent of the nation's allotment of flue-cured tobacco acreage will not be planted or harvested in 1970. North Carolina's unused allotment has increased steadily from 25,000 acres in 1967 to 30,000 acres in 1968 and 35,000 acres out of a state allotment of 416,000 acres in 1969.

As they always have to some extent, small landowners can continue to make a crop only by cooperating with one another—swapping and sharing their labor, their equipment and their land. One man who has a good allotment but poor land might enter into a loose arrangement with his neighbor who has only a fractional allotment but the soil to produce the kind of tobacco that will bring higher prices on the market. A man who has unusually good soil or the skill and the time to produce plant beds may do nothing but supply his neighbors with plants and take a portion of their ripe tobacco as payment.

One measure of the small grower's plight is that he has begun to drop his fierce independence and mistrust of any judgment but his own. The militant National Farmers Organization began organizing in the Southeast last spring and currently has local chapters in more than half of North Carolina's 100 counties, plus several counties in the other tobacco states. Its greatest success so far has been with the hog and grain farmers, but small tobacco farmers also are beginning to join and even more are likely to sign with the next year. NFO organizers have said their main effort in the region in 1970 will be in the tobacco fields, among the small farmers.

In North Carolina, which has more individual farms than any other state except Texas, 42,000 small farms went under between 1959 and 1964. It is doubtful that even NFO tactics can do more than slow the attrition.

33 / THE COMING OF THE HUMANOIDS

Neil P. Hurley

Science fiction has proven in the last 50 years to have a greater accuracy of prediction than, as a rule, demographers, economists and political forecasters. The reason lies partly in the fact that the authors of science fiction have intuitively grasped the inexorable dynamic behind the mechanization process.

In science fiction we see portrayed the uttermost limits of mechanization's logic, an extreme rationalistic view which arbitrarily arranges parts and techniques into utilitarian patterns without concern for ultimate purposes. Since the all-absorbing process of "automatization" is self-justifying, its inevitable term is a machine which is not a machine. Since Karel Capek's *R.U.R.* in 1921, dramatists, novelists and short story writers have played fancifully, sometimes frighteningly, with the idea of a robot which could simulate human behavior. In its most perfect incarnation, the robot takes on such life-like appearance as to be called an android or humanoid. The growing spate of fiction on androids is beginning to constitute a new literary category within the larger *genre* of science fiction.

We are all familiar with the heart transplant operation. In his short story, *The Fires of Night*, Dennis Etchison asks about replacing vital organs with, say, a plastic heart, a latex stomach, a fiberglass ribcage. He then poses the next logical question: Is it murder to kill someone who was part flesh, part plastic and metal? Etchison asks: "What was the point—25 per cent 50 per cent 75 per cent?—at which the part that is human dies and the oiled, punched, guaranteed factory parts take over? How do you know when you stop being a person who is part machine, and become merely a machine that is part human?" The most logical step in prosthetics would obviously be the installation of a miniature computer in a human cranium to serve as the command and control center for artificial intelligence.

Such a step in the mechanization process leads us unequivocally to the case of the android, a subject whose wider implications may be

---

discerned by a perusal of contemporary science fiction. In Norbert Wiener's *The Human Use of Human Beings* (1950), the author spoke of the Faustian compulsion to apply "know-how" without determining "know-what." This seems to be true of us Americans, who, unlike the Greeks seldom view the harnessing of nature's powers with split emotions. Wiener speaks of the great figure of Prometheus, defying the gods of Olympus by bringing fire down from heaven to earth, as "the prototype of the scientist." If science constructs a thinking machine without any power of learning, then it will necessarily be a literal-minded servant of man. However, that is not, as we shall see, the ultimate development in bio-engineering. Here science fiction can aid by supplying a good number of robot scenarios which permit us in the early stages of thinking machines to ponder the social and ethical implications of lens-eyed mannikins replete with synthetic skin, steel tendons, ball-bearing joints and preset responses. With this in mind, we may now pass to a selective sampling of android fiction in order to pierce the curtain of the future.

One distinguished science fiction writer, Isaac Asimov, implies that programming circuits in servomechanisms could be made to follow the three master principles of the world's ethical systems: (1) Every robot is to protect men, even allowing himself to be destroyed if necessary; (2) Every robot must defer to legitimate authority, even if disagreeable; and (3) Every robot is to insure his own self-preservation as long as it is compatible with Rule 1. Asimov's Rules of Robotics are common enough in the plots of other authors so that detection of an android may pivot on some test involving a violation of the altruistic nature of robo-psychology.

Contrasted with the benevolent, albeit deterministic, behavior of androids is the range of purposes to which their human masters put them. Nowhere is the application of automation for automation's sake better seen than in the typical entertainment story involving androids. Often the customary behavior of androids serves to increase the convenience, the efficiency and the pleasures of human beings. One boxing manager trains his fighter assidously for a championship bout by using an android as a sparring partner, an android capable of stimulating the pugilistic style of any boxer, living or dead. One night the fighter, without his manager's knowledge, inadvertently inserts in his mechanical "sparring partner" a programming subroutine which simulates himself. The result is an ironic death caused by fighting his automated *alter ego*. Richard Mathieson's story, *Steel*, deals with a similar Faustian compulsion to match human energy against mechanical force. Thus we find that "thinking robots," as highly intelligent and powerful means, are subservient to indifferent, at times trivial, ends.

In James Causey's *The Show Must Go On*, we see hate bars employed in order to siphon off the brimming aggressions of human beings. A similar therapy consists in the vicarious and cathartic sensations which human spectators at a circus derive in watching android performers accomplish perilous feats of strength and dexterity. The story ends with the accidental destruction of a female android by a beast. This pleases the crowd so much that every evening a similar tragedy is scheduled, thus recalling the "pan and circenses" psychology of the Roman amphitheatre in the days of Nero. Robots, as we see, are expendable in themselves, and must serve even such trivial ends of human beings as victims of a spectator sport.

Ron Goulart presents a less gruesome but no less disturbing story of android behavior in *Badinage*, a 1984-ish tale of the broad sanctions which a Credit Authority possesses in a totally cashless society. Goulart's android is a mechanical Iago, plotting to keep in perpetual indebtedness the story's protagonist, who, like Othello, finally recognizes the moral tilt in the robot's behavior and seeks to destroy him. Goulart has a subtle critical sense about the "law of irresistible use" implicit in the mechanization process, a law which seems to say that if a process can be automated, it will be automated. His imaginative concern has led to stories about android-staffed colleges, hospitals, old age homes and missions. Here the purposes which androids serve are more utilitarian, less casual.

The question of deviant behavior, implicit in Badinage, is more elaborately developed in Shelley Lowenkopf's *The Addict*. In addition to a pathological attraction for devouring fiction literature, Lowenkopf's female robot has been programmed to feel shame and modesty as well as superiority in the presence of non-humanoid robots. (The implication of caste and racial discrimination is clear.) Lowenkopf suggests that the solution for eccentric androids is much simpler than for human beings—reprogramming of the computer tapes. This "robotherapy" eliminates anomic responses and guarantees social conformity according to the prevailing cultural "definition of the situation" in keeping with whatever is acceptable behavior. In these instances we have clearly medical and social ends being called into play regarding the dispositon of automata.

The mechanization process not only permits progressive improvements on one and the same android but most especially between one generation of androids and a later one. Since robots may be improved till they acquire human appearance, the advanced model of android is capable of multiple responses and branching decisions as complex as those made by today's "man-in-the-street." In his story, *Evidence*, Isaac Asimov presents a superior android with a highly developed positronic brain. Having already served as district attorney, the android runs for the office of mayor and wins. Although neither omniscient nor infallible, the android mayor offers certain advantages to his constituency. Because of the first of the Three Laws of Robotics, he will never hurt human beings, even through corruption or tyranny. Undoubtedly the twenty-first century will see political decision-making being done by thinking robots.

Once androids reach a stage of technical development where they cannot be distinguished from human beings, the possibility arises of serving as convenient "stand-ins" for persons. The issue of "replica-presence," as it is called, furnishes material for a large number of "android" science writings, particularly in the ability of life-size marionettes to satisfy adequately emotional needs for company, conversation, and even love. In *The Changeling,* Ray Bradbury presents a wealthy man who, tired of his mistresses and desirous of solitude, purchases automatic replicas of himself to keep six women happy. Bradbury, unaware of the giant pun he created in his story of "sex-location," caught the essential preoccupation of those who, like T.S. Eliot, S. Giedion, Marshall McLuhan, Arnold Toynbee, Lancelot Law Whyte and Archibald MacLeish, lament the dissociation of thought and feeling in contemporary industrial society.

This split is described even more dramatically by Robert F. Young in *Juke Doll.* In this short story, Young depicts how the human void for affection is filled by a "doll-friend," who, even more than the paper-doll of popular music fame, is faithful to its human master. Speaking demurely in an electronic voice, this carefully-assembled puppet is found to be merely the extension of the master-puppeteer's strategy. While all the other plots mentioned earlier have philosophical and ethical overtones, the case of the "humanoid" and its power of "replica-presence" presents moral and metaphysical difficulties of the first magnitude.

When does an android cease being a literal-minded slave of human masters and become autonomous, or truly humanoid? Norbert Wiener gives the answer in *The Human Use of Human Beings,* saying that the machine "which can learn and can make decisions on the basis of its learning, will in no way be obliged to make such decisions as we should have made, or will be acceptable to us." Such is the case in Henry Kuttner's *Those Among Us,* an attention-arresting plot about an android, cast so perfectly in the image of man as to represent a threat to his fellow androids. Situated in the twilight zone of the organic and the inorganic, this humanoid undergoes the identity crisis of "the stranger," that outsider who must traffic convivially with others who know exclusively those rules of the game inside of which they are meaningful actors. Kuttner taxes to the utmost the principle of identity which underlies Western rationalism from the time of Aristotle: Can A be A and non-A at one and the same time? In other words, can a machine be human? One of Kuttner's characters indicates the alarming convergence of a possible man-machine incarnation: "When the first successful humanoid was produced by the robots." Here we have a giant hall of mirrors with an infinite series of human and mechanical reflections and counter-reflections.

The same identity crisis emerges from William F. Nolan's *The Joy of Living,* in which a mechanical bride (apologies to Marshall McLuhan!) is accepted by a widower for both his personal solace and his children's tutelage. Having developed an affective tie for her human husband, the pseudo-wife, Margaret, pleads eloquently not to be discarded on the argument that, in creating her, man imparted his own qualities of compassion and feeling. One finishes the story with an ambivalent reaction, of deep awe and grateful acquiescence, not at all dissimilar to the mingled feeling inspired by the Genesis account of the creation of man from the slime of the earth and of woman from his side. We are at the heart of the dilemma posed by the mechanization process. Is not the technologist somewhat like Prometheus defying the limits placed by the Gods of Olympus, in order to bring fire from heaven to earth?

It is true, as Buckminster Fuller has pointed out, that the discoverer always ventures into the outlaw area. It is important, however, that we know the antinomies implicit in all frontier-transcending enterprises, the sense of awe which should accompany our decision to chart the unknown. Norbert Wiener says that the application of "know-how" with little "know-what" is definitely Promethean, inevitably bringing its own punishment with it. This typical awareness of the Greek outlook is needed if man is to refrain from the Promethean urge to transfer to the machine made in his likeness, the responsibility for his choice of good and evil, without continuing to accept a full responsibility for that choice. Therein should be the indissolubly wedded elements of awe and acquiescence, the "Allelujah" of creaturely respect with the "Amen" of human creation.

Mankind must awake to the discovery that we set an irreversible course. The writings of Pitt, McCullough, Wiener, Shannon, Pierce and Roseblith, to name a few of the leading names in the field of engineering biophysics, point to a cybernetic world where "feedback" arrangements could produce a high order of consciousness with a corresponding capacity for language and interpersonal communication. Is human voluntary action, after all, more than a choice among psychic tropisms so that the direction of commitment is given by the most useful resolution of decision vectors? If it is not, then androids will compete with men and perhaps overthrow them as Samuel Butler warned in the eighteenth century. His famous book, *Erewhon,* speaks of machines which could conquer mankind through the use of men as instrumental accomplices. If, on the other hand, man has an immortal soul which only God can create, then there can be no serious identity crisis as raised by mechanization's blind pursuit of technical virtuosity and efficiency. The crux is in the matter of ends and not just means. If our purposes are clear then we can hallow the means.

Philosophy and theology aside, the problem still remains for all of us, just as for scientists such as Norbert Wiener, of approximating human rational performance by machines. After all, the physical identity of an individual does not consist in matter alone but "in a certain continuity of process, and in the memory by the organism of the effects of its past development." This simulation of essentially spiritual characteristics is the basis of a very unusual story by Charles Beaumont called *Last Rites*. Extremely sick, a long-standing friend of a priest calls him to his bedside and raises the issue of a humanoid soul: "If your friend were suddenly to reveal himself to you as a machine, and he was dying, and wanted very much to go to Heaven—what would you do?" The suspense of the tale lies in whether the question is hypothetical or biographical. Is the priest's friend an authentic human or the faultless blueprint projection of some master bio-engineer? Beaumont never tells us what the priest discovers after he anoints his friend.

One could go on documenting the insights raised by science fiction writers concerning "thinking robots." More imperative at this point is a public awareness that this "revolutionary revolution" to use Aldous Huxley's apt expression, is upon us. Before his death in California, Huxley told a reporter that his "Brave New World" was coming into being faster than he had anticipated. It is not yet a quarter of a century since Mark I was developed by Harvard's Howard Aiken. Since that time we have vastly improved on this cathode-ray tube model with miniaturized transistor models capable of playing chess, composing poetry and music, and designing art patterns. The idea of a tiny computer contained within an android skull is a logical step within the dynamics of the mechanization process. William F. Nolan says in the preface to his anthology, *The Pseudo-People*:

> "The birth of the first android, therefore, is a lot closer to us than we might imagine. Artificial hearts, lungs and arteries are already being developed in science; the artificial brain is the next major step toward the creation of humanized robots."

Ethicians, philosophers, moral theologians and behavioral scientists would do well to take science fiction more seriously, and most especially that body of literature which deals with robots, androids and humanoids. It is more possible to direct the mechanization process in the earlier stages of its course than when it has almost come to term in its definitive impact on society. Much concern over the spurious, even noxious, effects of technology arise out of the *fait accompli*, the distasteful, perhaps poisonous, fruit of seeds planted much earlier. In a very real sense, the future has already begun, as Robert Jungk wrote some years back. Those who may doubt that the future of androids has already begun should visit Disneyland in Southern California where regularly scheduled performances are held of a "replica-presence" of Abraham Lincoln: this truly amazing robot sits, stands, takes steps, makes gestures and speaks, even if imperfectly. If we can reproduce an Abraham Lincoln in Disneyland, what is to prevent science from bringing a Winston Churchill back to rule England?

34 / THE AMERICAN ACADEMY 1970

Judson Jerome

"Why do students come here? What do they really want?" Assembled deans and faculty of a new community college look at me and shrug. The answer is obvious. A professor of engineering states it with a cynical laugh: "Fact is, what they want is the diploma." We regard that motive as ignoble. "Suppose," I ask, "you gave them that when they came. 'Here's your degree—your A.A.,*' you tell them. 'Now is there anything else we can do for you?'" Silence. We grin together in complicity. We'd be out of jobs. And the students, of course, would miss out on their education. . . .*

Their *what?* Among the many metaphorical ways in which we try to understand what we are doing, we sometimes think of education as though it were a *thing*. You get it by going to college. If you get a degree, you have it. When you have it, it entitles you to a job and a place in society. It is a commodity, acquired with a special kind of currency—college credit—acceptable at a solid rate of exchange at the various

---

From *Change*, September/October 1969. Reprinted by permission of the author and the author's agent.

institutions in an international network. The student turns in credits for his degree like a book of green stamps. A credit is a unit of time: three hours per week for a quarter or semester, a device for symbolizing the conversion of energy and time into a diploma. We measure our productivity in the network by counting the credits we generate. Education is a kind of piecework.

That is a partial view. All metaphors are partial views. The currency is that of a vast and expanding Fifth Estate, perhaps more powerful than the Lords Spiritual, the Lords Temporal, the Commons and the daily press in influencing minds and shaping public policy. Simultaneously it is a remarkably homogenous and hierarchical system with widespread agreement about premises, standards, levels, definitions of quality. In one sense it is the great leveler; in another it is the opposite: its business is to select and classify. Its business is also to modify human material, grinding slow but exceeding small.

It is a religion. An anthropologist studying the graduation exercises at one of our great universities (the buzzard costumes, the pomp and prayer, the rites of passage) or at lesser universities, public or private colleges, junior colleges, technical schools, military institutes, seminaries, high schools, even junior high and grade schools, could draw some very accurate conclusions about our national worship of classification, labeling and stratification, all conducted with a sanctimony implying the scrolls are duplicated in heaven. He should hurry to complete his study while the natives still perform their rituals in the established fashion. Had he observed in June of 1969, his data would have been colored by co-eds in riot helmets, red fists on the backs of academic gowns, impertinent posters and mass walkouts.

This is a revolution, or a series of revolutions. As late as the Spring of 1968, Christopher Jencks and David Riesman, in *The Academic Revolution,* were able to announce that the professors had seized the palace and had consolidated their rule like a military junta. They foresaw an era of peace and order, but even as their book appeared, Columbia and the Sorbonne were seething and erupting in violence. They described a monolithic orthodoxy that is becoming crazed with cracks before our eyes.

To our wars in Asia and in our cities we have had to add the war on our campuses, and this third war may provide the most sensitive clues of all in helping us to understand the cultural transformation we are experiencing. The violent explosions on the surface are, of course, merely symptoms of subterranean turbulence and pressure, the steamy flux within. Not only in the colleges are the old standards in doubt, all purposes questioned, the very modes of perception and measurement changing. But traveling through the Fifth Estate, observing, listening, we can tell a great deal about what is happening, and what is bound to happen.

Each morning we board up the shattered windows and open the doors for business as usual. The American high school senior this fall is already toting up his scores, guessing his class rank (248/1057?), consulting his counselor, poring over catalogues which tell him nothing, visiting campuses, sending off for application forms. Yet increasingly the demoralization and confusion in the colleges are permeating the high schools, where underground papers flourish and demonstrations are becoming more common. Prospective freshmen are more bewildered, fearful and alienated than they are enthusiastic or hopeful. Parents tell me their kids are turned off by school at an earlier and earlier age. The pressures of the senior year drive many beyond frenzy into stupor. "I told him he either goes to college or gets a job," one parent, a research chemist, said. "I'm not going to have him loafing around home."

The threat of having to take a menial job may well drive the young man into college, dumping him, purposeless and unmotivated, into the lap of an advisor. ("Might as well get your general requirements out of the way while you're deciding what interests you.") He will find himself in classes where professors will anxiously wheedle him with relevance or slice at him with sarcasm. He will be assigned to a dormitory with other young men in similar states of emotional paralysis. ("It's the freshmen who bring in the pot," an upperclassman told me. "They get it from high school. If we want some, we get it from the freshmen.") And in this context he will set out to get educated.

On their applications, students give a number of reasons for wanting to be admitted to college: to learn about the world, to learn how to do things, to explore new roles, to assert maturity, to develop individuality, to have greater freedom, to engage in the solution of social problems. But behind the stated reasons is another, usually unexpressed: they have nowhere else to go. The society seems to have less and less use for men and women under twenty-one, and students sense it, knowing they are expensive burdens, feeling undefined, unneeded, clumsy and overgrown. It is common to hear of high school students who can find no college which interests them until the April panic when the music stops and they rush frantically for any available chair.

In this seller's market, the colleges entice and haughtily reject. *Les belles dames sans merci*. State universities frankly use the first two years to flunk out large percentages. From the time the student starts high school he is told that his performance is important because he must *qualify*, and as a college junior he still must qualify—now for graduate study. For the most academically successful students the B.A., like the high school diploma, provides hardly a breather. Life—or whatever it is one is getting ready for, qualifying for—shimmers always ahead like a mirage. Sooner or later the student is likely to ask, "Who needs it?" He finds mirages to inhabit nearer at hand.

If we look at the educational system from the top instead of the bottom of the mountain, that disaffected high school student, that freshman or sophomore, seems a distant concern. The masses keep surging forward, being admitted—a gritty inconvenience. One threads through them on the way to the laboratory or library. They seem a noisy, silly lot—occasionally dangerous. We herd them off the street into classrooms to watch us on television. We set our graduate students (but not the aces, whom we want for our own research) to tending them.

There is general agreement up here on the peaks that the purpose of the university is the advancement of knowledge (which is terminology we use for getting and completing contracts). For this business we need highly qualified, highly specialized professors, and graduate students committed to *becoming* highly qualified, highly specialized professors. We need administrators who know where the bodies are buried around Washington. We need computers, cyclotrons, lasers, field trips, per diems. Rightly or wrongly we have sold our society on the proposition that the key to national security, growth, development and welfare is in the headlong pursuit of scientific and technical knowledge, shadowed (in order) by information about society and "humane learning" in such fields as history, philosophy and literature. Nearly twenty billion dollars of the federal budget goes into research; untold other billions from industry go into research; and a large proportion of it all pours into the universities.

Three classic functions of higher education are thus uncomfortably fused. The more-or-less official doctrine is that the colleges provide liberal education—the general knowledge, the cultivated skills, the intellectual development—needed by every man, and especially by the leaders of society. Their second function is to generate their own professors, and we are told that the man who can best convey liberal education to the undergraduate is one who is actively engaged at the frontier of a specialized field. In practice, this second function far outweighs the first in importance, creating institutions on the German model, top-heavy in preoccupation with graduate studies and postgraduate scholarship, with consequent neglect of the undergraduate program and general education. The pursuit of knowledge for its own sake, or for the sake of the advancement of human culture, is a luxury we associate with nineteenth- and early twentieth-century scholars, such as the independently wealthy anthropologists who funded their own expeditions.

With the research needs of World War II came the third and now dominant function: commissioned work for public and private agencies.

Most of this research is—or is called—pure, but its focus is determined by forces external to the university itself. And it has created an economic base more or less independent of tuition. At major private universities, such as M.I.T. or the University of Chicago, only about fifteen to twenty per cent of total income is derived from tuition; up to seventy per cent is likely to come from the government for sponsored research. The graduate programs, which are reputedly more expensive than undergraduate programs, make it possible to accept research contracts because the graduate programs supply cheap technical manpower. It almost seems as though the universities might close down their undergraduate programs altogether, at some financial advantage, and survive entirely on research.

The universities have become specialists in consumption. They gobble their way into government, particularly its juiciest flank, the military. They gobble their way into industry. They gobble the substance of foundations. They gobble the rich. They gobble tuitions, of course, like canapés. But it is a diet which makes hungry where most it satisfies. Ultimately contracts increase operating costs beyond what they recompense, grants create programs which continue with their own inertia; even gifts tend to add to operating expenses, and since tuition covers only a portion of educational costs, every student is an additional liability. Yet payrolls must be met; we must have more contracts, more grants, more special programs, more gifts, more students paying higher tuitions. The rim of the whirlpool widens and widens.

So powerful and attractive is this research function, it skews the whole system of higher education. Though only a small number of the more than 2,400 colleges and universities in the country obtain an appreciable proportion of their income from research funds, most of the rest have become, in effect, feeder institutions for the giants—or are aspiring to become giants themselves. Whether our hypothetical high school senior starts his freshman year at a municipal college, a branch of a state university, a private liberal arts college, a church-related college, or in the undergraduate program of one of the major universities, he is likely to find even his beginning courses taught by specialists, designed to produce specialists, leading in linear fashion to graduate work. His professors (or graduate-assistant teachers) will have their ambitions set upon achieving the kind of publication and research that attracts attention among the professionals. They will be interested in Joe Frosh if he shows aptitude for and commitment to their specialties. There are exceptional colleges, and exceptional teachers in every college; but essentially the system of higher education is only incidentally, and then somewhat reluctantly, related to the personal growth and education of Joe Frosh.

We should have predicted that if we were to lock up seven million bright and healthy people in a network alien to their lives—one which systematically denies their manhood and womanhood, ignores them as individuals, subjects them to tremendous pressure to achieve ends with which they do not identify—there would eventually be trouble. We not only did not predict the trouble, but even now we refuse to see its implications. The blissful complacency of the academic world before the Free Speech Movement at Berkeley in 1964 is equalled only by the vexed complacency of the academic world in 1969. We ask, sometimes plaintively, sometimes belligerently, why can't we just have law and order? Why can't we stamp out these symptoms?

We have been forced to do some soul-searching, and certainly there have been some modifications and concessions. But there is little movement toward the fundamental changes required to convert the system to better social use. At graduation time two years from now we may have steel mortarboards clamped to our helmets, we may wear gas masks and bulletproof gowns while a cordon of police marches in to "Pomp and Circumstance," unless by then we have at least begun to alter radically the nature of the university and its function in society.

EDUCATION FOR EVERYMAN

Sorry, closed: this college temporarily out of order.

sign on Franconia College campus, 1968

Can anything be changed until everything is changed? Sometimes I think, as the SDS leaders do, that we should let the whole contraption grind to a halt. Let government and industry keep their money and do their own research; if they want employees trained and tested and certified, let them do it. If foundations want scholarship, let them support scholars—with no undergraduate education to confuse the issue. Let the rich name office buildings after themselves. If we want to exempt prosperous youth from the military, let's figure out a more direct way of doing it than inflicting them on professors. If we need to keep the young off the labor market, let's introduce youth pensions. If we need to provide ways for young women to meet young men, let's build youth centers. If we want to preserve the culture of our civilization, let's expand the libraries and museums. In short, let's sort out our needs and resources to see whether there aren't better ways of doing things than relying on the Rube Goldberg Edufactory.

As for education itself, we seem to have forgotten what it is all about. I have watched a handicapped child go eagerly to school and reflected that the normal children I know do not want to go to school that badly. The special education people seem to know some things we other educators could benefit by. They automatically accept children for what they are. They are pleased at progress and do not punish failure. They assume that when a child does something wrong, he does it in an effort to do right. They recognize they are dealing with a wide variety of individuals with different patterns and rates of learning. They assume their mission is one of assisting growth and development; that if a child is not interested, not engaged, not learning, the staff needs to reexamine itself and the program. They assume that hostility has some cause, and that it is better to deal with the cause than to repress the hostility. Faced with tantrums, they do not make speeches about law and order. When there is general disorder, they do not accuse their pupils of conspiracy.

College education has become, *de facto,* compulsory. I am sick of hearing remarks about our "privileged" youth in higher education. If a person is born white and middle class, he is required to serve sixteen to eighteen years of his life in custodial institutions, never mind the Army. I have talked to students in dozens of colleges, and I hear what we all know but rarely admit: students are in college because their parents and their society demand that they be there. Socially, we require the degree for serious participation—let the chips fall where they may, which is usually on the underclass. "Go ahead with your Afro-American studies," a faculty member said to a black student, "but why ask us for a degree?" The student laughed: "*We* don't want the degree. You want us to have it." In fact, we punish them if they don't get it. Let's not talk any more about the advantages of higher education. They are like the advantages of obeying the law.

Our students are half-persuaded they need the credentials, but they see no connection between the credentials and what college and life demand of them. Some are so disenchanted by the array of vocations available to them—with or without degrees—that they stay in college as the lesser of two evils. Most simply do not know what else to do with themselves. Some say they are avoiding the draft, but if the draft were ended they would still stay in college as long as they could. And yet they talk of getting rid of requirements, not of learning. They talking of getting *out,* as though they were serving sentences. But they don't want out, either; bad as it is, college is a kind of sanctuary.

It reminds one of the rites of passage of primitive cultures in which young men assume with gravity and joy the role of manhood in the tribe. To become an adult should be a sacred honor. But we live in a nation in which children don't want to grow up. This is not because we have made childhood so delightful and carefree; it is because membership in our society is repugnant to those who stand on its threshold. It is pointless to berate a whole generation for laziness, weak character, immaturity, lack of commitment, escapism and ambivalence. Too few American adults regard their own membership as a sacred honor. Something has gone foul in the deep core of our society. Always in human experience maturation has been spiced with disillusionment; but has any culture ever so failed to win the allegiance of its young?

Compulsory education is a contradiction in terms, a central miscalculation about the nature of learning. With the best of intentions we made education not only available to but required of everyone. But in education as in love, compulsion destroys the pleasure and the inherent rewards.

To lock everyone into a compulsory system we had to resort to massive standardization. We could not do it without making education primarily a state function, with laws to insure compliance. I wonder whether education and state are not at least as incompatible as church and state. There is nothing inherently contaminating about using tax funds to make educational resources available—open to the citizenry for free use. But once attendance is required and curriculum is subject to state control there is no protection from indoctrination.

We could not do so massive a job without collaborative arrangements with the major sources of power and funds, which means the fabled military-industrial complex. (Recently a student at Earlham College referred casually to "the military-industrial-university complex.") To make democracy work we needed an informed electorate, but arranged matters so that the intellectual establishment could be manipulated by anti-intellectual forces. And by definition, an establishment must refrain from offending many students, parents, taxpayers or politicians, and so be grey as an Associated Press dispatch. (That, incidentally, is another system which seeks to inform but succeeds in neutralizing; newspapers from Maine to Georgia to Oregon carry much the same news, reported in the same bloodless, impotent and official way.)

It is irrelevant that the wire services are free enterprises and that many of our schools, colleges and universities are private. The fact that the highest credentials available are produced by private universities, such as Harvard, Yale, Princeton, Columbia, Chicago and Stanford, does not mean these universities are any more free of the system. Indeed, they epitomize it. The repressive element is not, finally, the state; it is the nationalized, professionalized orthodoxy of the system itself. The opinions, standards, assumptions and competitive pressures of academic colleagues at M.I.T. and Brandeis and Fordham and Rice and Duke hold Berkeley in check—even more than does the Governor of California.

The business of the university is the production of scholars and research scientists, in spite of the fact that, once produced, they have nowhere to go but into the system which finds it so difficult to maintain them. The professoriate tends to describe the university as "an institution that justifies itself by its output of scholarship" (Jacques Barzun in *The American University*); it tends to oppose any kind of vocational training, any emphasis upon experience or social service or "life" (a word which Barzun regards as cant, confusing our educational mission).

In short, professors like to think of what they are doing in terms of pure intellectual development, and they tend to recognize as indices of success such things as Woodrow Wilsons, high scores on GRE's, acceptance by a "good" department of sociology, or publication in a scholarly journal. If we maintain those standards of excellence and drive as many students as we can toward them, we must support the enterprise with the grants and projects which enable graduate students and scholars to work together on the forefront of knowledge, to produce visible (publishable) results, and we are back in the cycle. When in doubt, accelerate.

It is a ladder propped against the air. A student's performance in elementary school is measured in terms of preparation for high school, and so on, in hierarchical order, until he is ready for postgraduate research in an academic discipline. Those who fall off the ladder can find their places in the world's lower echelons. But if by some miracle all students entering kindergarten next year were equally qualified intellectually and economically, there would be no reason other than laziness or perversity why they should not all graduate some twenty-one years later from Columbia or its counterpart with doctoral degrees, prepared to advance knowledge in the discipline of their choice. What a society we would have then. It is, as Harris Wofford has said, as though we geared the whole machine to produce the .8 per cent who eventually receive Ph.D.'s. It is as though the teacher's function were to mold children in the image of the teacher's professor.

To be sure, the professoriate tells us repeatedly that the university is not for everyone and that we are mistaken in trying to make it so. Some say we should kick out of our colleges all but the real students, the gentlemen scholars, those who share the professors' commitment to work in the academic disciplines. That would be a good solution except for the fact that most of such professors would promptly be out of jobs, and the few who remained would not have the laboratories, libraries and salaries they conceive of as necessary for their work.

Imagine such a purge of our institutions. Cull those Barzun calls the mandarins, who are there not to learn but to qualify. Cull the anti-intellectuals, the militants, the experience-seekers, the group-gropers and T-groupers, the great washed masses who are none of these but who are content to be herded along, not wanting to rock the boat, not wanting to risk their degrees and jobs and deferments. Cull the sycophants, the hustlers, the socialites, the influence peddlers and seekers, the red-necks. Cull the lost flower children, searching for their identity, confused about their goals, drifting in fuzzy clouds of introspection. Cull—of course—the athletes, the flashy frat boys, the sex hounds, the drug cult, the pranksters, the collegiate rah-rah crowd. Cull the adolescent rebels who are chronically opposed to all authority because they cannot stand their parents. Cull women. Cull draft-dodgers. Cull the inadequately prepared, the products of poor schools, the stupid, the lazy, the disadvantaged, the spoiled. Cull blacks who are not willing to accept the standards and goals of our educational institutions. Cull the vocationally oriented, the teachers back for summer school who only want a raise. Cull dilettantes, the bored, the culture-seekers. Cull the childish, not mature enough to be away from home. On one end of the log remains Mark Hopkins. On the other end is a mirror.

In a way such professors are like their students, uneasy in prosperity. They won, as Jencks and Riesman say, the academic revolution. They have achieved prestige, influence, security. Now they are vexed by the responsibilities of power, sated by the rewards of success, and yearn backward toward a more pastoral image of themselves—the rumpled scholar in his book-lined study advising the eager student burning out his eyes in tireless, selfless inquiry, the pursuit of Truth—however arcane and remote from the world's affairs. They suffered poverty, sure, but had the comfort of stimulating intellectual fellowship, the camaraderie of specialists, the consuming engagement of the human spirit with the mysteries of the unknown. I imagine these professors, in their Brooks Brothers suits, in bars and hotels of Washington between consultations at the Pentagon, getting together to remember the good old days. They think of themselves puttering around impoverished labs, stringing together equipment with baling wire, spilling nitroglycerine into fuller's earth and accidentally discovering dynamite, bequeathing the proceeds to the cause of Peace. It's like a hippy's dream of a Canadian homestead.

It has been pointed out often that adolescence is a modern invention, and though nothing in our literature would recommend that state of mind, we seem bent on extending it to everyone in the culture from nine to ninety. But be cautious about calling it a privilege or one of the "extraordinary accomplishments" of higher education. What has happened is that through improving nutrition and improving the communications media, we have enabled people to mature physically and intellectually at earlier ages, and we have failed to adjust our educational system accordingly; we have, in fact, increased the years of schooling without accommodating them to physical and intellectual maturity. We have made it extremely difficult for able individuals to be self-directing and independent until later and later in their lives. This may indeed have something to do with campus unrest—but it is a failure, not an achievement. Its victims see it as part of a pattern of human enslavement.

The kids are not so brain damaged, yet, that they will let this happen to them indefinitely. Through their efforts in conjunction with other social forces, higher education is about to be transformed, and the emerging pattern may be unrecognizable and distasteful to many of us formed by and committed to the present system. But quality should be possible within it if our universities commit themselves to creating excellence within new and necessary forms.

I believe our colleges will move in the direction of becoming community centers. This development started with the storefront churches, universities of the streets, the storefront museums. Some at present are extensions of college programs; others are independent agencies. The physical plants of our colleges can, to a large extent, be adapted to this new purpose; the moated citadels of present campuses should break up, and more neighborhood programs and establishments (many of them rather transient and easily dismantleable) will appear. Educational institutions would then be more like libraries or museums, with facilities available on a drop-in basis to citizens of all ages. Now the intention of such centers is to reach marginal people, those who have gotten off the educational ladder and need means of reentry to the system. But the ladder itself may be abandoned, and these new community centers might then replace schools and colleges as we now know them altogether.

Museum and *library*. These are words with connotations of passivity, quite inappropriate to community centers. But the connotation need not be. The Boston Children's Museum holds classes, conducts workshops, field trips, supplies instructional kits—a whole range of guided activities and prepackaged resources which provide structured study for those who want it. In addition to exhibits and active programs, there will surely be at our future colleges back-up collections of materials and resources, such as the holdings of the American Museum of Natural History in New York City, with its enormous accumulation not on display, its vast research program employing dozens of scholars and specialists, all supporting an educational program through which these materials are adapted for public use and instruction.

If our colleges convert themselves to the model of community centers, they would make their facilities and activities more open to the public (perhaps on a fee basis for some). They would not concern themselves, for the most part, with matriculation, graduation or registration. They would operate to a large extent in after-school, after-work hours, and on weekends. A twelve-year-old girl and sixty-year-old man might find themselves side-by-side at potting wheels. Programmed material would be available. There would be no standard time units, such as semesters or quarters: the institution would run year-round, with offerings beginning and ending at a variety of times.

Certification would not be the object but would be provided for those who want it, primarily on a unit basis—certificates indicating that a person is competent in programming computers, in analytic geometry, in intermediate French. If the concept of the degree persists, degrees would be available for those whose certified work added up to preestablished requirements. Insofar as possible, examination should not be by those engaged in instruction; the dynamics should be to get the learner and his instructor on the same side against ignorance—and the examiner. (If an employer is concerned about the skills and knowledge of a prospective employee, it is his job to measure them, and not to accept the word of the educational institution.) Similarly, advanced study programs might begin with entrance tests, but there is little reason for examination at the *end* of a unit of study. The relevant question is not what the student knows then, but what he knows when he begins his next task.

The college as community center would perform many of the functions it now performs, and many in addition; but its stance in the community would be quite different. It would not be designed for any particular age group. There would be no ritual of admission, no predetermined requirements for leaving. It would invite the conception of education as continuous and lifelong. It would probably not provide living accommodations, though specialized transient housing might be developed as a parallel operation, perhaps offering apartments linked electronically to the college. There would be no parietal rules, except those applying to any rented property.

The kinds of research and service projects now associated with universities would continue to be conducted, but without a forced relationship between these activities and education. Some staff members would be researchers; others would be engaged in creating and updating instructional material—pamphlets, books, slides, tapes, films, charts, exhibits. Others would be engaged in instruction, in classes or in counseling. Some staff might combine more than one function. But there would be no expectation that the variety of jobs we presently associate with a college professor—lecturer, discussion leader, scholar, advisor, administrator, politician and policeman—need be united in one person. Staff members would do what they want to do, and do well.

Such institutions could be public or private in their financing. Miami-Dade Junior College already is well on the way to offering an educational smorgasbord as part of a county public school system. Consider, too, the YMCA, the Jewish Community Centers, park programs, cooperatives and clubs with educational programs. If there are no general requirements for all students, no set curriculum, no admission and exit qualifications, publicly financed education is much less a threat to intellectual freedom. Private institutions could be supported by combinations of membership and service fees, organizational or charitable support and governmental support, as they are now.

Even children might use such institutions, instead of schools. There could be a sign-in, sign-out arrangement for the information of parents, but there would be no custodial function except—as in a library or swimming pool—rules to prevent injury and disturbance of others. If children know they are free to choose, they might well want to spend more time at such a place than they now spend at school.

The function of educators and educational institutions is to facilitate learning. Some kinds of learning require that the institution provide special facilities or instruction. But many or most kinds of learning do not require teachers at all. The college of the future will be a kind of broker, making contacts and contracts, helping people into situations in which they can learn. There is less and less need for colleges to attempt to simulate the world in their classrooms, libraries, studios and laboratories for instructional purposes. This is both too expensive and unnecessarily artificial. "The world," said one student recently returned from a year at a field study center in Hawaii, "is *there*." What we need to develop is more skill and efficiency in using the learning resources already around us—nature, our existing libraries, our industries, community organizations, homes, even the universities now in operation. Colleges and universities duplicate their facilities wastefully when the same resources could better be spent in developing communication and transportation and cooperative arrangements.

We need to find out what people need to know and, with guidance, advice and negotiation, make it possible for them to learn. This means job placement, negotiating the terms by which a person can study with a master, arranging for library and auditing privileges at nearby universities, planning a trip to Europe, or helping to work up a bibliography. It means, sometimes, teaching a course, but that in general is an inefficient way of enabling people to learn.

We need to certify and interpret learning which has already taken place. Too often we are faced with people who have, by one means or another, learned what they need to know in order to do a job, but they are prevented from doing it because they lack credentials. Completely independent of their instructional function, our educational institutions need to establish a credential service—collecting and evaluating job reports, recommendations, publications and other evidence of past learning, giving tests (such as civil service examinations), helping match qualifications to jobs. The idea that the only way people get educated is by being enrolled in institutions is long obsolete. We need new testing offices, independent units, indifferent to where or how or over what period of time a person learned, concerned only with *what* he learned and how it can be usefully interpreted.

We are obsessed with credentialism in our society. For one thing, we should simply do less of it, limiting our certificates to what we know and can attest to. At present, our colleges are rightfully accused of issuing bogus currency, for though they honor among themselves transferred credit in History of Philosophy or Evolution or Social Conflict, they haven't the least notion of what such credit validates. We give degrees of great market value, but the degrees testify to almost nothing, give us almost no grounds for predicting what a given graduate knows or can do. Society will not change overnight, and thus there is a continuing practical need of credentials; but we can move in the direction of issuing certificates that are reliable, descriptive, that attest to quality in some verifiable way. And there is no reason why this function need be confused with teaching and learning; there are many reasons why it should not be.

The college of the next decade—of next year—need have no specific geographic location. (Our campuses too often separate students from life rather than involving them in it.) It would consist of a set of functions. Like a trademark, its word would attest to a level of quality, a style. It would operate a network of facilities (among them, community education centers) in many locations. Its students would move freely among the facilities, availing themselves of what they need. This may sound like a scattered and impersonal institution, so highly individualized that its students are lonely in their educational quest. But one of the traditional functions of a college—and a good one, if it does not interfere with other functions—is that of a retreat. Colleges and private institutes are now developing highly specialized and sometimes consciously therapeutic retreats, and this tendency is sure to continue. In addition to community centers, with their free flow and chance groupings, our colleges could manage isolated, lodge-like facilities, to which people could go for a few days, a weekend, a week, a month, for meditation, association with others, personal renewal, and to participate in seminars lasting perhaps six or eight weeks. Participants (no more than about a dozen in each seminar) would be of all ages, all varieties of social and educational status. Away from family and usual acquaintances, they would meet daily for two or three hours of intense mutual examination of their purposes and the ways they are going about opening up their lives.

These functions of the future college—community education centers, educational agencies, retreats—are concerned with the individual's growth and learning, but have little to do with the advancement of knowledge itself. Colleges will also, undoubtedly, continue to manage institutes such as those currently on the educational scene, problem-oriented and trans-disciplinary, facilitating the collaboration of specialists in addressing critical human concerns. Institutes serve a kind of R and D function for society, and it is appropriate that they be sponsored by colleges and universities rather than industry or the government. Universities collect the necessary expertise and they stand a chance of being fairly disinterested, operating somewhat like the judiciary, with no commitment except a general one to truth, justice and human welfare. The institutes, as part of a network of educational services, would work on contracts, projects, services, both in collaboration with other organizations and on their own initiative. Part of their function would be, of course, educational. But their primary commitment would be to solving problems, not to instruction. They would be funded in such a way that they could pay, at least minimally, their learner-researchers, but in no way would the institutes serve as devices for production under the guise of instruction.

One of the concerns of educators has been to insure distribution in education, or, as we often put it, an exposure to the principal areas of human learning. We have assumed that on this general base the student will specialize increasingly as he proceeds up the educational ladder. That theory has, ironically, led to a hideous devaluation of general education. Barzun, for instance, uses the haughty term *propaedeutic* to describe that stuff through which one plows before getting down to the serious business of specializing, an attitude that is widely shared both by teachers and students. But not only has this theory been weakened by the knowledge explosion, which has made it literally impossible to give any student even a reasonable sampling of the content of the major fields of knowledge, it is faulty on other grounds.

The fact is we don't know at what period in a person's life he is best able to consider inter-relationships between areas of knowledge, but it is not likely to be when he is in grade school or high school or the first two years of college. On the other hand, if a student of, say, fifteen takes on some part-time work for an institute of urban housing, he will necessarily learn something about how people live, and if curious, he may learn something about politics, economics, law, sociology, architecture and city planning. Specialization need not limit him; it may indeed be the best way to broaden him. And setting to work at that age on a responsible job may help him break the syndrome of adolescence. If we let him out of school more hours of the day, in other words, he might more rapidly become a person instead of a boy. (There is evidence to show that intellectual growth accompanies and increases with emotional growth, that experiential education stimulates abstract learning.)

Those distressed by the emerging pattern of education may be concerned that it does little to inculcate discipline. But truly valuable discipline must come from within, not be imposed; it is the discipline of the artist. I doubt that any student ever acquired such discipline by having rigorous standards imposed upon him by a disciplinarian in a classroom. Others will be concerned that the new education makes inadequate provision for sequence and order in learning, but the validity of sequentialism (like that of compartmentalism, essentialism and credentialism) has been shattered in modern experience. It is simply impossible to make a case today that there is a proper and necessary order in which things can be learned, or that we can define an essential body of knowledge which all men should share.

In that state of relativity, what guarantee have we that our cultural heritage can be preserved? Is nothing of the past worth saving? In this shopping-center model of education, will the consumer have any guidance or direction other than fad? Will education be so responsive to market analysis that there will be nothing but trash on the shelves? The first answer is that we no longer have much choice. The day has ended when the educational system can be used with impunity to colonize minds. Necessity is a rigid and authoritarian professor; she will help us sort out what is worth saving from our cultural heritage. We will not have to invent the wheel again with each generation; the value of the wheel is self-evident, even to student militants. The elements of our heritage either are enduring, or they will not endure.

Before we become too alarmed at the encroachment of tomorrow, we should remember that our professionalized system of higher education is a callow invention, modeled on nineteenth-century German institutions and developed to its present position of power in response to the technological demands of World War II, hardly a heritage that need be sanctified with rhetoric about cultural heritage. Whatever is indeed essential about Western civilization (about human civilization, for that matter) has been carried as a chalice through generations of turmoil and social change without the honor guard of an educational establishment to protect it. I care about Shakespeare, but I trust his memory more readily to those outside the academy than to those within it whose love is motivated by an institutional need to pick over his carcass in search of publishable footnotes.

American higher education is thoroughly capable of adapting to fundamental change, if only it will. It is a pity that those of us involved must be scared into change by outbreaks of anarchy. It is a pity we cannot more willingly take advantage of the fluidity of our times, the availability of resources, the vitality and engagement of our students, and the bewilderment of a society in the throes of revolutionary change. It is a pity we cannot show intellectual initiative rather than panic and rigidity at a time when the need is so great and the possibilities are so abundant.

EPILOGUE / ISSUES FOR CONSIDERATION

1. How will changes in the economic institution affect the role of the worker in American society?
2. Are changes within the higher education system likely to reflect changes needed within the society at large?
3. Will technological advances like those described by Hurley have an effect on the differentiation of American society?
4. Discuss what you see as some of the blocks to changes in higher education which Jerome suggests are needed.
5. Do changes within the discipline of sociology reflect broader changes within society?

ABCDE7987654321